Security Issues and Threats in Ubiquitous Computing

Security Issues and Threats in Ubiquitous Computing

Madelyn Trent

www.willfordpress.com

Published by Willford Press,
118-35 Queens Blvd., Suite 400,
Forest Hills, NY 11375, USA

ISBN: 978-1-64728-487-9

Cataloging-in-Publication Data

Security issues and threats in ubiquitous computing / Madelyn Trent.
    p. cm.
Includes bibliographical references and index.
ISBN 978-1-64728-487-9
1. Ubiquitous computing. 2. Ambient intelligence. 3. Embedded computer systems.
4. Embedded Internet devices. 5. Wireless communication systems. 6. Electronic
data processing--Distributed processing. I. Trent, Madelyn.
QA76.5915 .U45 2023
004--dc23

For information on all Willford Press publications
visit our website at www.willfordpress.com

Contents

Permissions

Index

Preface

The main aim of this book is to educate learners and enhance their research focus by presenting diverse topics covering this vast field. This is an advanced book which compiles significant studies by distinguished experts in the area of analysis. This book addresses successive solutions to the challenges arising in the area of application, along with it; the book provides scope for future developments.

The concept of ubiquitous computing is used in computer science, software engineering and hardware engineering for computing which can take place in any format, any device and at any location, unlike desktop computing. The traditional view of computing systems has been irreversibly changed by the recent technical developments in hardware and software. They not only contain linked servers but also include a wide variety of embedded and pervasive devices, which lead to the development of ubiquitous computing systems. Cryptanalysis methodologies and tools are used to enhance the security of the ubiquitous computing environment, by providing protection and controlling access to data. Cryptanalysis is the process of examining information systems for understanding hidden aspects of the systems. It involves the study of theoretical and practical cryptographic mechanisms intended to provide privacy and security. This book unravels the recent studies on ubiquitous computing. It will elucidate the concepts and innovative models around security issues and threats in ubiquitous computing systems. The book will help the readers in keeping pace with the rapid changes in this field.

It was a great honour to edit this book, though there were challenges, as it involved a lot of communication and networking between me and the editorial team. However, the end result was this all-inclusive book covering diverse themes in the field.

Finally, it is important to acknowledge the efforts of the contributors for their excellent chapters, through which a wide variety of issues have been addressed. I would also like to thank my colleagues for their valuable feedback during the making of this book.

Madelyn Trent

Part I
Ubiquitous Devices: An Overview

Ubiquitous Devices: Challenges and Solutions

Mirosław Kutyłowski, Piotr Syga, and Moti Yung

Abstract In this chapter we focus on two important security challenges that naturally emerge for large scale systems composed of cheap devices implementing only symmetric cryptographic algorithms. First, we consider threats due to poor or malicious implementations of protocols, which enable data to be leaked from the devices to an adversary. We present solutions based on a watchdog concept— a man-in-the-middle device that does not know the secrets of the communicating parties, but aims to destroy covert channels leaking secret information. Second, we deal with the problem of tracing devices by means of information exchanged while establishing a communication session. As solutions such as Diffie-Hellman key exchange are unavailable for such devices, implicit identity information might be transmitted in clear and thereby provide a perfect means for privacy violations. We show how to reduce such risks without retreating to asymmetric algorithms.

1.1 Introduction

The popularity and wide spread of ubiquitous systems requires us to focus our attention on possible threats and challenges that are either not present or are easy to solve in other environments. Quite often, a user of such a system is in possession of multiple severely constrained devices that may communicate with others without the user's explicit consent or knowledge. Since the user has no direct control over the messages that are exchanged, a malicious manufacturer may aim to leak users' secrets over a covert channel created when random values should be transmitted. The problem is acute, since due to cost factors it is hard to defend against it—e.g., by going through a tough certification process.

M. Kutyłowski · P. Syga
Wrocław University of Science and Technology, Wrocław, Poland

M. Yung (✉)
Columbia University, New York, NY, USA
e-mail: moti@cs.columbia.edu

Another threat which is specific to ubiquitous systems is the possibility of tracking a device even if it communicates over encrypted channels: e.g., establishing a shared key by two devices may enable identifying these devices. Device tracking may result in various personal threats, ranging from profiling the device holder (resulting in targeted advertisements) to criminal activities such as stalking and impersonation. Apart from risks to the individuals, there is a threat of massive tracking being done for illegal business purposes, organized crime, or subversive or terrorist purposes, as well suppressing personal freedom. So far, methods for preventing tracking have not been adequately developed. In this chapter we identify the aforementioned threats and present some solutions that are feasible in ubiquitous systems.

The chapter is organized into two main parts. In Sect. 1.2 we focus on the threat posed by a device designed to leak the user's secrets via covert channels. As a countermeasure against leaking information in supposedly random parts of a communication, we propose using a watchdog device. We describe modifications of cryptographic primitives that allow the use of a watchdog: in Sects. 1.2.3.1 and 1.2.3.2 we discuss commitments, in Sects. 1.2.3.3 and 1.2.3.4 we focus on generating and answering challenges, and Sect. 1.2.3.5 is devoted to distance bounding. In Sect. 1.3 a privacy aspect of the protocols is discussed, in particular we aim to prevent the adversary from identifying a device as partaking in two different communications. Section 1.3.2 discusses some basic ideas for coping with communication linking in ubiquitous systems using predistributed keys. In Sect. 1.3.3 we present a notion of using 'general pseudonyms', common to a group of devices, in order to preserve their privacy, whereas in Sects. 1.3.4 and 1.3.5 we discuss modifying the transmitted keys by a permanent evolution in the former case, and by transmitting the identifiers with a pseudorandom perturbation in the latter.

1.2 Malicious Devices and Watchdog Concept

1.2.1 Attacks by Malicious Devices

In ubiquitous systems, controlling hardware devices in terms of their security features may be a major problem. Methods such as certification of products, strict manufacturing regimes and controlling the supply chain might be relatively costly compared with the purpose and application area of such systems. On the other hand, there are numerous smart methods to cheat users: a device may look inoffensive, while it may leak secret data to an adversary using various types of covert channels. In fact, no extra message has to be sent: covert channels can be hidden in regular innocent-looking messages. The main problem areas are:

1. Protocol steps where random elements are created by a malicious device and subsequently presented in some form.
2. Erroneous executions where (random) faults in protocol execution may encode information.

Note that in the second case there might be no security alert. For instance, distance bounding protocols explicitly admit failures.

While the most effective methods of the types mentioned in point 1 require asymmetric cryptography (see, e.g., [590]), there are possibilities to create narrow covert channels even if a random string is processed with, say, a hash function. Assume for instance that the device chooses r at random, while $\text{Hash}(r)$ is available to the adversary. Assume that a malicious device executing the protocol intends to leak bits of a string μ of length 2^l. Assume also that it has a secret key k shared with the adversary, who is observing the communication channel. Instead of just choosing r at random, computing $\text{Hash}(r)$, and presenting it, the following steps are executed:

1. choose r at random, $s := \text{Hash}(r)$, $z := \text{Hash}(s, k)$,
2. parse z as $a||b||\ldots$, where a consists of l bits and b consists of m bits,
3. goto 1, if the m-bit substring of μ starting at position a is different from b,
4. output s.

Of course, this is a *narrow channel*, as m must be small enough so that an appropriate r can be found in a reasonable time—in practice we are talking about a few bits per protocol execution. Note that this procedure works for any hash function. It works also if the loop may be executed only a limited number of times and, during the last loop execution, steps 2 and 3 are omitted. Unfortunately, if a device is delivered as a black-box, then the possibilities to inspect what the device is doing are severely limited. There are only a few exceptions (see, e.g., [94]).

1.2.2 Active Watchdog Concept

The general idea is that a device is controlled by its dedicated watchdog coming from a source independent from the device manufacturer and the device provider. The watchdog should detect malicious operation or make it ineffective, given that no access to the internal operation of the device controlled is granted. A watchdog is an active device, modeled as follows:

- it controls the whole communication between the device and the external world,
- it can delete and change all messages,
- it may challenge the device during extra interactions executed by them.

The idea of separating the tasks between two independent devices is an old concept [136]. The same concerns supervising computation correctness by an external unit [97]. Nevertheless, it has attracted more attention in the post-Snowden era, being used, among others, in a solution guarding against subversion attacks on cryptographic devices—see the paper [31] and an extension [510].

1.2.3   Solution Strategy

We propose the following general approach for transforming cryptographic protocols into versions involving a watchdog:

- the proposed changes in a protocol should be minimal, preferably exactly the same protocol should be executed by other protocol participants,
- we identify the basic components of the protocol that enable creating covert channels and for each of them provide a modified secure version.

The main problem areas are the steps that are either nondeterministic or not verifiable by the protocol partners and external observers. This concerns in particular choosing elements at random. However, we have also to consider deterministic steps if their correctness can be verified only with a delay—note that in the meantime the session can be interrupted due to, for example, a real or claimed physical fault.

From now on we use the following terminology:

Device   a potentially malicious device to be controlled,
Watchdog   a watchdog unit controlling the Device,
Reader   the original partner in the protocol executed by the Device.

Apart from that, we talk about an adversary that may observe and manipulate communications between the Watchdog and the Reader, while the adversary has no access to communications between the Watchdog and the Device (including, in particular, all Device's output.)

1.2.3.1   Commitments: Problems with Solutions Based on Hash Functions

Cryptographic hash functions are frequently used to generate commitments in lightweight protocols for ubiquitous devices. Due to their one-wayness, it is hard to build a broad subliminal channel, however the following attacks are still possible:

- choosing the committed value in a malicious way (e.g., from a small subspace),
- creating a narrow covert channel according to the method described on page 5.

For this reason, forwarding a hash value by the Watchdog should not occur unless the hash argument has been randomized by the Watchdog. One may attempt to randomize a hash value in the following naïve way:

1. the Device chooses r' at random, computes $c' := \text{Hash}(r')$ and sends c' to the Watchdog,
2. the Watchdog selects ρ at random and returns it to the Device,
3. the Device computes the final value $r := r' \oplus \rho$ (where $\oplus$ stands for the bitwise XOR operation) and sends the final commitment $c := \text{Hash}(r)$.

The problem with this approach is that in the case of standard hash functions, the Watchdog cannot check that c has been computed correctly without retreating to very complicated procedures (more expensive than simple commitments based on symmetric cryptography) or disclosing r. However, revealing the committed value must not occur before the moment when this value is transmitted to the Reader. Indeed, the Watchdog might transfer this value prematurely—we cannot exclude the possibility that the Watchdog and the Reader are colluding.

Recall that randomization of the hash argument is easy for Pedersen commitments:

- the Device chooses r' and s' at random and computes $c' := g^{r'} \cdot h^{s'}$, it presents c' to the Watchdog,
- the Watchdog chooses r'', s'' at random computes $c := c' \cdot g^{r''} \cdot h^{s''}$ and:
  - sends r'', s'' to the Device,
  - sends the commitment c to the Reader,
- the Device computes the committed values: $r := r' \cdot r''$, $s := s' \cdot s''$.

Unfortunately, such commitments require implementing asymmetric cryptography, while we have assumed that we are limited to symmetric methods. Concluding, as it seems very hard to overcome the problems related to hash functions that are not based on asymmetric cryptography, we must focus on symmetric encryption. Note that symmetric encryption has to be implemented on most ubiquitous devices to encrypt messages, so reusing it for commitments may reduce the implementation cost and simplify the hardware requirements.

1.2.3.2 Commitments Based on Symmetric Encryption

We assume that the encryption function works with n-bit keys and converts n-bit blocks into n-bit ciphertexts. Hence each key defines a permutation on n-bit blocks. We assume that the encryption scheme is resistant to known-plaintext attacks.

The second assumption is that given a ciphertext c, for most plaintexts t there is a key k such that $c = \text{Enc}_k(t)$.

Basic Commitment Mechanism
1. choose a plaintext t and a key k at random,
2. compute $c := \text{Enc}_k(t)$,
3. present (t, c) as a commitment for k.

In order to open the commitment (t, c) one has to present k. The commitment opening test is $\text{Enc}_k(t) \overset{?}{=} c$. Note that breaking the commitment is equivalent to a successful known-plaintext attack. Of course some care is required when choosing the encryption scheme, as each single bit of the key has to be secure against cryptanalysis.

Controlled Commitment Mechanism
1. The Device creates a commitment (t', c') for k' using the basic mechanism (i.e., $c' := \text{Enc}_{k'}(t')$ and t' is a single n-bit block), and presents (t', c') to the Watchdog,

2. The Watchdog chooses n-bit blocks θ and κ at random and presents them to the Device,
3. The Device recomputes the basic commitment:

$$t := t' \oplus \theta, \quad k := k' \oplus \kappa, \quad c := \mathrm{Enc}_k(t)$$

and presents c to the Watchdog,
4. the Watchdog chooses α at random and computes

$$t := t' \oplus \theta, \quad \zeta := \mathrm{Enc}_c(\alpha)$$

5. The Watchdog presents the final commitment (t, α, ζ) concerning the element k to the Reader.

Note that the Watchdog has no control over the correctness of execution of the third step and therefore the Device can potentially install a covert channel in c. However, at this moment c is hidden behind the commitment (α, ζ) chosen by the Watchdog. So in particular, the potential covert channel is hidden as well.

However, it is necessary to note that the Device should not be given the freedom to interrupt the protocol execution. Otherwise the Device could selectively interrupt the execution depending on the values of t and k and in this way leak some secret bits.

Opening the commitment is controlled by the Watchdog in the following way:

1. the Device presents k' to the Watchdog,
2. the Watchdog computes $k := k' \oplus \kappa$ and aborts if

$$c' \neq \mathrm{Enc}_{k'}(t'), \quad \text{or} \quad c \neq \mathrm{Enc}_k(t' \oplus \theta),$$

3. the Watchdog presents k to the Reader,
4. the Reader computes $\bar{c} := \mathrm{Enc}_k(t)$, and accepts the opening if $\zeta = \mathrm{Enc}_{\bar{c}}(\alpha)$.

Note that breaking this commitment by the adversary is at least as hard as known-plaintext cryptanalysis. Namely, for a (plaintext, ciphertext) pair (α, ζ) one can choose t at random and present it to the adversary. Indeed, for any key ψ that is a solution for (α, ζ), for most values t there is a key k such that $\psi = \mathrm{Enc}_k(t)$.

1.2.3.3 Encrypted Random Challenge

We assume that the protocol requires the Device to send a random challenge r as a ciphertext $\mathrm{Enc}_k(r)$ for the key k shared with the Reader. The following protocol enables the Watchdog to control the situation:

1. the Watchdog sends a commitment θ to an element α chosen at random (for this purpose the basic commitment from Sect. 1.2.3.2 can be used),

2. the Device chooses r' at random, computes $s := \mathrm{Enc}_k(r')$ and sends s to the Watchdog,

3. the Watchdog computes $\sigma := \alpha \oplus s$ and sends

- σ to the Reader,
- α to the Device (if necessary, the Watchdog attaches also an opening to the commitment).

With this approach, the random challenge is $r = \mathrm{Dec}_k(\sigma)$.

For the Device, the final shape of r is unpredictable so there is no way to hide information in r. On the other hand, the Watchdog cannot influence r (for instance, enforce repetition of the same r), as α has to be determined before the (random) ciphertext s is presented to it.

Note that if the random challenge is presented in clear, then a simplified version of the above procedure can be used.

1.2.3.4 Answers to Challenges

One of the moments when information can be leaked to the adversary is when the Device is responding to a challenge sent by the Reader by computing some deterministic algorithm, but any verification procedure for the response requires knowledge of a key shared by the Reader and the Device. This key must not be available to the Watchdog due to security reasons. In this case no censorship by the Watchdog is possible. On the other hand, the Reader may discover the manipulation when it is already too late, since the malicious message has been already on the air, available to the adversary.

The solution to this problem is to encrypt the communications from the Watchdog to the Reader with a random session key that is unknown to the Device. Such an encryption results in randomization destroying, any covert channel.

The procedure to establish the session key is as follows:

1. the Reader creates a commitment u to a random key z' and sends u to the Watchdog of the Device,

2. at the same time the Reader creates a ciphertext $c_0 = \mathrm{Enc}_k(z')$ with the key k shared with the Device, and sends it to the Device through the Watchdog,

3. the Device decrypts c_0 and reveals z' to its Watchdog,

4. the Watchdog checks the correctness of z' against the commitment u and chooses a key z at random,

5. the Watchdog sends $\mathrm{Enc}_{z'}(z)$ to the Reader,

6. from now on, in the current session all messages forwarded by the Watchdog from the Device to the Reader are additionally encrypted with the key z.

Note that for the steps 1 and 2 one can apply the procedures from Sects. 1.2.3.2 and 1.2.3.3. Thereby, the protocol can be secured against a malicious Reader as well. Note also that the Device knows z' so it could learn z from $\mathrm{Enc}_{z'}(z)$. However, the

Device cannot access the communication channel without help from the Watchdog. Consequently, it does not know $\text{Enc}_{z'}(z)$.

For the adversary, the situation is just the opposite: it has access to $\text{Enc}_{z'}(z)$, but it does not know z' and cannot learn it from the colluding Device, as there is no communication channel between them.

1.2.3.5 Distance Bounding Protocols

A distance bounding protocol [112] is executed when the physical presence of the Device in a close proximity of the Reader needs to be verified. This is particularly important in scenarios concerning access control in the presence of hardware tokens. By utilizing the timing delays between sending out a challenge bit and receiving a response, the Reader can calculate an upper bound on the distance to the verified device, and, if the Device is outside the intended perimeter, abandon the protocol.

The main and most problematic part in distance bounding protocols is the Rapid Bit Exchange (RBE) phase that is key to calculating the distance based on the response time. Typically, it is executed by a Device and a Reader as follows:

1. the Device and the Reader share m-bit strings r_0 and r_1 (computed from a shared secret and a nonce transmitted in clear),
2. for $i = 1, \ldots, m$, the following steps are executed:

   (a) the Reader sends a pseudorandom bit $c[i]$,
   (b) the Device responds immediately with $r_{c[i]}[i]$.

3. The Reader aborts the protocol if the answers of the Device have not been obtained within (strict) time limits or not all of them are correct.

The RBE phase is potentially a source of problems:

- The Device can send bits different from $r_{c[i]}[i]$ just to create a covert channel. Incorrect responses might be interpreted not as malicious activity of the Device, but as an attempt by an adversary standing between the Device and the Reader to cheat about the distance.
- Convincing the Watchdog about the correctness of the responses is a challenge: during the RBE phase there is no time for exchange of messages between the Device and the Watchdog and for nontrivial computations.

The solution presented below is based on blinding the responses with a one-time pad, where the random key is transported via the Device to the Watchdog in a secure way. It consists of the three phases described below:

PREPARATION: During this phase a blinding string is prepared. Namely, a session key z shared between the Watchdog and the Reader is established, as described in Sect. 1.2.3.4. However, instead of using it for encapsulation of messages it is used as a seed for creating a pseudorandom bit string $B(z)$.

RBE: RBE is executed as in the standard protocol except that the
                        Watchdog, after receiving the ith response $A[i]$ from the
                        Device, converts it to

$$A'[i] := A[i] \oplus B(z)[i]$$

                        and forwards $A'[i]$ to the Reader.

VERIFICATION: Aside from the usual operations, the Reader additionally
                        removes the blinding by XORing each $A'[i]$ with $B(z)[i]$.

1.3 Privacy

Deploying ubiquitous systems means not only substantial advantages for many
application areas, but at the same time emerging and significant privacy problems.

For instance, if device identifiers are explicitly transmitted when two devices
establish a communication session, then it is relatively easy to create a global
tracking system and misuse the information collected in this way. Note that in the
case of symmetric cryptography, one cannot first securely establish a session key
(e.g., with the Diffie-Hellman protocol), and then send the identifiers encrypted with
this key. Theoretically, parties A and B sharing a symmetric key k may recognize
each other without transmitting any identifier:

1. party A chooses a nonce n at random and for each of its partners i:

   (a) chooses a nonce n_i at random,
   (b) computes $M_i = \text{Enc}_{k_i}(n, n_i)$, where k_i is the key shared with this partner,

2. party A broadcasts $(n, M_1, M_2, \ldots,)$,
3. party B decrypts each M_i with all shared keys it knows; if the first half of the
   plaintext is n, then this is the right key and it responds with n_i.

The obvious problem with such a protocol is its lack of scalability, so it cannot be
applied in large-scale ubiquitous systems.

Fortunately, in the case of ubiquitous systems the size of the system may be an
advantage: even if the adversary can monitor communication at many places, one
can assume that the adversary is not omnipresent and consequently only a fraction
of the interactions are available to him. Some defense methods are based on this
fact.

Another factor that may hinder adversarial actions is that a device may have some
a priori knowledge about its potential communication partners and therefore its
computation effort can be limited to these partners. On the other hand, an adversary
having no idea who is attempting to communicate may be forced to consider all
possible pairs of partner devices—the computational effort in this case might be
higher by an order of magnitude. Moreover, it may lead to many false candidates—
while for the attacked device this problem does not arise, as its range of partner
choices is limited.

The rest of this section is devoted to diverse methods that at least reduce the privacy risks without retreating to asymmetric cryptography.

1.3.1 Symmetric Protocols and Deniability

From the point of view of privacy protection, symmetric cryptography leads to fewer problems than advanced methods based on asymmetric cryptography. Namely, if all cryptographic secrets used to execute a protocol are available to both parties executing the protocol, then a valid transcript of a protocol execution can be created by either party of the protocol. Therefore such a transcript cannot be used as a proof that an interaction has taken place.

Let us note that the situation might be different if a secret for symmetric cryptography is known only to one party of the protocol. For instance, if a device D is authenticated by presenting a token s, where Hash(s) is a one-time key publicly known as belonging to D, then presenting s may serve as a proof that an interaction with D has taken place.

1.3.2 Identity Hiding with Random Key Predistribution

When tools such as Diffie-Hellman key exchange are unavailable, random key predistribution may help to protect the initial information exchange. According to this approach, a session is initiated as follows:

Phase 1 (key discovery):   the communicating devices find keys from the key predistribution scheme that they share,

Phase 2 (identity disclosure):   the devices exchange their identity information, and communication is protected with the shared keys found in Phase 1,

Phase 3 (authentication and key establishment):   the devices continue in a way tailored to the declared identity information, encryption may be based on bilateral keys and not on the keys from the key predistribution.

Let us recall a few details of key predistribution schemes. There is a global key pool $\mathcal{K}$ of size N. We assume that each device i has an individual key pool $\mathcal{K}^{(i)}$ consisting of keys $k_1^{(i)}, \ldots, k_n^{(i)}$. If devices i and j meet, they identify a key (or keys) in $\mathcal{K}^{(i)} \cap \mathcal{K}^{(j)}$ (shared keys).

There are certain details about how to choose the subsets of keys to ensure that the set of keys $\mathcal{K}^{(i)} \cap \mathcal{K}^{(j)}$ is nonempty. The basic approach is to choose random subsets—then due to the birthday paradox there is a fair chance of a key being shared if $n \approx \sqrt{N}$. Another approach is to consider a projective space and assign keys corresponding to a line to each device—note that in a projective space every two lines intersect [124].

Key predistribution may reduce the privacy risks during identity information exchange as most of the devices in the vicinity of devices A and B initializing an interaction will not be able to access the information exchanged in Phase 2. However, some details have to be implemented carefully:

- In Phase 1 a device cannot simply send identifiers of the keys it holds as this set of identifiers would serve as its implicit identifier and can be abused to trace it.
- An adversary that knows a key k from the pool (e.g., as a legitimate user) would be able to trace all interactions in Phase 2 between devices for which k is the shared key. Even worse, the adversary may attempt to learn as many keys from the pool as possible, e.g., by hacking its own devices.

In the following we recall a few techniques that reduce these risks.

1.3.2.1 Key Discovery with a Bloom Filter

Bloom filters can be used as a compact data structure to enable discovery of shared keys in a relatively secure way. A Bloom filter is a bit array of length, say, 2^l. In order to "insert" keys $k_1, \ldots, k_t$ into a filter a device A performs the following steps:

1. initialize a Bloom filter F as an array of zeroes,
2. choose a nonce η at random,
3. for each $i \le t$ "insert" the key k_i into the filter:

   (a) for $j \le m$ compute $\text{Hash}(\eta, k_i, j)$, truncate it to the l most significant bits, getting $h_{i,j}$ (m is a Bloom filter parameter),
   (b) set the bits of F to 1 in the positions $h_{i,1}, \ldots, h_{i,m}$,

When a device B receives the filter F together with the nonce η, for each key it holds it can perform a similar calculation and check whether F holds only ones in the computed positions. If there is even a single 0, this key is not shared with A. Otherwise, it is a candidate shared key. For some details see [332].

Of course, depending on the size of the Bloom filter, the number of keys inserted into the filter and the parameter m, there might be false candidates. In order to inform A about the candidate keys one can reply with a Bloom filter created for the candidate keys. A few interactions of this type should suffice to narrow the set of candidates to the set of shared keys on both sides.

1.3.2.2 Multiple Shared Keys

For the sake of privacy preservation, it is useful to design the key predistribution scheme so that two devices share multiple keys. Then during Phase 2 the devices sharing keys, say, $k_{i_1}, \ldots, k_{i,w}$, encrypt each message with all these keys. For instance, one can use single encryption with a key $K := \text{KGF}(k_{i_1}, \ldots, k_{i,w}, nonce)$ where KGF is a key generation function, and $nonce$ is a nonce exchanged in the clear.

The advantage of this approach is that the adversarial device needs to know all keys $k_{i_1}, \ldots, k_{i,w}$ to decrypt the communications of Phase 2. Of course, some keys from the list may be known to the adversary—due to the key predistribution mechanism.

1.3.2.3 Epoch Keys

Paradoxically, reducing the number of keys in a pool may be advantageous. According to [146], each device holds the following:

long term keys: These are the keys from a key predistribution scheme. Long term keys are used only to decrypt ciphertexts containing epoch keys,

epoch keys: These keys are used for establishing communication links within their epoch as described in previous subsections.

From time to time the system provider runs the following steps:

1. new epoch keys are generated at random,
2. for each key k from the pool of long term keys, the corresponding ciphertext $C := \mathrm{Enc}_k(\eta)$ with a MAC is created, where η is an epoch key selected for k,
3. the ciphertexts of the epoch keys are disseminated to the devices.

There might be different ways of dissemination. For example, it might be done by broadcasting over a public radio channel or handling the new epoch keys when a device logs into the system.

The crucial property of this approach is that the number of epoch keys is N/m, where N is the number of long term keys, and that an epoch key is assigned to m long term keys when creating the ciphertexts described above. The parameter m could be a small constant such as 4. If each device holds $n \approx \sqrt{N}$ long term keys, and m is a small constant, then the expected number of epoch keys shared by two devices is approximately m.

Using epoch keys has advantages from the point of view of privacy protection:

- As the number of shared keys increases the probability that a different device can follow the communication in Phase 2 is significantly reduced. For instance, for $m = 2$ the probability changes from n/N to

$$\frac{\binom{n}{2}}{\binom{N/2}{2}} \approx \frac{n^2/2}{N^2/8} = 4 \cdot \left(\frac{n}{N}\right)^2 .$$

As typically $\frac{n}{N} \ll 1$, the progress is significant.
- Devices A and B may share epoch keys for two reasons:

  - A and B share a long term key, so consequently they share the epoch key encrypted with this long term key,
  - the same epoch key has been encrypted with different long term keys possessed, respectively, by A and B.

In the second case the same pair of long term keys does not necessarily correspond to the same epoch key during the next epoch. So an adversary that may follow A and B in one phase cannot automatically continue to do so in the next epoch.

1.3.3 Overloading Identifiers

The idea is to follow the approach used in human society: in everyday life we do not use unique identifiers (like personal identification numbers), but ambiguous identifiers such as first names (in Europe), family names (in China), etc. Despite the fact that the same identifier is used by a large number of people, there is almost no confusion in social interactions. For ubiquitous systems, we can mimic this approach. Namely, we assume that:

- The number of devices is large, say N, however in each local environment the number of devices is at most m, where $m \ll N$,
- Apart from its main unique identifier, each device holds k identifiers from a pool of size M, where $M \ll N$ and k is a small constant,

Now, the concept is that in a local environment each device occurs under one of its short IDs [147]. The process of joining such an environment involves using one of its short identities not yet in use there so far. The chances of having such an identifier available might be surprisingly high due to the famous power-of-two-choices phenomenon [46]. The crucial point in this approach is to determine how many short identifiers are needed globally, as minimizing their number provides better privacy protection. One can show that this process proceeds successfully for m participants (i.e., they always have the ability to choose an unused identifier) with probability at least p if the number of short identifiers N is approximately

$$\left(-\frac{m^{k+1}}{(k+1)\ln(1-p)} \right)^{1/k} .$$

1.3.4 Pairwise Keys Evolution

If a device has no asymmetric cryptography implemented, then establishing a bilateral key with another device is a problem. In small scale systems, we can deploy such keys in a secure environment during the manufacturing phase. Unfortunately, this is no longer possible in most large-scale application scenarios. So, the common solution is to pair two devices in a private environment and hope that electronic communication has not been tapped there. Only in a limited number of cases the key (or some auxiliary information) can be carried by the user and inserted into both devices. Indeed, a device may have no appropriate interface for such direct communication with the user (e.g., a keyboard). Another issue is that users might feel annoyed by the need for such manual work.

A pragmatic solution to this problem was presented in [499]:

- One can assume that the adversary is not omnipresent, hence it misses some number of successful communications between each pair of devices.
- Each time two devices meet, they change the bilateral key in a random way, i.e., if the shared key is k, then new key is $F(k, i)$, where $i \le n$ is chosen at random and $F(k, i)$ means k with its ith bit flipped.

This approach has the advantage that the bilateral key evolves in an unpredictable way and, after a small number of successful interactions it, becomes uniformly distributed in the key space. If during this time the adversary is not monitoring communication, then it loses control entirely over the shared key: indeed in the case of m subsequent changes the adversary would have to check more than $\binom{n}{m} > (\frac{n}{m})^m$ possibilities.

An additional advantage of this approach is that if a device A gets cloned, then a partner B of A can talk with only one version of A—evolution of keys will lead to a lack of synchronization and consequently detection of the presence of clones.

One can modify the scheme so that recovering past versions of the key becomes impossible: if F is, say, a hash function, then learning the current version of the key (e.g., by breaking into the device) does not reveal even the previous key. Despite the limited randomness in the process, key evolution has comparable properties to key unpredictability [331].

In a similar way, one can let the identifiers evolve.

1.3.5 Transmission with Errors

Transmitting the same encrypted identifiers during Phase 2 of the algorithm from Sect. 1.3.2 allows the adversary to set it as a temporary identifier for that user. To do so, the ciphertext has to be randomized. The obvious way to create non-repeatable messages is to include a nonce, namely instead of sending $c = \text{Enc}_k(A)$, A selects a nonce η and transmits $\hat{c} = \text{Enc}_k(A \oplus \eta)$ together with η. However, one can arrange this in a more clever way. The modified procedure is as follows:

- A chooses at random a string η with a (relatively) small Hamming weight,
- A computes $\hat{c} := \text{Enc}_k(A \oplus \eta)$ and sends it to a partner (say B), with which it expects to share the key k.
- B computes $\hat{A} := \text{Dec}_k(\hat{c})$ and looks for identifiers D of its partners such that the Hamming weight of $\hat{A} \oplus D$ is small. The identifier of A is among these candidates, and if the parameters are chosen properly there is only a small chance of having any other candidate on the list. Such false candidates may be eliminated easily using bilateral keys.

From the point of view of the adversary, holding a lot of keys the situation is more complicated. It may hold many false candidates for the key k used in this phase. As $\text{Dec}_{k'}(\text{Enc}_k(A \oplus \eta))$ provides unpredictable results, it may happen that it is close enough to some valid identifier U. In this way the adversary may get a lot of data confusing its tracing attack.

1.4 Conclusion and Future Directions

In this chapter, we focused on pointing out some of the challenges in developing large scale networks of severely constrained devices. Due to computational constraints the traditional approach to multiparty security and privacy has to give way to methods based on symmetric cryptography and information obfuscation. While considering threats caused by malicious protocol implementation, we presented several schemes utilizing an additional device, a watchdog, that may be provided by a third party, and hinders any covert channel aimed at secret leakage.

Future directions include inspecting the possibilities of leakage prevention in the case of collusion between a reader and a device. The additional device described in Sect. 1.2 prevents understanding of the messages exchanged between the verified device and the reader, however as the watchdog is not integrated into the device there is no guarantee that the device and the reader are not creating a covert channel. A natural approach would be to enable the possibility of signal jamming by the watchdog, however this solution is ineffective due to power requirements. Moreover, since each user may be in possession of multiple devices, the case of a single watchdog responsible for all a user's devices and batch authorization might be considered.

In the second part of the chapter, we pointed out the problem of violating privacy requirements, especially via user tracking, in ubiquitous systems. One of the major challenges is establishing a shared key, as 'generating' a new one with methods derived from the Diffie-Hellman protocol is not feasible and using a constant pool of predistributed keys allows a tracking adversary to identify devices during the key discovery phase. We described some methods based on a key evolution approach and on the obfuscation of information. The latter is obtained by utilizing hash functions or introducing a small error into the transmitted message. It should be noted that these solutions are not fully satisfactory, at least if we are confined to symmetric methods. If asymmetric cryptography can be used, then the situation is quite different (see Chap. 5).

Acknowledgments Authors "Mirosław Kutyłowski and Piotr Syga" supported by Polish National Science Centre, project OPUS no 2014/15/B/ST6/02837.

Part II
Symmetric Lightweight
Cryptographic Primitives

2

Lightweight Cryptographic Primitives: A Brief Categorized Catalog

Aleksandra Mileva, Vesna Dimitrova, Orhun Kara, and Miodrag J. Mihaljević

Abstract The main objective of this chapter is to offer to practitioners, researchers and all interested parties a brief categorized catalog of existing lightweight symmetric primitives with their main cryptographic features, ultimate hardware performance, and existing security analysis, so they can easily compare the ciphers or choose some of them according to their needs. Certain security evaluation issues have been addressed as well. In particular, the reason behind why modern lightweight block cipher designs have in the last decade overwhelmingly dominated stream cipher design is analyzed in terms of security against tradeoff attacks. It turns out that it is possible to design stream ciphers having much smaller internal states.

2.1 Introduction

Lightweight cryptography aims to deploy cryptographic algorithms in resource-constrained devices such as embedded systems, RFID devices and sensor networks. The cryptographic community has done a significant amount of work in this area, including design, implementation and cryptanalysis of new lightweight cryptographic algorithms, together with efficient implementation of conventional cryptography algorithms in constrained environments (see the Lightweight Cryp-

A. Mileva (✉)
Universitet "Goce Delcev", Štip, Republic of Macedonia
e-mail: aleksandra.mileva@ugd.edu.mk

V. Dimitrova
University "Ss Cyril and Methodius", Skopje, Republic of Macedonia

O. Kara
Department of Mathematics, IZTECH Izmir Institute of Technology, Izmir, Turkey
e-mail: orhunkara@iyte.edu.tr

M. J. Mihaljević
Mathematical Institute, Serbian Academy of Sciences and Arts, Belgrade, Serbia

tography Lounge,[1] [89, 260, 391]). Most recent cryptographic competitions such as NIST's SHA-3 Cryptographic Hash Algorithm Competition[2] and eSTREAM project[3] (with the Profile 2) had requirements that support implementations for highly constrained devices. Additionally, NIST currently is working on a special call[4] to create a portfolio of lightweight algorithms through an open standardization process.

The lightweightness of a given cryptographic algorithm can be obtained in two ways, by optimized implementations with respect to different constraints or by dedicated designs which use smaller key sizes, smaller internal states, smaller building blocks, simpler rounds, simpler key schedules, etc. There are several relevant metrics for assessing lightweight algorithms, such as power and energy consumption, latency, throughput and resource requirements [404]. Power and energy consumption are important for devices that are battery-oriented or energy harvesting. Latency is the time taken to perform a given task, and is important for applications where fast response time is necessary (e.g., Advanced Driver Assistance Systems), while throughput can be defined as the rate at which the plaintext is processed per time unit, and is measured in Bps.

Resource requirements are expressed differently in hardware and software implementations. In the hardware case, they are described as gate area, expressed by logic blocks for FPGAs or by Gate Equivalents (GEs) for ASIC implementations. However, these measures highly depend on the particular technology, so it is not possible to do a fair and relevant comparison of the lightweight algorithm implementations exactly across different technologies. In the software case, resource requirements are described as number of registers, RAM and ROM consumption in bytes. ROM consumption corresponds in fact with the code size.

Hardware implementations are suitable for highly constrained devices. For example, on the low end, low-cost passive RFID tags may have a total of 1000–10,000 gates, with only 200–2000 budgeted for security purposes [309]. Software implementations are suitable for less constrained devices, and they are optimized for throughput and energy consumption.

Some design choices related to dedicated lightweight cryptographic algorithms have influences on the security margins. For example, smaller key sizes such as 80 bits or 96 bits are in conflict with the current NIST minimum key size requirement of 112 bits. Smaller block and output sizes in some algorithms may lead to plaintext recovery or codebook attacks. Simpler key schedules may enable different attacks using related keys, weak keys, etc. Smaller internal state (IS) and digest sizes in hash functions may lead to collision attacks. Simpler rounds sometimes means that more iterations are required to achieve security.

---

[1] https://cryptolux.org/index.php/Lightweight_Cryptography.

[2] Part 2.B.2, Federal Register Notice (2 November 2007).

[3] http://www.ecrypt.eu.org/stream/call/.

[4] https://csrc.nist.gov/CSRC/media/Projects/Lightweight-Cryptography/documents/Draft-LWC-Submission-Requirements-April2018.pdf.

The main objective of this chapter is to offer to practitioners, researchers and all interested parties a short categorized catalog of existing symmetric lightweight primitives with their main features, some details about known software and hardware performance, and existing security analysis, to enable selection according to specific needs. These cryptographic primitives can be categorized into five areas: block and stream ciphers, hash functions, message authentication codes, and authenticated encryption schemes. As a consequence of the simplicity which provides lightweightness, the security evaluation of lightweight stream ciphers appears as an issue of top importance, and so a number of illustrative elements relevant for cryptanalysis of lightweight encryption techniques have been pointed out as well.

It can easily be observed that (see Sect. 2.2) almost all of the recently designed lightweight ciphers are block ciphers. The requirement for unnecessarily large internal states results in extra hardware area cost which definitely hinders designing ultralightweight stream ciphers. We analyze the arguments behind this criterion and propose to loosen it by justifying the security analysis in Sect. 2.3. We believe this adoption will promote the design and even the analysis of lightweight stream ciphers.

2.2   Catalog of Lightweight Cryptographic Primitives

The catalog of lightweight cryptographic primitives is divided in five categories: block and stream ciphers, hash functions, message authentication codes, and authenticated encryption schemes.

2.2.1   Block Ciphers

Block ciphers encrypt one block of plaintext bits at a time, to a block of ciphertext bits, through multiple rounds, and using a secret key. Each round is a sequence of several simple transformations, which provide confusion and diffusion [522]. In each round, a round key is used, which is derived from the secret key using a key schedule algorithm. According to the algorithm structure, block ciphers can be divided into several types:

- Substitution Permutation Network (SPN)—each round consists of substitution (S-) and permutation (P-) boxes. Usually, S-boxes are non-linear transformations and provide confusion, while P-boxes are linear and provide diffusion.
- Feistel Network (Feistel)—divides the input block into two halves, L_i and R_i, and in each round, the output block is $(L_{i+1}, R_{i+1}) = (R_i, L_i \oplus F(R_i, K_{i+1}))$, where F is the round-function (introduced by H. Feistel [209]).

- Add-Rotate-XOR (ARX)—only three operations are used: modular addition, rotation and XOR.
- Generalized Feistel Network (GFN)—divides the input block into n parts, and each round consists of a round-function layer and a block-permutation layer, which usually is a cyclic shift. If the round-function is applied only to one part, we speak about Type-1, and if it is applied on the $n/2$ parts, we speak about Type-2 GFN. If there is an additional linear layer between the two layers, we speak about Extended GFN [78].
- LFSR-based—in the round function they use one or more Linear Feedback Shift Registers (LFSRs) in combination with non-linear functions.
- LS-design—each round combines linear diffusion L-boxes with non-linear bitslice S-boxes, and they are aimed at efficient masked implementations against side-channel analysis [247].
- XLS-design—a variation of the LS-design, that uses the additional ShiftColumns operation, and Super S-boxes [306].

There are also tweakable block ciphers, which in addition to the key and the message have a third input named tweak, and they must be secure even if the attacker is able to control the tweak input. Each tweakable block cipher can be seen as a family of permutations in which each (key, tweak) pair selects one permutation.

The standard block cipher approach can be made lightweight by using smaller key sizes (e.g., 80 or 96 bits), smaller block sizes (e.g., 64 bits), smaller or special building blocks (e.g., 4-bit S-boxes, no S-boxes at all, or recursive diffusion layers), simpler key schedules (e.g., selecting a key schedule where bits from the master key are selected as round keys), smaller hardware implementation, involutive encryption, etc. AES-128 belongs in this group also, because there are ASIC implementations of it with an area of just 2400 GE[426] on 0.18 μm technology, but it cannot be applied in every scenario. In Table 2.1, we give a summary of the known lightweight block ciphers, sorted in alphabetical order, with their type, key and block size in bits, number of rounds, used technology and number of GEs if known, and we give the best known attacks in Table 2.2. KASUMI used in UMTS, GSM, and GPRS mobile communications systems, 3-Way and MANTIS are considered insecure. Additionally, CLEFIA and PRESENT are part of the ISO-29192-2 standard, while HIGHT, MISTY1 and AES are part of the ISO/IEC 18033-3:2010 standard.

For fair and consistent evaluation and comparison of software implementations of lightweight block and stream ciphers, one can use a free and open-source benchmarking framework FELICS (Fair Evaluation of Lightweight Cryptographic Systems) [182]. Currently, the assessment can be done on three widely used microcontrollers: 8-bit AVR, 16-bit MSP and 32-bit ARM, and extracted metrics are the execution time, RAM consumption and binary code size, from which one single value "Figure Of Merit" (FOM) is calculated. Table 2.3 presents some details about software performance of some lightweight block ciphers with the current best FELICS results for encryption of 128 bytes of data in CBC mode (scenario 1 in [182]), sorted according to the FoM measure, where the lowest result is the best.

Table 2.1 Lightweight block ciphers (characteristics)

Name	Ref	Type	Key size (bits)	Block size (bits)	No. of rounds	Techno. (µm)	No. of GEs
3-Way	[164]	SPN	96	96	11	–	–
AES-128	[166]	SPN	128	128	10	0.18	2400
CLEFIA	[527]	Type-2 GFN	128/192/256	128	18/22/26	0.13	2604 [16] (CLEFIA-128)
DESL/DESLX	[361]	Feistel	56/184	64	16	0.18	1848/2168
Fantomas	[247]	SPN+LS-design	128	128	12	–	–
FLY	[317]	SPN	128	64	20	–	–
GOST revisited	[487]	Feistel	256	64	32	0.18	651
GRANULE	[54]	Feistel	80/128	64	32	0.18	1288/1577
HIGHT	[283]	ARX+Type-2 GFN	128	64	32	0.25	3048
ICEBERG	[541]	SPN	128	64	16	–	–
ITUbee	[315]	Feistel	80	80	20	–	–
KASUMI	[1]	Feistel	128	64	8	0.11	2990 [586]
KATANn /		LFSR-based	80	$n \in \{32, 48, 64\}$	254	0.13	1054 ($n = 64$)
KTANTANn	[126]					0.13	462 ($n = 32$)
KLEIN	[239]	AES-like SPN	64/80/96	64	12/16/20	–	–
LBlock	[583]	Feistel	80	64	32	0.18	1320
LEA	[282]	ARX+GFN	128/192/256	128	24/28/32	0.13	3826

(continued)

Table 2.1 (continued)

Name	Ref	Type	Key size (bits)	Block size (bits)	No. of rounds	Techno. (μm)	No. of GEs
LED	[252]	AES-like SPN	64/128	64	32/48	0.18	966/1265
Lilliput	[78]	Extended GFN	80	4	30	0.065	1581
MANTIS$_r^a$	[68]	SPN	128+64 tweakey	64	$r \in \{5, 7\}$	–	–
mCrypton	[372]	SPN	64/96/128	64	12	–	–
MIBS	[299]	Feistel	64/80	64	32	0.18	1396
Midori	[51]	AES-like SPN	128	64/128	16/20	0.09	2450/3661
MISTY1	[398]	Feistel	128	64	8	–	–
Mysterion	[306]	SPN+XLS-design	128/256	128/256	12/16	–	–
Noekeon	[165]	SPN	128	128	16	–	–
PICARO	[485]	Feistel	128	128	12	–	–
Piccolo	[526]	GFN	80/128	64	25/31	–	–
PRESENT	[101]	SPN	80/128	64	31	0.18	1075/1391
PRIDE	[17]	SPN	128	64	20	–	–
PRINCE	[105]	SPN	128	64	12	0.13	3491
PRINTcipher	[333]	SPN	80/160	48/96	48/96	0.18	402/726
PUFFIN2	[569]	SPN	80	64	34	0.18	1083
RC5-12	[502]	ARX+Feistel	128	64	12	–	–
RECTANGLE	[598]	SPN	80/128	64	25	0.13	1599.5/2063.5
RoadRunneR	[63]	Feistel	80/128	64	10/12	–	–
Robin	[247]	SPN+LS-design	128	128	16	–	–
SEA	[542]	Feistel	$n = m(6b)$	n	odd[b]	–	–

SKINNY[a]	[68]	SPN	(64, 128, 192)/(128, 256, 384) tweakey	64/128	(32, 36, 40)/(40, 48, 56)	0.18	(1223, 1696, 2183)/(2391, 3312, 4268)
Simeck	[588]	Feistel	64/96/128	32/48/64	32/36/44	0.13	549/778/1005
SIMON	[65]	Feistel	64/(72, 96)/(96, 128)/(96, 144)/(128, 192, 256)	32/48/64/96/128	32/36/(42, 44)/(52, 54)/(68, 69, 72)	0.13	1234 (SIMON 128/128)
SPARX	[181]	ARX+SPN	128/128/256	64/128/128	24/32/40	–	–
SPECK	[65]	ARX+Feistel	64/(72, 96)/(96, 128)/(96, 144)/(128, 192, 256)	32/48/64/96/128	22/(22, 23)/(26, 27)/(28, 29)/(32, 33, 34)	0.13	1280 (SPECK 128/128)
TWINE	[544]	Type-2 GFN	80/128	64	36	0.09	1799
QARMA[a]	[39]	SPN	128/256	64/128	16/24	–	–
XTEA	[436]	Feistel	128	64	64	0.13	3490
Zorro	[227]	AES-like SPN	128	128	24	–	–

[a]Indicate tweakable block ciphers

[b] $\frac{3n}{4} + 2(\frac{n}{2b} + \lfloor b/2 \rfloor)$

Table 2.2 Lightweight block ciphers (best known attacks)

Name	Ref	Best known attack: data complexity/memory/time complexity
3-Way	[164]	**Practical** related-key attack [320], 1 related key pair, 2^{22} CPs
AES-128	[166]	Biclique key-recovery attack [545]: 2^{56} / $-$ /$2^{126.13}$
CLEFIA	[527]	Impossible differential attack [106]: $2^{114.58}$ / $2^{83.16}B$ /$2^{116.16}$
DESL/	[361]	Linear cryptanalysis on DES [311]: $2^{39} - 2^{41}$ DES evaluations
DESLX		Related-key attack on DESX[474]:$2^{3.5}$ KPs/$-$ / 2^{56} DES evaluations
Fantomas	[247]	$-$
FLY	[317]	$-$
GOST revisited	[487]	Single-key KP differential attack [159]: 2^{64} / $2^{70}B$ /2^{179}
GRANULE	[54]	$-$
HIGHT	[283]	Biclique cryptanalysis [15]: 2^8 / $\_$ /$2^{126.07}$
ICEBERG	[541]	Differential cryptanalysis [543]: 2^{63} CPs /2^{96} enc. on 8 rounds
ITUbee	[315]	$-$
KASUMI	[1]	**Practical** related-key attack [192]: 4 related keys, 2^{26} / 2^{30} B / 2^{32}
KATANn/	[126]	Meet-In-The-Middle attack on KTANTANn [104]
KTANTANn		$(3, 2, 2)$ pairs/ $-$/$(2^{75.17}, 2^{75.044}, 2^{75.584})$
KLEIN	[239]	Truncated differential attack [497]: $2^{48.6}$ / 2^{32} /$2^{54.9}$ on KLEIN-64
LBlock	[583]	CP related-key impossible differential attack[584]: 2^{63} / $-$ /$2^{75.42}$ on 24 rounds
LEA	[282]	$-$
LED	[252]	Random-difference distinguishers [443]: $-$ / $2^{60}B$/$2^{60.3}$ on 40 rounds LED-128
Lilliput	[78]	Key-recovery attack with the division property [512]: 2^{63} / $-$ /2^{77} on 17 rounds
MANTIS$_r$	[68]	**Practical** key-recovery attack [185]: 2^{28} / $-$ /2^{38} enc. on MANTIS$_5$
mCrypton	[372]	Related-key impossible differential cryptanalysis [388]: $(2^{59.9}, 2^{59.7})$ / $(2^{63.9}, 2^{55.7})B$ /$(2^{74.9}, 2^{66.7})$ on 9 rounds
MIBS	[299]	Biclique cryptanalysis [519] (MIBS-80): 2^{52}/$-$ /$2^{78.98}$
Midori	[51]	Key-recovery attack for the class of 2^{32} weak keys in Midori64 [250]: 2/$-$ /2^{16}
MISTY1	[398]	Single-key integral attack [56]: 2^{64}/$-$ /$2^{69.5}$
Mysterion	[306]	$-$

(continued)

Table 2.2 (continued)

Name	Ref	Best known attack: data complexity/memory/time complexity
Noekeon	[165]	Many related keys (weakness) [334]
PICARO	[485]	Related-key attack [129]: $2^{99}/2^{22} B /2^{107.4}$
Piccolo	[526]	Biclique cryptanalysis [15]: $2^4/- /(2^{79.07}, 2^{127.12})$
PRESENT	[101]	Biclique cryptanalysis (PRESENT-80) [15]: $2^{22}/- /2^{79.37}$
PRIDE	[17]	Multiple related-key differential attack [167]: $2^{41.6}/- /2^{42.7}$
PRINCE	[105]	Multiple differential attack [128]: $2^{57.94}/2^{61.52} /2^{60.62}$ on 10 rounds
PRINTcipher	[333]	Invariance subspace attack [359] applicable to $2^{52}/ 2^{102}$ weak keys: 5 CPs/ $-$/ negligible
PUFFIN2	[569]	Differential attack [95]: $2^{52.3}$ CPs/$- /2^{74.78}$
RC5-12	[502]	Differential attack [88]: 2^{44} CPs
RECTANGLE	[598]	Related-key differential attack [521]: $2^{62}/2^{72} B/2^{67.42}$ on 19 rounds
RoadRunneR	[63]	$-$
Robin	[247]	Key-recovery attack for the weak key set of density 2^{-32} [360]: 1 CP/$- /2^{64}$
SEA	[542]	$-$
SKINNY	[68]	Related-tweakey impossible differential attacks [23]: $2^{71.4}/2^{64} /2^{79}$ up to 23 rounds
Simeck	[588]	Linear hull attack with dynamic key-guessing techniques [491]: $(2^{31.91}, 2^{47.66}, 2^{63.09})/ -/(2^{61.78}, 2^{92.2}, 2^{111.44})$ add. and $(2^{56.41}, 2^{88.04}, 2^{121.25})$ enc.
SIMON	[65]	Differential cryptanalysis on 12/16/19/28/37 reduced-round SIMON-32/48/64/96/128
SPARX	[181]	Truncated-differential attack [24]: $2^{32} /2^{61}/2^{93}$ on 16 rounds (SPARX-64/128)
SPECK	[65]	Differential cryptanalysis [537]: $2^{125.35}/2^{22}/2^{125.35}$ on 23 rounds of the SPECK-128/128
TWINE	[544]	Impossible differential and multidimensional zero correlation linear attack [373]: $2^{62.1}$ KPs/ $2^{60} B / 2^{73}$ (TWINE-80)
QARMA	[39]	$-$
XTEA	[436]	Related-key rectangle attack [380]: $2^{63.83} / - / 2^{104.33}$ on 36 rounds
Zorro	[227]	Differential attack [55]: $2^{41.5} / 2^{10} / 2^{45}$

KP—Known Plaintext
CP—Chosen Plaintext

Table 2.3 The current best FELICS results for scenario 1: Encrypt 128 bytes of data in CBC mode

	AVR			MSP			ARM			
	Code	RAM	Time	Code	RAM	Time	Code	RAM	Time	
Cipher	(B)	(B)	(Cyc.)	(B)	(B)	(Cyc.)	(B)	(B)	(Cyc.)	FoM
Speck	966	294	39,875	556	288	31,360	492	308	15,427	5.1
Speck	874	302	44,895	572	296	32,333	444	308	16,505	5.2
Simon	1084	363	63,649	738	360	47,767	600	376	23,056	7.0
Simon	1122	375	66,613	760	372	49,829	560	392	23,930	7.2
RECTANGLE	1152	352	66,722	812	398	44,551	664	426	35,286	8.0
RECTANGLE	1118	353	64,813	826	404	44,885	660	432	36,121	8.0
LEA	1684	631	61,020	1154	630	46,374	524	664	17,417	8.3
SPARX	1198	392	65,539	966	392	36,766	1200	424	40,887	8.8
SPARX	1736	753	83,663	1118	760	53,936	1122	788	67,581	13.2
HIGHT	1414	333	94,557	1238	328	120,716	1444	380	90,385	14.8
AES	3010	408	58,246	2684	408	86,506	3050	452	73,868	15.8
Fantomas	3520	227	141,838	2918	222	85,911	2916	268	94,921	17.8
Robin	2474	229	184,622	3170	238	76,588	3668	304	91,909	18.7
Robin⋆	5076	271	157,205	3312	238	88,804	3860	304	103,973	20.7
RC5-20	3706	368	252,368	1240	378	386,026	624	376	36,473	20.8
PRIDE	1402	369	146,742	2566	212	242,784	2240	452	130,017	22.8
RoadRunneR	2504	330	144,071	3088	338	235,317	2788	418	119,537	23.3
RoadRunneR	2316	209	125,635	3218	218	222,032	2504	448	140,664	23.4
LBlock	2954	494	183,324	1632	324	263,778	2204	574	140,647	25.2
PRESENT	2160	448	245,232	1818	448	202,050	2116	470	274,463	32.8
PRINCE	2412	367	288,119	2028	236	386,781	1700	448	233,941	34.9
Piccolo	1992	314	407,269	1354	310	324,221	1596	406	294,478	38.4
TWINE	4236	646	297,265	3796	564	387,562	2456	474	255,450	40.0
LED	5156	574	2,221,555	7004	252	2,065,695	3696	654	594,453	138.6

2.2.2 Stream Ciphers

Stream ciphers encrypt small portions of data (one or several bits) at a time. By using a secret key, they generate a pseudorandom keystream, which is then combined with the plaintext bits to produce the ciphertext bits. Very often the combining function is bitwise XORing, and in that case we speak about binary additive stream ciphers. The basic security rule for stream ciphers is not to encrypt two different messages with the same pair of key/IV. So, stream ciphers usually have a large keystream period, and a different key and/or IV should be used after the period elapses. Each stream cipher usually has an initialization phase with some number of rounds (or clock-cycles), followed by an encryption phase. A fast initialization phase makes a given cipher suitable for encrypting many short messages, while when several large messages need to be encrypted, stream ciphers with a fast encryption phase are more appropriate.

The standard stream cipher approach can be made lightweight by using: smaller key sizes (e.g., 80 bits), smaller IV/nonce sizes (e.g., 64 bits), a smaller internal state (e.g., 80 or 100 bits), simpler key schedules, a smaller hardware implementation, etc. Table 2.4 lists the known lightweight stream ciphers in alphabetical order, with their main parameters and details about hardware implementation, and Table 2.5 provides the best known attacks. One can notice that all eSTREAM Profile 2 candidates that were not selected as finalists are not in the table. Also, according to the hardware implementations, ZUC, ChaCha and Salsa20 cannot really be considered as lightweight. While Lizard uses 120 bit keys, its designers claim only 80-bit security against key-recovery attacks. A5/1 used in GSM protocol, E0 used in Bluetooth, A2U2, and Sprout are considered insecure.

Additionally, Enocoro and Trivium are part of the ISO/IEC 29192-3:2012 standard, and Rabbit is part of ISO/IEC 18033-4:2011. SNOW 3G was chosen for the 3GPP encryption algorithms UEA2 and UIA2, while ZUC was chosen for the 3GPP algorithms 128-EEA3 and 128-EIA3. The profile 2 eSTREAM portfolio includes Grain v1, MICKEY 2.0 and Trivium. There is an IETF implementation of the ChaCha20, published in RFC 7539, with 96-bit nonce and maximum message length up to $2^{32} - 1B$ that can be safely encrypted with the same key/nonce, as a modification.

2.2.3   Hash Functions

A hash function is any function that maps a variable length input message into a fixed length output. The output is usually called a hashcode, message digest, hash value or hash result. Cryptographic hash functions must be preimage (one-way), second preimage and collision resistant.

Usually the message is first padded and then divided into blocks of fixed length. The most common method is to iterate over a so-called compression function, that takes two fixed size inputs, a message block and a chaining value, and produces the next chaining value. This is known as a Merkle-Damgård (MD) construction. The sponge construction is based on fixed-length unkeyed permutation (P-Sponge) or random function (T-Sponge), that operates on b bits, where $b = r + c$. b is called the width, r is called the rate (the size of the message block) and the value c the capacity. The capacity determines the security level of the given hash function. There is also a JH-like sponge in which the message block is injected twice.

The main problem of using conventional hash functions in constrained environments is their large internal state. SHA-3 uses a 1600 bit IS, and its most compact hardware implementation needs 5522 GE [471] on $0.13\,\mu m$ technology. On the other hand, SHA-256 has a smaller IS (256 bit), but one of its smaller hardware implementations uses 10,868 GE [211] on $0.35\,\mu m$ technology.

Lightweight hash functions can have smaller internal state and digest sizes (for applications where collision resistance is not required), better performance on short messages, small hardware implementations, etc. In some cases, for example tag-based applications, there is a need only for the one-way property. Also, most tag protocols require hashing of small messages, usually much less than 256 bits.

Table 2.4 Lightweight stream ciphers (characteristics)

Name	Ref	Key size (bits)	IV/nonce (bits)	IS (bits)	Output size (bits)	Max. keystream bits per (key, IV/nonce)	No. of init. rounds/cycles	Techno (μm).	No. of GEs
A2U2	[173]	61	64	95	1		var.	–	283 estimated
A5/1	[92]	64	22	64	1	228	86 + 100	–	–
BEAN	[350]	80	64	160	2		81	–	–
CAR30	[172]	128	120	256	128	$>2^{122}$	160	–	–
CAvium	[511]	80	80	288	1	–	144	–	–
ChaCha	[79]	256	64	512	512	2^{73}	8/12/20	0.18	9110 [270]
E0	[96]	8–128	26 + 48	132	1		240	–	–
Enocoro	[574, 575]	80/	64	176/	8	2^{35}	40/	0.18/	2700/
		128(v2)		272		2^{67}	96	0.09	4100
Fruit-80	[228]	80	70	80	1	2^{43}	160	0.18	960
Grain	[266, 267]	80(v1)/128	64/96	160/256	1	2^{43}	160	0.13	1294/1857 [240]
LILLE	[53]	80	80	80/100/120	40	$2^{32} \cdot 40$	720	0.09	911/991.6/1076.4
LIZARD	[253]	120	64	121	1	2^{18}	128+128	0.18	1161
MICKEY 2.0	[48]	80/	80/	200/	1	$2^{40}/$	260/	0.13	3188/
		128	128	320		2^{64}	416		5039 [240]
Plantlet	[421]	80	90	110	1	2^{30}	320	0.18	928

Rabbit	[98]	128	64	513	128	2^{71}	4+4	0.18	3800
RAKAPOSHI	[148]	128	192	320	1	2^{64}	448	–	–
Salsa20	[80]	256	64	512	512	2^{73}	20	0.18	9970 [270]
SNOW 3G	[204]	128	128	576	32		32	–	–
Sprout	[27]	80	70	89	1	2^{40}	320	0.18	813
Trivium	[127]	80	80	288	1	2^{64}	1152	0.35	749 [409]
Quavium	[555]	80	80	288	1	2^{64}	1152	–	3496 estimated
WG-8	[207]	80	80	160	1	2^{160}	40	0.065	1786 [587]
ZUC (v 1.6)	[205]	128	128	560	32		32	0.065	12,500 [378]

Table 2.5 Lightweight stream ciphers (best known attacks)

Name	Ref	Best known attack: data complexity/memory/time complexity
A2U2	[173]	**Practical** key-recovery attack [524] under the KP attack model $210/-/2^{24.7}$
A5/1	[92]	**Practical** Time-Memory tradeoff attack [92] 2sec KPs/ 2^{48} preprocessing steps to compute $300GB/\ 2^{24}$
BEAN	[350]	Distinguishing attack [13] with 2^{17} keystream bits
CAR30	[172]	–
CAvium	[511]	–
ChaCha	[79]	Multi-bit differential attack [143]: $2^{28}\ /-/\ 2^{233}$ on 7 rounds
E0	[96]	**Practical** key-recovery attack [381] using the first 24 bits of $2^{23.8}$ frames and 2^{38} computations
Enocoro	[574, 575]	–
Fruit-80	[228]	–
Grain	[266, 267]	Fast near collision attack [595]: $2^{19}\ /\ 2^{28}/\ 2^{75.7}$ on Grainv1
LILLE	[53]	–
LIZARD	[253]	Distinguishing attack [52]: $-/2^{76.6}/2^{51.5}$ random IV enc
MICKEY 2.0	[48]	Practical related key attack [179] with 65/113 related (K,?IV) pairs and 0.9835/0.9714 success rate
Plantlet	[421]	Distinguishing attack [422]
Rabbit	[98]	Differential fault analysis [330] with $128 - 256$ faults: $-/2^{41.6}B/2^{38}$
RAKAPOSHI	[148]	Related key attack [297]: 2^{38} chosen IVs/$-/\ 2^{41}$
Salsa20	[80]	Multi-bit differential attack [143]: $2^{96}\ /-/\ 2^{244.9}$ on 8 rounds
SNOW 3G	[204]	Multiset distinguisher [90]: 2^8 on 13 rounds
Sprout	[27]	Many, e.g., key recovery attack [50]: $-/-/2^{66.7}$ enc.
Trivium	[127]	Key-recovery attack [224]: 2^{77} on 855 rounds
Quavium	[555]	–
WG-8	[207]	Related key attacks [180] with one related key 2^{52} chosen IVs/$-/\ 2^{53.32}$
ZUC (v 1.6)	–	

KP—Known Plaintext

Tables 2.6 and 2.7 list the cryptographic and implementation properties of the known lightweight hash functions. ARMADILLO is considered insecure. Lesamnta-LW, PHOTON, and SPONGENT are part of the ISO/IEC 29192-5:2016 standard.

2.2.4 Message Authentication Codes

A message authentication code (MAC) protects the integrity and authenticity of a given message, by generating a tag from the message and a secret key. MAC

Table 2.6 Lightweight hash functions (cryptographic properties)

Name	Ref	Construction	Type of compression function	Message digest (bits)	IS (bits)	Rate (bits)	Preimage	Second preimage	Collisions	Best known attack
ARMADILLO2	[49]	MD	BC with data-depend. bit transpositions	80/128 /160/192/256	256/384 /480/576/768	48/64 /80/96/128	$2^{80}/2^{128}$ $/2^{160}/2^{192}$ $/2^{256}$	$2^{80}/2^{128}$ $/2^{160}/2^{192}$ $/2^{256}$	$2^{40}/2^{64}$ $/2^{80}/2^{96}$ $/2^{128}$	**Practical** free-start collision attack [435] $2^{8.9}/2^{10.2}/2^{10.2}/$ $2^{10.2}/2^{10.2}$
DM-PRESENT	[102]	MD	PRESENT in Davies-Meyer mode	64	64	80 / 128	2^{64}	2^{64}	2^{32}	Multi-differential collision attack [343] $2^{29.18}$ hash comp. on 12 rounds
H-PRESENT	[102]	MD	PRESENT in double-block-length c.	128	128	64	2^{128}	2^{128}	2^{64}	–
GLUON	[77]	T-sponge	Based on Feedback with Carry Shift Register	128/160/224	136/176/256	8/16/32	$2^{128}/2^{160}$ $/2^{224}$	$2^{64}/2^{80}$ $/2^{112}$	$2^{64}/2^{80}$ $/2^{112}$	Preimage attack [469] 2^{105} complexity
Lesamnta-LW	[281]	MD	Type-1 GFN 64–round BC in LW1 mode	256	256	128	2^{120}	2^{120}	2^{120}	–
LHash	[582]	P-Sponge	18-round Feistel-PG	80/96	96/96	16/16	$2^{64}/2^{80}$	$2^{40}/2^{40}$	$2^{40}/2^{40}$	–

(continued)

Table 2.6 (continued)

Name	Ref	Construction	Type of compression function	Message digest (bits)	IS (bits)	Rate (bits)	Preimage	Second preimage	Collisions	Best known attack
PHOTON	[251]	P-Sponge	12 round AES-like permutation	80/128/160/ 224/256	100/144/196/ 256/288	(20,16)/16/ 36/32/32	$2^{64}/2^{112}/$ $2^{124}/2^{192}$ 2^{224}	$2^{40}/2^{64}/$ $2^{80}/2^{112}$ 2^{128}	$2^{40}/2^{64}/$ $2^{80}/2^{112}$ 2^{128}	–
QUARK	[33]	P-Sponge	Grain-like permutation 544/704/1024 rounds	136(u)/176(s) /256(d)	136/176/256	8/16/32	$2^{128}/2^{160}$ 2^{224}	$2^{64}/2^{80}$ 2^{112}	$2^{64}/2^{80}$ 2^{112}	–
sLiSCP	[20]	P-Sponge	Type 2 GFN Simeck	160/160/192	192/256/256	32/64/64	$2^{128}/2^{128}$ 2^{160}	$2^{80}/2^{96}$ 2^{96}	$2^{80}/2^{96}$ 2^{96}	–
SPN-Hash	[144]	P-Sponge	SPN permutation in JH mode 10 rounds	128/256	256/512	128/256	$2^{128}/2^{256}$	$2^{128}/2^{256}$	$2^{64}/2^{128}$	–
SPONGENT	[100]	P-Sponge	PRESENT-like permutation 45/70/90 /120/140 r.	80/128/160 /224/256	88/136/176 /240/272	8/8/16/16 /16	$2^{80}/2^{120}$ $/2^{144}/2^{208}$ $/2^{240}$	$2^{40}/2^{64}$ $/2^{80}/2^{112}$ $/2^{128}$	$2^{40}/2^{64}$ $/2^{80}/2^{112}$ $/2^{128}$	Linear distinguishers [2] on 23 rounds of the SPONGENT permutation

Table 2.7 Lightweight hash functions (implementation properties)

Name	Ref	Techno. (μm)	No. of GEs	Throughput (Kbps @ 100kHz)
ARMADILLO	[49]	0.18	(2923/4353/5406/6554/8653) vs. (4030/6025/7492/8999/11,914)	(27/250/250/25/25) vs. (109/1000/100/100/100)
DM-PRESENT	[102]	0.18	(1600/1886) vs. (2213/2530)	(14.62/22.9) vs. (242.42/387.88)
H-PRESENT	[102]	0.18	2330 vs. 4253	11.45 vs. 200
GLUON	[77]	–	2071/2799.3/4724	12.12/32/58.18
Lesamnta-LW	[281]	0.09	8240	–
LHash	[582]	0.18	817/817/1028	2.40/2.40/(1.81, 0.91)
PHOTON	[251]	0.18	(865/1122/1396/1736/2177) vs. (1168/1708/2117/2786/4362)	(2.82/1.61/2.7/1.86/3.21) vs. (15.15/10.26/20/15.69/ 20.51)
QUARK	[33]	0.18	(1379/1702/ 2296) vs. (2392/2819/4640)	(1.47/2.27/3.13) vs. (11.76/18.18/50)
sLiSCP	[20]	0.065	2271/3019/3019	29.62/44.44/22.22
SPN-Hash	[144]	0.18	(2777 / 4625) vs. (4600 / 8500)	(36.1 / 35.8) vs. (55.7 / 111.3)
SPONGENT	[100]	0.13	(738 / 1060 / 1329 / 1728 / 1950) vs. (1127 / 1687 / 2190 / 2903 / 3281)	(0.81 / 0.34 / 0.4 / 0.22 / 0.17) vs. (17.78 / 11.43 / 17.78 / 13.33 / 11.43)

schemes can be constructed from block ciphers (e.g., CBC-MAC (part of the ISO/IEC 9797-1:1999 standard) or OCB-MAC [504]), from cryptographic hash functions (e.g., HMAC (RFC 2104)), etc. Three lightweight security architectures have been proposed for wireless sensor networks: TinySec [316], MiniSec [382] and SenSec[370]. TinySec and MiniSec recommend CBC-MAC and the patented OCB-MAC, while SenSec recommends XCBC-MAC, for which there is an existential forgery attack [238], and all suggest the use of 32-bit tags. 32-bit security is not enough—the recommended size is at least 64 bits.

Design choices for lightweight MACs include shorter tag sizes, simpler key schedules, small hardware and/or software implementations, better performance on very short messages, no use of nonces, and generation from lightweight block ciphers and hash functions. Some lightweight MACs are listed in Table 2.8, and the best known attacks against these MACs are provided in Table 2.9.

2.2.5   Authenticated Encryption Schemes

Authenticated encryption (AE) schemes combine the functions of ciphers and MACs in one primitive, so they provide confidentiality, integrity, and authentication of a given message. Besides the plaintext and the secret key, they usually accept variable length Associated Data (AEAD schemes), a public nonce, and an optional secret nonce. AD is a part of a message that should be authenticated, but not encrypted.

Lightweight authenticated encryption schemes are presented in Table 2.10, and the best known attacks against these schemes are provided in Table 2.11. Sablier and SCREAM/iSCREAM are considered insecure. The hardware implementation is given with encryption/authentication and decryption/verification functionalities.

2.3   Illustrative Issues in Security Evaluation of Certain Encryption Schemes

As a consequence of the simplicity which makes them lightweight, the security evaluation of lightweight encryption schemes arises as an issue of top importance. However, constraints on chapter space limit our discussion of the security evaluation. Consequently, this section shows only a number of illustrative issues relevant for the cryptanalysis of lightweight encryption techniques. In the first part, a generic approach for security evaluation is discussed, and in the second an advanced dedicated approach is pointed out.

Table 2.8 Lightweight MACs (characteristics)

Name	Ref	Type	Key size (bits)	Block size (bits)	Tag size (bits)	No. of rounds	Techno. (μm)	No. of GEs
Chaskey	[428]	Permutation-based MAC	128	128	≥64	8 (12)		3334.33 GE [356] estimated
LightMAC	[384]	New parallelizable mode with BC and two keys	2 × 80/128	64/128	64/128	Depends of used BC	–	–
SipHash-2-4	[32]	ARX-based keyed hash function	128	256	64	2 + 4 4 fin. rounds	–	–
TuLP	[238]	PRESENT BC in ALRED construction	80/160	64/128	64	14	0.18	2252/2764

Table 2.9 Lightweight MACs (best known attacks)

		Best known attack: data / time complexity
Chaskey	[428]	Differential-linear attack [369] $2^{48}/2^{67}$ on 7 rounds
LightMAC	[384]	–
SipHash -2-4	[32]	–
TuLP	[238]	–

2.3.1 Reconsidering TMD Tradeoff Attacks for Lightweight Stream Cipher Designs

We can simply divide the tradeoff attacks against ciphers into two groups, key recovery attacks and internal state recovery attacks. The first tradeoff attack against symmetric ciphers was introduced by Hellman [268] to illustrate that the key length of DES was indeed too short. Hellman prepared several tables containing DES keys. In general, the tradeoff curve is $TM^2 = N^2$ where T is the time complexity and M is the memory complexity. N is the cardinality of the key space. Here, the data complexity $D = 1$ since only one chosen plaintext is used to define a one way function which produces the (reduction of the) ciphertext of the chosen plaintext for a given key. Then, the tables are prepared during the precomputation phase. In practice, one generally considers the point $T = M = N^{2/3}$ on the curve since the overall complexity also becomes $N^{2/3}$. The precomputation phase costs roughly $O(N)$ encryptions. This is a generic attack which is applicable to any block cipher. Therefore, we can say that the security level diminishes to $2k/3$-bit security during the online phase of the Hellman tradeoff attack where k is the key length of a block cipher. However, one must pay a cost equivalent to exhaustive search to prepare the tables during the precomputation phase.

Stream ciphers also suffer from the same affliction by tradeoff attacks in that their keys can be recovered with an effort of $2^{2k/3}$ for each of them during the online phase. Stream ciphers consist of two parts. The initialization part uses an IV and a key to produce a seed value S_0. Then, S_0 is used to produce the keystream sequence through a keystream generator. While a state update function updates the internal states S_i, an output function produces the keystream bits (or words) z_i. It is possible to define a one way function from the key to the first k bits of the keystream sequence by choosing an IV value and fixing it. This is similar to the case of tradeoff attacks on block ciphers with a chosen plaintext. However, the attack may only be mounted on a decryption mechanism since it may not be possible to choose the IV during the encryption. Then, by preparing the Hellman tables, one can recover a key in $2^{2k/3}$ encryptions using $2^{2k/3}$ memory. The precomputation is 2^k. This is similar to the Hellman attack. Therefore, stream ciphers are prone to tradeoff attacks as with block ciphers in the key recovery case.

The other category of tradeoff attacks is aimed at recovering internal states of stream ciphers, rather than keys. Babbage [47] and Golić [236], independently, introduced another type of tradeoff curve $DM = N$ to recover an internal state.

Table 2.10 Lightweight authenticated encryption schemes (characteristics)

Name	Ref	Type	Key (bits)	Nonce (bits)	IS (bits)	Block/rate (bits)	Tag (bits)	Techno. (μm)	No. of GEs
ACORN v3[a]	[581]	SC (LFSR)	128	128	293	1	128	–	–
ALE	[103]	SC (AES, LEX leak)	128	128	256	128	128	0.065	2700
APE	[22]	Sponge (different hash f.) e.g., PHOTON-196	160[d]	36n[d] (opt.)	196[d]	36[d]	160[d]	0.18	1634[d]
ASC-1	[300]	SC (AES, LEX leak CFB-like mode)	256	56	512	128	128	0.065	4964 [103]
Ascon[a]	[186]	Sponge (SPN)	96/128	96/128	320	64 (128 for Ascon-128a)	96/128	0.009	2570 (7970) Ascon-128 [245] (SCA-protected)
C-QUARK	[36]	Sponge (LFSR, NFSR)	256	64	384	64	≥ 64	0.09	4000
FIDES	[87]	Sponge (AES-like, 16 rounds)	80/96	80/96	160/192	10/12	80/96	0.09	793–2876/ 1001–4792
Hummingbird-2	[200]	Hybrid (SPN)	128	64	128	16	128	0.13	2159-3220
Helix	[215]	SC (ARX)	256	128	160	32	128	–	–
Joltik[b]	[304]	tweakable BC (Joltik-BC)	64/80/96/ 128+64/48/96/64 tweak	32/24/48/32	64	64	64	–	2100/2100/ 2600/2600 (estimated)
KETJE[a]	[82]	Sponge (Keccak-f)	k≤ 182/ k≤ 382	182-|k|/ 382-|k|	200/400	16/32	64	–	–
LAC[c]	[596]	SC (LBlock-s, LEX leak)	64	80	144	48	64	–	1300 (estimated)

(continued)

Table 2.10 (continued)

Name	Ref	Type	Key (bits)	Nonce (bits)	IS (bits)	Block/rate (bits)	Tag (bits)	Techno. (μm)	No. of GEs
NORX32 v.3[a]	[35]	Sponge (LRX, 4/6 rounds)	128	64	512	320	128	0.018	62,000
NORX8 /NORX16	[34]	Sponge (LRX, 4/6 rounds)	80/96	32	128/256	40/128	80/196	–	1368/2880 (estimated)
Sablier[c]	[594]	SC (LFSR)	80	80	208	16	32	–	1925 (estimated)
SCREAM[b] /iSCREAM	[246]	tweakable BC (SPN+LS-designs)	128+128 tweak	8–120	128	128	128	–	–
sLiSCP	[20]	Sponge (Type-2 GFS+Simeck)	80/112/128	80/80/128	192/192/256	32/32/64	80/112/128	0.065	2289/2289/3039
TriviA-v2 /uTriviA	[132]	SC (Trivium-like)	128	128	384	64	128	0.065	21,521 / 16,748

[a] Indicates CAESAR Round 3 candidate
[b] Indicates CAESAR Round 2 candidate
[c] Indicates CAESAR Round 1 candidate
[d] In this case APE is used with PHOTON-196

Table 2.11 Lightweight authenticated encryption schemes (best known attacks)

Name	Ref	Best known attack: data complexity/memory/time complexity
ACORN v3	[581]	–
ALE	[103]	Forgery attack [324]: $2^{40}/-/2^{110}$
APE	[22]	–
ASC-1	[300]	–
Ascon	[186]	Key-recovery attack [371]: $2^{103.9}$ time on 7 out of 12 rounds ASCON-128
C-QUARK	[36]	–
FIDES	[87]	State-recovery/forgery attacks [184]: 1KP/$(2^{15}, 2^{18})/(2^{75}, 2^{90})$
Hummingbird-2	[200]	Related key-recovery attack [525]: 24 pairs of related keys/$-/2^{40}$
Helix	[215]	Key-recovery attack [432]: 2^{17} CP/$-/2^{88}$
Joltik	[304]	–
KETJE	[82]	–
LAC	[596]	Differential forgery attack [368] with probability $2^{-61.52}$
NORX32 v.3	[35]	–
NORX8/NORX16	[34]	–
Sablier	[594]	**Practical** state/key recovery attack [213]: $-/-/2^{44}$
SCREAM/iSCREAM	[246]	**Practical** forgery attack [530] with 2 queries
sLiSCP	[20]	–
TriviA-v2/uTriviA	[132]	–

One can pick out the point $D = M = N^{1/2}$ to get an overall complexity of $N^{1/2}$. Then, storing $\sqrt{N}$ internal states with their outputs (keystream parts with an appropriate length), one can recover a keystream used during encryption/decryption if it is loaded in the table. We need roughly $\sqrt{N}$ data to ensure a remarkable success rate. So, it is conventionally adopted that $\sqrt{N}$ should be larger than 2^k as a security criterion just to ensure that the internal state recovery attack through tradeoff is slower than the exhaustive search. This simply means that the internal state size should be at least twice as large as the key size. This extremely strict criterion has played a very crucial role in raising extra difficulties in designing lightweight stream ciphers.

Another highly effective tradeoff attack for internal state recovery is the Biryukov-Shamir attack [91]. This simply makes use of Hellman tables. But, instead of recovering just one specific internal state, it is enough to recover only one of D internal states. Then, preparing just one Hellman table is an optimum solution and the table can contain N/D states. So, the precomputation phase is around $O(N/D)$ and the tradeoff curve is $TM^2D^2 = N^2$ where D is bounded above by $\sqrt{T}$ since the number of internal states contained in just one table is limited to avoid merging of collisions. We can pick out the point on the curve where time and memory are equal and maximize the data, namely $T = M = N^{1/2}$ and $D = N^{1/4}$. We need $N^{1/2}$ to be larger than 2^k if we want the online phase of the attack to be slower than an exhaustive search. This again simply implies that the internal state size should be at least twice as large as the key size.

The condition on the size of the internal states of stream ciphers makes designing ultralightweight stream ciphers too difficult. Indeed, there are several ultralightweight (say less than 1000 GE) block ciphers recently designed, such as PRESENT [101], LED [252], KTANTAN [126], Piccolo [526], and SIMON/SPECK [65], whereas there are almost no modern stream ciphers with hardware area cost less than 1000 GE.

The security margin for state recovery attacks through tradeoff techniques is k bits, whereas it is much less, $2k/3$ bits, for the key recovery attacks, although any information about the key is assumed to be more sensitive than any information about the internal states. One can produce any internal state once the key is recovered. However, recovery of an internal state may reveal only one session of the encryption/decryption with the corresponding IV. Hence, it seems that the more sensitive data are, contradictorily, protected less against tradeoff attacks!

The security level of tradeoff attacks to recover internal states should be the same as the security level of tradeoff attacks to recover keys, just to be fair. So, the online phase of a tradeoff attack should be at least $2^{2k/3}$ instead of 2^k. Similarly, the precomputation should be not faster than exhaustive search. In this case, $D = M = N^{1/2} \geq 2^{2k/3}$ for the Babbage-Golić attack. Then, N should be at least $2^{4k/3}$. The same bound is valid for Biryukov-Shamir attack since the smallest overall complexity is attained when $T = M = N^{1/2}$.

The precomputation phase of the Biryukov-Shamir attack is roughly N/D; which is simply $N^{3/4}$ when $D = N^{1/4}$. So, the precomputation phase is more than 2^k. This means that it is slower than an exhaustive search. On the other hand, the precomputation phase of the Babbage-Golić attack is M, and hence if the data is restricted to at most $2^{k/3}$ for each key we have $M \geq 2^k$ and hence the precomputation phase will be slower than an exhaustive search.

It seems it is enough to take the internal state size as at least $4k/3$, not at least $2k$, for security against tradeoff attacks. This simply implies that it is possible to design lightweight stream ciphers with much smaller internal states. However, it is an open question how to design stream ciphers with very small internal states. The security is generally based on the largeness of the states.

2.3.2 Guess-and-Determine Based Cryptanalysis Employing Dedicated TMD-TO

This section presents an illustrative framework for cryptanalysis employing guess-and-determine and time-memory-data trade-off (TMD-TO) methods using the results of security evaluations of the lightweight stream ciphers Grain-v1, Grain-128 and LILI-128, reported in [415, 416], and [417], respectively.

2.3.2.1   Generic Approach

Certain stream ciphers can be attacked by employing the following approach: (1) Assuming the availability of a sufficiently long sample for recovering an internal state, we develop a dedicated TMD-TO attack which allows recovery of the internal state for a certain segment of the available sample. (2) The dedicated TMD-TO attack is developed over a subset of the internal states in which certain parts of the internal state are preset or algebraically recovered based on the considered keystream segment. Assume that the state size is ν and that certain bits (say β) of the internal state are fixed according to a specific pattern. Then, with this information, for the corresponding keystream segment, we try to obtain some more bits (say γ) of the internal state. The final goal is to recover the unknown bits of the internal state $\delta = \nu - \beta - \gamma$ by employing a suitable TMD-TO attack. Accordingly, the cryptanalysis is based on the following framework:

- preset certain bits of the internal state to a suitable pattern (the all-zeros pattern, for example);
- for a given m-bit prefix (usually an m-zeros prefix) of the keystream segment, algebraically recover up to m bits of the internal state assuming that the remaining internal state bits are known;
- recover the assumed bits of the internal state by employing the dedicated TMD-TO attack.

2.3.2.2   Summary of Cryptanalysis of Grain-v1 Employing Guess-and-Determine and Dedicated TMD-TO Approaches

The internal state of Grain-v1 consists of 160 bits corresponding to the employed nonlinear and linear feedback shift registers NFSR and LFSR, respectively. For a given parameter m, let $\Omega^{(m)}$ be a subset of all internal states where three m-length segments of all zeros exist which implies that the state generates m consecutive zero outputs. Let the vectors $\mathbf{b}^{(i)}$ and $\mathbf{s}^{(i)}$ be the states of the NFSR and LFSR, respectively, at the instant i, $\mathbf{s}^{(i)} = [s_i, s_{i+1}, \ldots, s_{i+79}]$ and $\mathbf{b}^{(i)} = [b_i, b_{i+1}, \ldots, b_{i+79}]$. Let $\mathbf{u}^{(i)}$ be the internal state of Grain-v1, and accordingly, $\mathbf{u}^{(i)} = [\mathbf{s}^{(i)} || \mathbf{b}^{(i)}] = [s_i, s_{i+1}, \ldots, s_{i+79}, b_i, b_{i+1}, \ldots, b_{i+79}]$. For a given parameter m, the set $\Omega^{(m)}$ is the set of internal state vectors defined as follows $\Omega^{(m)} = \{\mathbf{u}^{(i)} | s_{i+25-j} = 0, s_{i+64-j} = 0, b_{i+63-j} = 0 , \quad j = 0, 1, \ldots, m - 1\}$. Consequently, the number of internal states belonging to $\Omega^{(m)}$ is upper-bounded by 2^{160-3m}.

The internal state recovery is based on the following: Whenever we observe an m-zeros prefix of a keystream segment, we suppose that the segment is generated by an internal state belonging to $\Omega^{(m)}$ and we employ a dedicated TMD-TO attack to check the hypothesis. The complexities of this cryptanalysis and a related one are illustrated in Table 2.12.

Table 2.12 An illustrative numerical comparison of two algorithms for cryptanalysis of Grain-v1

Approach	Time complexity of processing	Space complexity of pre-processing and processing	Time complexity of pre-processing	Required sample
Cryptanalysis reported in [416]	$\sim 2^{54}$	$\sim 2^{78}$	$\sim 2^{88}$	$\sim 2^{72}$
Cryptanalysis reported in [385]	$\sim 2^{53}$	$\sim 2^{78}$	$\sim 2^{78}$	$\sim 2^{82}$

3

Symmetric Encryption Algorithms: Design and Analysis

Vasily Mikhalev, Miodrag J. Mihaljević, Orhun Kara, and Frederik Armknecht

Abstract In this chapter we provide an overview of selected methods for the design and analysis of symmetric encryption algorithms that have recently been published. We start by discussing the practical advantages, limitations and security of the keystream generators with keyed update functions which were proposed for reducing the area cost of stream ciphers. Then we present an approach to enhancing the security of certain encryption schemes by employing a universal homophonic coding and randomized encryption paradigm.

3.1 Introduction

The concept of ubiquitous computing brings new challenges to the designers of cryptographic algorithms by introducing scenarios where classical crypto primitives are infeasible due to their costs (such as hardware price, computational time, and power and energy consumption). In this chapter we provide an overview of selected recent approaches which deal with such challenges.

An approach [27] which allows one to realize secure stream ciphers with state size beyond the bound which was previously considered to be the minimum is summarized in Sect. 3.2. The main idea is to use so-called keystream generators with keyed update functions (KSGs with KUF) where the secret key is involved not only in the initialization phase (as is common practice) but during the entire encryption process. After explaining the advantages [27] of KSGs with KUF in resisting Time Memory Data Tradeoff (TMDTO) attacks [47, 237] together with

V. Mikhalev (✉) · F. Armknecht
University of Mannheim, Mannheim, Germany
e-mail: mikhalev@uni-mannheim.de

M. J. Mihaljević
Mathematical Institute, Serbian Academy of Sciences and Arts, Belgrade, Serbia

O. Kara
Department of Mathematics, IZTECH Izmir Institute of Technology, Izmir, Turkey

practical issues and limitations on their implementation in hardware[421], we describe the stream cipher Sprout which was designed in order to demonstrate the feasibility of the approach [27], and its improvement Plantlet where the security weaknesses of Sprout were fixed [421]. In Sect. 3.3 we present a generic attack [314] against such KSGs that implies a design criterion. Section 3.4 presents an approach to security enhancement of certain encryption schemes employing universal homophonic coding [397] and a randomized encryption paradigm [503]. The approach summarized in this section has been reported and discussed in a number of references including [413, 418, 452] and [420]. A security evaluation of this encryption scheme has been reported in [452] from an information-theoretic point of view, and a computational-complexity evaluation approach is given in [420].

3.2 Keystream Generators with Keyed Update Functions

3.2.1 Design Approach

Stream ciphers usually provide a higher throughput than block ciphers. However, due to the existence of certain TMDTO [47, 91, 237] attacks, the area size required to implement secure stream ciphers is often higher. The reason is the following. The effort of TMDTO attacks against stream ciphers is $O(2^{\sigma/2})$, where σ is the internal state size. Therefore, a rule of thumb says that to achieve κ-bit security level, the state size should be at least $\sigma = 2 \cdot \kappa$. This results in the fact that a stream cipher requires at least $2 \cdot \kappa$ memory gates which are the most costly hardware elements in terms of area and power-consumption. In this section we discuss an extension [27, 421] of the common design principle, which allows for secure lightweight stream ciphers with internal state size below this bound.

We start the description of the new approach for stream ciphers design by giving the definition of the KSG with KUF [27]:

Definition 1 (Keystream Generator with Keyed Update Function) A keystream generator with a *keyed update function* comprises three sets, namely the key space $\mathscr{K} = GF(2)^\kappa$, the IV space $\mathscr{IV} = GF(2)^\nu$, and the variable state space $\mathscr{S} = GF(2)^\sigma$. Moreover, it uses the following three functions

- an initialization function $\mathsf{Init} : \mathscr{IV} \times \mathscr{K} \to \mathscr{S}$
- an update function $\mathsf{Upd} : \mathscr{K} \times \mathscr{S} \to \mathscr{S}$ such that $\mathsf{Upd}_k : \mathscr{S} \to \mathscr{S}$, $\mathsf{Upd}_k(st) := \mathsf{Upd}(k, st)$, is bijective for any $k \in \mathscr{K}$, and
- an output function $\mathsf{Out} : \mathscr{S} \to GF(2)$.

The internal state ST is composed of a variable part $st \in \mathscr{S}$ and a fixed part $k \in \mathscr{K}$. A KSG operates in two phases. In the *initialization phase*, the KSG takes as input a secret key k and a public IV iv and sets the internal state to

$st_0 := \mathsf{Init}(iv, k) \in \mathscr{S}$. Afterwards, the keystream generation phase executes the following operations repeatedly (for $t \geq 0$):

1. Output the next keystream bit $z_t = \mathsf{Out}(st_t)$
2. Update the internal state st_t to $st_{t+1} := \mathsf{Upd}(k, st_t)$

The main difference between KSGs with KUF and the KSGs traditionally used as a core of stream ciphers is that the next state is now computed not only from the current variable state st_t (as is commonly done) but also from the fixed key k.

We now explain why stream ciphers built based on the KSGs with KUF have advantages in resisting TMDTO attacks over classical KSGs. The goal of the TMDTO attacker is the following: given a function $F : \mathscr{N} \rightarrow \mathscr{N}$ and D images $y_1, \ldots, y_D$ of F, find a preimage for any of these points, i.e., determine a value $x_i \in \mathscr{N}$ such that $F(x_i) = y_i$. Typically, these attacks consist of two phases: a precomputation (offline) phase, and a real-time (online) phase. At first the attacker precomputes a large table using the function F (offline phase). In the online phase the attacker gets D outputs of F and checks if any of these values is included in the precomputed table. In the case of success, a preimage has been found. Obviously, an attacker can increase the success probability by either precomputing more values in the offline phase or collecting more data in the online phase where the optimal trade-off is usually given as $|D| = \sqrt{|\mathscr{N}|}$.

The goal of a TMDTO attack in the context of KSGs is to recover one internal state as this allows us to compute the complete keystream. To this end, let $F_{\mathsf{Out}} : \mathrm{GF}(2)^\sigma \rightarrow \mathrm{GF}(2)^\sigma$ be the function that takes the internal state $st_t \in \mathrm{GF}(2)^\sigma$ at some clock t as input and outputs the σ keystream bits $z_t, \ldots, z_{t+\sigma-1}$. Then, the attack translates to finding a preimage of F_{Out} for a given keystream segment with the search space being $\mathscr{N} = \mathscr{S}$ and an effort of at least $\sqrt{|\mathscr{S}|} = 2^{\sigma/2}$. This implies the above-mentioned rule of selecting $\sigma \geq 2\kappa$.

To understand the motivation behind the design principle given in Definition 1, we introduce the notion of keystream-equivalent states which is important for analyzing the effectiveness of a TMDTO attack. Let $F_{\mathsf{Out}}^{\mathrm{compl.}}$ be the function that takes as input the initial state and outputs the maximum number of keystream bits. If no bound is given by the designers, we assume that the maximum period of 2^σ keystream bits is produced. An attacker is interested in any internal state that allows the keystream to be computed:

Definition 2 (Keystream-Equivalent States) Consider a KSG with a function $F_{\mathsf{Out}}^{\mathrm{compl.}}$ that outputs the complete keystream. Two states $st, st' \in \mathscr{S}$ are said to be *keystream-equivalent* (in short $st \equiv_{\mathrm{kse}} st'$) if there exists an integer $r \geq 0$ such that $F_{\mathsf{Out}}^{\mathrm{compl.}}(\mathsf{Upd}^r(st)) = F_{\mathsf{Out}}^{\mathrm{compl.}}(st')$. Here, Upd^r means the r-times application of Upd.

For any state $st \in \mathscr{S}$, we denote by $[st]$ its equivalence class, that is $[st] = \{st' \in \mathscr{S} | st \equiv_{\mathrm{kse}} st'\}$.

Now, let us consider an arbitrary KSG with state space $\mathscr{S}$. As any state is a member of exactly one equivalence class, the state space can be divided into ℓ distinct equivalence classes:

$$\mathscr{S} = \left[st^{(1)} \right] \dot{\cup} \ldots \dot{\cup} \left[st^{(\ell)} \right] \tag{3.1}$$

Assume a TMDTO attacker who is given some keystream (z_t), based on an unknown initial state st_0. In this case if none of the precomputations are done for values in $[st_0]$, the attack will fail. This implies that the attack effort is at least linear in the number ℓ of equivalence classes. Hence we can see that if we design a cipher such that $\ell \geq 2^\kappa$, such a cipher will have the required security level against trade-off attacks.

Let us now take a look at the minimum time effort for a TMDTO attack against a KSG with a KUF. We make in the following the assumption that any two different states $ST = (st, k)$ and $ST' = (st', k')$ with $k \neq k'$ never produce the same keystream, that is $F_{\mathsf{Out}}^{\mathrm{compl.}}(ST) \neq_{\mathrm{kse}} F_{\mathsf{Out}}^{\mathrm{compl.}}(ST')$. Hence, we have at least 2^κ different equivalence classes. As the effort grows linearly with the number of equivalence classes, we assume in favor of the attacker that we have exactly 2^κ equivalence classes. This gives a minimum time complexity of 2^κ. This means that, in theory, it is possible to design a cipher with a security level of κ regardless of the length σ of its variable state.

3.2.2   On Continuously Accessing the Key

In most cases the workflow of ciphers looks as follows. After the encryption or decryption process is started, the key is loaded from some non-volatile memory NVM into some registers, i.e., into some volatile memory VM. We call the value in VM a *volatile value* as it usually changes during the encryption/decryption process and the value stored in NVM, the *non-volatile value* or *non-volatile key* which remains fixed. It holds for most designs that after the key has been loaded from NVM into VM, the NVM is usually not involved anymore (unless the key schedule or the initialization process needs to be restarted). But the design approach discussed in Sect. 3.2.1 requires that the key which is stored on the device has to be accessed not only for initialization of the registers but continuously in the encryption/decryption process. The feasibility of this approach for different scenarios was investigated in [421].

It has been argued there that continuously accessing the key can impact the achievable throughput. To this end, two different cases need to be considered. The first one is when the key is set once and is never changed and the second one is when it is possible to rewrite the key. The types of NVM (e.g., MROM and PROM) which can be used in the first case, allow for efficient implementations where accessing the key bits induces no overhead. However, the key management is very difficult here.

In the second case, i.e., for those types of NVM which allow the key to be rewritable (such as EEPROM and Flash), severe timing limitations for accessing the NVM may occur. In particular, it depends on how the key stored in NVM needs to be accessed. In some cases, implementation of ciphers which require continuous access to the randomly selected bits of the key stored in rewritable types of NVM may lead to a reduction of the throughput up to a factor of 50 [421]. However, designs that require sequential access to the key bits are almost unaffected, irrespective of the underlying NVM type.

With respect to area size, there is no big difference whether the key has to be read only once or continuously during encryption, since the logic for reading the key (at least once) has to be implemented anyway. Small extra logic may be needed for synchronization with an NVM cipher which should not be clocked unless key material is read from NVM.

3.2.3 The Stream Ciphers Sprout and Plantlet

The design principles discussed in Sect. 3.2.1 have been demonstrated by two concrete keystream generators with keyed update function, namely Sprout and Plantlet. Both ciphers have a similar structure (see Fig. 3.1) which was inspired by Grain-128a [14]. The differences are the following:

1. Sprout and Plantlet have shorter internal state size compared to any of the Grain family ciphers [265]
2. They use the round key function to make the state update key-dependent

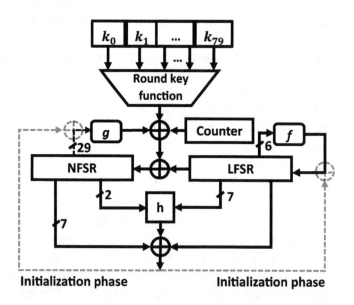

Fig. 3.1 Overall structure of the Sprout and Plantlet ciphers

3. The counter is used in the state update in order to avoid situations where shifted keys result in shifted keystreams

The design of Plantlet actually builds on Sprout but included some changes to fix several weaknesses [50, 203, 355, 387]. The main differences between Plantlet and Sprout are the following:

1. Plantlet has a larger internal state size compared to Sprout. The difference was introduced in order to increase the period of the output sequences and to increase resistance against guess-and-determine attacks
2. In both ciphers, the round key function cyclically steps through the key bits, which is well aligned with the performance of different types of NVM as mentioned before. However, in Sprout the key bits are only included in the NFSR update with a probability of 0.5, i.e., only if the linear combination of several state bits is equal to 1. This has been exploited by several attacks so in Plantlet the next key bit is added unconditionally at every clock-cycle.
3. Plantlet uses a so-called double-layer LFSR which allows for high period and at the same time avoids the LFSR being initialized with all-zeroes

For full specifications we refer the reader to [27, 422].

Implementation Results We used the Cadence RTL Compiler[1] for synthesis and simulation, and the technology library UMCL18G212T3 (UMC 0.18 μm process). The clock frequency was set to 100 kHz. For different memory types Sprout requires from 692 to 813 GEs, whereas Plantlet needs from 807 to 928 GEs. Note that the smallest KSG which follows the classical design approach needs at least 1162 GEs if the same tools are used for implementation [421].

Security As already mentioned, several serious weaknesses [50, 203, 355, 387] were shown to exist in Sprout, whereas Plantlet, to the best of our knowledge, remains secure for the moment.

3.3 A Generic Attack Against Certain Keystream Generators with Keyed Update Functions

In this section, we describe a generic attack against the following type of Keystream Generators with a Keyed Update Function (Definition 1):

Definition 3 (KSG with Boolean Keyed Feedback Function) Consider a KSG with a KUF as in Definition 1. Let Upd_i denote the Boolean component functions of the update function Upd, that is $\mathsf{Upd}(k, st) = (\mathsf{Upd}_i(k, st))_i$. We call this a KSG with a Boolean KFF (Keyed Feedback Function) if only one component function depends on the secret key. That is, there is an index i^* such that all other component

---

[1] See http://www.cadence.com/products/ld/rtl_compiler/pages/default.aspx.

functions with index $i \neq i^*$ can be rewritten as $\mathsf{Upd}_i(k, st) = \mathsf{Upd}_i(st)$. We call $\mathsf{Upd}_{i*}(k, st)$ the keyed feedback function and denote it by $f_{\mathsf{Upd}}(k, st)$.

When we say the "feedback value", we mean the output of the keyed feedback function $f_{\mathsf{Upd}}(k, st)$. The most prominent examples of KSGs with a Boolean KUF in the literature are Sprout [27] and its successor Plantlet [421] (see Sect. 3.2.3). Even though several attacks against the cipher Sprout have been published [50, 203, 355, 387, 593], only little is known about the security of the underlying approach (see Sect. 3.2.1) in general. In the following, we explain the only existing generic attack [314] that implies a design criterion for this type of ciphers.

The attack is a guess-and-determine attack that is based on guessing internal states from the observed output. Its efficiency heavily relies on the guess capacity, which we define next:

Definition 4 For a given KSG with a Boolean KFF having a σ-bit internal state, a κ-bit key, and f_{Upd} as its Boolean keyed feedback function, we define the *average guess capacity* as

$$\mathrm{Pr}_g = \frac{1}{2} + 2^{-\sigma} \sum_{st} \left| \frac{\#\{k : f_{\mathsf{Upd}}(k, st) = 0\}}{2^{\kappa}} - \frac{1}{2} \right|.$$

The average guess capacity simply indicates how accurately we can guess the feedback value $f_{\mathsf{Upd}}(k, st)$ when we know the internal state but we do not know the key. The following attack [314] applies to the case of $\mathrm{Pr}_g > 1/2$ which eventually allows us to formulate a necessary design criterion.

The core of the attack is an internal state recovery algorithm (see Algorithm 1). It tests, for a given internal state whether it can consistently continue producing the observed output bits. To this end, it produces the feedback values (the outputs of the Boolean keyed feedback function) for the next states by either determining them from the output if that is possible or first checking and then guessing them. It consists of two parts: determining the feedback value is done by Algorithm 2 and checking the candidate state and then guessing the feedback value if the state survives, is achieved by Algorithm 3. It is obvious that Algorithm 2 produces only one feedback value for each clock. Similarly, Algorithm 3 first checks if a candidate state can produce the output. So, it survives with a probability of one half and the surviving states will have two successors. Hence, neither Algorithm 2 nor Algorithm 3 will propagate the total number of states to be checked.

Each candidate state has successors for consecutive clocks and a set of feedback values produced by Algorithm 1. On the other hand, we count the number of mismatches for each feedback value. We say that a feedback value is a mismatch if it is not the suggested value obtained through its internal state. If the probability that the feedback value is equal to 0 (or 1) for a given state is higher than one half, then 0 (or 1) will be the suggested value of that state.

Assume we clock the generator α_{ter} steps to check each state. Then, we expect roughly $\alpha_{ter}/2$ mismatches for a wrong state and $\alpha_{ter}(1 - \mathrm{Pr}_g)$ mismatches for

---

Algorithm 1 Internal state recovery

1: **Input:** Non-empty set of internal state candidates, $\mathbb{S}$; keystream $\{z_{t+1+\theta_f}, \ldots, z_{t+\theta_f+\alpha_{ter}}\}$; the maximum number of clocks for each test, α_{ter}; average guess capacity, $\Pr_g$; miss event probability ϵ

2: Set $\epsilon_{ter} = \sqrt{\frac{-\ln \epsilon}{2\alpha_{ter}}}$ and $\alpha_{thr} = \alpha_{ter}(1 - \Pr_g + \epsilon_{ter})$

3: Initialize CUR and NEW as two empty sets and load all the states in $\mathbb{S}$ into CUR

4: Set $\#MM(st)$ to 0 for each state st in CUR and make a copy of CUR as the *roots*

5: **for** each clock i from t to $(t + \alpha_{ter} - 1)$ **do**

6:     **for** each state st in CUR **do**

7:         Compute $\Pr_g(st)_f$

8:         **if** $\Pr_g(st)_f = 0.5$ **then**

9:             Set $fb_{sugg} = 0$

10:         **else**

11:             Set fb_{sugg} as the feedback value of st suggested through f_{Upd}

12:         **end if**

13:         **if** $f_{\mathsf{Upd}}(k, st)$ of st can be determined from the output bit $z_{i+1+\theta_f}$ **then**

14:             Run *Determine Procedure* (Algorithm 2)

15:         **else**

16:             Run *Check-and-guess Procedure* (Algorithm 3)

17:         **end if**

18:     **end for**

19:     Terminate if NEW is empty and give no output

20:     Copy NEW to CUR

21:     Empty NEW

22: **end for**

23: **Output:** the roots in CUR as the candidates for the correct state at clock t

---

Algorithm 2 Determine procedure

1: Determine the feedback value as $f_{\mathsf{Upd}}(k, st)$ from the corresponding output bit

2: Update st by clocking it with the feedback value fb_{det}

3: **if** $fb_{sugg} \neq fb_{det}$ (it is a mismatch) **then**

4:     Increment $\#MM(st)$ by one

5: **end if**

6: **if** $\#MM(st) \leq \alpha_{thr}$ **then**

7:     Add updated st with $\#MM(st)$ and its root to NEW

8: **end if**

---

a correct state. This provides us with a distinguisher to recover the correct state without knowing the key. We set a threshold value α_{thr}, between $\alpha_{ter}(1 - \Pr_g)$ and $\alpha_{ter}/2$ and simply eliminate the states whose number of mismatches exceeds α_{thr}. We expect all the wrong internal states to be eliminated for a well-chosen pair $(\alpha_{ter}, \alpha_{thr})$ and only the correct state is expected to survive. Theorem 1 suggests appropriate values for α_{ter} so as to obtain a given success rate. Then we fix the threshold value accordingly, in Algorithm 1 in its third line.

Algorithm 3 Check-and-guess procedure

1: **if** the output of st is equal to the actual output at the corresponding clock **then**
2:      Make two copies st_0, st_1 of st with $\#MM(st_0) = \#MM(st_1) := \#MM(st)$
3:      Set the feedback value to 0 for st_0 and update st_0 and 1 for st_1 and update st_1
4:      **if** $fb_{sugg} = 0$ **then**
5:          Increment $\#MM(st_1)$ by one
6:      **else**
7:          Increment $\#MM(st_0)$ by one
8:      **end if**
9:      **if** $\#MM(st_0) \leq \alpha_{thr}$ **then**
10:          Add st_0 along with $\#MM(st_0)$ to NEW and set the root of S as its root
11:      **end if**
12:      **if** $\#MM(st_1) \leq \alpha_{thr}$ **then**
13:          Add st_1 along with $\#MM(st_1)$ to NEW and set the root of st as its root
14:      **end if**
15: **end if**

The performance of Algorithm 1 depends heavily on how many clocks we should go further to eliminate all the wrong states without missing the correct state. This is determined by the success rate of the algorithm which in turn is dominated by the guess capacity (Definition 4) as stated in the following Theorem 1 [314]:

Theorem 1 *Let* $\Pr_g > 1/2$ *be the guess capacity of a given KSG with Boolean KFF having internal state size* σ. *For a given* $0 < \epsilon < 1$, *if* α_{ter} *is greater than or equal to*

$$\frac{1}{(2\Pr_g - 1)^2} \left(\sqrt{-2\ln\epsilon} + \sqrt{2\ln 2 \cdot (\sigma - 1)} \right)^2 ,$$

then the success rate of the attack in Algorithm 1 is at least $1 - \epsilon$ *and the number of false alarms is less than one in total.*

The average guess capacity of Sprout is 0.75. Hence it is possible to recover its correct state without knowing the key by eliminating a wrong state in roughly 122 clocks [314]. Checking roughly 2^{40} states (which are called "weak states" and loaded into a table in the precomputation phase), one can recover the key in roughly 2^{38} encryptions [314]. On the other hand, Algorithm 1 becomes infeasible when $\Pr_g$ approaches $1/2$. Plantlet (Sect. 3.2.3) has a guess capacity of $1/2$, so Algorithm 1 is not applicable to Plantlet. Concluding, the attack above implies a new security criterion: the guess capacity of the feedback function of a KSG with Boolean KFF should be one half in order to avoid state recovery attacks that bypass the key.

3.4   Randomized Encryption Employing Homophonic Coding

3.4.1   Background

In [503], several approaches to including randomness in encryption techniques are discussed, mainly in the context of block and stream ciphers. Randomized encryption is described [503] as a procedure which enciphers a message by randomly choosing a ciphertext from a set of ciphertexts corresponding to the message under the current encryption key.

Homophonic coding was introduced in [249] as a source coding technique which transforms a stream of message symbols with an arbitrary frequency distribution into a uniquely decodable stream of symbols which all have the same frequency. The universal homophonic coding approach [397] is based on an invertible transformation of the source information vector with embedded random bits, and this approach does not require knowledge of the source statistics. The source information vector can be recovered from the homophonic coder output without knowledge of the random bits by passing the codeword to the decoder (inverter) and then discarding the random bits.

A number of randomized encryption techniques have been reported: In [234], a probabilistic private-key encryption scheme named LPN-C whose security can be reduced to the hardness of the LPN problem was proposed and analysed. An approach for the design of stream ciphers employing error-correction coding and certain additive noise degradation of the keystream was reported in [201]. A message is encoded before the encryption so that the decoding, after mod 2 addition of the noiseless keystream sequence and the ciphertext, provides its correct recovery. Resistance of this approach against a number of general techniques for cryptanalysis, was also considered in [201]. Joint employment of randomness and dedicated coding has been studied for enhancing the security of the following block-by-block encryption schemes: (1) in [418], where the basic keystream generator security is enhanced by employing a particular homophonic coding based on embedding of random bits; (2) in [413, 419] and [414] randomness and dedicated coding were employed for enhancing the security of the compact generators of pseudorandom vectors; (3) in [322] and [577] channel coding was employed to increase the security of a DES block cipher operating in the ciphertext feedback (CFB) mode. Also, certain issues of randomized encryption were considered in [321, 570] and [313].

3.4.2   Encryption and Decryption

The ciphering technique given in this section originates from the schemes reported in [322, 414, 418], and it corresponds to the randomized encryption schemes proposed and discussed in [452]. The design assumes the availability of a source of pure randomness (for example, as an efficient hardware module) and that a suitable error-correcting coding (ECC) technique is available. This availability means that the implementation complexities of the source of randomness and the ECC do not imply a heavy implementation overhead in suitable scenarios.

The scheme employs a homophonic approach for a purpose different from the ones this coding techniques were designed for. The main purpose is not just randomization of the source message vectors (the goal of homophonic coding) nor secrecy without a secret key (the goal of wire-tap channel coding) but enhancing the cryptographic security of certain encryption schemes by employing the underlying features of homophonic or wire-tap channel coding. The goal is the security enhancement of a cryptographic keystream generator for encryption by employing a dedicated coding scheme where the codewords provide additional "masking" of the keystream vectors employed for encryption. The encryption scheme in Fig. 3.2 performs modulo 2 addition of the outputs of the encoding block and the keystream generator which can be considered not only as "masking" the message vector with a vector generated by a secret key, but also as masking the keystream vector by a randomized mapping of the information vector.

We assume that the encryption from Fig. 3.2 employs concatenation of the following coding algorithms: (1) a universal homophonic coding [397] which performs the following mapping $\{0, 1\}^{\ell} \rightarrow \{0, 1\}^{m}$, $\ell < m$, and (2) a linear block error-correction code which performs $\{0, 1\}^{m} \rightarrow \{0, 1\}^{n}$, $m < n$, and which provides reliable communication over a binary symmetric channel with a known probability of bit complementation. Please note that any suitable binary

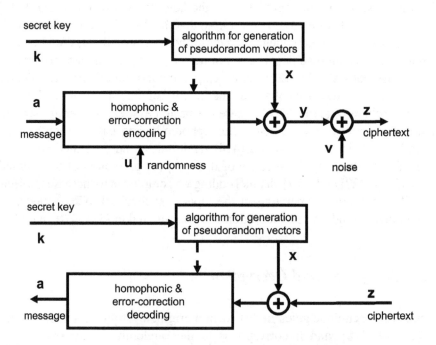

Fig. 3.2 Model of a security enhanced randomized encryption within the encoding-encryption paradigm: the upper part shows the transmitter, the lower part—the receiver [452]

linear block code designed to work over a binary symmetric channel with crossover probability p could be employed. There are a lot of these coding schemes reported in the literature and one which best fits into a particular implementation scenario (hardware or software oriented) could be selected. We consider a communication system displayed in Fig. 3.2 where some message $\mathbf{a} = [a_i]_{i=1}^{l} \in \{0, 1\}^l$ is sent to a transmitter over a noisy channel and the following operations at the transmitter and receiver.

At the Transmitter To ensure reliable communication, a linear error-correcting encoder $C_{ECC}(\cdot)$ is used, that maps an m-bit message to a codeword of $n > m$ bits, using an $m \times n$ binary code generator matrix $\mathbf{G}_{ECC}$. A homophonic encoder $C_H(\cdot)$ is added prior to $C_{ECC}(\cdot)$, which requires the use of a vector $\mathbf{u} = [u_i]_{i=1}^{m-l} \in \{0, 1\}^{m-l}$ of pure randomness, i.e., each u_i is the realization of a random variable U_i with distribution $\Pr(U_i = 1) = \Pr(U_i = 0) = 1/2$. The encoding $C_H(\mathbf{a}||\mathbf{u})$ may be described by an $m \times m$ binary matrix $\mathbf{G}_H$ such that

$$C_H(\mathbf{a}||\mathbf{u}) = [\mathbf{a}||\mathbf{u}]\mathbf{G}_H, \ \mathbf{G}_H = \begin{bmatrix} \mathbf{h}_1 \\ \vdots \\ \mathbf{h}_l \\ \mathbf{G}^C \end{bmatrix} \tag{3.2}$$

where $\mathbf{G}^C$ is an $(m-l) \times m$ generator matrix for an $(m, m-l)$ linear error-correction code C, and $\mathbf{h}_1, \mathbf{h}_2, \ldots, \mathbf{h}_l$ are l linearly independent row vectors from $\{0, 1\}^m \setminus C$.

We get a joint encoding $\mathbf{a} \in \{0, 1\}^l \mapsto C_{ECC}(C_H(\mathbf{a}||\mathbf{u})) \in \{0, 1\}^n$, which may alternatively be written as

$$C_{ECC}(C_H(\mathbf{a}||\mathbf{u})) = C_{ECC}([\mathbf{a}||\mathbf{u}]\mathbf{G}_H) = [\mathbf{a}||\mathbf{u}]\mathbf{G}_H\mathbf{G}_{ECC} = [\mathbf{a}||\mathbf{u}]\mathbf{G} \tag{3.3}$$

where $\mathbf{G} = \mathbf{G}_H\mathbf{G}_{ECC}$ is an $m \times n$ binary matrix containing the two successive encoders at the transmitter.

The codeword sent is finally an encrypted version $\mathbf{y}$ of $C_{ECC}(C_H(\mathbf{a}||\mathbf{u}))$ given by $\mathbf{y} = \mathbf{y(k)} = C_{ECC}(C_H(\mathbf{a}||\mathbf{u})) \oplus \mathbf{x}$ where $\mathbf{x} = \mathbf{x(k)} = [x_i]_{i=1}^{n} \in \{0, 1\}^n$ is a pseudorandom vector needed for encryption, which is generated by either a keystream generator, or by a block cipher working in the cipher feedback mode (CFB) as in [322] and [577]. Notice the important dependency of $\mathbf{x} = \mathbf{x(k)}$ in the secret key $\mathbf{k}$. Also note that, for simplicity of the exposition, the data employed for generation of the pseudorandom vectors $\mathbf{x}$, which are publicly known (like a public seed and a synchronization parameter) are not explicitly shown. Finally, the model includes the assumption that the concatenation of the binary vectors $\mathbf{x}$ appears as a pseudorandom binary sequences and from a statistical point of view is indistinguishable from a random binary sequence.

At the Receiver The noisy communication channel is modeled by the addition of a noise vector $\mathbf{v} = [v_i]_{i=1}^{n} \in \{0, 1\}^n$, where each v_i is the realization of a random variable V_i with $\Pr(V_i = 1) = p$ and $\Pr(V_i = 0) = 1 - p$. The receiver obtains $\mathbf{z} = \mathbf{z(k)} = \mathbf{y} \oplus \mathbf{v} = C_{ECC}(C_H(\mathbf{a}||\mathbf{u})) \oplus \mathbf{x} \oplus \mathbf{v}$ and starts by decrypting $\mathbf{y} = (C_{ECC}(C_H(\mathbf{a}||\mathbf{u})) \oplus \mathbf{x} \oplus \mathbf{v}) \oplus \mathbf{x} = C_{ECC}(C_H(\mathbf{a}||\mathbf{u})) \oplus \mathbf{v}$. He then first decodes $C_H(\mathbf{a}||\mathbf{u})$. In the case of a successful decoding, he computes $\mathbf{a}$ using C_H^{-1} and informs the transmitter he could decode. Otherwise he asks the transmitter for a retransmission. This assumes noiseless feedback between the receiver and the transmitter.

3.4.3   Security Evaluation

Information-Theoretic Security In [452], the above model of randomized encryption schemes was studied from an information-theoretic point of view. The goal was to analyze the security enhancement provided by the wiretap encoding, in terms of secret key $\mathbf{k}$ equivocation, that is, the uncertainty that an adversary faces about the secret key, given all the information he could collect during passive or active attacks. This analysis demonstrated a gain in unconditional security, and thus confirmed the security benefit of the additional wiretap encoder, through tight lower bounds (Lemmas 1 and 2 in [452]) and asymptotic values (Theorems 1 and 2 in [452]) of the secret key equivocation. The cost of this enhanced security is only a slight-to-moderate increase in the implementation complexity and the communications overhead. However, it also revealed that if the same secret key is used for too long, the adversary may gather large enough samples for offline cryptanalysis. The uncertainty then decreases to zero. Then starts a regime in which a computational security analysis is needed to estimate the resistance against secret key recovery, which motivated the current paper.

Computational Complexity Security Mihaljević and Oggier [420] presents a security evaluation of the considered technique in a chosen plaintext attack scenario, which shows that the computational complexity security is lower bounded by the related LPN (Learning from Parity with Noise) complexity in both the average and worst cases. This gives guidelines for constructing a dedicated homophonic encoder which maximizes the complexity of the underlying LPN problem for a given encoding overhead.

Note Recall that in a chosen plaintext attack (CPA) scenario, the claim that a scheme is secure in an information-theoretic sense means that even an attacker with unlimited resources for recovering the secret key, in the considered evaluation scenario, faces complete uncertainty about the secret key employed for encryption, i.e., a set of equally probable candidates for the true secret key will exist. On the other hand, a claim that an encryption scheme is secure in a computational-complexity sense means the following: Although the secret-key could be recovered in a CPA scenario, and so it is not possible to claim information-theoretic security, the computational complexity of this recovery is as hard as solving a problem which belongs to a class of proven hard problems, as the LPN problem is.

3.5   Conclusion and Future Directions

We have presented some advances in the design and security evaluations of some contemporary symmetric encryption techniques which provide a good trade-off between the implementation/execution complexity and the required security.

In one direction, we have demonstrated the use of keystream generators with keyed update functions to provide the same security level at much smaller hardware area costs. In particular, we have shown that the security limitations which were believed to be imposed by the size of the state can be improved to offer a much better trade-off between hardware requirements and security. In the other direction, we have described the use of homophonic encoding for security enhancement of certain randomized symmetric encryption schemes.

Also, we have discussed certain generic approaches for security evaluation of the considered encryption schemes. The encryption schemes based on keyed update functions were evaluated against a dedicated guess-and-determine attack. The randomized encryption schemes were evaluated based on generic information-theoretic and computational-complexity approaches. We believe that there is plenty of room for further work in this area, and other innovative schemes should be investigated. We have found that employment of keyed update functions and results from coding theory are particularly promising ideas for the design of advanced encryption schemes and we plan to explore them further in the near future.

4

The ISO/IEC Standardization Process for Simon and Speck

Tomer Ashur and Atul Luykx

Abstract Simon and Speck are two block cipher families published in 2013 by the US National Security Agency (NSA). These block ciphers, targeting lightweight applications, were suggested in 2015 to be included in *ISO/IEC 29192-2 Information technology—Security techniques—Lightweight cryptography—Part 2: Block ciphers*. Following 3.5 years of deliberations within ISO/IEC JTC 1 they were rejected in April 2018. This chapter provides an account of the ISO/IEC standardization process for Simon and Speck.

4.1 Introduction

By their very nature, cryptographic algorithms require large-scale agreement to enable secure communication. Standardization by bodies such as ANSI, IEEE, and ISO/IEC is important means by which industries and governments achieve such agreement. The standardization process can be effective for agreeing upon trustworthy, secure, and efficient cryptographic algorithms when conducted in the open, as was the case with AES [444]. Yet opaque standardization processes lend themselves to subversion, as exemplified by Dual-EC [472].

In recent years, standardization bodies have initiated projects to understand the need for lightweight cryptographic algorithms. We shed light on the ISO/IEC standardization process, one not well understood by the general public, by delving into how cryptographic algorithms are scrutinized and determined to be fit for standardization. To this end, we present a chronological description of the events that led to removal of the NSA block ciphers Simon and Speck [64] from

T. Ashur (✉)
imec-COSIC, KU Leuven, Leuven, Belgium

TU Eindhoven, Eindhoven, The Netherlands
e-mail: tomer.ashur@esat.kuleuven.be

A. Luykx
imec-COSIC, KU Leuven, Leuven, Belgium

Table 4.1 Simon's
parameters

Block size ($2n$)	Key size (mn)	Rounds (T)
32	64	32
48	72	36
	96	36
64	96	42
	128	44
96	96	52
	144	54
128	128	68
	192	69
	256	72

consideration in the ISO/IEC process, spanning 5 years from their initial public release. We aim to educate the wider public and academic community about the process which leads governments and industries to agree upon the algorithms which secure their digital communications.[1]

4.2   Simon and Speck

Simon and Speck are two block cipher families designed by the NSA and published in 2013 [64]. Each family has ten variants differing in their block- and key- sizes. Both ciphers aim to be extremely efficient on resource constrained platforms, with Simon targeting hardware implementation and Speck software implementation.

4.2.1   Simon

A member of the Simon family is denoted Simon$2n/mn$ where $2n$ is the block size and mn is the key size. For a list of block- and key-size pairs see Table 4.1. All variants use a balanced Feistel structure iterating a simple round function using only XOR's, bitwise AND's and cyclic bit rotations. Simon's round function is depicted in Fig. 4.1.

For all variants, the key schedule is an LFSR operating on m words.

The number of rounds for each variant, which was a big source of contention during the standardization process, as well as the round dependent constants, can also be found in Table 4.1.

---

[1]The authors have been actively participating in the discussions surrounding this project as ISO/IEC JTC 1/SC 27/WG 2 experts. This chapter is an account of their personal experiences.

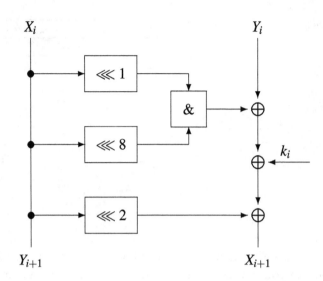

Fig. 4.1 One round of Simon (without the final swap operation)

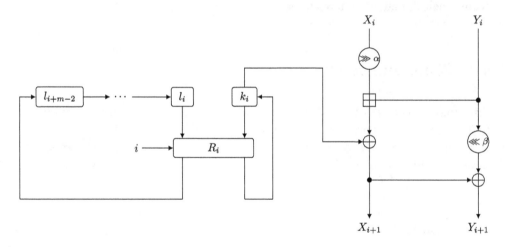

Fig. 4.2 One round of Speck and its key schedule

4.2.2 Speck

Similar to Simon the Speck family includes ten variants, differing in their block- and key- sizes. A member is denoted Speck$2n/mn$ where $2n$ is the block size and mn is the key size. Speck builds on the ARX design paradigm and the cipher is composed of three operations: modular Addition, Rotation, and XOR (hence the name ARX).

While efficient in software, ARX operations are known to have slow diffusion. Usually, this slow diffusion mandates employing a large number of rounds (see e.g., [214]) to be secure. However, as discussed in the sequel, the designers argued that they have a good understanding of the cipher's diffusion and settled for a relatively small number of rounds.

Table 4.2 Speck's parameters

Block size ($2n$)	Key size (mn)	(α, β)	Rounds (T)
32	64	(7, 2)	22
48	72	(8, 3)	22
	96	(8, 3)	23
64	96	(8, 3)	26
	128	(8, 3)	27
96	96	(8, 3)	28
	144	(8, 3)	29
128	128	(8, 3)	32
	192	(8, 3)	33
	256	(8, 3)	34

To reduce implementation size, the designers reuse Speck's round function for the key schedule, feeding in the round number as the round key and outputting one subkey word in every round. Depicted in Fig. 4.2 are the round function and the key schedule for Speck. The pairs of possible block- and key- sizes, and the rotation constants α and β for each variant are listed in Table 4.2.

4.3 Simon and Speck's "Design Rationale"

A standard practice in modern block cipher design is to provide a design rationale explaining the design decisions (e.g., the choices of round constants, number of rounds, rotation amounts, etc.), and the expected security of the new algorithm. There is no particular structure to a design rationale, but it usually includes a description of the attacks the designer attempted to apply against the algorithm, and some reasoning about why the designer believes the algorithm to be secure (e.g., using the wide-trail strategy). If the cipher has additional features (such as being an involution) they are also described and explained in the design rationale.

The purpose of the design rationale is twofold. First, it allows a cryptanalyst to quickly discard attacks that have been attempted and ruled out by the designer. Secondly, it provides a general idea about how secure the algorithm should be. Once new attacks are found against an algorithm they can be compared with the expected security reported by the designer to see how serious they are.

An important component to establishing confidence in a new algorithm's security is the teamwork between the designer and third party cryptanalysts. While the designer has the "home advantage" of understanding the internals of their algorithm, the cryptanalyst enjoys an unbiased view that allows them to see things that might have been overlooked by the designer.

This is why it came as a surprise that the NSA chose not to provide any security design rationale for their algorithms. The lure of analyzing newly released NSA-ciphers proved tempting for many, as the vacuum the NSA left behind was quickly filled with third party analysis such as those in [5, 6, 18, 19, 183].

As a result of substantial resistance to their attempts to standardize Simon and Speck in ISO—discussed further below—the designers finally offered to ISO what they called a "design rationale" in April 2017. As per the request from ISO experts, this so-called design rationale was made public to the crypto-community via the ePrint repository in June 2017 [66].[2] The purpose of releasing this design rationale is stated in Sect. 4.4:

> A desire has been expressed that we publish our analysis of Simon and Speck, and we certainly understand the wish to have insight into our analysis. Therefore, we would like to address that here. We will begin by addressing how we as the design team considered the standard block cipher attacks and their applicability to the security of the SIMON and SPECK design.

However, the joy of finally having a design rationale was short-lived. While the document is heavy on selling the algorithms' efficiency, the security part of the design rationale is practically non-existent. A careful reading of [66, Sec. 4] reveals that it includes no new information regarding the algorithms' security, and merely cites publicly known third party analysis. In particular, three caveats which we now describe in detail raised questions about whether this so-called design rationale was published in good faith.

4.3.1 Lack of New Information

Rather than explaining the attacks the design team attempted, the authors quote the work of others without committing to any particular security claim. The so-called security analysis opens with:

> As the limiting attacks on Simon and Speck have been observed to be differential and linear attacks, it is important to understand the linear and differential properties of the algorithms. Fortunately, this has been a focus of the academic research, and it was an area we paid considerable attention to in our design effort.
> The design team used standard techniques (Matsui's algorithm, SAT/SMT solvers) to determine optimal differential and linear paths for Simon and Speck. We agree with the results obtained by outside researchers.

Reading this, the expectation was that the design team would explain in detail the methods used to bound the length of differential and linear paths[3] and release their tools so that the results they obtained can be reproduced. Instead, they proceeded to describe academic works, sometimes veiling published results as original work by the design team.

---

[2]We remind the reader that the algorithms were published in June 2013, i.e., 4 years prior.

[3]The designers use the term "path" in place of the more common terms "characteristic" and "trail" and we will follow suit.

Moreover, it is a known secret that differential and linear paths do not give the full picture due to the "multipath effect".[4] The designers also acknowledge this and wrote for Simon:

> As has been noted by various authors [3, 4, 19, 138, 490, 523], Simon has a strong multipath effect, largely because of the simplicity of its round function ... We might very conservatively estimate that the number of rounds admitting detectable linear correlations (12, 16, 20, 29, and 37) increases by 50% or so, in the worst case.

How this number (50%) was obtained remains unknown.

Similarly, the multipath effect for differences in Speck is simply stated without explanation:

> For Speck, there is also a slight multipath effect for differences and so an additional round or two can be gained, as noted by Song et al. [537]

and the multipath effect for linear approximation is not quantified at all:

> The linear paths tend to exhibit a stronger multipath effect, but the best linear attacks for Speck are still worse in every case than the best differential attacks.

To understand how the design team determined these numbers is crucial not only for understanding the security of Simon and Speck, but if properly done it can help in improving the security of other algorithms.

4.3.2   Choice of the Number of Rounds

A major source of contention within ISO was the lack of any information on how the round numbers were chosen. Table 4.1 gives the number of rounds for the various variants of Simon. We can see from this table that there does not seem to be any rule for choosing the number of rounds (or "stepping", as it is called in [66]). For example, moving from Simon48 with $m = 3$ to $m = 4$ does not change the number of rounds, while the same change adds two more rounds for Simon64 and Simon96, and 3 more rounds for Simon128.

The only concrete claim in [66] is about the security margins.[5] The designers say:

> Thus, the design team set the stepping with the aim of having security margins comparable to those of existing and trusted algorithms, like AES-128. After 4 years of concerted effort by academic researchers, the various variants of Simon and Speck retain a margin averaging around 30%, and in every case over 25%. The design team's analysis when making stepping decisions was consistent with these numbers.

---

[4]The term "multipath effect" used by the designers is also known as the "clustering effect", "differential effect", or "linear hull effect".

[5]The security margin is the difference between the number of rounds that can be attacked and the actual number of rounds.

In an attempt to determine the real security margins, ISO experts tried to piece together all the claims made by the designers. First, we looked at the best paths given in [66]:

> The design team determined that the single path probabilities (and linear correlations) dip below $2^{-\text{block size}}$ for 12, 16, 20, 29, and 37 rounds for Simon 32, 48, 64, 96, and 128, respectively.

Then, for the multipath effect they argue:

> Simon has a strong multipath effect, largely because of the simplicity of its round function ... We might very conservatively estimate that the number of rounds admitting detectable linear correlations (12, 16, 20, 29, and 37) increases by 50% or so, in the worst case.

That an additional round on each side of a Feistel network can be attacked is acknowledged:

> And then first/last round attack ideas must be factored in.

Pasting all these pieces of information together reveals that except for the case of Simon32/64, which retains a security margin of 37.5%, the remaining security margins for all other variants are below 30%, ranging between 12.5–27.8% with numbers that tend to decrease for the larger block sizes. The exact figures can be found in Table 4.3.

For Speck, the so-called design rationale focuses on differential cryptanalysis:

> the stepping was based on the best differential paths, which tend to be stronger than the best linear paths. See [223]. The single difference path probabilities dip below $2^{-\text{block size}}$ for 10, 12, 16, 18, and 21 rounds for Speck 32, 48, 64, 96, and 128, respectively.

The multipath effect is not quantified and the report only reads:

> For Speck, there is also a slight multipath effect for differences and so an additional round or two can be gained, as noted by Song et al. [537].

Table 4.3 Remaining security margins for Simon

Variant	Number of rounds	Longest path	150%	150% + first/last round trick	Remaining security margin (rounds)
32/64	32	12	18	20	37.5% (12)
48/72	36	16	24	26	27.8% (10)
48/96	36	16	24	26	27.8% (10)
64/96	42	20	30	32	23.8% (10)
64/144	44	20	30	32	27.3% (12)
96/96	52	29	43.5	45.5	12.5% (6.5)
96/144	54	29	43.5	45.5	15.7% (8.5)
128/128	68	37	55.5	57.5	15.4% (10.5)
128/192	69	37	55.5	57.5	16.7% (11.5)
128/256	72	37	55.5	57.5	20.1% (14.5)

A method which uses the key recovery procedure to attack additional rounds is mentioned:

> Dinur [183] shows that an r-round differential distinguisher yields at least an $(r + m)$-round attack, where m is the number of words of key.

For linear cryptanalysis the designers make a vague statement:

> The best linear paths for Speck are notably weaker than the best difference paths, with squared correlations dropping below $2^{-\text{block size}}$ in fewer rounds than is necessary for the difference path probabilities. This agrees with what was found (through non-exhaustive searches) in [223].

Then they cite again someone else's work, but only for Speck32, Speck48, and Speck64:

> In [377], it's proven that for Speck 32, Speck 48, and Speck 64 the squared correlations fall below $2^{-\text{block size}}$ in 10, 11, and 14 rounds, respectively.

The multipath effect is again mentioned, but not in a meaningful way:

> The linear paths tend to exhibit a stronger multipath effect, but the best linear attacks for Speck are still worse in every case than the best differential attacks.

In the case of Speck, not only does no variant retain a security margin of 30% as is argued in [66], but also the largest security margin is 18.2% for Speck32/64. The exact figures can be found in Table 4.4.

We stress that the estimation of the remaining security margin given here is very generous. It assumes that no path longer than those already found exists (which the designers refused to confirm), that the first/last round trick can indeed only be applied to a single round on each side, and that unlike Speck, key recovery attacks against Simon cannot extend beyond the statistical property being used.

Table 4.4 Remaining security margins for Speck

Variant	Number of rounds	Longest path	Multipath effect (+2)	Multipath effect + m	Multipath effect + m + first/last round trick	Remaining security margin (rounds)
32/64	22	10	12	16	18	18.2% (4)
48/72	22	12	14	17	19	13.6% (3)
48/96	23	12	14	18	20	13% (3)
64/96	26	16	18	21	23	11.5% (3)
64/144	27	16	18	22	24	11.1% (3)
96/96	28	18	20	22	24	14.3% (4)
96/144	29	18	20	23	25	13.8% (4)
128/128	32	21	23	25	27	15.6% (5)
128/192	33	21	23	26	28	15.2% (5)
128/256	34	21	23	27	29	14.7% (5)

Even under these generous assumptions the security margins seem slightly on the unsafe side. Surprisingly, it appears that the security margin decreases with the block size and that for about half of the variants the security margin is below (sometimes well below) the claimed 25%. In particular, by the time this so-called design rationale was finally released, only the 128-bit variants of Simon and Speck were considered for standardization in ISO with their extremely small security margins.

After facing these comments, the designers updated [66] and changed the 50% figure for the multipath effect to 25% adding a footnote which reads:

> The original version of this paper said 50% here, but noted that this was "very conservative." This led to confusion by some, who interpreted 50% as an exact value, rather than the very conservative upper bound we intended it to be. This is supported by the literature (see, e.g., [138]) and by our internal analysis. Indeed 50% is a significant overestimate; 25% appears to be a more accurate estimate. We apologize for the lack of clarity here, and note that even if future advances increased the 25–50% Simon would still be secure.

In fact, this footnote is liberal with the facts. In a private correspondence between the design team and one of the ISO experts, the former writes:

> Interestingly, for 18 rounds, it appears that there *is* likely a distinguisher. However, it's not a slam dunk ... However, I think the existence of such a distinguisher could likely be supported by analytic arguments...

4.3.3   Misquoting Existing Work

Following an extended discussion about differential and linear paths the designers proceed to briefly discuss other, less notable attacks. When reading this section with an expert's eye it becomes clear that some of the claims are outdated, either intentionally or unintentionally. One claim stands out in particular in the paragraph discussing slide and rotational attacks. The designers write:

> Both Simon and Speck employ round counters to block slide and rotational properties ...
>   We note that, as with many block ciphers, the counters are essential elements of the designs; without them there are rotational attacks. In fact a very early analysis paper described a rotational attack on Speck, but it only worked because the authors of that paper mistakenly omitted the counter (see [6] (20130909 version)). Also see [28].

The uninformed reader may understand this paragraph to mean that rotational attacks are avoided by injecting round constants into the state and that this approach is supported by Ashur and Liu [28]. While adding round constants is indeed a common countermeasure against rotational attacks, the aforementioned [28] actually presents a novel method for building rotational distinguishers despite the algorithm's use of round constants. To drive the point home [28] exemplified the new method by building a rotational property for Speck. It is therefore not surprising that [376], a follow-up work to [28] used this method to build the longest distinguisher against certain variants of Speck using rotational cryptanalysis (surpassing differential and linear cryptanalysis which were deemed by the designers to be the limiting attacks).

4.4 The ISO/IEC JTC 1 Standardization Process

The work in ISO/IEC JTC 1 is done at two levels: expert- and country-level. Officially, members of JTC 1 are countries, and, more particularly, national standardization bodies (NBs) within these countries. In various stages of the standardization process (e.g., amending an existing standard, canceling a project, approval of Committee Drafts (CD), etc.) NBs are requested to vote on certain questions via a procedure called a *formal ballot*.

Meetings are held every 6 months, each time in a different country. The national bodies send national *experts* to the meetings to discuss the ballots' results, which happen between these meetings, and resolve comments and disagreements.

The rules for how standards are developed in JTC 1 are governed by the ISO/IEC Directives Parts 1–2 [295, 296], which are publicly available documents. In particular, [295, Sec. 2] (Development of International Standards) outlines the various steps a project should follow before being accepted as a part of an international standard.

Being international and market-driven in nature, the work of ISO/IEC JTC 1 focuses around the concept of *consensus*. The importance of reaching consensus is described in [295, Foreword]:

> Consensus, which requires the resolution of substantial objections, is an essential procedural principle and a necessary condition for the preparation of International Standards that will be accepted and widely used. Although it is necessary for the technical work to progress speedily, sufficient time is required before the approval stage for the discussion, negotiation and resolution of significant technical disagreements.

A more refined procedure for determining whether consensus has been reached appears in [295, Sect. 2.5.6], which we mention further below.

When developing a new standard or amending an existing one, an editor and possible co-editor(s) are assigned to the project. The role of the editor is to manage the comments received from the various stakeholders, resolve them, and integrate the changes into the draft text. Target dates are also set for each project. A project that does not meet its target dates is automatically canceled, although extensions are possible.

For a better understanding of the standardization of Simon and Speck, and its resulting cancellation, we now briefly explain some of the important stages of the process.

Study Period

The standardization process for a new algorithm starts with a Study Period (SP). In this, a Call for Contributions (CfC) is drafted and sent to stakeholders. The stakeholders are requested to provide their views on the new proposal. The CfC usually includes questions about the necessity for the new proposal, its security, possible use cases, how it compares to algorithms in existing standards, etc.

The decision to initiate a new working item as a result of an SP is made by the experts participating in the following meeting, and approved by NB ballot.

Working Draft (WD)
Once it has been decided to initiate a project, a working draft is circulated among the experts associated with the Working Group (WG) in charge of the project. The role of the project editor is to receive, resolve, and integrate comments from the experts to build consensus. A Working Draft (WD) usually undergoes several revisions until the experts agree that it is ready to progress to the Committee Stage as a Committee Draft (CD).

Committee Stage (PDAM, Proposed Draft Amendment)
The committee stage is the principal stage at which comments from NBs are taken into consideration. Once the Working Group experts agree that a draft proposal is mature enough to progress to the Committee Stage, a ballot is sent to all NBs which are requested to vote to approve this draft. While NBs are obliged to vote, the internal process through which the NBs vote is decided is governed by its own internal working procedures. When an NB wishes to vote to reject a proposal, they must also provide justification. Many of the national bodies do not have the required expertise to evaluate all proposals they receive and they either abstain or automatically approve proposals, by default.

The goal of the Committee Stage is to reach consensus among the national bodies involved. The definition of consensus is given in [217] and [295, Sect. 2.5.6]:

> Consensus: General agreement, characterized by the absence of sustained opposition to substantial issues by any important part of the concerned interests and by a process that involves seeking to take into account the views of all parties concerned and to reconcile any conflicting arguments.
>
> NOTE: Consensus need not imply unanimity. . . . in case of doubt concerning consensus, approval by a two-thirds majority . . . may be deemed to be sufficient for the committee draft to be accepted for registration as an enquiry draft; however, every attempt shall be made to resolve negative votes.

Further Stages
A consensual proposal that has been approved in the committee stage goes through more stages until its final publication. Since Simon and Speck, the subjects of this chapter, did not make it past the committee stage we do not explain the further stages here, and refer the interested reader to [295, Sec. 2].

4.5   The Standardization Process of Simon and Speck in ISO/IEC 29192-2

ISO/IEC 29192 [218] is a standard managed by the Joint Technical Committee (JTC 1) of the International Organization for Standardization (ISO) and the International Electrotechnical Commission (IEC). The standard is managed by

Subcommittee 27 (SC 27) which is responsible for *information and IT security.* Within SC 27, the standard is edited by Working Group 2 (SC 27/WG 2) which is responsible for *cryptography and security mechanisms.* ISO/IEC 29192 itself is a multipart standard dealing with *lightweight cryptography* and Part 2 deals with *Block ciphers.*

The standardization process of Simon and Speck was improper from the outset. It involved premature submission of the algorithms, assignment of the Simon and Speck designers as the project editors, using erroneous procedures to promote the algorithms, refusal to respond to technical questions and a generally adversarial approach towards the process. For brevity, we describe in the sequel the timeline of the standardization process starting from the initial study period and until the project was finally canceled.

Mexico City, Mexico (October 2014)
The idea to include Simon and Speck as part of ISO/IEC 29192-2 was formally launched in the WG 2. A Study Period (SP) was initiated in November 2014 and there was a Call for Contributions for a period of 18 weeks.

Kuching, Malaysia (April 2015)
The responses in the study period were registered. Responses from 4 NBs were received: two supporting the standardization (Russia and the US) and two objecting (Norway and Germany). A presentation was given by Doug Shors discussing the comments submitted by the NBs.[6]

The meeting report indicates that a discussion was held about some of the submitted comments, resulting in a compromise which extended the study period by 6 months to request further input on the algorithms' security, while also allowing a Preliminary Working Draft (PWD) to be circulated in parallel. Interestingly, the most critical question in the Study Period, Question 1, "Should SIMON and SPECK be included in ISO/IEC 29192-2?" is not addressed in the meeting report despite negative responses from some NBs. It is this meeting summary that would later be used by the editors to argue that a decision to include Simon and Speck in ISO/IEC 29192-2 had already been made and could not be contested anymore.

The new Call for Contributions and the Preliminary Working Draft were circulated in May 2015 and June 2015, respectively. At this point, the new CfC no longer included any question of whether Simon and Speck should be standardized, suggesting that the NSA had already decided by then to act in a way that was adversarial to the process.

Jaipur, India (October 2015)
The circulation of the extended CfC following the previous meeting resulted in several experts' comments. About half of the experts commented that the security

---

[6]Doug Shors and Louis Wingers are two NSA employees listed as part of Simon and Speck's design team. They were assigned as co-rapporteurs for this study period, and later as co-editors of the project.

of Simon and Speck was not yet fully understood, and additional information, preferably in the form of a design rationale, was requested.[7]

In parallel, two responses to the Preliminary Working Draft, editorial in nature, were received. Both the comments made in the study period and the ones on the Preliminary Working Draft were discussed in a presentation by Louis Wingers. In this presentation, Wingers argued that providing a design rationale was not the designer's job, and that cryptanalysis of both algorithms had stabilized such that no new results were expected to be published.[8]

Not mentioned in the meeting summary is a discussion that was held about past involvement of the NSA in sabotaging cryptographic standards, e.g., Dual-EC. One of the NSA experts, Debby Wallner, who was also involved in the standardization of Dual-EC, referred to it as the "elephant-in-the-room" and claimed that they had apologized for it and that it was time to move on.[9]

Also not reflected in the summary is a request by Wallner to have a country-level vote during the meeting in order to decide how to proceed with the project. This vote, which has no grounds in the ISO directives, had to be later ratified using the correct procedure. By then, the meeting summary had already noted that the study period should be terminated and that a first Working Draft should be circulated.

Tampa, Florida, USA (April 2016)

Simon and Speck's Working Draft (WD) was circulated on November 2015 with a commenting period of 17 weeks (until March 2016). Aside from editorial remarks, the comments received make it clear that many experts did not trust the security of these algorithms. Another concern raised by experts was that many experts disagreed with the editors' decision to leave variants of Simon and Speck with a 48-bit block size in the draft.

In their Disposition Of Comments (DoC), the editors refused to address the security concerns raised by the experts, virtually marginalizing what seems to be the majority's opinion; quoting from the first paragraph of their response:

> The decision to initiate this Amendment which includes SIMON and SPECK has already been made.

Reading the comments about small block sizes, the editors decided to shift the discussion outside of their own project, and started yet another Study Period (SP) dealing with the more general question of small block sizes.

In conclusion, the meeting report writes:

> The session ended by trying to determine how to move forward. To do this, Debby Wallner (US) requested that a straw poll be taken to decide if the proposed Amendment should move

---

[7]This would be a recurring theme in the standardization of Simon and Speck.

[8]This is yet another recurring theme in the standardization of Simon and Speck. This claim was made by the NSA in each and every meeting, and was always defeated by the time of the next meeting.

[9]Since the discussion about Dual-EC is not reflected in the meeting summary, it is reproduced here from memory.

to second working draft or to the ballot stage. All experts in attendance were asked and the result was 16 to 8 in favor of a second working draft with 8 abstentions.

Such numbers, especially in a preliminary stage, show that the algorithms did not enjoy the wide support required for standardization. Nevertheless, since it was the editors' responsibility to implement the decisions, they concluded the meeting, writing:

> The Editor will now draft a new Call for Contributions which will make three requests. First, a request to outline security concerns with the use of a 48-bit block cipher. Secondly, a request for potential use cases for a 48-bit block cipher. Finally, a request for any updates on the ongoing security evaluation of SIMON and SPECK.

Abu Dhabi, UAE (October 2016)

Indeed, another Working Draft was circulated on June 2016 with a commenting period of 15 weeks (until September 2016). Surprisingly, the Working Draft only included questions about the block size, and about new cryptanalytic results, completely ignoring the mistrust expressed by the majority of experts. As a result, comments about this working draft were limited to the questions asked and referred only to the block size.

In their Disposition of Comments, the editors resolved to remove the 48-bit variants of Simon and Speck and leave the other block sizes.[10] They also resolved all editorial comments and declared that a consensus has been reached and that the draft was ready to progress to Committee Stage.

Hamilton, New Zealand (April 2017)

Simon and Speck's 1st PDAM was circulated on December 2016 requesting that votes and comments be sent until February 2017. The result of this ballot showed that 15 NBs voted to approve the proposal (some with comments), 8 voted to disapprove, and 26 abstained. This result showed not only that the algorithms do not enjoy consensus, but also even the 66% minimal threshold was not met.

Many of the comments from the National Bodies listed the absence of a design rationale as a factor in their disapproving vote. Other comments also mentioned that 64-bit block ciphers were inherently insecure against generic attacks.[11] In their preliminary Disposition of Comment the editors announced that they would provide a design rationale for the algorithms:

> The editors will provide documentation that discusses the design rationale and the design team's security analysis for SIMON and SPECK.

---

[10]Since the efficiency of the two algorithms, which was its main selling point, was always presented with respect to the smaller variants of the algorithms, it is interesting how the smaller variants have been slowly phased out of the proposed standard, leaving only the larger variants whose efficiency was never thoroughly discussed and that do not fare as well as the alternatives.

[11]The Sweet32 attack [86] was published around this time and was a factor in many of the decisions of the NBs.

but the editors refused to address the comments about small block sizes. Following a heated discussion in the meeting itself, they announced that they would remove all variants of Simon and Speck with block size smaller than 128-bits.

Berlin, Germany (October 2017)

The so-called design rationale was circulated together with the 2nd PDAM asking again the national bodies to approve or disapprove this project within 8 weeks. This time, the results were that 15 countries voted to approve the draft (some with comments), and 7 voted to disapprove. This vote, while still not consensual, at least met the 66% threshold allowing the secretariat to deem such vote consensus.

The so-called design rationale and the problems that arise from it were analyzed in Sect. 4.3 and most of these comments were also submitted as part of the National Bodies (NBs) justifications for disapproval. The editors refused to address these comments, and provided the following standard answer to comments from NBs:

> The editors regret that [Country X] feels that there is insufficient design criteria provided for SIMON and SPECK in order to determine their inclusion in ISO/IEC 29192-2. ... No further design rationale will be provided by the editors for SIMON and SPECK. The editors stand behind their position that all the documents previously referenced as a part of this Disposition of Comments do indeed provide sufficient information to determine that SIMON and SPECK are indeed secure.

A particular focus was put in this meeting on how the number of rounds was chosen for the algorithms. The NSA editors argued that Tables 4.3 and 4.4 are a misunderstanding and that

> Any native English speaker would immediately understand what we were trying to say in the design rationale.

When asked to elaborate about this decision for the sake of the non-native English speakers in the room, they simply refused. Furthermore, the editors also refused to answer the following two questions posed to them:

- When releasing the algorithms in 2013, was the NSA aware of all attacks that were later published by the academic community against these algorithms?
- Is the NSA aware of additional attacks, beyond those already discovered and published by the academic community?

Their refusal to answer these questions, together with the insufficient quality of the design rationale, was enough to demonstrate that "sustained opposition to substantial issues" still existed, and it was decided that a 3rd PDAM should be circulated.

Wuhan, China (April 2018)

The 3rd PDAM was circulated on December 2017, again asking for the support of national bodies within 8 weeks (until February 2018). This time, 14 countries voted to approve the draft (some with comments), and 8 voted to disapprove. The Disposition of Comments was not distributed prior to the meeting and was made available to participants only in the meeting itself. The project editors could not attend the meeting in-person and the editing session was performed via Skype. At this point, it was made clear that the editors had given up on reaching consensus. They refused to address the concerns raised by the NBs, and simply said that they requested that a 4th PDAM be circulated. In response, some of the experts suggested that since it is clear that a consensus cannot be reached due to the refusal to provide further information, the project should be canceled.

Following a discussion about the proper procedure to make this decision, the WG2 conveners decided to hold an internal vote. Each country participating in the meeting would cast a single vote for one of the following options: (1) cancel the project; (2) proceed to a 4th PDAM; and (3) abstain. Of the 16 countries represented in the room, 8 voted to cancel the project, 4 voted to move to a 4th PDAM, and 4 abstained. This decision was later ratified by SC27, the parent committee to WG2.

The justification for cancellation reads:

> Working Group 2 (WG 2) feels that both algorithms included in the amendment are not properly motivated and their security properties are not sufficiently understood. An attempt was made by the designers to publish a design rational (ePrint 2017/560) which was not enough to convince WG 2 experts. Requests to disclose additional information about the way the algorithms were designed were refused by the designers.
>
> It appears that a stalemate has been reached where the amendment cannot reach the required majority of 66% to move from PDAM to DAM stage. This issue seems to already reflect badly on ISO's reputation in what media attention it receives. It also has an adverse effect on the collaborative nature of the work within ISO which seems to polarize around this and spill over onto other projects. Therefore, WG 2 experts believe that it is best to cancel the project and not standardize these algorithms.
>
> WG 2 wishes to convey that not including the algorithms in ISO/IEC JTC 1/SC 27 standards is not a statement about the security or the quality of the algorithms nor about the work done by the designers nor the editors. Since the decision to move forward from a PDAM stage requires consensus decision (even if not unanimity) it simply means that given the available information and the opposing opinions about the security of the algorithms they do not enjoy the level of confidence required for inclusion in ISO/IEC JTC 1/SC 27 standards.

Part III
Lightweight and Ultra-Lightweight Authentication Protocols

5

Electronic ID: Design and Implementation

Lucjan Hanzlik and Mirosław Kutyłowski

Abstract This chapter is devoted to the design and implementation of electronic ID (eID) such as ePassports and electronic personal identity documents. We present an overview of existing and emerging concepts, both concerning threats and possible countermeasures. Thereby we aim to shed light on the development of ubiquitous systems, where many artifacts will require strong electronic identification with similar properties to those in the case of eIDs issued for humans.

5.1 Application Scenarios

The initial reason to develop an electronic identity document (eID)—an identity document with an electronic layer—was to prevent its forgery. The problem is that purely visual security measures have their limitations. The introduction of the electronic layer changed the situation substantially.

After introducing the electronic layer into identity documents it became evident that there are multiple opportunities to design and/or improve systems requiring strong authentication. The first obvious example is the eGate automatic border control.

5.1.1 Remote vs. Local Use

The motivation for designing eID systems comes from situations such as automated border control and enabling eGovernment applications. The first option is presenta-

Lucjan Hanzlik
Stanford University and CISPA, Stanford, CA, USA

M. Kutyłowski (✉)
University of Science and Technology, Wrocław, Poland
e-mail: miroslaw.kutylowski@pwr.edu.pl

tion of an eID to a reader and processing all information locally. The second option is using an eID as a secure token that enables us to create authenticated connections with a remote terminal. An alternative is to use no eID and realize its functions using an ID infrastructure. Each option has its advantages and disadvantages:

Option 0: Virtual ID An ID document contains data that may be fetched from an appropriate registry. So one can use a "virtual ID document" containing only a key to a database (e.g., an ID number printed on a sheet of paper). There are certain advantages of this approach: a negligible technical effort for issuing and delivery of an ID document, and ease of ID document updating and revocation. However, this solution has also substantial disadvantages:

- The service operator (as well as a cyber criminal that breaks into the system) is aware of all activities concerning identity verification. This violates the data minimization principle of security engineering.

- In the case of a system failure (e.g., due to a cyber attack, telecommunication infrastructure failure, etc.), all activities requiring identity verification are suspended.

- There is a non-negligible communication latency and overhead.

- Responding to a query should be preceded by checking the rights to get an answer. This is hard if the verifier has no eID.

Option 1: Local Use An eID token holding crucial ID data and verifiable for its originality has substantial advantages in certain situations:

- The presence of an eID is indirect proof of the physical presence of its holder.

- Identity and data verification does not require online access despite strong guarantees originating from the eID issuer.

- Interaction with a chip may enable biometric verification without the involvement of any external database. The biometric data obtained by the reader can be directly compared with data stored in the eID. Consequently, any security breach in the system would not expose the biometric data of the whole population.

Option 2: Remote Use In this case an eID serves as a secure cryptographic token for remote authentication. The advantages of this approach are as follows:

- An eID is involved in the authentication process as a "what you have" and a "what you know" component, since typically an eID requires us to provide the user's activation password.

- In remote authentication it is hard to check that the user is really on the other side of the line. An eID serves as indirect proof of this presence: its participation in a protocol execution is checked in a cryptographic way, while one can reasonably assume that the owner of the eID would not borrow/give it to a third person.

5.1.2 Actors and Scenarios

Determining the actors of the process involving an eID enables us to see the variety of solutions associated with this term. Below we list a number of cases:

- **Owner–eID–Reader:** Example: border control booth.
  A traveler presents their ePassport to an eGate. No border control officer is involved in this process (unless additional processing is needed or the traveler needs assistance). The holder of the ePassport is involved in the protocol as biometric data are scanned and compared with the data stored in the ePassport. In some data protection scenarios, providing the password of the ePassport holder is required.
- **eID–Reader:** Example: vending machine with age verification.
  A vending machine selling stuff for adults only (alcohol, etc.) has to verify the age of the buyer. The process must work smoothly without annoying the buyer. The protocol should guarantee that a genuine eID is involved, and that this eID has been issued for a person that has reached the legal age. No other data about the eID holder should be revealed.
- **Owner–eID–Reader–Terminal:** Example: submitting claims to an e-government authority.
  In this case the reader serves as a man-in-the-middle transmission device located between the eID and the remote terminal. It provides technical means to establish a channel between them, while the essential part of the protocol is run between the eID and the terminal. The second role of the reader is to enable authorization of the eID owner to perform some actions with the eID—such as signing a digital document submitted to the terminal.
- **eID–Reader(s)–eID:** Example: vehicle to vehicle communication.
  In the near future a new application area may emerge where autonomous devices, such as vehicles, communicate directly and make decisions about their behavior. In many cases this will require strong authentication. For instance:

  – One has to recognize non-authorized devices that may work in a malicious way or merely misuse the protocol for their own profit.
  – It might be necessary to identify traffic rules violators and vehicles responsible for traffic accidents.

  At the same time the privacy of the authenticating parties should be protected.
- **eID–PC:** Example: user presence verification.
  In certain cases a user operates a terminal and apart from the initial authentication we need continuous verification of their presence. This concerns cases such as operating a terminal for performing certain financial operations or safety-relevant operations (e.g., in railway or air traffic). We have to make sure that an unauthorized person will not be able to perform any action when the authorized person leaves the terminal without closing a session.
  Another major application area is medical services and, in particular, authenticating medical records presented to an insurance company. Evidence of presence

created together with a patient's eID is required in order to witness a medical transaction.

- **Owner–eID–PC:** Example: signature creation.

  An eID may enable us to create digital signatures that are legally equivalent to handwritten signatures. In this case the eID holds signing keys and creates signatures provided that the eID owner explicitly gives their consent.

5.1.3   Goals of Protocol Execution

The execution of a protocol with an eID may serve different purposes. Below we list those that are either currently in operation or claimed as a near target:

- **identity data confirmation**: confirming data regarding the owner that are either printed on the eID or otherwise available for the verifier (e.g., a face image of the eID holder),
- **attribute confirmation**: an eID shows no identification information (including indirect ones such as the eID's serial number), instead it presents (authenticated) attributes of the eID owner,
- **key exchange**: the eID and the terminal establish a mutually authenticated secret key for establishing secure communication,
- **authentication and proof of eID's presence**: a volatile or non-volatile proof of the eID presence, in the second case the proof can be used against third parties,
- **authentication and proof of user's presence**: we check that the owner holds an eID participating in a protocol (the difference with the previous case is that the eID holder is involved in the process, for instance through biometric or password verification),
- **terminal authentication**: authentication of the (remote) terminal concerning its identity and access rights,
- **confirming owner's consent**: providing an (implicit) proof that the owner of the eID has agreed to something.

5.2   Threats and Security Requirements

5.2.1   Assets

The first type of asset concerns secret and private information:

- **password:** a password or a PIN number used to activate the electronic layer of the eID or used in a password authentication protocol,
- **secret key:** a secret key used for eID or terminal authentication,

- **personal data:** data about the document owner including name and other identification attributes that are printed on the physical layer of the identity document,
- **sensitive data:** data stored in the electronic layer of the eID, which are not present on the physical layer (typically, biometric data about the document owner: iris scan, fingerprint, etc.).

On the other hand, there are assets related to a property or state of a protocol execution. The following assets fall into this category:

- **authenticity of data:** we consider the integrity and originality of the data stored in the memory of the eID,
- **authenticity of eID:** the integrity and originality of the eID as a device,
- **confidentiality of communication:** preventing access of unauthorized parties to data exchanged over communication channels established with an eID,
- **access limited to authorized terminals:** limiting access to sensitive data to authorized terminals,
- **privacy of eID usage and location:** confidentiality of data regarding eID usage, including for instance the identity of terminals involved in an interaction, the interaction time, and the data exchanged.

    Note that in some scenarios a proof that the document interacted with a reader is required. However, in general user privacy should be protected and access to the data should be confined to authorized parties.
- **robustness:** an eID must work properly regardless of previous, possibly faulty, executions.

5.2.2 Threats

A major threat against identification documents is **forgeries**. An attacker may attempt to create a fake eID that behaves like a genuine one and presents data that will be accepted just like in the case of interaction with a genuine eID.

An adversary may attempt to **clone** an eID.

A clone can be used by a person with a similar appearance as well as in remote applications, unless protection via biometric authentication or password verification continues to work effectively. In particular, eID cloning may enable identity theft with profound consequences. Note that breaking the secret key of an eID may be regarded as a partial forgery or cloning.

Another threat is using an eID without the **owner's consent**. This is particularly likely in the case of wireless communication, where interaction with an eID can be initiated even without the owner's knowledge. Typically, an eID is secured via a password either entered manually by the owner or read optically from the document's surface.

Since the password has usually low entropy (e.g., 4–6 digits in the case of a PIN) it might be guessed by an adversary. A common protection mechanism is to block an eID after a limited number of failed attempts, but this would allow an adversary to mount a denial of service attack—especially in the case of wireless communication. In the case of non-blocking passwords, an adversary can try to guess the correct password using a brute-force dictionary attack. If the protocol execution is artificially slowed down so that a single interaction takes, say, 2 s, the threat is only reduced.

On the other hand there is a threat of offline attacks, where the attacker analyzes transcripts of communications between the eID and honest as well as dishonest readers. Another scenario is simply leaking passwords from a malicious reader.

A different kind of threat comes from malicious terminals that interact with the electronic layer of an eID and attempt to receive more data than allowed. This may concern eID identity (e.g., if no password has been provided by the eID holder) or sensitive data such as biometric data (if the terminal has not been properly authenticated). In any case we are talking about **escalating access rights** via bypassing the access control mechanism employed by the eID. Note that breaking the secret key used for terminal authentication is essentially a step of such an attack.

Malicious terminals as well as parties observing communication may use an interaction with an eID to convince a third party of their location and activities. In the weaker form of **location and activity tracing** an attacker derives these data for its own purposes, e.g., by observing interaction or initiating a session with the purpose of learning the identity of eIDs within its range.

An adversary can also try to extract personal data by **eavesdropping** on secure and authenticated communication between an honest eID and an honest reader/terminal. To perform this kind of attack, the adversary has to break the confidentiality of the communication channel or hijack a session already established.

In Table 5.1 we summarize the dependencies between the above assets and threats.

5.3 Cryptographic Protocols for eIDs

In this section we present some cryptographic protocols that are implemented and used in various existing eID solutions and which tackle the problems described above.

5.3.1 Preventing eID Forgeries

A simple approach adopted, among others, by the ICAO (International Civil Aviation Organization) (see [291]), is to store all relevant data $D_1, \ldots, D_n$ in the electronic layer, compute $h := \text{Hash}(\text{Hash}(D_1), \ldots, \text{Hash}(D_n))$ and an electronic signature of the eID issuer on h. Then, it is possible to check the signature and verify that the data $D_1, \ldots, D_n$ are authentic. (Note that it is also possible to verify

Table 5.1 Threat-asset dependency table

Threat/asset	Password	Secret key	Personal data	Sensitive data	Authenticity of data	Authenticity of eID	Communication confidentiality	Limited access	Usage/location privacy
eID forgery	✓				✓	✓			
eID cloning	✓	✓	✓	✓		✓			?
Owner's consent			✓	✓			?	✓	✓
Escalating access rights			✓	✓					✓
Location and activity tracing									✓
Eavesdropping	✓		✓	✓			✓	✓	✓

the signature when only some D_i are given, while for the remaining values D_j only Hash(D_j) is presented.) What is more, this data can be compared with the data stored in the physical layer of the document.

The solution presented is called *Passive Authentication* (PA).

Unfortunately, it provides no protection against eID cloning as all digital data stored in the eID can be presented to a reader in the course of a normal interaction.

5.3.2 Enforcing Owner's Consent

An access control mechanism based on an activation password can be deployed in order to protect against using an eID without the owner's consent, Unfortunately, it can turn out to be ineffective. There are at least two attack scenarios:

1. an adversary is communicating directly with an eID,
2. an adversary is eavesdropping on an interaction between honest parties.

In the former case, the adversary may try all possible passwords by starting an interaction with the eID. However, the eID may increase its response time to say 1–2 s in order to slow down the attack.

Moreover, the password may include a code printed on the eID in a *machine readable zone* (MRZ) and optically read by the reader. This code may have much higher entropy than human memorizable passwords.

Because of this latter scenario, the password cannot be transmitted in a form that would enable the adversary to learn it and reuse it later to communicate with the eID. This has been taken into account in a solution adopted by the ICAO called Basic Access Control (BAC). In this protocol a fixed password corresponding to an eID is used (1) to encrypt random nonces used to derive a session key, and (2) to create MACs authenticating the nonces. If on any side an incorrect password is used, then the protocol will fail. The password is derived from data scanned optically from the MRZ area—therefore an ePassport must be *shown* by its owner. Unfortunately, BAC allows an offline attack, i.e., given a transcript of a communication an adversary can apply a brute-force dictionary attack to learn the password [375].

The successor to BAC—Password Authenticated Connection Establishment (PACE) introduced by the German Federal Office for Information Security (BSI) in 2008—changes the situation. It becomes impossible to verify a password guess given only a transcript of a communication between an eID and a reader. The PACE protocol consists of four main phases (see Fig. 5.1 for details):

1. sending a ciphertext $\text{Enc}(K_\pi, s)$ to the reader, where s is random and the key K_π is derived from the password,
2. using a mapping function based on the secret s to derive new parameters $\hat{\mathbb{G}}$ with a new generator $\hat{g}$ for the Diffie-Hellman protocol,
3. applying Diffie-Hellman key exchange to derive a master secret key K,
4. exchanging message authentication tags T_R, T_C based on a key derived from K.

eID:	reader:
password π, parameters $\mathbb{G}$	password π, parameters $\mathbb{G}$
PROTOCOL EXECUTION	

eID		reader
$K_\pi = \text{KDF}(\pi)$		$K_\pi = \text{KDF}(\pi)$
choose $s \leftarrow \mathbb{Z}_q$		
$z = \text{Enc}(K_\pi, s)$	$\xrightarrow{\quad z \quad}$	
		$s = \text{Dec}(K_\pi, z)$
$\cdots\cdots\cdots\cdots\cdots\cdots$ Mapping Function $\cdots\cdots\cdots\cdots\cdots\cdots$		
$\hat{\mathbb{G}} = \mathbf{Map}(\mathbb{G}, s)$		$\hat{\mathbb{G}} = \mathbf{Map}(\mathbb{G}, s)$
choose $y_C' \leftarrow \mathbb{Z}_q^*$		choose $y_R' \leftarrow \mathbb{Z}_q^*$
$Y_C' = \hat{g}^{y_C'}$	$\xleftarrow{\quad Y_R' \quad}$	$Y_R' = \hat{g}^{y_R'}$
abort if $Y_R' = Y_R$	$\xrightarrow{\quad Y_C' \quad}$	abort if $Y_C' = Y_C$
$K = Y_R'^{y_C'}$		$K = Y_C'^{y_R'}$
$K_{\text{Enc}} = \text{KDF}_{\text{Enc}}(K)$		$K_{\text{Enc}} = \text{KDF}_{\text{Enc}}(K)$
$K_{\text{Mac}} = \text{KDF}_{\text{Mac}}(K)$		$K_{\text{Mac}} = \text{KDF}_{\text{Mac}}(K)$
$K_{\text{Mac}}' = \text{KDF}(K, 4)$		$K_{\text{Mac}}' = \text{KDF}(K, 4)$
if $\text{Verify}(K_{\text{Mac}}', (Y_A', \mathbb{G}), T_R) = 0$,	$\xleftarrow{\quad T_R \quad}$	$T_R = \text{Mac}(K_{\text{Mac}}', (Y_C', \mathbb{G}_1))$
then abort		
$T_C = \text{Mac}(K_{\text{Mac}}', (Y_R', \mathbb{G}_1))$	$\xrightarrow{\quad T_C \quad}$	if $\text{Verify}(K_{\text{Mac}}', (Y_B', \mathbb{G}), T_C) = 0$,
		then abort
key $= (K_{\text{Enc}}, K_{\text{Mac}})$		key $= (K_{\text{Enc}}, K_{\text{Mac}})$

Fig. 5.1 PACE protocol

There are two variants of the mapping function specified in the ICAO standard: Generic and Integrated Mapping. In the former case, $\hat{g} = h \cdot g^s$, where h is the secret key generated using a standard Diffie-Hellman protocol for parameters $\mathbb{G}$. In the latter case, $\hat{g} := \text{Hash}(s, r)$ where r is a random number chosen by the reader.

The security of the Generic Mapping version of the protocol is based on the following argument. We can create a virtual protocol, where h is not derived by the Diffie-Hellman protocol but is a random element. Such a change cannot be detected by an adversary performing an offline attack due to the hardness of the Diffie-Hellman Problem. However, in the virtual protocol all data exchanged are stochastically independent of s. Therefore, it is impossible to derive any information about s. A similar argument applies to Integrated Mapping. Note that $\hat{g}$ never occurs in the communication and the values Y_C', Y_R' are uniformly distributed, as the group used has a prime order. The only relation to $\hat{g}$ is hidden in the way the protocol partners derive K. However, again we can consider a virtual protocol where K is replaced by a random element. The change is not observable to the attacker even if they learn the key K. Some partial security proofs for the PACE protocol were presented by Bender et al. [72] and for the PACE Integrated Mapping by Coron et al. [153].

An important feature of password-based schemes is how to respond to authentication attempts with a wrong password. In any case, a failed attempt is information indicating incorrectness of the password. The important point is that no other information should be revealed to the attacker. Note that PACE has this property: first, the ciphertext of a random number s does not reveal any information about the password dependent encryption key. Second, the random challenges exchanged within the final Diffie-Hellman key exchange are stochastically independent of the password. The password dependent message T_C is sent *after* positive verification of T_R—so T_C is not transmitted, if the password is incorrect!

5.3.3 EID Authentication and Preventing Cloning

The threat of eID cloning is also called an *impersonation attack*, since a user of a cloned eID may impersonate its legitimate owner. This kind of attack can be easily performed in the case of passive authentication, as all data in an eID are also available outside it. An obvious remedy to this problem is to use an eID public key as part of the data authenticated by the document issuer, store the corresponding secret key in the memory of the eID, and run an authentication protocol based on these keys. Obviously, this solution makes sense only if it is infeasible to export the secret key from the eID.

The ICAO standard for Machine Readable Travel Documents specifies two cryptographic protocols that can be used to authenticate a chip. The first is called Active Authentication (AA) and relies on the challenge-response paradigm. The terminal sends a challenge to the ePassport, which responds with a signature under this challenge. Finally the terminal verifies the signature with respect to the public key stored in the authenticated data read from the ePassport's memory.

The second solution called Chip Authentication v.2 (ChA v.2) was introduced by the BSI as part of the so-called Extended Access Control (EAC) protocol stack, where within the same protocol the rights of the terminal are checked. ChA v.2 is a static Diffie-Hellman protocol: it is simply the Diffie-Hellman key exchange protocol where the challenge from the eID is replaced by its public key, say $y = g^x$. As in the Diffie-Hellman key exchange protocol deriving the shared key is possible provided that one knows the discrete logarithm of the challenge, the ability of the eID to derive the secret key serves as evidence that it knows the secret key x.

The main advantage of ChA v.2 is that it generates a new session key that can be used to secure communication between the eID and the terminal. Note that the protocols discussed in the previous subsection establish a secure channel between the eID and a reader, which is not necessarily part of the terminal. For example, if the eID is used for online activities the card reader is at best a part of the user's system.

The main disadvantage of both solutions is that they require additional computations that are expensive, i.e., exponentiations. For this reason the ICAO adopted

eID:		reader:
choose $y_C \leftarrow_R \mathbb{Z}_q^*$		choose $y_R \leftarrow_R \mathbb{Z}_q^*$
$Y_C = g^{y_C}$	$\xleftarrow{\quad Y_R \quad}$	$Y_R = g^{y_R}$
abort if $Y_R \notin \langle g \rangle \backslash \{1\}$	$\xrightarrow{\quad Y_C \quad}$	abort if $Y_C \notin \langle g \rangle \backslash \{1\}$
$h = Y_R^{y_C}$		$h = Y_C^{y_R}$
$\hat{g} = h \cdot g^s$		$\hat{g} = h \cdot g^s$

Fig. 5.2 Generic mapping of PACE

a protocol called PACE with Chip Authentication mapping (PACE-CAM) that combines PACE with authentication of the eID [298]. The initial part of the protocol is exactly the same as in the case of PACE Generic Mapping (see Fig. 5.2)—which is important for reasons of backwards compatibility and the costs of upgrading the protocols. However, in the final part of the protocol the eID must show the discrete logarithm of its challenge Y_C with respect to its public key pk_C as the generator. Note that the eID cannot pass the protocol without being able to derive h and this requires knowledge of y_C such that $Y_C = g^{y_C}$. As the eID has to present a w such that $Y_C = pk_C^w$, it follows that $pk_C = g^{y_C/w}$ where y_C and w are both known to the eID. Consequently, after checking that $Y_C = pk_C^w$ the terminal can safely conclude that the eID knows the discrete logarithm of pk_C.

Leakage Resistance The protocol PACE-CAM may serve as an example of a possible defense against malicious or poor implementations. One of the critical threats for this protocol is the danger of leaking the discrete logarithm of pk_C (thereby enabling cloning of the eID concerned).

Assume that during protocol execution the eID first chooses y_C and later computes $w = y_C/sk_C$ (as in [73]). Then obviously the key sk_C is exposed in case a weak random number generator has created y_C. In [257] the computations are performed in a slightly different way. Namely, $Y_C = pk_C^w$, for w chosen at random, and there is no computation of w during the final stage. The most important feature is that the value y_C does not appear at all. However, the element h has to be computed by the eID in a slightly different way: instead of computing $h = Y_R^{y_C}$, the eID computes $h = (Y_R^w)^{sk_C}$. The exponentiation with sk_C can be executed in a separate hardware zone which performs no other operation. In this way the secret key sk_C is essentially secure even if the adversary has access to all values outside this hardware zone.

Particular care is needed in the case of protocols using signatures such as DSA and Schnorr. In this case leakage of ephemeral random values leads to leakage of the long time secret keys and it seems that there is no simple remedy for this problem.

5.3.4   Authenticating the Terminal and Its Rights

A terminal that has guessed or knows the activation password of an eID may attempt to read sensitive data from the eID. Since it knows the activation password it can interact with the eID, but should not necessarily be able to access all data. This problem is solved by Terminal Authentication v.2 (TA v.2), which in fact is a standard challenge-response protocol: the eID generates a random nonce and the terminal responds with a signature of this nonce and a fingerprint of an ephemeral public key—this public key is the challenge for the static Diffie-Hellman key agreement executed as part of ChA v.2. For the sake of signature verification the terminal presents a certificate of its public key. The certificate declares in particular which data from the eID the terminal is allowed to read. To verify the authenticity of the certificate, the document verifies a chain of certificates supplied by the terminal. The first supplied certificate is verified using the root of trust, i.e., a public key of the issuer stored inside the eID (for details see Sect. 5.4).

5.3.5   Proof of Interaction

In this scenario we consider a malicious reader/terminal that tries to sell a transcript of communications or interactions to a third party. Such a transcript may contain valuable information about the document owner (e.g., location, services used). The best protection one can achieve is that a reader/terminal can create a protocol transcript (including values normally available only to the reader/terminal) that is indistinguishable from transcripts originating from real executions. This should also concern executions where a reader/terminal deviates from the protocol description. Then a transcript presented by a reader/terminal has no value to a third party.

In general, any protocol implemented in an eID should support deniability: neither the eID nor the terminal/reader should be able to prove that an interaction with the eID has taken place and had a given form. Note that AA provides a strong proof of interaction for third parties, while for ChA v.2, PACE, PACE-CAM the deniability property is fulfilled. For TA v.2 a signature collected from the terminal is a proof of interaction (with an unspecified eID).

5.3.6   Passive Tracing

Protocols such as PA enable tracing—an eID responds with explicit identification data. The situation is slightly better for BAC. However, once the adversary learns the secret key used by the eID of the traced person to set up connections, the adversary can make trial decryptions of all recorded communications and identify those of the traced eID. The situation is different for protocols such as PACE and PACE-CAM—where identity information is revealed after establishing a secure channel. Even password related data are transmitted in a very careful way—via a ciphertext of a random value s. For ChA v.2 the situation is slightly more complicated: if PACE is executed first, then ChA v.2 is secured by the secret channel established by PACE. Otherwise, transmission of the public key used for static Diffie-Hellman reveals the identity of the eID. This was one of the reasons for designing ChA v.3, where the protocol starts with the regular Diffie-Hellman key exchange.

5.3.7 Eavesdropping

While most of the discussed protocols run key exchange protocols and automatically support confidentiality of the established session, there are some subtle issues concerning for instance the threat of hijacking of a session. Especially if the protocols are executed one after another, the protocol partners need to be sure that in the meantime an adversary has not taken over the communication on one side. For instance, TA v.2 and ChA v.2 are coupled by a signature created during TA v.2 execution for a fingerprint of the terminal's ephemeral key used during execution of ChA v.2. Similarly, while PACE is not resilient to MiTM attacks (by an adversary knowing the password), it seems to be infeasible to run an active attack enabling the eID and the reader to establish the shared key K, so that it would be known also to the adversary.

Summary

Table 5.2 depicts threats addressed successfully by the protocols discussed above.

Table 5.2 Threats addressed by the discussed protocols

Threat/protocol	PA	PACE	ChA v.2	TA	PACE-CAM
eID forgery	✓		✓		✓
eID cloning			✓		✓
Lack of owner's consent		✓			✓
Unauthorized data access				✓	
Location and activity tracing		✓			✓
Eavesdropping		✓	✓	Indirectly	✓

5.4   PKI

In standard situations the Public Key Infrastructure (PKI) is built on top of trust relations. A user chooses *roots of trust*—entities that are trusted by him. A root of trust can delegate trust to other entities, creating a *chain of trust*. In the end, the user will accept/trust any entity that can prove itself to be a member of a chain of trust. To confirm trust relations, the entities issue certificates signed with their secret keys.

A similar approach could be implemented in the eID scenario, but we face substantial technical problems. The hardware chip of an eID might be severely limited in computational power and memory size. Storing many roots of trust and verifying long chains of trust would immediately make an eID solution quite inefficient. For this reason a simplified approach has been adopted:

- the root of trust is set to one entity, namely *the country verifying certificate authority* (CVCA),
- the CVCA delegates its rights to domestic and foreign document verifiers that delegate rights to terminals—so the trust chains have a length of at most 2,
- certificates have a form enabling easy verification on hardware with limited resources (*card verifiable certificates*, CVC).

This PKI allows for interoperability between passports issued by different countries. However, in order to inspect a passport, a document verifier must be trusted by the document owner's CVCA, which requires cooperation between two countries. Practically it turns out to be a problem.

Another serious problem is revoking certificates. In a standard situation it is implemented using certificate revocation lists (CRL) and an online certificate status protocol (OCSP). In the case of eID systems this may lead to technical problems:

- an eID has no memory available for storing CRLs,
- an eID has no direct access to the OCSP server,
- verification may turn out to be too slow from a practical point of view,
- an eID has no internal battery and therefore no internal clock. It can only store the time last seen, so a terminal may authenticate itself with an outdated CRL.

The solution implemented in ePassports is to use short-term certificates for terminals. Thereby, a terminal that has to be revoked simply does not receive a new certificate.

5.5   Challenges for eID Systems

In this section we focus on some fundamental issues that do not concern eIDs directly, but nevertheless are crucial for their success in practice.

Deployment of eIDs Due to financial costs, the deployment of eIDs has to be a continuous process, where the production capacities are used evenly over time.

Hence invalidating eIDs and replacing them with new ones on a large scale might be infeasible. Unfortunately, one cannot exclude that a security flaw or an exploit will be found after deployment. Therefore it would be reasonable to design in advance pragmatic strategies for such situations which are not based on replacement.

As an eID is issued for a long period of time (typically 10 years in the case of personal ID documents and passports), inevitably many generations of eIDs will have to coexist and interact with the existing systems. On the other hand, if a user gets a new eID replacing the expired one, they should be able to continue all activities as the same person. This might be a problem, since transferring the signing keys from the old eID to a new eID might be technically impossible or forbidden due to, e.g., requirements for "secure signature creation devices".

Malicious Provider/Document Issuer Before an eID is given to its owner it has to go through procedures implemented by the hardware and software provider and the document issuer responsible for personalization of the eID. These procedures may be not strict enough and/or depend on the internal policies of these parties. This can open doors for implementing trapdoors or intentional creation of security weaknesses.

A malicious hardware provider can implement secret backdoors that reveal the secret keys of the eID (created during personalization) or provide a means to trace the eID. Similar backdoors can be implemented in software by the document issuer. A malicious issuer can still infer information about users, even if the software is somehow protected (e.g., installed by a different authority). In many cases the secret keys used by the cryptographic protocols can be generated on-card (i.e., by the eID without revealing the secret key to anyone). However, the owner of the document has no *guarantee* that this is how the keys have been generated. What is more, in many cases the secret keys cannot be generated on-card since secret system keys have to be involved.

A different attack technique is to use a flawed random number generator that would allow an attacker to predict the secret key generated by the document and break any protocol based on randomness generated by an eID. The problem can be also caused by a flawed software library. This was the case for the Estonian eID, where many RSA moduli were created in a way that made their factorization easy.

Interoperability While in the area of biometric passports we have to deal with a de facto worldwide standard, in the case of personal ID documents there are a variety of different solutions and concepts. At the same time, the expectation is that an eID may interact with any system and communicate with any reader. This is costly and hardly possible from the technical point of view. The problem has been recognized by the European Union as an obstacle to the internal market. The eIDAS regulation [546] attempts to find a solution to this problem. The approach chosen by eIDAS is as follows. Assume that an eID J attempts to connect to a terminal T in a third country. Then:

- the terminal T redirects the connection request of J to an online authentication service A of the country of origin of J,

- *A* runs the verification process,
- after a positive answer from *A* the terminal *T* establishes a connection with *J*.

Unfortunately, this approach has limited usability:

- it does not work for the offline eID–reader scenario,
- a reader must run all protocols notified in the EU,
- when the authentication service learns that the eID is active at some place. for some protocols the online authentication service can learn the session key and be able to eavesdrop on the communication.

Sometimes cooperation between eID providers is limited, e.g., due to different approaches to personal data protection (such as for the EU versus the US).

User–eID interaction While declaratively users pay attention to their own security, the standard behavior is to trade security for convenience. A good eID system should take this into account. On the other hand, a user has to be given a minimal level of control over their eID. This should include in particular the possibility to:

- temporarily block their own eID,
- get a record of their former activities.

In existing systems, there are limited possibilities to suspend or invalidate an eID based on inserting entries into a central database. This is not enough to prevent lunchtime attacks, where an eID is seized by an adversary for a short time. To keep track of eID activity one could deploy for instance a transaction counter or some more sophisticated solution (see, e.g., [349].

5.6   Future Directions

Composability The main goal of eID protocol designers should be composability. That is, given a limited number of cryptographic procedures it should be possible to implement all required functionalities and even leave room for new applications. This approach not only ensures that an eID can be created with cheaper hardware (i.e., less code means less memory used), but also makes it easier to create and reuse a formal security analysis.

Extensions The protocol stack implemented in an eID should allow extensions. In particular, it should be possible to build new security features on top of the existing stack.

Simple Protocol Changes If a security flaw is found, the protocol designers should focus on simple fixes that make only small changes to the existing protocols. This would not only simplify the security analysis of the new protocol but also speed up the certification process. What is more, the same approach should be taken in the case of an extension to existing protocols. A good example is the PACE-CAM protocol, which is only slightly different from PACE, but significantly improves it.

Acknowledgments Both authors "Lucjan Hanzlik and Mirosław Kutyłowski" have been supported by Polish National Science Centre, project OPUS no 2014/15/B/ST6/02837.

6

Ultra-Lightweight Authentication Protocols: A Critical Analysis

Xavier Carpent, Paolo D'Arco, and Roberto De Prisco

Abstract In this chapter we provide a *critical look* at the state of the art in ultra-lightweight authentication protocols. We start by outlining the features of the current ubiquitous and pervasive computing environment that have motivated the development of the ultra-lightweight paradigm which uses only basic arithmetic and logical operations. We emphasize its goals and its main challenges. Then, we focus our attention on the authentication problem. We use an abstract framework for modeling the protocols proposed over the years, in order to discuss their design strategies and the security and privacy properties they aim to achieve. After that, we survey the weaknesses and the common pitfalls in both the design and the analysis of ultra-lightweight authentication protocols. Finally, we conclude the chapter by discussing some fundamental ideas and research directions.

6.1 Introduction

6.1.1 A Fully Connected World of Small Devices

Small and inexpensive devices are becoming increasingly important in today's technological infrastructures. Modern computing paradigms, pervasive in nature, involve methods for monitoring the status of physical objects, capturing meaningful data, and communicating the data through network channels to processing servers. In many cases, the endpoint elements of connected systems are small and inexpensive devices attached to physical objects. These devices carry identifying information, and are used to achieve certain functionalities: to open and lock doors, control a heating system, catalog items in a shopping basket, identify objects,

X. Carpent
University of California, Irvine, CA, USA

P. D'Arco · R. D. Prisco (✉)
University of Salerno, Fisciano, Italy
e-mail: robdep@unisa.it

operate anti-theft systems, and much more. Wireless communication plays an important role in this landscape, especially in dealing with moving objects where Radio and Near-Field frequencies are commonly used. In the specific case of Radio-Frequency Identification (RFID), there are "Tags" and "Readers". Tags are tiny devices used to label objects; they contain data and communicate with the readers. Readers are bigger devices that collect and forward information to a backend server that processes the data. RFID tags are already widely deployed to track objects (e.g., goods dispatched in a distribution hub). Tags, in their most basic form, the *passive* one, have no battery: they receive their energy wirelessly from the reader. Tags are extremely cheap, with costs in the order of few cents. They are severely constrained in terms of computing power.

In general, small devices, in all forms currently available, are the weak link in the system (e.g., see [579] for a recent attack), and good solutions to the security and privacy concerns are of paramount importance. In particular, *authentication*, the process through which two entities confirm their identities to each other, is a fundamental step for the development of secure applications.

6.1.2   Authentication: Protocol Classification and Physical Constraints

Unfortunately, the authentication problem, in the ultra-lightweight setting, is a challenging one. Indeed, the devices' limitations severely impact the design of the protocols. In [139] a coarse classification partitions authentication protocols into 4 categories: *full-fledged*, *simple*, *lightweight*, and *ultra-lightweight*. The division is based on the capabilities of the constrained devices. Full-fledged protocols allow the use of public-key and symmetric-key cryptography. Thus, they can fully exploit standard cryptographic tools. Simple protocols rely on a limited number of cryptographic functionalities like pseudo-random numbers generation and hashing. Lightweight protocols further restrict the usable cryptography. They avoid hashing, and resort to using simpler operations like CRC checksums. Finally, ultra-lightweight protocols rely only on basic arithmetic and logical operations (modular addition, and, or, xor, etc.).

Although the above classification does not provide an exact distinction among the various classes, we still adopt it since it has been used in several papers that have appeared in the literature. In this chapter we are concerned with very small computing elements, like passive RFID tags, and with ultra-lightweight authentication protocols for such devices. It is very likely that a large percentage of tomorrow's interconnected world will consist of ultra-lightweight computing elements. Indeed, as observed in [308], although technological advances allow us to build inexpensive devices with improved capabilities at the same price, usually the market dictates the use of increasingly cheaper devices with the same capabilities. Hence, we should expect to keep dealing with the least powerful ones.

What exactly are the limitations imposed by these inexpensive devices? In [26] the authors provide a detailed description of the constraints.[1] These constraints are mostly influenced by hardware factors: chip size, power consumption, and clock speed. A standard measure for the computing power of such devices is the number of Gate Equivalent (GE) elements, which reflects the number of logic gates that the circuit integrated on the device consists of.

Let us consider RFID tags as an example. An RFID tag can communicate at very slow rates (typically under 200 kb/s), and this imposes, assuming that authentication has to happen within a reasonable time limit (e.g., 150 ms), an upper bound on the size of the total communication that the protocol can use. RFID tags usually consists of no more than 2000 GEs. Such a limit is imposed by the available physical area and by the cost of the device. Most of the gates are used for the tag's basic functionalities, and only a small fraction of them remain available to implement an authentication protocol. The cheapest RFID tags are passively powered. They receive power through an electromagnetic field, radiated from the reader; this limits the total power consumption that can be used in a single run of the authentication protocol. The power available to the tag is inversely proportional to the maximum distance at which the tag and the reader have to operate: a greater distance implies less available power and this imposes limits on the clock speed (a typical limit is 100 kHz) and, consequently, on the number of instructions that the tag is allowed to execute to finish a run of the protocol within a given time bound. Another limitation of RFID tags is the total number of memory bits: a typical limit is 2048 bits.

Finally, notice that authentication protocols often rely on random or pseudo-random number generators. Passive RFID tags can hardly afford such a component. There exist low-cost pseudo-random generators, but they still pose a substantial burden for an RFID tag. A generator might require the use of more than 1000 GEs, which is more than half of the total number of GEs usually available on these devices.

6.1.3   Design Challenges

Authentication can be achieved in several ways. Standard authentication protocols exhibit a *challenge-and-response* structure, and exploit public-key or symmetric-key cryptography. Sometimes they require the presence of a trusted third party. In all cases, the parties involved in the protocols must be able to execute the required cryptographic algorithms (e.g., encrypting a piece of data using AES). So it goes without saying that standard authentication protocols are not tailored for ultra-lightweight devices. Thus, ultra-lightweight authentication protocols using

---

[1]The title of [26] uses the term "lightweight", but its authors do not use the classification proposed in [139]. The discussion provided in [26] is, indeed, about ultra-constrained devices, like RFID tags.

only elementary operations are needed. It should therefore not come as a surprise that achieving the same security levels as those offered by standard authentication protocols might be much more difficult, or perhaps even impossible.

Thus, the real challenge posed by ultra-lightweight authentication is obtaining the highest possible level of security, given the hardware constraints. Part of the challenge concerns the development of a formal model that can be used to assess the security and privacy achieved by ultra-lightweight authentication protocols.

Nowadays, security assertions are expressed in terms of formal mathematical models for describing problems and analyzing proposed solutions. In particular, security assertions are expressed in formal mathematical terms, cryptographic protocols are built upon computational hardness assumptions, and proofs assume the form of mathematical reductions. As we will argue in the following sections, ultra-lightweight cryptography should be tackled with a similar rigorous approach. We might have to rethink, or to appropriately adapt, the formal framework within which ultra-lightweight protocols are designed and security and privacy assertions about them are assessed.

6.1.4   Organization of the Chapter

In Sect. 6.2 we provide a general concise framework which captures the common structure of known ultra-lightweight authentication protocols, and we discuss the design strategies and properties they aim to achieve. Then, in Sect. 6.3, we point out the limits of achieving security by using very constrained computing devices which allow only simple operations. Specifically, we survey the weaknesses and the common pitfalls in the design of ultra-lightweight authentication protocols. In Sect. 6.4, we elaborate on the importance of using security and privacy models, and provide suggestions for sound design strategies. Finally, in Sect. 6.5 we provide some conclusions.

6.2   Ultra-lightweight Authentication Protocols

Ultra-lightweight mutual authentication protocols appeared in the literature around 2006. M^2AP [467], LMAP [466] and EMAP [465] were the first protocols designed to be executed on circuits equipped with only a few hundred gates. They were collectively identified as the *UMAP family*. In the following year, another protocol, called SASI [139], addressed some of the weaknesses present in those protocols. SASI received considerable attention both from cryptanalysts and designers. However, like its predecessors, it was quickly broken in a few months. Surprisingly, plenty of similar protocols followed, and its "structure" is still being used.

Almost all proposed ultra-lightweight mutual authentication protocols can be seen as instances of one general framework. Three entities are involved: a tag, a reader and a backend server. The channel between the reader and the backend server is assumed to be secure, but the channel between the reader and the tag is public and is susceptible to attacks. To simplify the description, we say that the reader performs some computations, even if the reader just forwards the messages and the backend server is the real entity that performs the computations.

Each tag has a *static identifier*, ID, which is hard-coded into the circuit at production time and is never revealed. Furthermore, the tag has a *pseudonym*, IDS, and a few *secret keys*, which are stored in the tag memory, and are usually updated after each successful execution of the protocol. All of these values are bit-strings of up to 100 bits. Common values are 64 and 96.

Readers are expected to be able to generate *random numbers* or *pseudo-random numbers*.

The backend server, for each tag with static identifier ID, stores in a table the pseudonym and the keys, which therefore are shared with the tag.

The authentication protocol consists in a few rounds. Typically, four.

Figure 6.1 depicts the structure of many ultra-lightweight authentication protocols. Here we provide a description of the messages:

- The *Hello* message is the starting message with which the reader activates the tag, providing it with the energy for the subsequent computation.

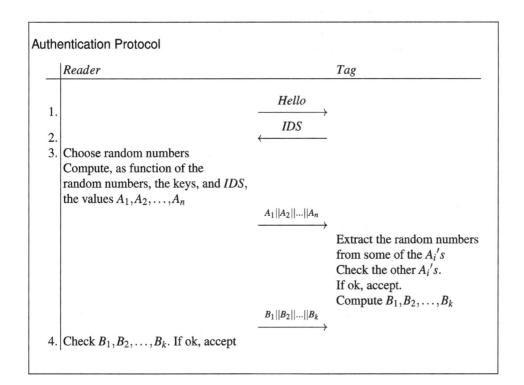

Fig. 6.1 General framework: steps of the authentication protocol

- The *IDS* is the current pseudonym, which the tag sends to the reader and initiates the subsequent authentication protocol.
- The sequence of values $A_1, A_2, \ldots, A_n$, computed by the reader, is usually used in the following form: the first values are a sort of *carriers* for fresh randomly or pseudorandomly generated numbers, while the last ones are the *true authenticators*, computed by using the random numbers, the secret keys and information shared between the reader and the tag. From some of the A_i's, the tag, by using the secret keys, retrieves the random numbers chosen by the reader. Then, by using the secret keys, the retrieved random numbers and some other shared information, the tag recomputes the remaining A_i's and checks that they match the ones received. Such a check aims at ensuring the integrity and the authenticity of the transmitted values.
- The values $B_1, B_2, \ldots, B_k$ are, finally, used by the reader as an acknowledgment that the tag has authenticated the reader, and to complete the authentication of the tag to the reader. They are generated and used in a similar way to the values $A_1, A_2, \ldots, A_n$.

At the end of a successful execution, the reader and the tag change the pseudonym *IDS* of the tag, and all the secret keys, by applying some updating functions. The updating functions use the *IDS* and the secret keys, as well as some of the random numbers, used in the last execution of the protocol. In particular, the updating function for the *IDS* uses also the static tag *ID*.

In practice, many protocols require the reader and tag to store both the new *IDS* and the sequence of secret keys, as well as the previous *IDS* and the previous sequence of secret keys. The reason is that the tag completes the protocol before the reader. If for some reason, adversarial or not, the reader does not complete the protocol, the tag updates the *IDS* and the secret keys while the reader does not. Then, at the subsequent execution, the reader and the tag do not recognize each other. Technically speaking, they are not *synchronized* anymore. By also keeping the old tuple of values, the authentication protocol can be modified in such a way that, if the reader does not reply to the new *IDS*, then the tag sends the old *IDS* again and the authentication protocol is executed using the old sequence of secret keys.

To exemplify the general framework, notice that in M^2AP and EMAP three values are sent from the reader to the tag, and two values are sent from the tag to the reader. In LMAP, SASI, and Gossamer [463], three values are sent from the reader to the tag and one value is sent from the tag to the reader. Moving ahead to more recent protocols, in KMAP [323], RCIA [431] and SASI$^+$ [431], three values are sent from the reader to the tag and one value is sent from the tag to the reader, while in SLAP [383] two values are sent from the reader to the tag, and one value is sent from the tag to the reader. However, some protocols slightly deviate from the general framework, e.g., RAPP [554] has one more round.

To get an idea of the computations, let us look at SASI. Denote by K_1 and K_2 two secret keys shared between the reader and tag, and by n_1 and n_2 two fresh random values generated by the reader. Moreover, we denote by $\oplus, \vee, +$ the xor, or and modular addition operators. Finally, denote with $Rot(s, \ell)$ a bit-string cyclic rotation function, which returns the string s rotated circularly to the left by ℓ positions. The three values, A_1, A_2 and A_3, computed by the reader, are:

$$A_1 = IDS \oplus K_1 \oplus n_1, \quad A_2 = (IDS \vee K_2) + n_2, \text{ and } A_3 = (K_1 \oplus \overline{K_2}) + (\overline{K_1} \oplus K_2),$$

where $\overline{K_1} = Rot(K_1 \oplus n_2, K_1)$ and $\overline{K_2} = Rot(K_2 \oplus n_1, K_2)$. Then, the value B_1, computed by the tag, is

$$B_1 = (\overline{K_2} + ID) \oplus ((K_1 \oplus K_2) \vee \overline{K_1})$$

The updating functions for the pseudonym and the keys are:

$$IDS = (IDS_{old} + ID) \oplus (n_2 \oplus \overline{K_1}), \quad K_1 = \overline{K_1}, \quad K_2 = \overline{K_2},$$

Having considered a sample computation, let us move to the basic requirement for an authentication protocol, that is, correctness: if the reader and tag initiate a protocol execution when they share at least one *IDS* and the corresponding sequence of secret keys, and no adversarial action or transmission error occurs, then they should successfully complete the execution and authenticate each other.

The main security and privacy goals in the design of ultralightweight authentication protocols are:

- **Resistance to desynchronization attacks.** An adversary should not be able to desynchronize the reader and tag.
- **Resistance to impersonation attacks.** An adversary should not be able to impersonate the reader to the tag or the tag to the reader.
- **Anonymity and resistance to tracking attacks.** The protocol should protect against any adversarial action aiming at identifying the tag, and should guarantee that the movements of a tag cannot be traced.
- **Resistance to replay attacks.** The protocol should be immune to attacks in which an adversary collects messages from protocol executions between the reader and tag and sends them again to the parties, in order to subvert some of the security and privacy properties.
- **Forward security.** Even if at a certain point the tag is compromised and the adversary gets the secret information stored in the tag's memory, the past communications should remain unaffected.
- **Resistance to leakage and disclosure attacks.** The protocol should not leak secret information under adversarial actions, and there is no way to get access to the secret information shared between the tag and reader.

Some of the above goals in certain applications should be guaranteed against a *passive* adversary, who just eavesdrops on the protocol executions, while others should hold with respect to an *active* adversary, who can intercept and modify the messages and interact with the parties.

In the next section we elaborate on the security and privacy properties. Indeed, in this area they are almost always expressed in an informal way, and as a *list of desiderata* that need to be achieved. No rigorous model is used to state clearly the goals and to prove the merits of a given protocol. The *proofs* are arguments aiming at convincing the reader of the goodness of the design. As shown in [169] in a case-study for the SASI protocol, this approach opens doors to unexpected consequences.

6.3 Weaknesses and Pitfalls

Ultra-lightweight protocols strive to achieve a strong level of both security and privacy while fitting extreme design constraints due to limited space, energy, and cost on RFID tags. Unsurprisingly, attacks on virtually all proposals in the literature have been published.[2]

As a result, no such protocol could reasonably be used in practice.[3] Although some lessons have been learned from these failures, and despite much advocacy for better screening from the research community, protocols repeatedly fall victim to common pitfalls, even in recent proposals. What follows is a short description of the prevailing weaknesses.

6.3.1 Poor Diffusion and Linearity

Many protocols use the so-called "T-functions" extensively. These are functions for which each bit in the output depends only on bits in the same or lower positions in the input. Binary operations (e.g., and, or, xor) and modular addition are T-functions.

By definition, in a T-function it is not possible that all output bits depend on all input bits, which is the ideal scenario for maximizing "diffusion", an important property in cryptographic primitives. This is particularly dangerous in cryptographic applications, lightweight or otherwise. The only reasonable way to address this shortcoming is by combining these operations with others which do not exhibit this characteristic. Unfortunately many designers do not follow this simple combination rule, and have proposed schemes entirely based on T-functions which are doomed to fail. LMAP [466] is an example of a protocol that uses T-functions exclusively, which was exploited in its cryptanalysis [464].

---

[2]It has been observed that ultra-lightweight protocols are "broken" with relative ease, very shortly after their publication. Avoine et al. [43] shows a short statistical study and concludes conservatively that most are broken in under 4 months.

[3]To the best of our knowledge, the Gossamer protocol [463] is the sole instance to not have any published attacks, although a number of weaknesses in its construction have been identified [130]. In addition, Gossamer is definitely more involved and, arguably, could hardly be considered "ultra-lightweight".

Linearity, i.e., the property that $f(a \odot b) = f(a) \odot f(b)$, is another source of trouble. The xor operation, rotations and other permutations are linear. Like T-functions, linearity is transitive (the composition of linear operations is linear), and some schemes have been shown to be entirely linear, which easily leads to attacks. Particularly notable and common examples are the many proposals in which security is based heavily on the use of Cyclic Redundancy Codes (CRCs). CRCs are designed to do channel error correction, but offer very little security if any at all.

6.3.2 Poor Message Composition

Securely designing the messages exchanged over an ultra-lightweight protocol is a difficult open problem. Keeping the secrets exchanged as secure as possible against any leakage is indeed a big challenge, particularly in such constrained environments. Generally speaking, the messages should guarantee good confusion (i.e., key mixing) and diffusion properties. That is, the secret key (or keys) should be thoroughly involved in the construction of the messages, and a subtle change in the secret should result in completely different messages. However, due to the constraints of ultra-lightweight protocols, messages are usually built using a handful of operations, and in many cases good confusion and diffusion levels are not obtained.

In LMAP for instance, the key update phase is defined by:

$$IDS^{(n+1)} = (IDS^{(n)} + (n_2^{(n)} \oplus K_4^{(n)})) \oplus ID,$$

where we can see that ID, a secret that the protocol is designed to protect, is simply xored with a mixture of public and secret values. This operation exhibits poor confusion and diffusion properties. Although exploitation of this varies in different attacks, this quite frequent feature heuristically leads to a major leakage of secret bits, as the rest of the message the ID is combined with may be biased, or be partially known by the adversary.

6.3.3 Biased Output

Another important weakness of many lightweight schemes is that some of the operations are biased, a property that in many cases leads to security vulnerabilities. This is typical of Boolean functions such as or ($\vee$) and and ($\wedge$), where $x \vee y$ and $x \wedge y$ have, for unbiased random bits x and y, heavily (75%) biased outputs, respectively, towards 1 and 0.

This can constitute a security weakness because these functions leak information for both of their arguments. For example, if $x \vee y = 0$, then $x = y = 0$, which discloses both the inputs. With a uniformly distributed input, this happens 25% of the time (similarly for and, of course). In some cases it is more than enough, after seeing some exchanges, to be able to completely recover all the inputs.

In LMAP, the reader sends $B = (IDS \vee K_2) + n_1$. The attacker can thus use $B + (2^L - 1)$ as a very good approximation to the unknown "shielded" nonce n_1 (on average, 75% of the bits are correct), and this approximation can be used later in other parts of the protocol to approximate the secret (see e.g. [44] for a full attack partially based on this).

6.3.4   Rotations

Rotations have been used for a long time in cryptography. Many modern block ciphers and hash functions such as BLAKE [37] or RC5 [502] rely on the ARX (addition, rotation, XOR) paradigm. Rotations are extremely cheap to implement in hardware, and they introduce diffusion, which complements nicely the modular addition and the XOR (which exhibit poor diffusion properties). Fixed-amount rotations are typically used in ARX designs, but data-dependent rotations, as first featured in the RC5 block cipher [502], also exist.

The SASI [139] protocol was the first ultra-lightweight authentication protocol to feature data-dependent rotations. Since then, most ultra-lightweight protocols have used them, and in many cases they are the weak spot for ad hoc attacks. In addition to linearity, the most important shortcoming of data-dependent rotations is that there are only L possible outputs. Mod n cryptanalysis [319] is also a promising tool for attacking schemes using rotations and additions, although it has never been applied in the cryptanalysis of an ultra-lightweight protocol, to the best of our knowledge. It has, on the other hand, been used to successfully attack block ciphers such as RC5P and M6, which use the same kinds of operation.

6.3.5   Vulnerability to Knowledge Accumulation

If partial leakage of a static secret occurs in a protocol, there is an obvious traceability issue. Indeed, it becomes possible for an attacker to correlate two leaked traces of an eavesdropped exchange. A typical example is recovering the least significant bit of the static identifier (see for instance [473], the first traceability attack on SASI). More importantly, an attacker is sometimes able to recover the full static secret after a few rounds. Indeed, different observations can be combined using Bayesian inference. An example of such an attack was the full cryptanalysis of SASI [44].

One of the initial goals of synchronized protocols[4] is to provide forward privacy. Forward privacy is a stronger notion than just privacy. Simply put, a protocol is said to be forward private if an attacker, having recovered the internal state (the dynamic values of the identifier and keys) of a tag, is not able to recognize the tag in past interaction traces. For a more formal definition, see [453]. Forward privacy cannot be achieved in a protocol if the secrets used in the exchange are all static. Indeed, if the attacker knows the secrets of a tag at some point, it also knows them in the past, since the secret does not change in the tag's lifetime. Therefore, messages sent by a tag in previous interactions can be recomputed, and recognized easily. Note that a changing secret is required for forward privacy, but it does not guarantee it (indeed, there are many synchronized protocols that are not private, and therefore not forward private).

A positive side effect of changing the secrets is that it might make it harder to obtain the full secret at any given time, if only a partial leakage is obtained at every authentication round. This seems to be a good feature as it is intuitively harder to hit a moving target than a static one. However, this does not necessarily make the full cryptanalysis impossible, just slightly harder, as has been demonstrated with the Tango attacks [273, 468].

6.3.6 Dubious Proofs of Security: Randomness Tests and Automated Provers

In many instances, some degree of security is allegedly claimed by verifying that the exchanged messages look random enough. For that, multiple sessions of the protocol are run and the exchanged messages are recorded and later analyzed using various randomness test batteries such as the well-known ENT [568], Diehard [394] and NIST [509]. Unfortunately this does not prove any security level (for instance, LMAP presented such a "proof" but was broken shortly after publication). Randomness may appear, not as a consequence of a well designed protocol, but simply as a result of employing nonces in message mixing. Randomness is not a sufficient condition, neither is it a necessary one. A trivial way of showing this is by thinking about highly formatted messages and how, even if a protocol is secure, due to formatting and padding of some or all of its messages these may not pass some randomness test.

Another popular but flawed way of proving security of proposed ultra-lightweight protocols is the use of logic modeling and formal protocol verification software.

A notable example is [492]. The scheme was broken in [464], despite being accompanied by a formal security proof in BAN logic. The authors mistakenly

---

[4]In synchronized protocols the parties, after each execution of the protocol, apply the same updating function to their secret keys and state information.

employed CRC (as recommended by the EPC-C1-G2 standard), but instead of using them as a simple error detection tool, employed them for encryption. In their idealized model, they identified their CRC usage as equivalent to encryption, so some of the BAN logic rules (for example R1: the message-meaning rule) did not hold anymore. This constitutes a common mistake, as an idealized scenario like the one modeled by BAN logic (with perfect, unbreakable and zero-leaking ciphers) never accurately models reality. The level of abstraction needed in the modeling phase basically makes it impractical for most realistic situations. This is, unfortunately, not only a limitation of BAN logic but, to different extents, is also in most formal models (GNY, etc.).

6.4   Towards a Sound Approach

6.4.1   State of the Literature

RFID technology has prompted many interesting challenges in the security and privacy research community, and designing a secure authentication protocol for very low-end tags is definitely one of them.

The field, however, has been the victim of an abundance of papers of dubious quality. Many research results either repeat mistakes (for new schemes) or past achievements (for attacks) or both. Recent protocols, with respect to previous ones, have been enhanced by using more involved transforms of the data stored in the tag's memory. However, the mistakes appear to be repeated: poor design choices, a lack of confusion and diffusion in the transforms, and informal fallacious security analyses to support the security claims [170]. This bad reputation, combined with a decline of interest in RFID security research as a whole, may have scared off many seasoned cryptographers, and contributed to the relative stagnation of the field.

Despite the current situation, which may seem to indicate that ultra-lightweight protocols are bound to fail, there is no clear evidence that designing a secure protocol with such constraints is impossible.

The field may nowadays be inactive, but there are many unanswered questions (and indeed, no practical, concrete, and trusted protocol emerged from it). While it is likely to reappear under a different guise, the problem of designing a secure authentication protocol while minimizing some aspects of its design (e.g., gate count), is not going away, and remains an interesting research question.

6.4.2   Promising Avenues

The need for cryptographic building blocks in low-end systems is definitely not unique to ultra-lightweight authentication protocols. A much larger research community is dedicated to so-called "lightweight cryptography", with countless applications.

In particular, significant efforts have been made to develop ciphers and hash functions suitable for lightweight authentication. A notable example is the KEC-CAK hash function [81], winner of the SHA-3 competition, that has excellent hardware performance. Furthermore, there are many ongoing efforts to develop special primitives with a stronger focus towards hardware footprint/performance, possibly trading off "some" security (e.g., reducing 128 or 256-bit security to 80) or other aspects, such as reducing block size, or software performance. Examples include the PRESENT block cipher [101] or the hash functions PHOTON [251] and QUARK [33].

Some of these, like BLAKE [37] or RC5 [502] are so-called Add-Rotate-Xor algorithms, that use the very same set of operations as ultra-lightweight protocols.

While not quite fitting the same extreme constraints imposed on ultra-lightweight protocols just yet, they are a stepping stone in that direction. They also benefit from much wider exposure and scrutiny, which bodes better for their overall security.

Ultra-lightweight protocols take a unique approach in that the entire scheme is designed, for instance, without using cryptographic building blocks as black boxes. It seems instead perhaps more promising to use standard authentication protocols with these lightweight primitives.

6.4.3   The Reductionist Approach

A deeply studied approach to the design of lightweight authentication protocols for RFID tags is the one provided by the $HB+$ protocol [310], which builds on the earlier HB protocol [284], introduced to efficiently authenticate a human to a computer. The security of these protocols is based on the difficulty of solving the *learning parity with noise* (LPN) problem [284]. Subsequently, several variants of $HB+$ have been proposed but almost all of them present some problems, e.g., [231–233, 457]. Unfortunately, according to [26], the HB-like protocols are not suitable for implementation on ultra-constrained devices. However, the identification of hard problems which allow the design of ultra-lightweight authentication protocols is a research direction which should not be abandoned.

Another interesting approach to designing an authentication protocol for RFID tags was proposed in [520]. Therein, a lightweight hash function, which can be used in RFID authentication, was described. The security of such a hash function is related to the security of the Rabin public key scheme. The idea is to compute an excellent numerical approximation for a *short window of bits* in the middle of the ciphertext produced by the Rabin encryption function. The Rabin encryption function uses a modulus of a particular form, in such a way that computing these bits for an adversary is as hard as breaking the full Rabin scheme. A basic version of the scheme was analyzed in [458]. As far as we know, the approach of [520] has not been followed by other significant proposals. We believe that this research line, which aims at reducing the computational burden while maintaining the security of the full protocol, or even in a more realistic way by paying a small loss compared to the full protocol, is worth pursuing in order to get an improvement in the field.

6.5 Conclusions

We have provided a short overview of the field: from our excursus, it seems clear that ultra-lightweight authentication is a challenging task, and that the present solutions are insufficient. The current state of knowledge is overall quite poor.

Perhaps, the first important open problem is to come up with a reasonable model for the class of ultra-lightweight protocols, in order to get an in-depth understanding of the possibilities and limits of these protocols.

Moreover, we note that, while most of the ultra-lightweight authentication protocols are broken, some are *more broken than others*: if one can impersonate a tag after 10^6 eavesdropped sessions, or after 1 such session, the two attacks effectively "break" the protocol in theory, but the question is does in practice the former represent an "acceptable" or "sufficient" level of security in some settings? It is quite unique to have this tradeoff between security and complexity measured, for example but not exclusively in GEs. We should think about this.

Finally, positive, promising avenues, which build on well-known cryptographic approaches and practices, are available. They are a good starting point to get new findings and to realize suitable solutions for the application market.

7

Relay Attacks and Distance Bounding: Mechanisms and Protocols

Gildas Avoine, Ioana Boureanu, David Gérault, Gerhard P. Hancke, Pascal Lafourcade, and Cristina Onete

Abstract We present the concept of relay attacks, and discuss distance-bounding schemes as the main countermeasure. We give details on relaying mechanisms, we review canonical distance-bounding protocols, as well as their threat-model (i.e., covering attacks beyond relaying) stemming from the authentication dimension in distance bounding. Advanced aspects of distance-bounding security are also covered. We conclude by presenting what we consider to be the most important challenges in distance bounding.

7.1 An Introduction to Relay Attacks and Distance Bounding

In this section, we first explain the concept of relay attacks. Then, we present distance bounding, the main countermeasure, but also discuss other ways of possibly counteracting relaying.

G. Avoine (✉)
Univ Rennes, INSA Rennes, CNRS, IRISA, Rennes, France
e-mail: gildas.avoine@irisa.fr

I. Boureanu
University of Surrey, Guildford, UK

D. Gérault · P. Lafourcade
Université Clermont Auvergne, Clermont-Ferrand, France

G. P. Hancke
City University of Hong Kong, Hong Kong, PR China

C. Onete
University of Limoges, XLIM, Limoges, France

7.1.1   Relay Attacks

A relay attack against two legitimate parties A and B is one whereby a man-in-the-middle C forwards A's messages to B and/or B's messages to A, unbeknown to them. In doing so, C wishes to obtain a facility meant for A and granted by B or vice-versa. For instance, C could get to fraudulently spend the funds associated with A's bank-card at a payment terminal embodied by B.

Relay attacks are hard to detect and deter, as they subvert all conventional cryptographic mechanisms potentially employed in the protocols: C only forwards the messages, and does not need to break the cryptography that is used. This is even more acute in the case of contactless applications: user A simply brings a token (e.g., a card or phone) within range of a reader B, and the protocol starts automatically, with no consent or input by the person who is getting the privilege. Thus, a relay attack can be mounted without hindrance.

7.1.2   Distance Bounding

The further A is from B, the longer the messages relayed by C from A take to arrive at B. Hence, imposing an upper-bound on the round-trip times (RTTs) of message-exchanges was proposed as a countermeasure in [83]. This lowers the probability of successful relay attacks. This mechanism is often referred to as *distance bounding (DB)*.

The idea of distance-bounding protocols is as follows: a *verifier* (e.g., an RFID reader) is equipped in the physical layer with a reliable clock that measures the RTTs of certain communication exchanges to check that a *prover* (e.g., a card) is no further than some allowed distance. So, at some point in the protocol, the verifier starts its clock, sends a challenge, and stops the clock when it receives the response. The measured time Δ_t corresponds to twice the time it takes for a message to travel from the prover to the verifier, plus the time taken by the prover to reply. Since no information can travel faster than the speed of light c, $d = \frac{\Delta_t \cdot c}{2}$ is an upper bound on the distance between the prover and the verifier. If the prover was any further than d, then it would mean that the messages traveled faster than light, which is impossible. Consequently, if d is short enough, then the verifier can deduce that the prover is within range. In other words, a time bound $\mathscr{B}$ can be a priori fixed such that, if $\Delta_t > \mathscr{B}$, then the verifier rejects the prover.

As described above, distance bounding would be just a *proximity-checking* mechanism. However, most distance-bounding protocols do not stop at proximity-checking. Instead, they also encompass a unilateral *authentication* dimension: the prover authenticates itself to the verifier. Authentication is generally achieved cryptographically: by using well-established primitives, such as signature schemes, HMAC, encryption, and others.

7.1.3 Other Relay-Countermeasures

Approaches to relay-counteraction other than distance bounding have been proposed. In his seminal paper [178], Desmedt proposed that a prover computed his exact location on earth, signed it, and sent it to the verifier. The inconvenience in this approach is that it requires one to trust the prover not to cheat. In addition, it requires a safe localization system, which is not trivial to realize. In particular, using the GPS technology does not seem to be a robust solution [242] due to the fact that the GPS signal is sensitive to obstacles and not accurate enough. In [133], position-based cryptography is further studied and proven to be impossible.

Another option against relay attacks is to measure the strength of the signal received by the verifier [347]: since it decreases as the distance increases, it gives indications about the distance from the prover. However, an attacker can amplify the signal to make the prover appear closer to the verifier, and defeat this approach.

Similarly, a solution based on sensing the local environment (for instance the air temperature) was proposed, with the idea that if the prover was actually close to the verifier, then it would sense similar values [561]. This approach however fails if the adversary is able to manipulate the value that is being sensed, which can be relatively easy to do.

To prevent relay attacks, one can also isolate the prover inside a Faraday cage [74] during the protocol, to make sure that it cannot communicate with external entities. While efficient, this solution is not very user friendly, and severely limits the usability of the system.

Finally, radio frequency fingerprinting [496] can be used. It identifies the devices based on variations in the signal features due to imperfections in the manufacturing process. However, such fingerprinting can be counterfeited [168].

Comparing all the aforementioned relay-countermeasures, distance bounding appears the most promising option to defeat relay attacks.

7.2 Relay Attacks in Practice

Relay attacks have been implemented against contact-based smart cards [189], contactless smart cards [256], and keyless car entry systems [221]. First, in Sect. 7.2.1, we discuss attacks against "unprotected systems". Then, in Sect. 7.2.2, taking into consideration the fact that distance-bounding type countermeasures are starting to be implemented, we consider more advanced practical relay strategies against systems thus "protected".

7.2.1   Basic Relay Strategies

A *basic relay* equates to the attack described in Sect. 7.1.

7.2.1.1   Purpose-Built Relays

There are several relay-attack implementations against radio frequency identification (RFID) systems using purpose-built attack proxies and relay links, which incur minimal delay in executing the attack, e.g., [221, 256, 548]. The conventional approach to implementing an attack uses custom-built attack proxies, using a combination of custom hardware and hacked readers [256, 548]. The proxy will first demodulate the data symbols from the reader or token, and then forward data over an analog radio link, e.g., a video channel [256], and this tends to introduce a delay in the order of a few to tens of microseconds (2–$20\,\mu s$). These implementations are also capable of active relay attacks, equivalent to a conventional man-in-the-middle or 'wedge' attack, which can modify communication with negligible additional delay, e.g., using an FPGA to reshape analog signals in real-time [256]. If the goal is to minimize the relay delay to less than a microsecond then the relay link can be implemented without demodulating the data first [221, 548]. In these cases, the proxies are either connected via a wire (120–500 ns delay), or forward data by direct up-mixing of the LF/HF carrier onto a UHF radio carrier for transmission (120–750 ns delay).

7.2.1.2   Off-the-Shelf Relays

It has also been shown that software-only implementations using off-the-shelf NFC-enabled mobile devices are effective, which simplifies the attack and allows any person with the right type of NFC-enabled mobile phone to implement a token emulator or a reader. These attacks can therefore use a standard phone as a proxy-reader and a second phone as a proxy-token and relay the data across Bluetooth, WiFi or the mobile data network [222, 392, 539]. Even though such attack implementations incur a larger attack delay (200-500 ms), these remain effective against real systems, as was demonstrated in an attack against Google Wallet [505]. There are an increasing number of non-mobile NFC devices, such as the Adafruit NFC breakout board, that easily connects with embedded hardware Arduino or Raspberry Pi, which could be used as readily available proxy platforms.

7.2.2 Advanced Relay Strategies

The relay attacks above were executed on systems that implemented no proximity checks. As systems start to implement such checks over conventional low-bandwidth communication channels there are practical strategies for gaining time that can hide the relay delay. Even if the attacker can gain part of a bit period, e.g., a few microseconds, it could leave enough time to mount one of the attacks in Sect. 7.2.1.

7.2.2.1 Early Send and Late Commit

If the attacker can send a challenge or response late but still get the prover or verifier to accept it as a valid message then that could also hide the relay delay. Receivers do not evaluate the bit value right at the beginning of the bit period T_B. To make the channel more reliable this evaluation is done later, in the middle or at the end of the bit period, which could be exploited to gain the attacker some time [149, 255]. For example, for NRZ (non-return to zero) coding the signal is high for the entire bit period for '1' and low for the entire bit period for '0', and the receiver samples only once in the middle of the bit period to determine the bit value, as shown in Fig. 7.1a. This means the attacker could start his response bit up to $T_A = T_B/2$ late, and still have the bit sampled correctly. Several receiver architectures, to be resistant to noise, integrate the signal across the entire bit period and evaluate the bit value at the end. In this case, the attack could 'late commit' by transmitting a larger, shorter signal later in the bit period and still achieve the same integration output at the time of bit value evaluation. If combined with early send, where the attacker guesses the value based on the observation of the first part of the bit period, the attack in Fig. 7.2 becomes possible. The attacker will guess the value of challenge C_i from the verifier early, and send it to the prover late. It will repeat this approach for the response R_i

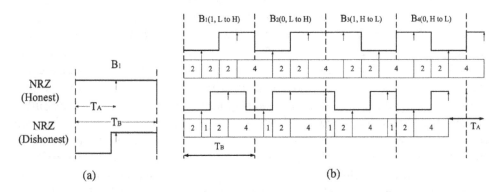

Fig. 7.1 Gaining attack time by exploiting channel characteristics. (**a**) Late commit for non-return to zero (NRZ) coding. (**b**) Speeding up Manchester code data clock [255]: Sampling clock is 8× time data clock (trigger and synchronization counter for sampling signal transition shown)

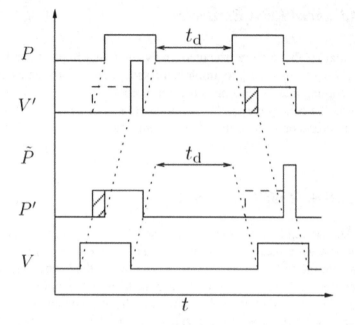

Fig. 7.2 Early send and late commit can make a Prover P appear closer than it really is. In the figure, one challenge round is relayed, with the dotted lines indicating the propagation time (the line stops and starts at transmission and reception). If the proxy-prover P' guesses C_i early, and the proxy-verifier V' commits late then the response R_i is received by the Verifier V at the same time as expected for a prover located at $\tilde{P}$ even though the Prover P is much further away [149]

that the prover sends to the verifier, and will therefore appear to be closer to the verifier than the true distance of the prover.

7.2.2.2 Speeding Up the Prover's Response

If the attacker can get the prover to provide the response earlier than expected by the verifier, then the relay delay could remain hidden, with the round-trip time of the message remaining within the bound. There are two approaches to making the prover process the challenge faster [255]. Smart tokens receive their system clock from the reader, with contact-based cards having a clock line and contactless cards recovering a clock from the received radio carrier. This allows the proxy-verifier to overclock the token, which causes the response to be calculated and transmitted earlier. If the token has its own, independent clock, then the attacker can also gain some time by exploiting data clock recovery from the data coding. For example, for Manchester coding ('1' is high to low, '0' is low to high) each bit period has an edge transition to which the receiver can synchronize its decoding data clock. If the transition is moved slightly ahead in each bit, as shown in Fig. 7.1b, then the receiver will sample earlier as the message is received and the message is decoded T_A faster than normal. This approach can also effect distance fraud if a dishonest prover is able to speed up its own response, either by calculating a response faster than expected or sending a correct response early, e.g., if the verifier sends a challenge followed by some framing bits and expects the provers to start calculating the response only once the entire message, including the stop frame bit, is received but instead the prover can send the correct response immediately after the challenge bit is received.

7.3 Canonical Distance-Bounding Protocols

In this section, we describe and discuss two protocols that can be considered the cornerstones of distance-bounding schemes. The Brands-Chaum protocol is the earliest distance-bounding protocol ever published, and is based on Beth and Desmedt's [83] idea that roundtrip times (RTTs) can detect mafia fraud. The Hancke-Kuhn protocol resurrected research interest in distance-bounding protocols, and was specifically designed for contactless devices.

7.3.1 General Structure

General Setup Distance-bounding schemes can use either symmetric- or public-key cryptography. In the symmetric-key scenario, the prover and verifier share a secret key K. For public-key primitives, the prover stores a private/public key-pair (sk_i, pk_i), for which the verifier only holds the public key. Each verifier is assumed to possess a clock able to measure roundtrip times (RTTs) with a fine-grained resolution (ideally, less than a nanosecond). In the protocol, the verifier uses the clock to measure RTT values for several so-called *time-critical* rounds.

General 3-Phase Structure The general structure of distance-bounding protocols follows these three phases (each consisting of zero, one, or multiple rounds of communication): session set-up, proximity checking, and verification. During *session set-up*, the prover and verifier exchange session-specific data and possibly pre-compute some values that will be used during the next stage. During *proximity checking*, the parties execute n fast phases of communication: the verifier generally starts the clock at the beginning of each round, and stops it at the end. The responses r_i sent by the prover, and the round-trip time (RTT) of each round are stored by the verifier. Finally, during *verification*, the verifier performs some cryptographic operations, may exchange some more messages with the prover, and it compares the measured RTT values of the proximity-checking phase with a threshold. At the end of this phase, the verifier must output an *authentication bit*, which is typically 1 if the prover is assumed to be legitimate and within a correct distance, and 0 otherwise.

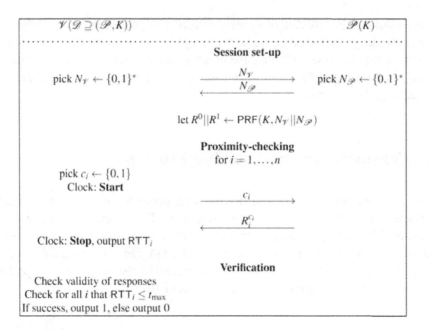

Fig. 7.3 The Hancke and Kuhn protocol between a prover $\mathscr{P}$ and a verifier $\mathscr{V}$. The notation $\|$ describes string concatenation

7.3.2   The Hancke-Kuhn Protocol

The protocol presented by Hancke and Kuhn [254] in 2005 performs symmetric-key distance bounding. It relies on a pseudorandom function (PRF), which takes two inputs, a key and a message, and outputs a string of fixed length (in our case, $2n$). Figure 7.3 depicts this protocol for a prover $\mathscr{P}$ and a verifier $\mathscr{V}$. At *session set-up*, $\mathscr{P}$ and $\mathscr{V}$ exchange nonces.[1] The two parties then use the PRF to map the key K and the concatenation of the two nonces to a bit-string of length $2 \cdot n$. This value is divided into a left and a right register of length n each, which we denote R^0 and R^1 respectively. During *proximity-checking*, in each of the n subsequent fast rounds, the challenger chooses a bit c_i at random, and the prover is expected to respond with the i-th bit from either the left response register (if $c_i = 0$) or from the right one. We denote these bits R_i^0 and R_i^1 respectively. For each round, the RTT is measured. At the end of the protocol, during *verification*, the prover is authenticated if, and only if, all the responses provided by the prover were correct, and if all the measured RTT values are under the $t_{\max}$ bound.

Design Intuition As long as the key K is unknown to an attacker, the PRF guarantees the security-crux herein: two independent response strings. Indeed, a man-in-the-middle attacker can relay the exact nonces used by an honest prover and

---

[1]In an early version of this protocol, only $\mathscr{V}$ sent a nonce; $\mathscr{P}$ did not. That version of the protocol is insecure against worst-case attackers; thus we choose to present a later version here.

verifier. This allows the adversary to establish two sessions (one with the prover, the other, with the verifier) which share the same response strings R^0 and R^1. This adversary can now use its session with the prover to extract data: before it receives the honest verifier's challenge, the adversary can query the prover with any kind of request. If the protocol were to rely on only one response string, the adversary could obtain the entire response and forward it to the attacker.

7.3.3 The Brands-Chaum Protocol

The public-key counterpart of the Hancke-Kuhn protocol was proposed by Brands and Chaum [113] and relies on commitment schemes and digital signatures. Commitment schemes allow users to temporarily hide a value; the commitment will also only open to that hidden value, and not to any other. Signature schemes are public-key primitives allowing a signer to generate signatures for a given message and a secret key; the signature can be verified for that message with the public key.

Figure 7.4 depicts an execution of the Brands-Chaum protocol. The session set-up and verification consist of one-message rounds each. During *set-up*, the prover chooses and commits (in a message C) to a number of responses to be used at proximity checking. Note that C *hides* the contents of the message, from both an attacker and the verifier. In each round of the *proximity-checking phase* the verifier picks a one-bit random challenge c_i and sends it to $\mathscr{P}$. The latter's response is $c_i \oplus r_i$, where r_i is the response bit to which the prover committed for this round. The values R_i and the measured RTT values are stored by the verifier. Finally, during *verification*, $\mathscr{P}$ sends to $\mathscr{V}$ the opening of the commitment C and a signature on the concatenated challenge and response values exchanged at proximity-checking. The

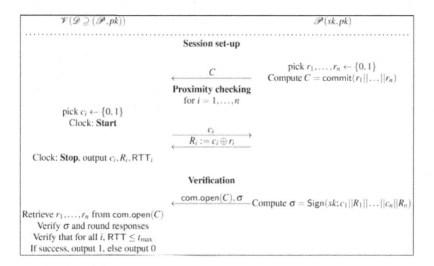

Fig. 7.4 The Brands–Chaum protocol for a prover $\mathscr{P}$ and a verifier $\mathscr{V}$

verifier retrieves the randomly-chosen r_i values from C and uses them to ascertain the validity of the prover's time-critical responses and the signature σ and R_i values. If these values verify and the measured RTTs are below the $t_{\max}$ bound, then the verifier authenticates the prover.

Design Intuition The commitment serves a dual purpose: it hides the values of r_i until they become useless to the attacker (i.e., until after the proximity-checking rounds); and the commitment compensates for the fact that the response values are chosen entirely by the prover. Finally, the commitment allows the verifier to retrieve the r_i values without exchanging or sharing any further keys with the prover. The commitment, however, does not authenticate $\mathscr{P}$; that is achieved by the signature σ. The signature also effectively prevents *pre-ask* strategies during the proximity-checking phase.

7.4   Distance-Bounding Threat Model and Its Formal Treatments

In this section, we present the main threats in distance bounding, and the state of formal security analysis in this field. We also review more recent protocols, comparing their advantages and disadvantages.

7.4.1   Main Threat-Model

Distance-bounding schemes are vulnerable to attacks other than relaying, issued out of the proximity-checking measure. For instance, any attack that makes the prover appear closer than it actually is defeats the purpose of a distance-bounding protocol, which is to compute a correct upper bound on this distance. The threats we present can be classified as attacks by outsiders and attacks by insiders. In the first category lies mafia fraud, where an unauthorized adversary attempts to be accepted by the verifier. In the second, comprising distance fraud, distance hijacking and terrorist fraud, a faraway dishonest prover attempts to be accepted by the verifier despite his distance.

7.4.1.1   Mafia Fraud (MF) [178]

In mafia fraud, an adversary $\mathscr{A}$ authenticates in the presence of a far-away honest prover. A mafia fraud typically involves a faraway prover, and two collaborating adversaries: one near the prover, and one near the verifier. The fraud succeeds if the authentication of the adversary located close to the verifier is accepted by the verifier.

7.4.1.2 Distance Fraud (DF) [113]

In distance fraud, a malicious prover located far away from the verifier attempts to convince the verifier that he is close. The fraud succeeds if the authentication of the faraway malicious prover is accepted.

7.4.1.3 Distance Hijacking (DH) [160]

Distance hijacking is a distance fraud in which honest provers are present near the verifier. This gives the malicious prover more surface of attack, so that some protocols are resistant to distance fraud, while being vulnerable to distance hijacking. For instance, in the Brands-Chaum protocol (Sect. 7.3.3), which is resistant to distance fraud, a faraway prover can eavesdrop on a session played by an honest prover P (located close to the verifier), send the final message before P does, and be authenticated in place of P. Distance hijacking succeeds if the verifier accepts the authentication of the faraway malicious prover.

7.4.1.4 Terrorist Fraud (TF) [178]

Terrorist fraud is an attack in which a malicious prover, located far away from the verifier, is helped by an accomplice located near the verifier. A trivial attack in this scenario would be that the prover simply gives all his secret keys to his accomplice. Since this attack cannot be prevented if the prover has access to his secret key, we make the additional assumption that the prover does not want the accomplice to impersonate him later. Hence, a terrorist fraud succeeds if the verifier accepts the authentication of the faraway prover through his accomplice, and the accomplice cannot authenticate on his own in a later execution of the protocol.

7.4.2 Provable Security and Formal Verification

Provable security is the field of research which aims at building formal, mathematical proofs of the security of systems or protocols. Early distance-bounding protocols were analyzed in an ad hoc fashion, so a call for provable security of distance bounding was needed. A preliminary framework [41] for modelling distance bounding paved the way to formal treatment of distance-bounding security.

In terms of formal security for distance bounding, we have: computational formalisms [110, 193], and symbolic ones [177, 401]. Computational models treat the messages as bitstrings and attackers as probabilistic polynomial-time algorithms trying to defeat cryptographic goals. Symbolic security verification represents messages as terms in a term algebra, abstracts the cryptographic primitives to black box functions and models attackers as rules manipulating the terms and black-box cryptographic functions. Due to these abstractions, symbolic models are easier to mechanize into automatic verifiers, yet generally an attack found in such models is more a logical flaw than a cryptographic-design problem.

7.4.2.1 Symbolic Verification

The two symbolic models permit us to use semiautomatic tools, Tamarin [406] and Proverif [93], respectively, to verify the security of distance-bounding protocols. They slightly differ in their approach: [177] models time and distance explicitly, while [401] abstracts this into some classification of the order of messages. However, they find similar attacks. Moreover, both methodologies take a step beyond the scope of previous computational models: they consider that the verifiers can be corrupted. Also, outside formalizations, in distance bounding, verifiers were traditionally considered honest (except when user privacy is considered).

However, as symbolic models, there are some attacks that they cannot find, due to the abstractions they make. For instance, if a prover is within the distance bound, it might be possible for a mafia-fraud adversary to flip challenge bits on the fly without being detected, which allows him to recover the secret key of the provers in some protocols [62]. This kind of attack can be found using the computational models, but not the symbolic ones, which abstract bitstrings to terms.

7.4.2.2 Provable Security

Due to abstracting the cryptographic primitives into black-boxes, symbolic-verification mechanisms also cannot detect attacks by "PRF programming" [108]. Some protocols, such as Swiss-Knife or Hancke-Kuhn, use a PRF to compute the response vectors. However, as noted in [108], the pseudorandomness of a PRF is only guaranteed if the adversary does not know anything about the involved key and if there is no oracle/reuse for/of the key anywhere else in the protocol. Yet dishonest provers in distance-fraud attacks do know the key of the PRF. And, in distance-bounding protocols such as the Swiss-Knife protocol [328], the key is re-used outside of the PRF call in forming the responses. So, [108] exhibit "programmed PRFs": dishonest provers can use the PRF to mount distance fraud, and man-in-the-middle attackers can adaptively chose inputs to mount mafia fraud. In turn, this means that in provably-secure distance bounding, care needs to be taken with security claims resting just on pseudorandomness.

For both symbolic and computational models, modelling terrorist fraud is a big challenge. The symbolic models for terrorist fraud are either too strong or too weak, and the computational ones are often tailored definitions proposed for specific protocols. For instance, SimTF [216] imposes restrictions on the communications between the prover and his accomplice, and in [109], the prover helps his accomplice several times instead of just once.

7.4.2.3 Provably-(in)Secure Protocols

Designing a distance-bounding protocol that is both efficient and provably-secure has proved a difficult task.

For instance, the Hancke-Kuhn scheme presented in Sect. 7.3 only provides sub-optimal mafia-fraud resistance (3/4 per round as opposed to the optimal 1/2); in addition, it is vulnerable to distance frauds by PRF-programming. Striving for optimal mafia- and distance-fraud resistance, Avoine and Tchamkerten [45] describe a scheme in which the proximity-check responses are inter-dependent: this strategy makes the per-round mafia-fraud security asymptotically approach the optimal bound of 1/2, but fails to thwart PRF-programming strategies. By combining a late authentication like Brands-Chaum and two pseudorandom response registers like Hancke-Kuhn, Kim et al. attempted to achieve optimal mafia- and distance-fraud resistance, as well as terrorist-fraud resistance [328]. However, its design includes a circularity in the use of the key which does not allow provable mafia-fraud resistance; in addition, its use of PRFs is problematic with respect to achieving distance-fraud resistance.

Protocols that provably guarantee the four properties described above are rare in the literature [40, 114]. The SKI protocols [110] introduced a new countermeasure to terrorist fraud by using a leakage function. This design is further refined and made efficient by Boureanu and Vaudenay [111, 325]. A recent protocol called SPADE [118] circumvents PRF-programming attacks by using one-time keys during the proximity-checking phase; in that case, terrorist-fraud resistance is achieved by adding in a backdoor. An extended family of protocols using the same basic designs was proposed in [42]; it can be instantiated with various primitives, achieving different degrees of provable security and privacy.

The reader is referred to extensive distance-bounding surveys, such as [40, 114].

7.5 Distance-Bounding Protocols in Practice

7.5.1 NXP's Mifare Technology

NXP is a world-wide semiconductor supplier especially involved in secure identification, automotive and digital networking industries. Mifare is a series of NXP's contactless products that includes four families, namely Classic, Plus, Ultralight, and DESFire. Mifare Plus (X and EV1) as well as Mifare DESFire (EV2) benefit from a distance-bounding protocol [445, 446]. Note that the DB protocols are not activated by default on these cards, and the data sheets do not explain how the system operator should evaluate the value of the round-trip time upper bound.

Although the protocols have not been publicly released, it is worth noting that

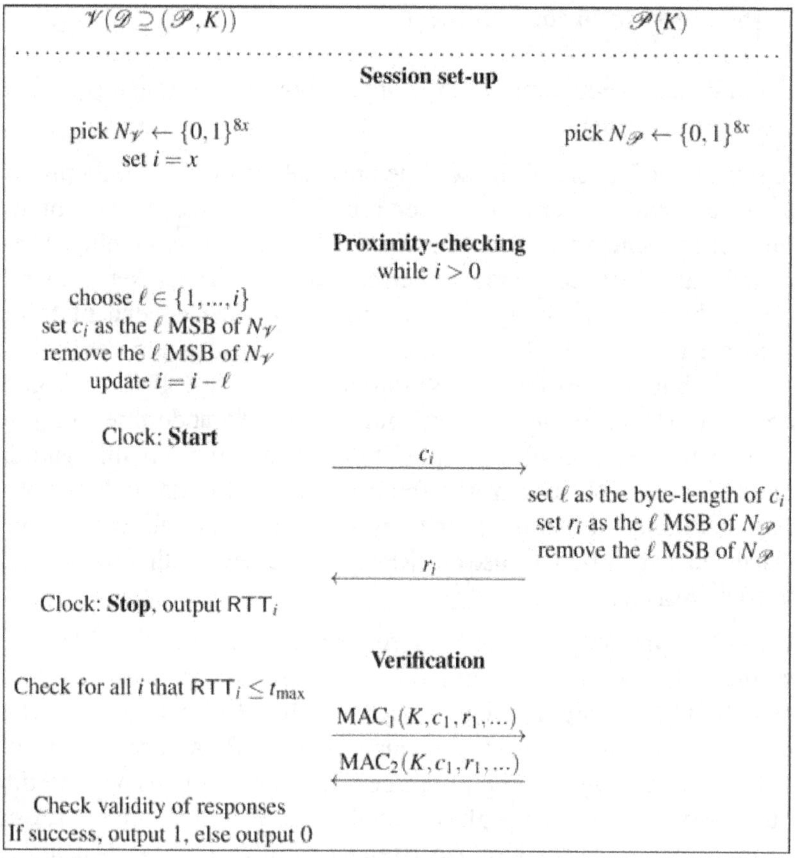

$$\mathcal{V}(\mathcal{D} \supseteq (\mathcal{P}, K)) \qquad\qquad\qquad\qquad\qquad \mathcal{P}(K)$$

. . . .

Session set-up

pick $N_{\mathcal{V}} \leftarrow \{0,1\}^{8x}$ pick $N_{\mathcal{P}} \leftarrow \{0,1\}^{8x}$
set $i = x$

Proximity-checking
while $i > 0$

choose $\ell \in \{1, ..., i\}$
set c_i as the ℓ MSB of $N_{\mathcal{V}}$
remove the ℓ MSB of $N_{\mathcal{V}}$
update $i = i - \ell$

Clock: **Start**

$$\xrightarrow{\qquad c_i \qquad}$$

set ℓ as the byte-length of c_i
set r_i as the ℓ MSB of $N_{\mathcal{P}}$
remove the ℓ MSB of $N_{\mathcal{P}}$

$$\xleftarrow{\qquad r_i \qquad}$$

Clock: **Stop**, output RTT_i

Verification

Check for all i that $\mathrm{RTT}_i \le t_{max}$

$$\xrightarrow{\quad \mathrm{MAC}_1(K, c_1, r_1, ...) \quad}$$

$$\xleftarrow{\quad \mathrm{MAC}_2(K, c_1, r_1, ...) \quad}$$

Check validity of responses
If success, output 1, else output 0

Fig. 7.5 Sketch of the patented NXP DB Protocol [303, 553]

NXP published several patents on distance-bounding protocols. Figure 7.5 depicts the protocol described in [303, 553]. In contrast to most DB protocols available in the literature, this NXP DB protocol is byte-oriented, meaning that the messages of the fast phase contain one or several bytes instead of a single bit. The byte-length x of the random values is not enforced in the patents, but suggested only. They can typically be 7 or 8 bytes. The fast phase is followed by a verification phase where MACs are exchanged. The MACs are computed "over the complete 7-byte random numbers and some information about the speed at which the [reader] and [transponder] operate". Note that "the random number ordering for the MAC input reflects the same split as during the sending of the proximity check commands." Obviously, the two final MACs must contain the message direction to avoid a trivial reflection attack. The NXP DB protocol is unlikely to be resistant to purpose-built relays—because the measurement resolution is probably not high enough to detect fast relays—but it might resist off-the-shelf relays.

7.5.2 3DB Technology

3DB Access AG is a Swiss company founded in 2013, by Boris Danev and David Barras. 3DB developed an integrated circuit that contains a distance-bounding protocol based on Ultra-Wide Band (UWB) pulses compliant to IEEE 802.15.4f. The technology allows a reader to estimate the distance to reach a given contactless receiver. It aims to avoid mafia-fraud attacks, but it does not consider the other frauds presented in Sect. 7.4 (e.g., it does not consider distance fraud). The distance range is 120 meters (line of sight) and the accuracy of the distance-bounding protocol is 10 cm according to the product's datasheet.[2] The 3DB technology specifically (but not only) targets the market of keyless entry and start systems (PKES), given that such systems are particularly vulnerable to relay attacks [221]. It is likely that most vehicles will be equipped with such a DB-friendly PKES in the future.

The protocol implemented in the 3DB technology, described in [531], is based on the Brands-Chaum protocol [113]. However, it takes the channel characteristics into account and includes countermeasures to thwart physical-layer attacks, in particular the "early detect and late commit" attack described in Sect. 7.2 that is mitigated since the basic symbol pulses have a very short period. These countermeasures rely on the reordering and blinding of the pulses. The reordering consists in applying a permutation to the pulse positions associated with each bit. The number of bits considered in the pulse reordering is actually an adjustable security parameter. The blinding consists in XORing the stream of pulses with a mask. The cryptographic primitives used to generate the permutation and the mask are not described. No attack has been suggested so far on these reordering and blinding techniques. Apart from security properties, UWB channels can also provide very accurate time-of-arrival measurement as the timing resolution achievable with a signal of bandwidth B, is $1/2B$.

7.5.3 Relay-Resistance in EMV

Relay attacks are particularly relevant in contactless-payment systems. Indeed, no PIN code or other payee-originating input is requested with such payments. Moreover, most contactless payment cards rely on ISO 14443, which is a standard available in most of today's smartphones. Consequently, performing a relay attack between a payment terminal and a payment card is as simple as uploading an app on a smartphone [567].

Indeed, using off-the-shelf smartphones and some in-house Android software, this relay threat was exhibited in practice by Chothia et al. [141] against the EMV (Europay, Mastercard and Visa) contactless-payment protocol; this is the most wide-

---

[2]Available at the 3DB Access AG Website, https://www.3db-access.com/, May 2018.

spread type for contactless payments. In their work, Chothia et al. also introduced a countermeasure to mitigate their own relay attack. Their so-called PaySafe protocol is put forward as a slight variant of the contactless version of PayWave, i.e., the EMV protocol used by Visa. In PaySafe, a new command is introduced into the EMV contactless protocol such that a calculation of the round trip times becomes possible for EMV readers. Namely, the reader sends a nonce to the card and expects that the latter will respond with a pre-generated nonce; the reader measures the time taken by the whole exchange and if it is beyond a pre-established bound, then the reader aborts the protocol. In PaySafe, the nonces used in this timed phase are encompassed in some other messages, included in a MAC issued by the card and keyed on a key the card shares only with the bank.

It is worth noting that PaySafe did not aim to be a full distance-bounding protocol (i.e., it did not mean to protect against the distance-bounding frauds presented in Sect. 7.4)

EMVCo—is the consortium behind EMV—give the EMV contactless payments' specifications in [199] (current version is 2.7, April 2018). Since 2016, these specifications include the possibility for a *relay-resistance mechanism*, which is inspired by PaySafe [141]. A friendly introduction to this protocol is provided in [563]. As of today, there are unfortunately no public figures about the number of MasterCard/Visa readers that benefit from this feature.

7.6   Current Challenges in Distance Bounding

7.6.1   Theory vs. Practice

Provable-security/formal-methods models for DB (see Sect. 7.4) generally do not capture accurately the DB threats shown in practice. For instance, one major assumption that most DB formal models make is that the computation on the prover's side, during the timed exchanges, is instantaneous or constant. In practice, as [141] showed, different cards have significantly distinct response-times, leading to practical attacks which cannot be easily found via theoretical tools.

Besides such coarse abstractions, other approximations are made by provable-security models for cryptographic-proofs to become possible. For instance, in some variants of the model in [193], no communication is allowed between colluding attacking parties during the timed phase (i.e., the coalition has to be active outside the timed phase). Or, in the formalism in [110], the time taken to compute over bits equal to 0 is always considered the same as that to compute over bits equal to 1, which—as Sect. 7.2 explained—is not always factually true. These two approximations entail that the respective models are too weak. But also there is the possibility that some formal security definition is too strong, i.e., that it would classify a protocol as insecure when in practice the protocol is secure (see [216]).

Last but not least, the theoretical DB protocols presented in Sect. 7.3 follow a design whereby the fast phase is generally formed of a repetition of a number of timed rounds, where each challenge/response is one bit. These designs (endorsed by formal models/proofs, etc.) were traditionally anchored in practice, and Sect. 7.2 alluded to this: i.e., a challenge given as a bitstring can lead to bit-by-bit early reads and therefore possible early responses by dishonest provers. But, *as of recently*, there seem to be mechanisms for these early-send attacks to be effectively counteracted by other ingenious, practical mechanisms in designs even in cases where the timed challenges/responses are bitstrings (see Sect. 7.5 or [531]). However, it is important to recall that the security of the DB design in [531] has not yet been formally analyzed, and the protocol only claims to protect against relay attacks, not other DB threats.

7.6.2 Application-Aware DB

In the formal models presented in Sect. 7.4 and even in the practical considerations given in Sect. 7.2, we saw that the DB threat-model has thus far been generally focused on this primitive in isolation; that is, it assumes an honest verifier, a dishonest prover and a malicious man-in-the-middle. However, as DB is adopted in different applications (e.g., PKES as per the above), these security considerations will need adjustments. To begin with, the verifier may be dishonest, or some threats—such as terrorist fraud—may become irrelevant, or specific anonymity concerns may be considered. In this space of fine-tuned threat models for DB, two lines have recently emerged [107, 326]. Namely, [107] advances a formal DB threat-model where a fine-grained level of corruption of the prover (i.e., white-box, black-box) is taken into account, such that each application can "pick and choose". In turn, this also leads to clear-cut, DB-security properties and even the exclusion of resistance to terrorist fraud, in some cases. Complementary to this, [326] recently advances a formal DB model with three parties, where the new party is a named piece of hardware and this also leads to a fine taxonomy of DB-security properties, with an application-ready nature.

DB efficiency is paramount, but it varies from application to application. A DB solution that can be acceptable on a smartphone, may be unacceptable on a simple, passive card. A series of research lines [111, 325] discussed the efficiency of DB protocols with "traditional" structure, i.e., following the designs presented in Sect. 7.3, from a theoretical-analysis viewpoint. At the same time, the practical solution for proximity-checking in PKES offered by 3DB (see Sect. 7.5) is extremely efficient in practice. However, this question of efficiency stands, especially if new DB solutions are to be given on top of different applications, such as EMV.

In DB adoption, there are also strong backwards-compatibility constraints. For instance, in EMV, the public-key infrastructure or the restrictions of keeping as close as possible to old-generation EMV cards/readers are such that a DB protocol, following the designs we saw in Sect. 7.3, is simply un-adoptable out of the box.

7.6.3 Specialist Implementations and Slow Adoption

On the one hand, PKES with relay-protection are finally becoming commercial—arguably due to relay attacks being exploited by fraudsters in the automotive sector. On the other hand, in DB-enhanced EMV contactless protocols (*à la* PaySafe), a dishonest party already has a tangible incentive to mount a distance-fraud attack;—a purchase receipt carries an intrinsic proof that the card was in the range of the reader. Yet, EMV with relay-protection is not widely deployed and, indeed, the markets do not appear to call for protocols to be enhanced with full DB-protection yet.

Should such DB frauds appear in practice, would we then see fully-fledged DB solutions being implemented for commercial purposes? Or, will the 5th generation of mobile networks (5G) and its increased spectrum and higher bands lead to the true rise of DB technology in the ubiquitous systems of the 2020s, and raise new DB research questions?

Part IV
Side Channel Analysis and Hardware Implementation

8

Side Channel and Profiling Attacks

Lejla Batina, Milena Djukanovic, Annelie Heuser, and Stjepan Picek

Abstract Side-channel attacks (SCAs) are powerful attacks based on the information obtained from the implementation of cryptographic devices. Profiling side-channel attacks has received a lot of attention in recent years due to the fact that this type of attack defines the worst-case security assumptions. The SCA community realized that the same approach is actually used in other domains in the form of supervised machine learning. Consequently, some researchers started experimenting with different machine learning techniques and evaluating their effectiveness in the SCA context. More recently, we are witnessing an increase in the use of deep learning techniques in the SCA community with strong first results in side-channel analyses, even in the presence of countermeasures. In this chapter, we consider the evolution of profiling attacks, and subsequently we discuss the impacts they have made in the data preprocessing, feature engineering, and classification phases. We also speculate on the future directions and the best-case consequences for the security of small devices.

8.1 Introduction

In 1996, Kocher demonstrated the possibility to recover secret data by introducing a method for exploiting leakages from the device under attack [338]. In other words, implementations of cryptographic algorithms leak relevant information

L. Batina
Radboud University, Nijmegen, The Netherlands

M. Djukanovic
University of Montenegro, Podgorica, Montenegro

A. Heuser
Univ Rennes, Inria, CNRS, IRISA, Rennes, France

S. Picek (✉)
Delft University of Technology, Delft, The Netherlands

about the data processed through physical side-channels such as timing [338], power consumption [339], EM emanation [493], and sound [225].

Side-channel attacks (SCAs) exploit weaknesses in the physical implementation of cryptographic algorithms rather than the algorithms themselves [389]. Those weaknesses stem from the physics of the underlying computing elements, i.e., CMOS cells, which makes it hard to eliminate such threats.

Numerous evaluation techniques, which generally involve some form of digital signal processing and statistical computations, have been proposed in the literature. Some of the most important methods include Simple Power Analysis (SPA) [339], Differential Power Analysis (DPA), and Template Attacks (TA) [135].

The SPA technique implies that the attacker aims at reconstructing the secret key using just a single trace of side-channel information, and it often exploits the difference in basic public-key operations such as double-and-add, or add-and-multiply [339]. Still, SPA is not possible if the observed signal-to-noise ratio (SNR) is not high enough. Consequently, most of the time developed countermeasures make SPA futile.

DPA techniques are based on the evaluation of many traces with varying input data for the targeted algorithm. After that step, a brute-force attack, testing sub-key hypotheses, is performed on a part of the algorithm (so-called "divide and conquer"). In the DPA approach, a large number of samples are used in order to reduce noise by averaging, and a single-bit power model is commonly adopted [339]. On the other hand, Correlation Power Analysis (CPA) represents a multi-bit power model in order to reduce the influence of noise on the possibility to execute a successful attack [115]. The main difference between these two techniques is that DPA is based on computing the difference between two trace sets, while CPA uses the correlation coefficient in order to calculate the dependency test. We often also say that the two use different side-channel distinguishers. Side-channel attacks using the above three techniques have been reported on a wide variety of cryptographic implementations, see, e.g., [154, 402, 410, 412, 434, 500] including some real-world applications [196].

In contrast to DPA, TA requires a profiling stage, i.e., a step during which the cryptographic hardware is under full control of the adversary to estimate the probability distribution of the leaked information and make better use of all the information present in each sample [135]. In this way, TA can provide a promising model of the real device, instead of using some a priori model.

TA is the best (optimal) technique from an information-theoretic point of view if the attacker has an unbounded number of traces and the noise follows the Gaussian distribution [277, 367]. After the template attack, the stochastic attack emerged using linear regression in the profiling phase [515]. In the years that followed, researchers recognized certain shortcomings of template attacks and tried to modify them in order to deal better with the complexity and portability issues. An example of such an approach is the pooled template attack where only one pooled covariance matrix is used in order to cope with statistical difficulties [142]. Alongside such techniques, the SCA community realized that a similar approach to profiling is used in other domains in the form of supervised machine learning. Consequently, some researchers started experimenting with different machine learning (ML) techniques and evaluating their effectiveness in the SCA context. Although mainly considering distinct scenarios and various ML techniques, all those papers tend to establish different use cases where ML techniques can outperform the template attack and establish themselves as the best choice for profiled SCA. More recently, we are witnessing the relevance of deep learning (DL) techniques in the SCA community with strong results in side-channel analyses, even in the presence of countermeasures.

8.2   Profiled Side-Channel Attacks

Profiled side-channel attacks estimate the worst-case security risk by considering the most powerful side-channel attacker. In particular, one assumes that an attacker can possess an additional device of which he or she has nearly full control. From this device, he obtains leakage measurements and is able to control the used secret key or at least knows which one is used. Knowing the secret key enables him to calculate intermediate processed values that involve the secret key for which he is estimating models. These models can then be used in the attacking phase to predict which intermediate values are processed and therefore carry information about the secret key. Commonly used models are the identity value or Hamming weight/distance.

Uniformly Distributed Classes Targeting intermediate variables, e.g., when loaded or manipulated on the device and resulting mostly in 2^n uniformly distributed classes where n is the number of bits of the intermediate variable.

Binomial Distributed Classes The Hamming Weight (HW) or the Hamming Distance (HD) of a uniformly distributed intermediate variable results in $n + 1$ binomially distributed classes.

8.2.1   Definition of Profiling Attacks

In this section, we consider side-channel attacks on block ciphers for which a divide and conquer approach can be utilized. Note that, as there exist operations within the block cipher which manipulate each block/chunk (e.g., bytes in Advanced Encryption Standard (AES)) independently and most importantly involving only one block/chunk of the secret key, an attacker only needs to make hypotheses about the secret key block/chunk instead of the complete secret key at once.

More formally, let k^* denote (a chunk of) the fixed secret cryptographic key that is stored on the device and let t denote (a chunk of) the plaintext or ciphertext of the cryptographic algorithm. The mapping y maps the plaintext or the ciphertext

$t \in \mathscr{T}$ and the key $k^* \in \mathscr{K}$ to an intermediate value that is assumed to relate to the deterministic part of the measured leakage x. For example,

$$y(t, k) = \text{Sbox}[T \oplus k], \qquad (8.1)$$

where $\text{Sbox}[\cdot]$ is a substitution operation. The measured leakage x can then be written as

$$x = \varphi(y(t, k^*)) + r, \qquad (8.2)$$

where r denotes independent additive noise and φ is a device-specific (unknown) deterministic function mapping the intermediate variable to the leakage space. In the rest of this chapter, we are particularly interested in multivariate leakage $\mathbf{x} = x_1, \ldots, x_D$, where D is the number of time samples, i.e., features (also called attributes or points of interest).

Now, it is considered that the attacker has the following information at his disposal to conduct the attack:

- *profiling phase:* N traces (measurements) $\mathbf{x}_{p1}, \ldots, \mathbf{x}_{pN}$, the secret key k_p^*, and plaintexts/ciphertexts $t_{p1}, \ldots, t_{pN}$, such that he can calculate $y(t_{p1}, k_p^*), \ldots, y(t_{pN}, k_p^*)$.
- *attacking phase:* Q traces $\mathbf{x}_{a1}, \ldots, \mathbf{x}_{aQ}$ (independent from the profiling traces), plaintexts/ciphertexts $t_{a1}, \ldots, t_{aQ}$.

In the attacking phase the goal is to make predictions about $y(t_{a1}, k_a^*), \ldots,$ $y(t_{aN}, k_a^*)$, where k_a^* is the secret key on the attacking device. Note, even before running the attack, there are several steps one could do in order to make the attack more powerful. These phases are depicted in Fig. 8.1.

8.2.2 Data Preprocessing

In the data preprocessing phase, the aim is to prepare the data in a way to increase the performance of side-channel analysis. There are several papers considering various data augmentation techniques in order to artificially generate measurements so as to increase the size of the profiling dataset. Cagli et al. propose two data

Raw data   Data preprocessing Feature engineering   Model selection,   Model validation
                                                        parameter
                                                        optimization

Fig. 8.1 Depiction of an end-to-end profiling attack

augmentation techniques they call Shifting and Add-Remove [122]. They use convolutional neural networks (CNN) and find data augmentation to significantly improve the performance of CNN. Pu et al. use a data augmentation technique where they randomly shift each measurement in order to increase the number of measurements available in the profiling phase [489]. They report that even such simple augmentation can effectively improve the performance of profiling SCA. Picek et al. experiment with several data augmentation and class balancing techniques in order to decrease the influence of highly unbalanced datasets that occur when considering HW/HD models [478]. They show that by using a well-known machine learning technique called SMOTE, it is possible to reduce the number of measurements needed for a successful attack by up to 10 times. Kim et al. investigate how the addition of artificial noise to the input signal can be beneficial to the performance of the neural network [329].

8.2.3 Feature Engineering

When discussing the feature engineering tasks, we can recognize a few directions that researchers follow in the context of SCA:

- feature selection. Here, the most important subsets of features are selected. We can distinguish between filter, wrapper, and hybrid techniques.
- dimensionality reduction. The original features are transformed into new features. A common example of such a technique is Principal Component Analysis (PCA) [25].

When discussing feature engineering, it is important to mention the curse of dimensionality. This describes the effects of an exponential increase in volume associated with the increase in the dimensions [71]. As a consequence, as the dimensionality of the problem increases, the classifier's performance increases until the optimal feature subset is reached. Further increasing the dimensionality without increasing the number of training samples results in a decrease in the classifier performance.

In the SCA community, there are several standard techniques to conduct feature selection:

- Pearson Correlation Coefficient. The Pearson correlation coefficient measures the linear dependence between two variables, x and y, in the range $[-1, 1]$, where 1 is a total positive linear correlation, 0 is no linear correlation, and -1 means a total negative linear correlation. The Pearson correlation for a sample of the entire population is defined by [301]:

$$Pearson(x, y) = \frac{\sum_{i=1}^{N}((x_i - \bar{x})(y_i - \bar{y}))}{\sqrt{\sum_{i=1}^{N}(x_i - \bar{x})^2}\sqrt{\sum_{i=1}^{N}(y_i - \bar{y})^2}}, \tag{8.3}$$

where $\bar{x}$ and $\bar{y}$ are the empirical means of x and y, respectively.

- SOSD. In [230], the authors proposed as a selection method the sum of squared differences, simply as:

$$SOSD(x, y) = \sum_{i, j > i} (\bar{x}_{y_i} - \bar{x}_{y_j})^2, \qquad (8.4)$$

where $\bar{x}_{y_i}$ is the mean of the traces where the model equals y_i. Because of the square term, SOSD is always positive. Another advantage of using the square is that it enlarges big differences.

- SOST. SOST is the normalized version of SOSD [230] and is thus equivalent by the pairwise student T-test:

$$SOST(x, y) = \sum_{i, j > i} \left((\bar{x}_{y_i} - \bar{x}_{y_j}) / \sqrt{\frac{\sigma_{y_i}^2}{n_{y_i}} + \frac{\sigma_{y_j}^2}{n_{y_j}}} \right)^2 \qquad (8.5)$$

with n_{y_i} and n_{y_j} being the number of traces where the model equals to y_i and y_j, respectively.

There are several more relevant works in the domain of feature selection and SCA. The work of Lerman et al. [367] compared template attacks and machine learning on dimensionality reduction. They concluded that template attacks are the method of choice as long as a limited number of features can be identified in leakage traces containing most of the relevant information. Zheng et al. looked into feature selection techniques but they did not consider machine learning options [600]. Picek et al. conducted a detailed analysis of various feature selection techniques where some are also based on machine learning (so-called wrapper and hybrid methods) [477]. They concluded that commonly used feature selection techniques in SCA are rarely the best ones and they mentioned L1 regularization as a powerful feature selector in many scenarios.

8.3 Template Attacks

In this section, we start by explaining the details of template attacks, and after that we give details about two techniques that emerged from template attacks—pooled template attacks and stochastic attacks.

8.3.1   Context of Template Attack

In the pioneering template attacks article of Chari, Rao, and Rohatgi, it is shown that template attacks apply advanced statistical methods and can break implementations secure against other forms of side-channel attacks [135].

In some works template attacks are built to classify the state of a byte, e.g., a key byte in RC4 [135, 498]. The weakness of these papers is the need to create 256 templates for each byte. Additionally, the template building process can only be guided by partial attack results. In [498], the authors reduce the number of points of a trace by using an efficient algorithm instead of the standard principal component analysis method, which increases the speed of selecting points of interest. Also, by introducing a preprocessing phase with the use of discrete Fourier transformation on traces, the authors improve the template attack results in practice.

Agrawal et al. develop two new attack techniques that extend the work of the previously mentioned research results [11]. The first is a single-bit template attack technique that creates templates from peaks observed in a DPA attack resulting with a high probability value of a single DPA-targeted bit. Their second, template-enhanced DPA attack technique can be used to attack DPA protected cards and consists of two steps: a profiling phase and a hypothesis testing phase. In the first, profiling phase, the attacker, who is in possession of a smart card with a biased RNG, builds templates, and in the hypothesis testing phase the attacker uses previously built templates to mount a DPA-like attack on a target card which is identical to the test smart card, but has a perfect RNG. The authors illustrate these two attack techniques considering unprotected implementations of DES and AES on smart cards.

Archambeau et al. take template attacks techniques a step further by transforming leakage traces in order to identify important features (i.e., transformed time instants) and their number automatically. Actually, they use the optimal linear combination of the relevant time samples and execute template attacks in the principal subspace of the mean traces creating a new approach, the principal subspace-based template attack (PSTA) [25]. The authors validate this approach by attacking the RC4 stream cipher implementation and an FPGA implementation of AES.

In the literature, the main focus is on template attacks aiming at recovering the secret key of a cryptographic core from measurements of its dynamic power consumption. But with scaling of technology, static power consumption grows faster and creates new issues in the security of smart card hardware. Therefore, Bellizia et al. proposed Template Attack Exploiting Static Power (TAESP) in order to extract information from a hardware implementation of a cryptographic algorithm using temperature-dependence of static currents as a source of information leakage [70].

8.3.2   Standard Template Attack

The template attack is based on the Bayesian rule and works under the simplifying assumption that the measurements are mutually independent among the D features given the target class. More precisely, given the vector of N observed attribute values x, the posterior probability for each class value y is computed as:

$$p(Y = y | \mathbf{X} = \mathbf{x}) = \frac{p(Y = y)p(\mathbf{X} = \mathbf{x} | Y = y)}{p(\mathbf{X} = \mathbf{x})}, \qquad (8.6)$$

where $\mathbf{X} = \mathbf{x}$ represents the event that $\mathbf{X}_1 = \mathbf{x}_1 \wedge \mathbf{X}_2 = \mathbf{x}_2 \wedge \ldots \wedge \mathbf{X}_N = \mathbf{x}_N$.

Note that the class variable Y and the measurement X are not of the same type: Y is discrete while X is continuous. So, the discrete probability $p(Y = y)$ is equal to its sample frequency where $p(\mathbf{X} = \mathbf{x} | Y = y)$ displays a density function. In most state-of-the-art models $p(\mathbf{X} = \mathbf{x} | Y = y)$ is assumed to be based on a (multivariate) normal distribution and is thus parameterized by its mean and its covariance matrix:

$$p(\mathbf{X} = \mathbf{x} | Y = y) = \frac{1}{\sqrt{(2\pi)^D |\Sigma_y|}} e^{-\frac{1}{2}(\mathbf{x} - \bar{x}_y)^T \Sigma_y^{-1} (\mathbf{x} - \bar{x}_y)}. \qquad (8.7)$$

8.3.3   Pooled Template Attack

In practice, the estimation of the covariance matrices for each class value y can be ill-posed mainly due to an insufficient number of traces for each class. The authors of [142] propose to use only one pooled covariance matrix to cope with statistical difficulties and thus a lower efficiency. Accordingly, Eq. (8.7) changes to

$$p(\mathbf{X} = \mathbf{x} | Y = y) = \frac{1}{\sqrt{(2\pi)^D |\Sigma|}} e^{-\frac{1}{2}(\mathbf{x} - \bar{x}_y)^T \Sigma^{-1} (\mathbf{x} - \bar{x}_y)}. \qquad (8.8)$$

The works in, e.g., [142, 476, 477, 481] showed that indeed the pooled version is more efficient, in particular for a smaller number of traces in the profiling phase.

8.3.4   Stochastic Attack

Compared to TA, the stochastic attack (SA) utilizes linear regression instead of probability density estimation [515]. One critical aspect of SA is the choice of regressors (aka base functions), as for example shown in [275]. A natural choice in the context of side-channel analysis is the bitwise selection of the intermediate variable, i.e., let $[\cdot]_b$ define the function selecting the bth bit and using the same intermediate variable as in Sect. 8.2.1 then

$$([\mathtt{Sbox}[T \oplus k]]_1 \quad [\mathtt{Sbox}[T \oplus k]]_2 \quad \ldots \quad [\mathtt{Sbox}[T \oplus k]]_n) \qquad (8.9)$$

is an n-dimensional vector used as regressors. One benefit of SA is the constructive feedback of side-channel leakage detection it might bring to the evaluator (see, e.g., [278]).

8.4 Machine Learning-Based Attacks

Machine learning encompasses a number of methods used for classification, clustering, regression, feature selection, and other knowledge discovering methods [423]. A typical division of machine learning algorithms is into supervised, semi-supervised, and unsupervised approaches. Each of those paradigms can also be used in SCAs—supervised (profiling) attacks, semi-supervised attacks (profiling), unsupervised (non-profiling) attacks.

In Fig. 8.2, we depict differences in the supervised and semi-supervised cases.

Supervised Techniques
The supervised approach assumes that the attacker first possesses a device similar to the one under attack. Having this additional device, he is then able to build a precise profiling model using a set of measurements while knowing the plaintext/ciphertext and the secret key of this device. In the second step, the attacker uses the earlier profiling model to reveal the secret key of the device under attack. For this, he additionally measures a new set of traces, but as the key is secret he has no further information about the intermediate processed data and thus builds hypotheses. The only information that the attacker transfers between the profiling phase and the attacking phase is the profiling model he builds.

When considering supervised machine learning and SCA, in recent years there have been numerous papers considering various targets, machine learning algorithms, and scenarios. Actually, the most common denominator for most of the work

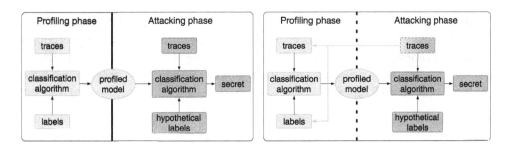

Fig. 8.2 Profiling side-channel scenario: supervised (left), semi-supervised (right)

is the fact that they attack AES [235, 274, 279, 285, 363–365, 367, 475, 476, 479, 481]. More recently, deep learning (DL) techniques started to capture the attention of the SCA community. Accordingly, the first results confirmed expectations, with most of the early attention being paid to convolutional convolutional neural networks [122, 329, 386, 482].

As far as we know, when considering machine learning-based attacks on other ciphers, there are only a few papers. Heuser et al. consider Internet of Things scenarios and lightweight ciphers where they compare 11 lightweight ciphers and AES in terms of their SCA resilience and conclude that lightweight ciphers cannot be considered to be significantly less resilient than AES [274, 276].

Semi-supervised Techniques

Semi-supervised learning is positioned in the middle between supervised and unsupervised learning. There, the basic idea is to take advantage of a large quantity of unlabeled data during a supervised learning procedure [517]. This approach assumes that the attacker is able to possess a device to conduct a profiling phase but has limited capacities. This may reflect a more realistic scenario in some practical applications, as the attacker may be limited by time or resources, or also face implemented countermeasures, which prevent him from taking an arbitrarily large amount of side-channel measurements while knowing the secret key of the device.

The first application of semi-supervised SCA was done by Lerman et al., where the authors conclude that the semi-supervised setting cannot compete with a supervised setting [366]. Note, the authors compared the supervised attack with $n + m$ labeled traces for all classes with a semi-supervised attack with n labeled traces for one class and m unlabeled traces for other unknown classes (i.e., in total $n + m$ traces). Picek et al. conduct an analysis of two semi-supervised paradigms (self-training and graph-based learning) where they show that it is possible to improve the accuracy of classifiers if semi-supervised learning is used [480]. What is especially interesting is that they show how semi-supervised learning is able to significantly improve the behavior of the template attack when the profiling set is (very) small.

8.4.1   Conducting Sound Machine Learning Analysis

Since it is not possible (in general) to expect machine learning techniques to give us theoretical observations or proofs of results, we need to rely on a set of procedures to run experiments such that the results are convincing and easy to reproduce. In the next section, we briefly discuss several steps to be considered in order to make the analysis more reproducible.

Datasets

When preparing the data for machine learning analysis, it is necessary to discuss the number of measurements, the number of features, and the number of classes (if known). Additionally, if the data come from different distributions, one needs to discuss those. If not all data from datasets are used, it is necessary to state how the samples are chosen and how many are used in the experiments. One needs to define the level of noise appearing in the data in a clearly reproducible way, e.g., using the signal-to-noise ratio (SNR). Finally, if some feature engineering procedure is used, it needs to be clearly stated in order to know what features are used in the end.

Algorithms

When discussing the choice of algorithms, first it is necessary either to specify which framework and algorithms are used or provide pseudo-code (for example, when custom algorithms are used). As a rule of thumb, more than one algorithm should always be used: the algorithms should ideally belong to different machine learning approaches (e.g., a decision tree method like Random Forest and a kernel method like Support Vector Machine (SVM)). Next, all parameters that uniquely define the algorithm need to be enumerated.

Experiments

Regarding the experiments, it is first necessary to discuss how the data are divided into training and testing sets. Then, for the training phase, one needs to define the test options (e.g., whether to use the whole dataset or cross-validation, etc.) After that, for each algorithm, one needs to define a set of parameter values to conduct the tuning phase. There are different options for tuning, but we consider starting with the default parameters as a reasonable approach and continue varying them until there is no more improvement. Naturally, this should be done in a reasonable way, since the tuning phase is the most expensive from the computational perspective and it is usually not practical to test all combinations of parameters.

Results

For the tuning phase, it is usually sufficient to report the accuracy. For the testing results, one should report the accuracy but also some other metric like the area under the ROC curve (AUC) or the F-measure. The area under the ROC curve is used to measure the accuracy and is calculated via Mann-Whitney statistics [580]; the ROC curve is the ratio between the true positive rate and the false positive rate. An AUC close to 1 represents a good test, while a value close to 0.5 represents a random guess. The F-measure is the harmonic mean of the precision and recall, where precision is the ratio between true positive (TP, the number of examples predicted positive that are actually positive) and predicted positive. The recall is the ratio between true positives and actual positives [488]. Both the F-Measure and the AUC can help in situations where accuracy can be misleading, i.e., where we are also interested in the number of false positive and false negative values.

8.5 Performance Metrics

When considering profiling SCA, there are three performance metrics we mention: accuracy, guessing entropy, and success rate. The accuracy is the proportion between the correctly classified measurements and all measurements:

$$ACC = \frac{TP + TN}{TP + TN + FP + FN}. \qquad (8.10)$$

TP refers to true positive (correctly classified positive), TN to true negative (correctly classified negative), FP to false positive (falsely classified positive), and FN to false negative (falsely classified negative) instances. TP, TN, FP, and FN are well-defined for hypothesis testing and binary classification problems. In the multi-class classification, they are defined in a one class vs. all other classes manner, and are calculated from the confusion matrix.

A side-channel adversary $A_{E_K,L}$ conducts an experiment $\mathsf{Exp}_{A_{E_K,L}}$, with time-complexity τ, memory complexity m, and making Q queries to the target implementation of the cryptographic algorithm. The attack outputs a guessing vector g of length o, and is considered a success if g contains correct key k^*. o is also known as the order of the success rate. The oth order success rate of the side channel attack $A_{E_K,L}$ is defined as:

$$\mathsf{SR}^o_{A_{E_K,L}}(\tau, m, k^*) = \mathsf{Pr}[\mathsf{Exp}_{A_{E_K,L}} = 1] \qquad (8.11)$$

The Guessing entropy measures the average number of key candidates to test after the attack. The **Guessing entropy** of the adversary $A_{E_k,L}$ against a key class variable S is defined as:

$$GE_{A_{E_K,L}}(\tau, m, k^*) = \mathsf{E}[\mathsf{Exp}_{A_{E_K,L}}] \qquad (8.12)$$

8.6 Countermeasures Against SCA

There are various countermeasures against SCAs that have been proposed over the years. A general approach focuses on decreasing the information gathered from the measurements:

- Noise Addition. Introducing external noise in the side-channel, shuffling the operations or inserting dummy operations in cryptographic implementations is often used as a countermeasure against SCAs. The basic objective is to reduce the signal-to-noise ratio (SNR) and thereby decrease the information gathered from measurements. Still, as shown already by Durvaux et al. [194], these countermeasures become insecure with increasing attack time.

- Dynamic and Differential CMOS Logic. Tiri et al. [557] proposed Sense Amplifier Based Logic (SABL)—a logic style that uses a fixed amount of charge for every transition, including the degenerated events in which a gate does not change state.
- Leakage Resilience. Another countermeasure, typically applied at the system level, focuses on restricting the number of usages of the same key for an algorithm. Still, generation and synchronization of new keys have practical issues. Dziembowski et al. introduced a technique called leakage resilience, which relocates this problem to the protocol level by introducing an algorithm to generate these keys [195].
- Masking. One of the most efficient and powerful approaches against SCAs is masking [134, 243], which aims to break the correlation between the power traces and the intermediate values of the computations. This method achieves security by randomizing the intermediate values using secret sharing and carrying out all the computations on the shared values.

8.7   Conclusions

In this chapter, we discussed profiling side-channel attacks where we started with data preprocessing and feature engineering. Then we presented several template-like techniques and afterward machine learning techniques. Next, we discussed how to conduct a sound machine learning analysis that should result in reproducible experiments. We finished the chapter with a short discussion on how to test the performance of SCA and what are some of the possible countermeasures to make such attacks more difficult.

9

Commercial, Open Source and Experimental Trace Acquisition Tools

Apostolos P. Fournaris, Athanassios Moschos, and Nicolas Sklavos

Abstract Side Channel Attacks are nowadays considered a serious risk for many security products and ubiquitous devices. Strong security solution providers need to evaluate their implementations against such attacks before publishing them on the market, thus performing a thorough assessment. However, this procedure is not straightforward and even with the appropriate equipment, it may require considerable time to provide results due to the slow process of collecting measurements (traces) and the inflexible way of controlling the tested implementation. In this chapter, we explore and overview the trace collection landscape for generic devices under test (including ubiquitous systems) highlighting and overviewing the latest trace collection toolsets and their shortcomings, but also proposing a trace collection approach that can be applied on the most recent, open source toolsets. We showcase our proposed approach on the FlexLeco project architecture, which we have developed in our lab, and manage to practically describe how an evaluator using the proposed methodology can collect traces easily and quickly without the need to completely redesign a control mechanism for the implementation under test.

9.1 Introduction

The transition of computing devices to the ubiquitous era, where the cyber world is merging with the physical world to bring an ever present layer of computer intelligence to everyday life objects, is bringing, among other things, cybersecurity and privacy into the physical world as an issue to be constantly considered. Due to IP interconnected cyberphysical systems, attackers can gain access not only to a victim's data but also to the victim's life itself, by controlling "smart"

A. P. Fournaris (✉)
Industrial Systems Institute/R.C. ATHENA, Patras, Greece
e-mail: fournaris@isi.gr

A. Moschos · N. Sklavos
Georgia Institute of Technology, Atlanta, USA

University of Patras, Patras, Greece

devices of urban and industrial systems, critical infrastructures and individual households [540]. This highlights the need for strong security features that must be installed on embedded systems. However, ubiquitous devices have several non-functional constraints like small processing power, low power consumption or small memory footprint, that prohibit the use of several traditional security and cryptography schemes (e.g., asymmetric cryptography). This has led to the redesign and simplification of existing security solutions (like TLS schemes and their cipher modes) or the development of cryptography algorithms especially designed for low performance devices (lightweight cryptography schemes [197]).

The design and evaluation of security schemes and cryptographic algorithms must take into account several parameters that are related to a scheme's crypto-graphic strength (addressed by cryptanalysis, formal security verification methods etc.), to its algorithmic performance (addressed by collecting and comparing per-formance and resource measurements) and to its resistance against implementation attacks like side channel and fault injection attacks [337]. Side channel attacks (SCAs) have a leading role in the design of modern cryptosystems, since they are the weakest point and they have been exploited by many well-known attacks in order to break otherwise unbreakable security/cryptography algorithms. SCAs can be easily applicable to ubiquitous, cyberphysical systems, where devices are left unattended in potentially security "hostile" environments (in remote, secluded areas, inside malicious user premises, etc.)

There is a broad research field related to various SCAs, aiming to exploit various physical characteristics of a device including timing, power consumption, electromagnetic emission, etc. The flagship SCA analysis methods are of statistical nature and can be categorized into horizontal attacks (using one or a few collected inputs) or vertical attacks (using many collected inputs). Among the most potent and successful such attacks are Differential Power Analysis (DPA) or Correlation DPA [390] as well as template, online template [58] and Mutual Information Attack (MIA) [229]. A simple review of the above advanced SCAs reveals that all of them require a considerable amount of collected leaked physical characteristic inputs in order to be effective.

Assessing if a security/cryptography scheme on a ubiquitous device is SCA resistant, is not a straightforward process. It usually follows two directions. In the first direction, a security scheme is evaluated against specific SCAs while the second direction is based on performing a generic information leakage assessment based on some statistical test. Student's or Welch t-test are two such tests that use statistical hypothesis testing in order to detect if one of a series of sensitive intermediate processes during a security procedure significantly influences the measurement data or (more often in a non-specific test) detect how different is a collected trace from random noise (indicating a bias addressed to exploitable information leakage).

Collecting inputs for SCA analysis is done using specialized equipment in a fairly cheap and easy way. However, when a huge number of inputs need to be acquired then the processing of an input (or trace, as they are usually denoted in the literature) becomes a very slow and cumbersome process. A restricted number of tools that help the acquisition of the needed traces for advanced SCA attacks exist. Most of them still require a considerable amount of time for trace collection and employ custom (to the cryptosystem at hand) control mechanisms. There are open source SCA trace collection setups widely used by the research community [451] but have either very primitive support or are built on low-cost equipment that cannot endure very sophisticated attacks without having software developed by an attacker [427]. Also, adjustments for different cryptographic devices under test are always needed, sometimes to a great extent. There exist a few commercial companies in this research field (Riscure [501], CRI[495]) that offer their own proprietary equipment to the prospective crypto-analysts at a prohibitively high cost, affordable only by high budget labs.

In this chapter we review the latest commercial, open source and experimental trace acquisition tools and focus on their benefits and drawbacks. We also highlight the need for a cheap, fast and automated process for sending and receiving data between a Device under Test (DUT) and a controller. We comment on the importance of efficient control loops of DUT in order to speed-up the trace acquisition process. Finally, we propose and describe a three step approach for controlling, functionally validating and SCA assessing a DUT that goes beyond the traditional control model that other solutions follow. Finally, we describe the use of our solution using an open source hardware/software trace acquisition platform that we have developed in our lab (FlexLeco project [427]) that consolidates the latest trends in trace collection tools and platforms.

The rest of the chapter is organized as follows. In Sect. 9.2, the major SCA categories and leakage assessment methodologies are described and evaluated according to the number of traces needed. In Sect. 9.3 we overview existing open source and commercial trace collection platforms and toolsets, and the proposed trace collection approach is described. In Sect. 9.4, we describe the use of the proposed approach on the FlexLeco project architecture, and discuss the benefits of the solution. In Sect. 9.4 conclusions are provided.

9.2   Side Channel Attacks, Leakage Assessment Methods and Problems

A typical side-channel attack (SCA) measurement and analysis setup consists of several components, including measuring equipment (e.g., a digital signal oscilloscope), a DUT controller component that handles attacker-to-DUT communication as well as a Personal Computer (PC). The PC is used by an attacker/evaluator for providing input to the controller and for analyzing, with the help of programming tools, the collected leakage trace measurements by applying signal processing techniques on them [390]. Possible additions to this classic SCA measurement collection and analysis setup could be some kind of pre-amplifier to boost the signals acquired by the measuring equipment (e.g., an oscilloscope), a differential cable to help reduce acquired measurements noise, electromagnetic probes for acquiring electromagnetic emanation signals, and some kind of tool that will speed up leakage trace capturing.

There are a large variety of DUTs that can be assessed for their SCA resistance using the above setup. Under the ubiquitous computing framework, small embedded system devices (e.g., RFID tags, wireless sensor network nodes, smart card devices), having lightweight versions of cryptographic algorithms, are the most prominent candidates to have SCA vulnerabilities. Assessing the SCA resistance of such devices can be achieved by evaluating the device when it is deployed and is fully operational (in that case the DUT is the whole device) or can be achieved by evaluating individually, in a controlled environment, a specific cryptography or security implementation that is meant to be deployed on the ubiquitous device. In the first case, SCA assessment is very hard to perform since, apart from security functions, on the DUT there are many operations, unrelated to security, that are being executed in parallel [219]. Such operations can be considered as hard-to-remove noise inside the collected traces [219]. In the second case, the DUT is not the full ubiquitous device but a specific security hardware or software implementation deployed on this device. No other operations are executed in the second case control environment, thus noise is minimized, enabling the evaluator to test many SCA resistance scenarios in depth.

When trace collection is needed for SCA analysis or assessment, the attacker/evaluator needs to pass the cryptography/security algorithm's expected input data each time from his control point (usually a personal computer) to the control component, which is responsible for sending the data to the DUT for one security/cryptography process to begin. After having set the right settings in the oscilloscope (e.g., sampling rate, time window capture, resolution capture) the attacker arms it. The attacker then sends a command to the DUT, for it to start performing the evaluated security process. Before the start of the process the DUT sends a triggering signal to the oscilloscope, warning it that the process is about to start and a trace capture must be performed. As soon as the trigger signal reaches the oscilloscope, it captures a leakage trace measurement (e.g., power consumption or the electromagnetic emanation, depending on the used probes) of the DUT. The attacker/evaluator then requests from the oscilloscope the captured trace for analysis at his PC. When the captured trace reaches the PC, various signal processing techniques are applied on it and it is used for side-channel analysis of the DUT. The above procedure (called loop round) is repeated for each new security/cryptography process we want the DUT to perform.

9.2.1   Side Channel Attack Categories

Adopting the formulation approach described in [60, 61, 220] we can model each security/cryptography computation C as a series of n different O_i operations (for $i \in \{0, 1, \ldots n - 1\}$) that each require inputs X_i (thus $O_i(X_i)$). We can also assume that each operation output can be considered as input to another operation during the C computation. Each operation O_i is linked to an information leakage variable L_i. A side channel attack is possible if there is some secret information s that is shared between O_i and its leakage L_i. The ultimate goal of a side channel analysis is, by using some strategy, to deduce s from a series of information leakage L_i values [220]. To achieve that we collect leakage traces L which are sequences (in time) $L = \{L_0, L_1, \ldots L_{n-1}\}$ and try to associate them with the computation C as a sequence of operations $C = \{O_0, O_1, \ldots O_{n-1}\}$.

SCAs follow either the vertical or horizontal leakage collection and analysis strategy, as originally described in [60]. In the vertical approach, the implementation is used N times using either the same or different inputs each time in order to collect leakage traces. Each trace is associated with the j-th execution of the computation. In the horizontal approach, leakage traces and related analysis is collected/performed from a single execution of the computation and each trace corresponds to a different time period within the time frame of this execution. As expected, in horizontal attacks the implementation input is always the same.

By associating and distinguishing specific patterns of O_i operations (consisting of a single or multiple operations) in a leakage trace L, an attacker can recover the secret s. Such an attack approach is typically followed in simple SCAs (SSCAs) that are mostly horizontal attacks meaning that they are mounted using a single leakage trace that is processed in time. Vertical SSCAs that need more than one leakage trace rely on comparative analysis for pattern matching between computations with different inputs. Vertical SSCAs require a few hundred leakage traces to be collected considering that averaging technique for noise reduction is applied between leakage traces of the same computation.

There exist several countermeasures that can thwart SSCAs, thus, more advanced attacks have been devised (i.e., Advanced SCAs (ASCAs)). ASCAs do not focus only on single operations or series of operations (e.g., O_i) but also on the computation operands (i.e., the operation inputs X_i) [61, 220]. ASCAs are focused on a specific subset of the calculation C (e.g., some O_i operations that are strongly associated with s) and examine how this subset behaves over a large collection of (e.g., N) leakage traces L_j associated with computations C_j with different inputs (where $j \in \{1, \ldots, N\}$). ASCAs on this subset of operations and associated leakage traces, exploit the statistical dependency between the calculation C for all X_j and the secret s. ASCAs follow the hypothesis test principle [60, 335] where a series of hypothesis $\acute{s}$ on s (usually on some bit j of s i.e., $\acute{s}_j{=}0$ or 1) are made and a series of leakage prediction values are found based on each of these hypotheses using an appropriate prediction model. The values of each hypothesis are evaluated against all actual leakage traces using an appropriate distinguisher δ for all inputs X_i so as to decide which hypothesis is correct.

Most ASCAs are of vertical nature and their success is highly related to the number of processed leakage traces. The most widely used ASCA vertical attack is Differential Attack (DSCA) originally proposed by Kocher in [336], which was later expanded into the more sophisticated Correlation SCA (requiring fewer traces to reveal the secret than DSCA) [21] and the collision correlation attack [99, 210, 425], which can be mounted even if the attacker does not have full control of the implementation inputs. There are, however, also horizontal ASCAs that apply differential or correlation statistics on a single leakage trace assuming that a subset of operations associated with the secret s appear many times in this trace. Finally, ASCAs can bypass strong SCA countermeasures (e.g., randomization/blinding) by combining horizontal and vertical approaches [59, 210, 220].

Following the above categorization (Vertical vs. Horizontal, SSCA vs. ASCA), we can include profiling SCAs like Template Attacks or Machine Learning Attacks [367] among the vertical ASCAs. Profiling attacks operate in two phases: Initially, they need to collect a series of leakage traces from a device under the full control of the attacker (with known inputs and secrets) so as to create a leakage model. In the second phase, the leakage model is used as a template or as the training set of a machine learning algorithm in order to recover a secret from a series of traces collected from a device (similar to the one used for profiling) not under attacker control.

9.2.2 Leakage Assessment Using t-Test

In addition to SCA resistance assessment based on the success of various SCAs, a generic methodology for finding information leakage from a DUT has been gaining ground. The dominant, generic, leakage assessment methodologies are based on Student's t-distribution following specific and non-specific t-tests [67, 516]. The goal is to detect any type of information leakage that occurs during the computation of security/cryptography functions in the DUT, at a certain n-th SCA order. [An SCA attack of order n appears when there exists an n set of intermediate variables that appear during the computation of the algorithm, such that knowing a few key bits (in practice fewer than 32 bits) allows us to decide whether two inputs (respectively two outputs) give the same value for a known function of these n variables.] Any sensitive computational intermediate operation O_i series that appears on the side channel as significantly different from random noise can potentially be detected using the above leakage assessment approach without conducting any specific SCA. This significant difference is enough to mark a DUT implementation as leaky and SCA insecure.

Test Vector Leakage Assessment (TVLA) is one of the most promising, generic, non-specific leakage detection techniques, initially proposed by Cryptography Research (CRI) [67]. The method is practically used as the first action towards assessing a system's SCA leakage. It consists of a univariate test that is performed on a series of traces obtained from a DUT. The DUT implementation is evaluated as non-leaky if the test throughout the duration of the DUT trace remains below a certain threshold, independently of the leakage model that might be used. More precisely, we test the case where there is no leakage (null hypothesis) versus the case where there is some leakage at a certain intermediate point $L(t)$ at time t. Let n_{tr} be the number of traces that the evaluator collects and n_s the number of samples in each trace. Following the notation of [597], and assuming that we have

N traces of n_s samples each, let $\mathbf{L} = \{L_1, \ldots, L_{n_s}\}$ be the leakage traces of a security/cryptography implementation, having mean values $\bar{L}_i$. For the traces null hypothesis to be true the expected leakage value $\bar{L}_{exp}$ should be the same as the measured value, if there is no leakage, i.e., $\bar{L}_{exp} = \bar{L}_i \ \forall i \in \{1, \ldots, n_s\}$. In practice, to perform the TVLA we conduct two experiments. In both experiments, we collect $N/2$ traces where the variable to be leakage assessed has a known, fixed, value and $N/2$ traces where this variable has a random value. This trace collection is done in an interleaved way by randomly choosing to acquire either a fixed trace or a random trace each time. After collecting the necessary traces, we perform a Welch's t-test as described in [516] and check the outcome against a threshold.

TVLA and all similar leakage assessment tests can provide an initial indication regarding SCA leakage but require huge amounts of collected traces in order to provide an accurate assessment result. In the case of symmetric key cryptography algorithms (e.g., in AES implementations) this number is in the order of millions (in [516] $N = 100$M traces for an AES evaluation). This number is reduced in Public Key algorithms (in the order of thousands of traces) yet still is hard to collect since each public key algorithm implementation trace consists of a very large number of samples n_s. From a trace collection perspective, TVLA is a very slow assessment method due to this high N number, and can become very frustrating for an SCA evaluator.

9.2.3   Practical Considerations in SCA Trace Collection

When, in practice, the above described SCA attacks are applied to actual, raw collected traces using real hardware or software implementations, their success rate is very low. This happens since in a trace, leakage information is mingled with a considerable amount of SCA-useless signals that we can consider here as "noise". Noise, as very accurately described in [411], can be external, intrinsic, quantization or algorithmic. External noise that is picked up from external to the DUT sources as well as intrinsic noise, due to the DUT's physical characteristics (capacitance, conduction, transistor, non-linear behavior, etc.), are not under the control of the attacker and the DUT SCA resistance designer, and must be removed or reduced by some appropriate trace preprocessing technique. On the other hand, quantization noise can be considerably reduced by using better trace collection equipment (with small A/D quantization for example). Algorithmic noise is usually designer infused on a DUT in an effort to increase randomness in data processing but also infused by computation functionalities unrelated to security, such as interrupts, pipelining, OS system calls, etc., these can very often appear in ubiquitous devices.

In order to practically make a successful SCA, noise cancellation techniques must be applied during or after trace collection in order to have clear and useful leakage traces. Traditional noise reduction techniques can be applied on traces after collection based on low-, band- or high-pass filtering after finding dominant frequencies using, for example, Fast Fourier Transform analysis or based on trace resampling where sample windows are specified and they are replaced by their average value [501]. However, many researchers apply the averaging technique to increase the signal-to-noise ratio and mount a successful attack. Using averaging, we collect T leakage traces with the same inputs and secret, then average them sample-per-sample to come up with a single, averaged leakage trace that contains a lot less noise than each individual trace itself. The technique is very popular (almost mandatory) in embedded system SCAs to remove noise, but it increases the needed number of collected traces by a factor of T since we need T trace collections for each SCA useful, averaged, leakage trace.

Another practical factor to be considered during trace collection, which also has an impact on the number of collected traces, is trace misalignment. This phenomenon happens when, after triggering a security/cryptography computation, the various O_i operations do not always appear at the same point in time in all leakage traces of this computation, even if the same inputs and secret are used. Misalignment can appear frequently in software based security computations (a common case in ubiquitous devices) since such computations run in parallel to other security-unrelated processes, or random events may happen that influence the computation execution sequence. Misalignment can also appear in hardware-implemented security computations when related SCA countermeasures are introduced in the computation flow. To solve the problem, SCA theory states that traces should be realigned using postcollection trace processing techniques [390]. However, in practice, for several cases of ubiquitous devices, traces are so misaligned that they become SCA useless and cannot be effectively realigned. Thus, there is a percentage of collected traces that due to misalignment should be discarded. This makes it imperative to collect more traces than those needed, having in mind that some of them will be useless due to misalignment. A rule of thumb in such cases is to collect 20% more traces than needed. This percentage can increase to 50% in highly misaligned traces (usually on ubiquitous software implementations).

9.3   Side Channel Attack Trace Collection Platforms

There exist several Security Test Labs and individual researchers who have proposed and manufactured their own ad hoc hardware boards [399, 532, 565] for trace collection. In the years following the discovery of SCAs, several Side-Channel Analysis measurement boards and evaluation setups emerged in the security community. The purpose of such boards is to provide a common platform for the aspiring attackers to mount their attacks and help them get low noise measurements in an easy way. Typically, they accommodate a general purpose device (a microprocessor, an ASIC, or an FPGA) serving as the DUT, connected with a controlling device (control component) on the same board (mainly some sort of microcontroller). There were also boards that accommodated signal-enhancing mechanisms on the same board to ease the oscilloscope's work [117]. Gradually the quality of the boards improved to such a degree that several of them found their way to the market for commercial use, with significant success.

There is limited variety of commercial SCA boards, each with its pros and cons. The Cryptographic Engineering Research Group (CERG) presented the FOBOS board [565, 566], which consists of two FPGA's, one for handling control tasks and one for the implementation of the cryptographic algorithm. The FOBOS board contains a Digital Clock Manager that produces frequencies in the range of 31.25 kHz up to 50 MHz for the Victim Board. The communication with the Control FPGA is performed through a software control loop that is responsible for transmitting the appropriate commands and the necessary data to the victim FPGA. The software loop is also responsible for the communication with the oscilloscope (currently supporting only Agilent oscilloscopes). Unfortunately, the FOBOS approach relies on old FPGA boards, is not capable of automated multiple trace collection through the provided control loop, is only applicable to a specific type of oscilloscope, and involves the PC in each trace collection (part of the control loop) which considerably burdens the collection speed.

The Tamper-resistance Standardization Research Committee (TSRC) released two trace collection hardware boards [399]. The first is INSTAC-8 which uses an 8-bit microcontroller and the second is INSTAC-32 with a 32-bit microcontroller as the control component and an FPGA chip as the DUT. Unfortunately, very limited information is provided on the clock frequencies and the communication methods that those two boards employed. Similarly to FOBOS, they also featured some custom-made software loops for the communication between the users and the victim chips. An evolution of the above approaches is the Sakura-Sasebo Project [354], which provides several choices regarding measurement boards. Initially, low-end-based chip boards were implemented, leading to the Sasebo-G, Sasebo-GII and Sasebo-W solutions, which for several years constituted the most widely used platforms for trace collection. Later, more sophisticated versions of those boards were launched, the Sakura-G, Sakura-X and Sakura-W. Both Sakura-G and Sakura-X contain two FPGAs each (a Control FPGA acting as the control component and a cryptography FPGA acting as the DUT), making them perfect for evaluation of hardware-implemented cryptographic algorithms, while Sakura-W was suitable for evaluation of smartcard security. Unfortunately, the boards are still supported by a primitive interface on the Control FPGA that enables the interfacing of a particular cryptographic algorithm with limited key-length. Also, the provided software loop in charge of data and command transmission to the Cryptographic FPGA is slow, oriented towards a specific algorithm with fixed key-length, and offers through a PC program very basic functionality only for a single trace capture per loop round.

An attempt to remedy this issue was made in the IAMeter project, which is focused exclusively on developing an efficient control loop for commercial and custom FPGA board platforms (including the Sasebo-G and GII boards) [307]. However, even this attempt can provide only a single trace collection per loop round, it is not capable of adjusting/controlling the DUT clock, and it relies heavily on PC-based configurations (including Python scripts along with MySQL databases queries) which slow the trace collection as a whole.

Recently, in an effort to provide a cheap SCA setup, the ChipWhisperer project [450] managed to provide a diverse tool-chain for embedded hardware security research. The ChipWhisperer featuring a CW1173-Lite board is suitable for capturing traces and attacking software cryptographic algorithms implemented in its Atmel XMEGA microcontroller, and it was recently upgraded to the CW1200-Pro version that offers additional ease-of-use on the process. ChipWhisperer though also provides the CW305-Artix FPGA board that specifically targets attacks on hardware cryptographic algorithms implemented in its ARTIX 7 FPGA as well as the OpenADC dongle that enables trace capturing directly from hardware devices (without the need for an oscilloscope). Both CW1173 and CW305 allow the modification of Victim's Chip frequency (e.g., the frequency range for the CW305-Artix board starts from 5 MHz and goes up to 160 MHz due to the onboard PLL (Phase Locked Loop)). The communication between the user and the Victim Chip in both boards relies on a software control loop called Chipwhipserer-Capture. This is a PC-based loop responsible for sending the appropriate data and commands to the Victim board. In the case of the CW305-Artix FPGA board the PC software loop is assisted by an onboard AVR microprocessor (partially acting as a control component).

Complete measurement and evaluation setups are provided by experienced security test laboratories with longtime presence in the hardware security community. BrightSight delivers the Sideways acquisition center. CRI-Rambus offers the DPA Workstation [495] which is a complete platform that enables the testing and analyzing of cryptographic chips and systems vulnerabilities, to power and electromagnetic (EM) side-channel attacks. Finally, Riscure launched the Inspector [501] which is an integrated test tool for side channel analysis and fault injection attacks on security devices. The above commercial setups offer SCA resistance evaluation/assessment on individual security/cryptography hardware and software implementations as well as on fully working DUT ubiquitous devices (e.g., embedded systems).

The gap between the measurement boards and the complete evaluation setups is huge when it comes to cost. Trace collection and SCA evaluation setups providing a complete package that includes measurement collection, side-channel attacks and DUT security analysis, have a considerable cost. On the other side, the cost of the measurement boards is much more affordable, nonetheless exploiting their capabilities to the full extent is not always supported by their manufacturers in terms of software or hardware tools.

9.3.1 Proposing a Fast Trace Collection Approach Beyond the Traditional Model

As the need for a huge number of traces for SCA evaluation and leakage assessment becomes considerable (in the presence of DUT with SCA countermeasures) the traditional SCA trace collection control loop model is not fast enough for efficient, practical, trace acquisition. The main bottleneck in such control loops is the presence of a PC device for providing inputs, collecting outputs and controlling each execution of the DUT security/cryptography implementation [427]. The solutions presented in the previous subsection, although they do not manage to eliminate the need for a PC inside the control loop, clearly indicate a tendency to migrate traditional PC-related functionality to other hardware or software entities that are closely associated with the DUT. In some solutions, the control loop operations are implemented in hardware and are downloaded on a dedicated control FPGA that is physically connected to the DUT. This is done in the Sasebo/Sakura project and in some ChipWhisperer (NewAE) technologies, just to name some examples. Hardware, however, is not flexible and thus cannot be easily adapted to different algorithms or assessment techniques. Similarly, control loop functionality is partially migrated on dedicated control loop ASIC microcontrollers or microprocessors that operate alongside a PC in order to implement the DUT control in software. Such solutions lack speed when transmitting DUT test vectors to the DUT itself since PC usage is still needed.

Therefore, it has become apparent that a different, updated approach to realize DUT control loops for SCA evaluation and leakage assessment is needed. In this work, considering the previous paragraph's described hardware and software control loop limitations, we propose an approach that relies on a hardware/software co-design solution for controlling the trace acquisition process. Extending and generalizing the work in [427], we propose a three-step SCA trace collection process. For this process to be possible, the control loop is not executed on a PC but exclusively on a microcontroller that is directly connected to the DUT. The microcontroller can be an ASIC (hard-core) or FPGA based (softcore) depending on the SCA trace collection board at hand. Using software that is executable on the microcontroller we gain the flexibility of a software control loop solution. Using the microprocessor that is directly connected (through a bus interface) to the DUT we gain very high control loop speed, which is not achievable using PC-based control loops. More information on such an architecture can be found in the use case example presented below.

In the first step of the proposed control trace collection process, denoted as the design phase, the evaluator can describe in a programming or scripting language (e.g., C, Python, JavaScript), using some developed Application Program Interface (API), the SCA trace acquisition experiment that needs to be performed. The experiment includes inputs that need to be provided to the DUT, specification of the security/cryptography operations that need to be executed, the execution sequence, the delay between experiment executions (in case the experiment needs to be executed more than once) and DUT output storage. The goal of the design phase is to fully specify the inputs, parameters and execution sequences of the experiment. The outcome of this phase is an executable file that can be transmitted to the microcontroller bootloader for execution.

The second step of the proposed control trace collection process, denoted as the execution phase, is focused on the execution of the designed experiment. This phase does not include any non-trivial transmission delays between the control loop entity (i.e., the microcontroller) and the DUT, since the bus connecting them is extremely fast, in contrast to the PC-based control loop where such transmission is done serially. During execution, the microcontroller control loop is responsible for transmitting the appropriate signals to the DUT so as to execute one or multiple times a security/cryptography operation as well as to generate appropriate trigger signals for trace collection by a DSO.

In the final step of the proposed control trace collection process, denoted as the trace processing phase, the execution of the experiment has been concluded and the experiment traces have been collected by the DSO. In this phase, post-collection operations are performed on the collected traces, like averaging and alignment but also operations related to the specificities of a particular experiment. This phase is performed on the DSO or on a PC with an appropriate digital signal processing toolbox, and it can be slow (depending on the post-collection operations that are executed). However, the performance delay is considerably smaller than when a PC is included in the control loop during an experiment.

9.4   A Use Case of a Flexible and Fast Platform for DUT SCA Evaluation

To showcase the applicability and effectiveness of the above-proposed three-step trace collection architecture and mechanism in action, we focus on the Flexible Leakage Collection (FlexLeco) project, which was recently published in [427]. the FlexLeco project was designed to match the latest trace collection challenges and to introduce a unified mechanism for applying various trace collection scenarios. It provides an architecture that tries to blend the reconfigurability of Software Control loops with the speed of Hardware Control loops. Taking advantage of the latest trace collection boards that utilize schemes with two FPGAs (one acting as the Control Unit and the other as the Device Under Test), the project created two generic hardware interfaces that enable fast communication between the two FPGAs, and managed to include an embedded softcore processor inside the Control FPGA, which is in charge of the Control Loop during the execution of trace collection scenarios. The project is currently instantiated on the boards of the Sakura/Sasebo project (Sakura-X and Sakura-G), but it can be modified to fit any board that adopts the approach of two distinct, hardware-isolated FPGA chips.

The FlexLeco architecture of Fig. 9.1, consists of two generic interfaces and an embedded softcore processor. Inside the Cryptographic FPGA a generic crypto-graphic interface is implemented for the communication of the Control Unit with the DUT. This interface contains two variable memory spaces (called "Hyperegisters") that handle the inputs and outputs of the DUT.

Inside the control FPGA exists a generic control interface that is directly connected with the embedded microprocessor (a Xilinx Microblaze for the Spartan-

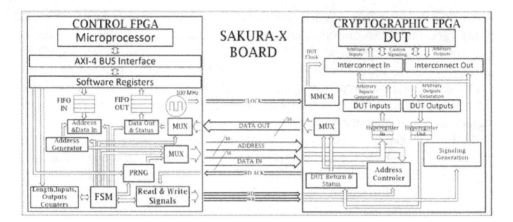

Fig. 9.1 General architecture

6 Control FPGA of the Sakura-X board), residing in the same FPGA. With this approach, the softcore microprocessor undertakes the duty of control and communication with the Cryptographic FPGA, through a hardware Finite State Machine implemented inside the control interface, which utilizes a custom hardware protocol between the two FPGAs. Data inputs to the DUT can be provided by the softcore processor, as well as from a hardware Pseudo Random Generator (PRNG) module (to support TVLA leakage assessment scenarios). The communication between the two FPGAs is performed using a 16-bit address bus, a 16-bit data bus for sending data to the crypto side and a 16-bit data bus for receiving data from the Cryptographic FPGA side.

The use of an embedded system design inside the control FPGA provides support for the proposed three-step trace collection approach thus allowing the execution of a software API on the microprocessor for the realization of the trace collection control loop. This API consists of reusable code functions that fit multiple trace collection scenarios and DUTs. Through these functions the control FPGA remains unchanged (no need for redesign or reprogram), regardless of the DUT inside the cryptographic FPGA, as it can be quickly reconfigured only by passing certain values to software registers inside the control interface. By setting code values to these registers, the control interface's Finite State Machine is ready to serve any updated cryptographic component inside the cryptographic FPGA. In this way, the control component can be permanently be downloaded inside the control FPGA's flash memory, thus negating the inflexibility issues that other hardware control loops present in their adaptability to different DUTs and scenarios.

The above-mentioned software API provides functions that, beside the initialization of the control loop, set up the leakage trace collection parameters (inputs/outputs number, bit-length, randomness), trigger encryption/decryption, send or receive plaintext/ciphertext values to FIFOs, and register and randomize input values.[1] By doing so, the attacker/evaluator can use the API functions to create any SCA or leakage assessment scenario to be executed inside the softcore microprocessor, omitting the slow, PC-based software control loops. In that sense, the FlexLeco solution fully supports and favors the design phase of the proposed trace collection approach of this chapter and provides to an SCA evaluator all the tools required to design diverse and complex SCA evaluation experiments.

The cryptographic interface on the cryptography FPGA side is primarily designed for testing specific security/cryptography hardware implementations. It is an open source HDL (Hardware Design Language) design that can be adapted to the DUT's cryptographic algorithm specifications during design time. By simply assigning appropriate values for five HDL generic parameters, the number of inputs, outputs and their bit length is adjusted to that of the DUT's algorithm. The generic interface is synthesized and downloaded whenever a new hardware implemented cryptography algorithm is tested.

Inside the cryptographic interface, a Digital Clock Manager has been included that provides different clock frequencies to the DUT and the interface. The frequency of the interface is the same as that of the other one inside the control FPGA, while the frequency of the DUT can be clocked as high as the component's critical path and the FPGA chip's functional specifications allow (or as low as the attacker/evaluator desires). By raising the frequency of the DUT, the evaluator is now able to use DSOs with low memory size buffers, thus fitting more traces on the time interval the DSO offers (as long as the DSO's sampling frequency allows it). The DCM's output frequencies update is a straightforward process done by changing a single parameter during the cryptographic FPGA's synthesis phase.

Presenting such flexibility and scalability, the FlexLeCo mechanism allows the evaluator to perform various trace collection scenarios like a Single-Encryption, a Single-Encryption with Rapid Block Mode (if an oscilloscope with such a feature is available) and a Multi-encryption mode [427], for different DUTs and with minimum overhead between the mode updates.

During any trace-collection scenario (Fig. 9.1), at design phase, the softcore microprocessor is set up so as to initiate communication transactions with the cryptographic FPGA, in which it either reads and sends the contents of the corresponding test vector records (i.e., plaintexts) or signals a random value generation (using an API function or the hardware PRNG) and transmits it to the DUT. We can design an experiment where this procedure continues until all of the test vectors on the microprocessor's memory have been sent to the cryptographic device (DUT) or until the needed number of random inputs is reached. After the design phase, the actual experiment is executed in the softcore microprocessor and post-collection operations may be performed. As an example of such postcollection operations, we showcase the Multi-encryption scenario, detailed in [427], which is enabled in the FlexLeco project in case an RBM (Rapid Block Mode) Digital

---

[1]Both software- and hardware-based randomization is supported through the PRNG module.

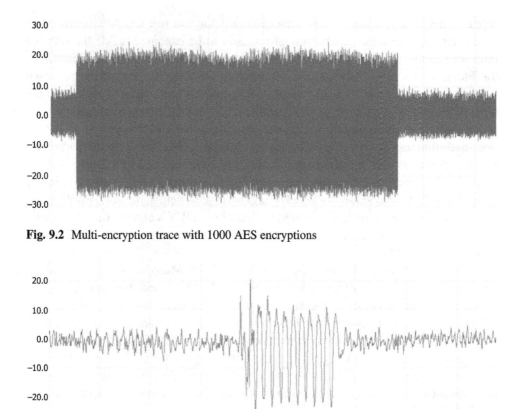

Fig. 9.2 Multi-encryption trace with 1000 AES encryptions

Fig. 9.3 Post-collection extraction outcome as a single AES leakage trace

Signal Oscilloscope is not available to the evaluator. During this scenario, the DSO starts capturing a continuous waveform (Fig. 9.2) of leakage traces starting from the first de/encryption and continuing for all de/encryptions until the end of the DSO's chosen time window. By setting up the appropriate time window, after execution phase, we capture a single continuous waveform that should contain the leakage traces of all the cryptographic processes we have instructed the DUT to execute. The split of this continuous multi-encryption waveform into individual single de/encryption traces is done during the trace processing phase. The outcome single encryption trace from this post-collection operation can be seen in Fig. 9.3. The whole process is considerably faster than if we tried to capture each de/encryption trace autonomously during the execution phase [427].

To qualitatively compare the proposed three-step trace collection approach of Sect. 9.3.1 as was realized using the FlexLeco project, we present Table 9.1 where our approach is compared with recent open source trace collection projects in terms of flexibility, usability and various post-collection feature supports. The presented results are collected from actual experimentation of the authors with the compared

Table 9.1 Leakage trace collection architectures qualitative features comparisons

Collection setup	Flexibility	Single encr.	Multi-encr.	Averaging	Ease-of use	Clock control
FlexLeco three step approach	High	Yes	Yes	Yes	High	5–230 MHz
Sakura/Sasebo [353]	No	Yes	No	No	None	No
ChipWhisperer [451]	Moderate[b]	Yes	Partial[c]	Yes	Moderate [b]	5–160 MHz
FOBOS [565]	No	Yes	No	No	Minimum[a]	Max. 50 MHz

[a] Hardware interfaces are unique for each cryptography DUT
[b] Hard to implement software control loop and tedious, time-consuming interfacing of different cryptographic DUTs
[c] Multi-encryption only with constant or random plaintexts

projects or from personal communication with the projects' developers. The table indicates that the three-step approach is flexible enough to rival existing and well-established solutions offered to the SCA community by Sakura and ChipWhisperer.

9.5 Conclusions

In this book chapter we focused on an important aspect of SCA analysis, evaluation and leakage assessment, which is the efficient and easy collection of needed SCA traces. We presented the traditional mechanism for collecting traces from DUT ubiquitous devices and commented on the drawbacks of this approach. After briefly describing dominant SCA attack categories and leakage assessment methodologies in view of their needed number of traces, considering also the high level of trace noise and possible misalignments that are ever present in ubiquitous devices, we concluded that the traditional model is not practically useful for ubiquitous systems SCA evaluation. To further explore the recent SCA trace collection and analysis landscape, we described the most prominent open source and commercial toolsets, both research and commercial. Most have shortcomings in terms of controlling in a flexible and easy manner the DUT to be SCA evaluated, thus giving us the motivation to propose a three-step trace collection methodology using a design, an execution, and a trace processing phase. To validate the applicability, efficiency, and ease-of-use of this proposed approach, we applied it to the FlexLeco project open source solution, which is highly compatible with our proposal. Using this use case we managed to easily design experiments and collect results even when we applied complex design scenarios, like the multi-encryption mode where multiple inputs are provided on the DUT, multiple traces are collected as one, and the actual single traces (that are usable for SCA evaluation or leakage assessment) are extracted after postprocessing. To conclude, the evaluation of our proposal and the exploration of the recent toolset landscape indicate that there is a need for a different model for trace collection. In this model, the trace collection DUT control functionality is migrated close to the DUT (on a device physically connected to the DUT) and not on a remote control entity (like a PC).

10

Random Number Generators: Testing and Certification

Darren Hurley-Smith and Julio Hernandez-Castro

Abstract This chapter focuses on the testing and certification of Random Number Generators (RNG). Statistical testing is required to identify whether sequences produced by RNG demonstrate non-random characteristics. These can include structures within their output, repetition of sequences, and any other form of predictability. Certification of computer security systems draws on such evaluations to determine whether a given RNG implementation contributes to a secure, robust security system. Recently, small-scale hardware RNGs have been targeted at IoT devices, especially those requiring security. This, however, introduces new technical challenges; low computational resources for post-processing and evaluation of on-board RNGs being just two examples. Can we rely on the current suite of statistical tests? What other challenges are encountered when evaluating RNG?

10.1 Introduction

Randomly generated values are sought after for a variety of applications, in which they are often vital. Cryptographic systems require random values to ensure that generated keys are unpredictable, making brute force attacks against those keys unfeasible. Even in the entertainment industry, there is a demand for randomness: lotteries and games both rely on random number generation to guarantee the fairness of the game in question.

However, random number generation is a non-trivial task. Deterministic Random Number Generators (DRNG), also known as Pseudo-Random Number Generators (PRNG), are incapable of truly random output [514]. PRNG achieve an *appropriate degree of randomness* by using an initial seed value to populate a proportionally far longer sequence of apparently random output. This form of random number generation is only unpredictable if the seed value remains unknown. To this end,

D. Hurley-Smith (✉) · J. Hernandez-Castro
University of Kent, Canterbury, UK
e-mail: darren.hurley-smith@rhul.ac.uk

most PRNG algorithms are periodically re-seeded from a natural source of entropy. The primary benefit of PRNGs is that they are usually extremely fast, especially when compared to the natural entropy sources used to seed them. This makes them highly attractive for use in computer systems, and in applications requiring high-volume RNG.

Physical sources of entropy can provide what is referred to as *true randomness*. True Random Number Generators (TRNG) use a broad array of different entropy sources as their key component but share several common characteristics. They do not require seeding to generate randomness and use a natural phenomenon as their entropy source. TRNGs can be classified further, as classical or Quantum Random Number Generators (QRNGs). To simplify matters, TRNG will refer to classical methods, and QRNG will refer to quantum methods from this point. TRNG utilize microscopic phenomena that generate statistically random noise signals. The photoelectric effect and thermal noise are two examples of classical entropy sources. QRNG operate on similar principles but instead make use of quantum phenomena. These include photon-counting, using a beam-splitter, or the observation of quantum shot-noise in MOS/CMOS devices.

All random number generators can be evaluated using statistical test batteries. Dieharder, Federal Information Processing Standard (FIPS) 140-1/2, and National Institute of Standards and Technology (NIST) SP800-22 [448] represent the three most common test batteries used for professional testing of random number generators. Manufacturers often use such tests to demonstrate the correct functioning of their products, but they are also used by third-parties to independently verify the randomness of a device. NIST and Common Criteria [407] provide guidelines and tests that have been independently developed to ascertain whether an RNG is non-random. These tests evaluate RNGs by identifying whether there is any observable bias, structure or predictability in an RNG's output. It is not possible to identify randomness, but non-randomness can be detected. Certification schemes make use of such tests to publicly acknowledge the robustness of computational security systems. Specific methodologies have been devised to guide and ensure the quality of these evaluations in the area of RNG validation.

Significant trust is placed in statistical testing to determine whether an RNG provides sufficiently random output. The aim of this chapter is to demonstrate that the challenges of statistical testing of randomness are far from solved. We evaluate a selection of contemporary TRNG to highlight issues in data collection, test correlation and the overuse of older test batteries to the exclusion of newer tests. As minuscule, integrated TRNG become more prolific through their use in Internet of Things (IoT) products, these considerations become all the more important.

The following sections discuss, in order: certification of RNGs and the standards/testing procedures that apply, the challenges faced during the collection of data from RNGs, and two sets of experimental results demonstrating issues in the appropriate selection of statistical tests for RNG evaluation.

10.2 Certification, Standards, and Testing

Many companies employ their own testing teams, to whom the responsibility of carrying out company mandated quality control falls. ID Quantique (IDQ) and NXP are two examples, both of whom perform varying degrees of testing on their products. In the case of products implementing cryptography, RNG testing is vital for the validation of the cryptosystem in question. However, in-house testing is insufficient for certification, with the exception of self-certification (as performed by IDQ). Testing must be performed by a third-party to ensure impartiality.

NIST is one example of a standards and testing institution. This US institute concerns itself with the advancement of measurement science, standards and technology. This body does not conduct testing or reward certificates itself but is responsible for the publication and impartial development of statistical test suites for randomness tests. Special Publications (SP) are created to circulate accepted developments in the field of RNG testing and formal verification of RNG. Of particular note are SP800-90B [449] and SP800-22 [448]. SP800-90B details specific tests for the entropy source and final outputs of PRNG and TRNG. SP800-22 details an extensive test battery suitable for use over PRNG and TRNG (including QRNG by association with TRNG).

Common Criteria (CC) is an international standard (ISO/IEC 15408). Unlike the NIST SP documents discussed previously, CC is a broad framework for the verification of computer security systems [407]. Functionality, construction, and assurance requirements are the core tenets of the CC. It is important to emphasize that this is a whole-system-security verification: RNG testing is only part of a larger verification process. However, it can be argued that RNG validation is a keystone for the certification of a computer-based security system. If the RNG is incapable of providing the appropriate output, then it is unlikely that the security system will be robust to the degree demanded by the CC.

To differentiate between different applications and their security requirements, the CC has developed the Evaluation Assurance Level (EAL) scheme. These numbered levels, from 1 to 7, reflect an increasing security requirement. At level 1, testing is cursory and reports provided by manufacturers are acceptable. As higher certifications are sought, more third party and design-stage tests by third parties are required. At levels 5+, spot checks of manufacturing plants and implementation of security critical systems are performed. NXP produces two CC EAL certified devices: the DESFire EV1 (EAL4+), and the DESFire EV2 (EAL5+).

The test methodology employed by the CC when testing RNGs is outlined in AIS-31 [327]. AIS-31 outlines the test methodology for entropy sources in computer-based security systems [327]. AIS-20 is referred to as the source of information for recommended tests and parameters for TRNG evaluation. Both documents have a TRNG focus, as they are aimed at the evaluation of the formal verification of entropy sources, not the PRNG algorithms that they may seed. As a result, hardware RNGs are the focus of these documents.

Table 10.1 Standards applied in the testing of selected RNGs

Manufacturer	Device	Cost €	Entropy source	Certifications/tests
NXP	DESFire EV1	0.59	Not disclosed	CC EAL4+
NXP	DESFire EV2	1.25	Not disclosed	CC EAL5+
IDQ	Quantis 16M	2900	Beam splitter	NIST SP800-22, METAS, CTL
IDQ	Quantis 4M	1299	Beam splitter	NIST SP800-22, METAS, CTL
IDQ	Quantis USB 4M	990	Beam splitter	NIST SP800-22, METAS, CTL
Comscire	PQ32MU	1211	Shot noise	NIST SP800-90B/C
				NIST SP800-22
				Diehard
Altus Metrum	ChaosKey	45	RBSJ[a]	FIPS 140-2

[a]Reverse biased semiconductor junction

Table 10.1 shows a selection of RNGs and their associated certifications. CC EAL, METAS, CTL, and FIPS 140-2 are applicable as certifications from their respective institutions. NIST SP800-22 indicates that the NIST methodology and test battery were applied when testing the RNG in question (whether internally or externally). Any RNG testing process requires a set of statistical tests. One of the earliest examples of a statistical test battery for randomness is Marsaglia's Diehard battery [393]. NIST SP800-22 provides a more expansive series of tests developed by Rukhin et al. [508]. The NIST battery contains 15 tests, which are evaluated in terms of uniformity and proportion of p-values for each test. There has been some criticism of the accuracy of these results. Marton and Suciu observed that false alarms were common and that more tests that SP800-22 suggests can be failed by otherwise robust RNGs [396]. NIST itself states that any failure is cause for further investigation, but does not suggest any specific follow up procedures for RNG testing. It is implied that further data collection and testing a larger number of target devices are initial approaches to the problem.

Dieharder is an extension of Diehard, integrating the SP800-22 tests and the original Diehard tests [116]. This brings the battery up to a total of 30 tests, with 76 variant tests in total. This battery requires a much larger body of test data than its predecessors. To test a stream of data with no rewinds with every test in the suite, one must collect 228 GB of data. This is far beyond the recommended parameters suggested by NIST and CC. A 4 GB sample would rewind 57 times under the same test conditions. If a sequence of repeats during a single execution of a given test, type-1 errors may be introduced. The test may report such repetition as a violation of its definition of randomness, and identify the sequence as non-random, when in fact it was just insufficiently large. This highlights the importance of appropriate data collection.

TestU01, developed by L'Ecuyer and Simard, is more of an RNG developer's toolbox than test battery [362]. However, it incorporates 5 different test batteries: Alphabits, Rabbit, Small Crush, Crush, and Big Crush. Each battery has a differing number of tests. Alphabits and Rabbit operate over bits, whilst the Crush batteries operate over floating point numbers between 0 and 1. Alphabits, Rabbit, and Small Crush complete in minutes over samples of 2 GB in size. Big Crush requires a large amount of data (or a constant stream of input from the target device) and can take hours to complete. McCullough et al. identify some potential issues with this toolset. Some tests are only able to read 32 bits and are more sensitive to errors in their most significant bits than their least significant bits [403]. To resolve this, they suggest that tests are performed over the sequences forwards and backwards. The issue here is that a test on live data cannot be performed in this manner. This limits many tests and prevents them from being used as live tests.

Another class of tests exists; continuous tests. These tests are designed to identify whether there have been hardware failures that lead to corruption or cessation of the entropy stream. FIPS 140-1/2 are designed with hardware in mind [121]. Both tests suites can be implemented in the circuitry of an RNG, providing a constant series of results regarding the health and functionality of the device. A core requirement of any continuous test is that no RNG should output two identical N bit blocks in succession. If this condition is not met, the device should cease function immediately and alert the user that it is not performing as expected. However, this does not detect more subtle flaws. The astute reader may also have deduced that requiring that no two N bit blocks be identical actually results in reduced entropy. This has an impact on the legitimacy of such tests when considering that the definition of an ideal RNG is one that is completely unpredictable. These tests are likely to be implemented alongside IoT TRNG implementations due to their efficient implementation in hardware, carrying the previous concerns to millions of potential devices.

The usage of NIST, Dieharder, TestU01, and other statistical test batteries can vary between institutions. NIST SP800-22 outlines minimum sample sizes and Dieharder implies these by rewinding samples if insufficient data is provided. However, during self-certification, some companies have been found to test small samples, below the suggested guidelines. This can cast doubt over the validity of their findings.

10.3 Challenges in Data Collection

For standalone RNG, data collection may be simple. However, there are no official certifications for standalone RNG. FIPS and CC both certify whole security systems, not individual elements, so even though RNG testing is key to this process, a standalone RNG that passes these tests still cannot be certified. Regardless, RNG testing as a part of whole system certification is a critical consideration. Data collection from certain integrated RNGs may not be trivial. As IoT devices represent a whole-system security implementation, they may be certified; RNG evaluation forms a critical part of any such evaluation process.

Black-box design is often employed by companies using licensed technology, or who need to protect their Intellectual Property (IP). This means that schematics of their security implementation, including RNG, may not be publicly accessible. For lower EAL awards, such obfuscation of technical detail may extend to inspectors and CC officials. At higher levels, non-disclosure agreements are required as a part of the certification contract between the petitioning company and the evaluating body. Such arrangements are expensive. Inspectors and independent testers have to be compensated for their times and the cost falls to the company requesting an evaluation at a given EAL. As a result, self-certification is common.

The speed with which an RNG may be read depends on a great many factors. In situations where the RNG is fully integrated, there may be additional overheads such as post-processing, use of a PRNG to *clean* TRNG output used as an entropy source, or simply a hard limit on output size and speed. A poignant example of this is the DESFire EV1 and EV2. These RFID cards do not directly expose their internal TRNG to the user, requiring that the user extracts random numbers using the authentication protocol instead. This protocol requires that both the card and reader exchange random values as part of their authentication handshake [289]. The 16 bytes values transmitted by the card can be collected and stored in a file for analysis using statistical tests for randomness [288]. This is a time-consuming procedure, as Table 10.2 shows. To collect 64 MB of data from the DESFire cards, approximately 12 days were required. The primary bottleneck in this process was the need to complete the authentication protocol before a second handshake could be initiated to gather additional 16-byte sequences. Attempting to terminate the protocol by switching off the reader, thus resetting the card, proved to be even more time-intensive [288]. This issue is shared by IoT devices, many of which implement integrated TRNGs.

IoT devices have a plethora of ways in which PRNG and TRNG may be implemented. The FRDM K64F board implements a TRNG, though the output is limited to making calls internally for use, or outputting values over an I/O pin in the form of unsigned integers. Though significantly faster than the EV1 and EV2, this is still much slower than most standalone TRNGs. The Red Bear Duo does not implement a local entropy source. An on-board PRNG must be supplied with off-device entropy, with no checks or continuous tests performed on-device. In a full-system implementation, such a device can make it difficult to identify where the flaw in its RNG occurs.

Table 10.2 RNG output speed of selected devices

	Sample size (MB)	Mean data rate (bit/s)
DESFire EV1	64	$4.93 \cdot 10^2$
DESFire EV2	64	$4.90 \cdot 10^2$
Quantis 16M	2100	$1.27 \cdot 10^8$
Quantis 4M	2100	$3.08 \cdot 10^7$
Quantis USB 4M	2100	$3.11 \cdot 10^7$
Comscire PQ32MU	2100	$2.48 \cdot 10^8$
ChaosKey	2100	$3.07 \cdot 10^7$

The standalone generators (Quantis, Comscire and ChaosKey entries in Table 10.2) are substantially faster, making data collection trivial by comparison. However, this does not mean that samples of appropriate size were tested.

SP800-90B states that an entropy source must provide 1,000,000 bits of sequential output for testing [449]. Concatenation of smaller sequences is tolerable if contiguous output to that size is not possible, but is undesirable. 1000 such sequences must be concatenated, according to NIST guidelines. SP800-22 extends these requirements by recommending that 100 samples of the aforementioned size are tested to validate the results [508]. AIS-31 and AIS-20 do not stipulate minimum sample sizes. John Walker states that, in their default configuration, the Diehard tests should be run over at least 100 MB of data [568].

With this in mind, the test reports of several TRNG manufacturers can be more thoroughly analyzed. IDQ states that their Quantis devices pass the Diehard and NISTSP800-22 batteries with no failure.[1] SP800-22 tests were conducted over 1000 samples of 1,000,000 bits in length. A significance level of 1% was maintained throughout this process. Diehard was used over a single sample of $1 \cdot 10^9$ bits. Our own tests confirm that IDQ's report of no failures is true, even for larger samples (ours were 2.1 GB in size). In this case, IDQ is a good example of a test protocol that is in line with the recommendations of test developers.

Comscire's PQ32MU, a QRNG that uses shot-noise as an entropy source, is a different story. Their NIST-Diehard report[2] shows that the number of tests has been reduced. The reduced sample size is one issue, but reducing the number of tests can result in the loss of certain capabilities. Unless the removed tests are wholly redundant, it is likely that their removal will impact the capability of the battery to detect certain types of non-randomness. The insufficient sample size is cited as the reason for excluding those tests. Comscire only tests this QRNG using 2 samples; one of $8 \cdot 10^7$ bits and another of $1 \cdot 10^6$ bits. This is drastically below the suggested sample size for Diehard. Even though these samples meet the requirements of NIST SP800-90B in the most basic sense, they still fall short of SP800-22's additional recommendations requiring the testing of at least 100 samples. Considering the ease with which samples can be generated from standalone RNGs such as these, it is surprising that a more robust test process is not used.

10.4 Appropriate Selection of Tests

The correlation between tests in a battery, and as a whole if the evaluation methodology involves multiple test batteries, must be considered. Statistical tests have a limited range of issues that they are able to identify in the target RNG. Test

---

[1]https://marketing.idquantique.com/acton/attachment/11868/f-004c/1/-/-/-/-/Randomness%20Test%20Report.pdf.

[2]https://comscire.com/files/cert/comscire-pq32mu-nist_diehard-validation-tests.pdf.

```
Entropy = 4.385614 bits per byte.

Optimum compression would reduce the size
of this 20180 byte file by 45 percent.

Chi square distribution for 20180 samples is 1266758.61, and randomly
would exceed this value less than 0.01 percent of the times.

Arithmetic mean value of data bytes is 56.5619 (127.5 = random).
Monte Carlo value for Pi is 3.611061552 (error 14.94 percent).
Serial correlation coefficient is 0.568671 (totally uncorrelated = 0.0).
```

Fig. 10.1 Example of Ent default output in byte mode [272]

batteries are intended to mitigate this issue by providing many statistical tests that evaluate different aspects of the target RNG, providing a broader analysis.

Hernandez-Castro et al. identify a degree of correlation between tests in the Ent battery. The Ent battery is a simple set of tests included in most Linux distributions as a simple statistical testing tool [568]. Ent includes tests for estimated entropy, compression, χ^2, arithmetic mean, Monte Carlo π, and serial correlation. Bit and byte level tests can be run over target sequences. Figure 10.1 shows the output of the Ubuntu 16.04 Ent utility in byte mode.

By degenerating an initially random sequence using a genetic algorithm, Hernandez-Castro et al. were able to observe the test results of Ent as the sequence slowly became more ordered and predictable [272]. The results demonstrate that many of the Ent tests have a degree of correlation. Entropy and compression tests analyze the same general attributes, both performing linear transformation and ceiling operations on a sequence. The χ^2 and excess statistics provided by the χ^2 test are also closely correlated. The conclusion of the paper recommends that the excess and compression statistics should be discarded.

Soto et al. explore the degree of correlation between tests in the NIST SP800-22 battery. Their work finds that the range of attributes evaluated by SP800-22 may be insufficient to recognize issues [538]. TRNG and QRNG are particular issues, as many examples of these RNGs have been developed since the development of SP800-22. Soto describes the independence of tests in this battery as an open problem.

Turan et al. provide a more recent analysis of SP800-22. Their work finds that the frequency, overlapping template (input template 111), longest run of ones, random walk height, and maximum order complexity tests produce correlated statistics [560]. This issue is most evident when using small samples or block sizes. Georgescu et al. build on Turan's work, identifying and examining the open problems in SP800-22 test correlation. The sample size is found to have a significant effect on the correlations between tests. The correlations identified by Turan et al. are confirmed, and their relationship with sample size explored in greater depth [226]. Such results demonstrate that every element of an RNG test methodology must be carefully examined to ensure a meaningful and unbiased result. Georgescu et al. conclude by stating that better tests than those implemented in SP800-22 may exist, as that battery is now quite old.

Researchers have commented on the ambiguity of SP800-22's hypothesis and statistical output, stating that more descriptive test output is required. Zhu et al. propose a *Q-value*, computed using test statistics prior to their consolidation to *p*-values [601]. The proposed statistic is more sensitive to total variation distance and Kullback-Leiber divergence. This overcomes some of the issues caused by correlations between the non-χ^2 level 2 tests of SP800-22 [601].

Dieharder implements many of the SP800-22 tests. As a result, it shares many of the criticisms levelled at SP800-22 [206]. TestU01 is a more recent battery aimed at allowing researchers to develop and evaluate their own RNGs, especially TRNGs. There is little critical literature regarding this battery at present, so the independence of tests in TestU01 is an open question at this time. Turan et al. comment on the presence of some tests that they have found to be correlated being implemented in the Crush batteries of TestU01 [560].

The diversity of a test methodology is related to, but separate from, the independence of tests. Where independence is a measure of how related the results from a set of tests may be, diversity is a measure of how many methods of evaluation are used in the analysis of an RNG. A common observation is that the isolated use of *p*-values is insufficient to fully characterize the randomness (or lack thereof) of a sequence. Research by Hurley-Smith et al. explores TRNG and QRNG in detail to identify flaws that were not detected by the most commonly used test batteries. In these analyses, test correlation and diversity are key topics.

10.4.1 Randomness Testing Under Data Collection Constraints: Analyzing the DESFire EV1

The first of these in-depth analyses was conducted over the Mifare DESFire EV1, an RFID card produced by NXP [379]. The DESFire EV1 is used as a part of the Transport for London (TfL) Oyster card scheme, as well as other loyalty and e-wallet schemes throughout Europe. As a device that can store cash value, it requires robust security to foster trust among vendors and users. The EV1 has achieved an EAL4+ certification, based on its full security implementation.

Table 10.3 shows the Dieharder results for 3 DESFire EV1 cards. As mentioned previously, data collection from the EV1 is challenging, requiring 12 days to obtain 64 MB of data. As a result, this was the largest amount of data able to be collected. A total of 100 cards were tested, with all 100 passing. The 3 cards shown in this table show the *p*-values reported by the Dieharder tests for all tests that can be performed on 64 MB of data without rewinds.

Card 3 shows a single failure of the Dieharder battery, for the count the ones test. However, this was not reproduced by any other card that was tested. Therefore, it is reasonable to conclude that the Dieharder battery does not identify any significant degree of non-randomness in the tested sequences.

Table 10.4 shows the pass rates for NIST tests. All SP800-22 tests were used over the EV1 samples we collected.

Table 10.3 Dieharder results [289]

Test	Card 1	Card 2	Card 3
Birthday spacings	0.18194520	0.61105583	0.78263630
Overlapping permutations	0.38044164	0.58693289	0.44201308
32×32 Binary rank	0.42920693	0.23409500	0.55699838
6×8 Binary rank	0.31311490	0.32387215	0.66137580
Bitstream	0.97724174	0.18743536	0.59532464
Count the 1's (stream)	0.17108396	0.74984724	0.87214241
Count the 1's (byte)	0.65870385	0.01287807	**0.00020194**
Parking lot	0.18078043	0.24200626	0.38128677
Minimum distance (2d sphere)	0.76328000	0.95091635	0.34980807
3d sphere (minimum distance)	0.23871272	0.20826216	0.39340851
Squeeze	0.62598919	0.08843989	0.77057749
Runs	0.99778832	0.62043244	0.90550208
	0.44719093	0.91228597	0.04870531
Craps	0.54077256	0.92769962	0.91803037
	0.57614807	0.94245583	0.95209393

The bold values indicate those tests which fail, but such a degree that they are well outside the bounds of confidence established by NIST (or in the case of Ent, our extrapolation of the NIST SP800-22 confidence bound of $a = 0.01$)

Table 10.4 NIST SP800-22 results [289]

Test	Card 1	Card 2	Card 3
Frequency	198/200	200/200	197/200
Block frequency	196/200	199/200	194/200
Cumulative sums	2/2	2/2	2/2
Longest run	196/200	198/200	198/200
Rank	198/200	199/200	197/200
FFT	197/200	199/200	198/200
Non-overlapping template	**147/148**	148/148	148/148
Overlapping template	198/200	198/200	198/200
Universal	198/200	198/200	198/200
Approximate entropy	197/200	198/200	196/200
Random excursions	8/8	8/8	8/8
Random excursions variant	18/18	18/18	18/18
Serial	2/2	2/2	2/2
Linear complexity	199/200	197/200	199/200

The bold values indicate those tests which fail, but such a degree that they are well outside the bounds of confidence established by NIST (or in the case of Ent, our extrapolation of the NIST SP800-22 confidence bound of $a = 0.01$)

Cards 1 and 3 both show some borderline results, notably in the Runs and Non-overlapping template tests. However, the majority of cards (98 of 100) passed this battery. This was a cause for concern: any failure is a cause for further investigation as stated by SP800-90B. As a result, further analysis was deemed necessary, and the

Table 10.5 Mifare DESFire EV1 ENT results for 64 MB of TRNG output [289]

	Card 1	Card 2	Card 3	Optimal
Entropy	7.999969	7.999989	7.999972	8
Optimal compress.	0	0	0	0
χ^2	**2709.10**	**973.07**	**2470.32**	256
Arith. mean	127.492921	127.500582	127.5006	127.5
Monte Carlo π est.	3.14167	3.142019	3.141909	3.14159
S. correlation	0.000008	0.000045	0.000093	0.0

The bold values indicate those tests which fail, but such a degree that they are well outside the bounds of confidence established by NIST (or in the case of Ent, our extrapolation of the NIST SP800-22 confidence bound of $a = 0.01$)

humble ENT battery was used as a starting point for a more generalized approach to our EV1 TRNG evaluation.

Considering Hernandez-Castro et al.'s work on the independent of Ent tests, the compression and excess statistics should be discarded. However, the full results of the Ent battery over 3 EV1 cards are shown in Table 10.5 for the sake of completeness.

All tests are passed, with the exception of the χ^2 test. For the 3 64-MB samples shown in Table 10.5, the χ^2 statistic is exceptionally poor. By comparison, a sequence that passes this test should have a χ^2 statistic of between 220 and 305. Even at a sample size of 1 MB, 100 DESFire EV1 cards failed this test. These results show that the values in the tested sequences are not uniformly distributed: there is a bias towards some byte values and away from others. Considering that the χ^2 test is such a trivial (and widely used) test of the distribution of values in a sequence, it is surprising that it would highlight issues in the output of the EV1's TRNG while Dieharder and NIST SP800-22 do not.

Non-uniform distribution of bytes is not an automatic indicator of non-randomness. It is not a good indicator of randomness, but it is also possible for a true source of randomness to produce a slightly biased sequence. However, as per the guidelines of AIS-20 and SP800-90B, a TRNG should provide an output that is functionally equivalent to that of a cryptographic PRNG. As a result, non-uniform byte distribution is a concern. The fact that there is bias is an important observation, but more important is the analysis of that bias.

Figure 10.2 provides a deeper examination of how bias is expressed by the TRNG output of 100 DESFire EV1 cards. Figure 10.2a shows the mean bias of 100 1-MB samples. The extreme deviation from the expected distribution of values is apparent in the square-wave of the plot. The expected distribution should result in a noisy, relatively evenly distributed set of byte values. A bias in the order of 10^{-5} is observed, with an almost evenly distributed bias among values that are deviated above or below the normal. To be precise, 127 values are biased above the normal, and 129 are biased below the normal.

Figure 10.2b refines the observations of the previous graph. Fourier approximation of the bias reveals that the distribution of byte values has a period (w) of

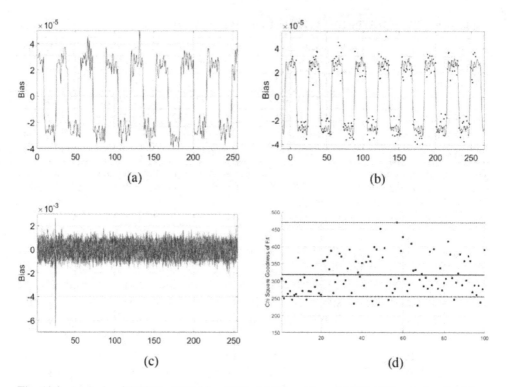

Fig. 10.2 Analysis of DESFire EV1 bias [289]. (**a**) Mean bias of 100 1-MB samples. (**b**) Mean Fourier approx. of 1 MB samples. (**c**) Mask test results. (**d**) χ^2 scores for 100 1-MB samples

-31.9918. This results in 8 oscillations throughout the 256 possible byte values, with a shift across the normal, observed every 32 values (approximately). Statistical analysis of the possible distribution of bits within these byte values shows that the under-occurrence of a specific bit-sequence can result in this very particular form of bias.

Figure 10.2c provides the results of a so-called *mask test*. The purpose of this test is to XOR each byte of a sequence with an 8-bit sequence, ranging from *0000000* through all intervening values to *11111111*. The sum of all sequences that resolve to zero after the XOR operation records the occurrence of that bit-sequence throughout a sample. This graph shows the composite of 100 1-MB sequences tested in this manner. It is immediately apparent that there's a significant deviation from the normal for mask *00011000*. For all cards, and for both 64 and 1 MB samples, this bias was observed. Following our responsible disclosure to NXP, it was suggested that this bias may be caused by an incorrectly implemented whitening-function: a function usually intended to remove bias from TRNG output.

Figure 10.2d shows the distribution of the χ^2 statistic for 100 1-MB EV1 samples. The statistics are proportionally lower than those seen for the 64 MB samples (Table 10.5). This is because sample size has a direct effect on the expression of bias within a sequence. Early experiments conducted by Hurley-Smith et al. demonstrated that the bias of the DESFire EV1 could not be observed at sample sizes smaller than 7.5 KB [288, 289]. This emphasizes the point made in Sect. 3 regarding data collection. The amount of data collected needs to meet a minimum size to reliably identify issues in the RNGs being tested. This minimum threshold is test-specific, requiring that the highest minimum sample size is identified by analysts prior to conducting an evaluation of an RNG. Furthermore, these experiments showed that even well-respected, proven statistical test batteries such as Dieharder and NIST SP800-22 were unable to identify the issue with the DESFire EV1. It is clear that it is possible to design a TRNG to pass these tests, but is it wise to rely on tests that can be designed for? Does designing to meet the finite and narrow requirements of Dieharder and NIST SP800-22 actually provide any guarantees of randomness? We argue that it does not.

10.4.2 Identifying Issues with Quantum Random Number Generators

The EV1 experiments provided an introduction to issues in using well-established statistical tests to identify non-randomness in TRNG. QRNGs are currently too large for RFID card or IoT device implementations, but miniaturization of quantum entropy sources is proceeding quickly, and proposals for IoT-scale QRNG have already been published. However, there are several open problems with the current generation of QRNGs and their evaluation.

Even when sample collection is not a problem, there can be issues. IDQ's Quantis range of QRNGs is based on an optical quantum source of entropy (a beam splitter). Comscire produces a rival product, the PQ32MU, which uses quantum shot-noise as its entropy source. Both companies provide multiple models of QRNG with varying speeds, all with appropriate statistical test results associated with their devices. As previously discussed, IDQ provides a relatively robust test report, though it is limited to Diehard and NIST SP800-22 tests. Comscire uses few and small samples, with a smaller number of tests, limiting the rigor of its test process significantly. None of the devices tested as a part of this work were validated using the AIS-31 methodology, nor were they certified (as there are no official certifications for standalone RNGs).

Data collection is not an issue from these devices, the Quantis devices provide data at a rate of 4 or 16 Mb/s, whiles the PQ32MU has an output speed of 32 Mb/s. As a result, collecting large amounts of data is trivial. A key difference in these two brands is that the Quantis generators do not implement on-board post-processing to remove bias, whilst the PQ32MU is an all-in-one product with post-processing performed on-device.

Table 10.6 shows the results for the EV1, Quantis generators and PQ32MU. Both raw and post-processed Quantis output is shown. EV1 data is tested for 64 MB samples over 100 cards. Quantis and Comscire QRNGs are tested over 100 2.1 GB

Table 10.6 Dieharder, NIST and TestU01 results

Device	Samples #	Dieharder passed	NIST SP800-22 passed	Alphabits passed	Rabbit passed	Small crush passed	Crush passed
DESFire EV1	100	100	98	0	0	–	–
Quantis 16M	100	100	100	54	60	93	47
Post 16M	100	100	100	95	87	91	82
Quantis 4M	100	100	100	3	7	91	3
Post 4M	100	100	100	91	82	93	86
Quantis USB	100	100	100	3	21	89	3
Post USB	100	100	100	90	81	97	80
Comscire PQ32MU	100	100	100	91	86	93	84

samples collected from one of each type of device. Ideally, more devices would be tested, but the cost was a limiting factor (the cheapest device, a 4M, costs €900).

All devices pass Dieharder, while all but 2 EV1's pass the SP800-22 tests. The TestU01 toolkit has been used, with 4 of its statistical test batteries used to evaluate all tested devices, including the EV1. Due to the sample size requirements of the Crush tests, EV1 data has not been tested for either Crush test. Immediately, the EV1 shows critical issues, failing the Alphabits and Rabbit batteries. The average failure rate is 1 of 4 tests for Alphabits, and 5 of 16 tests for Rabbit. This shows how the simple addition of a new test battery can instantly reveal weaknesses that the better-known batteries cannot identify.

Raw Quantis samples, especially those of the 4M and its USB variant, also perform very poorly on Alphabits and Rabbit. They also perform very poorly in Crush, but a significant number of samples pass the Small Crush tests. This could be because the Small Crush battery has many tests in common with SP800-22, leading to a correlation between the results. Post-processing cleans up many of these issues, but not completely. Most notably, Alphabits, Rabbit and Crush test results improve dramatically, with the most drastic change being the jump from 3 passed tests for the 4M under Alphabits, to 91 passes. This shows that appropriate use of a QRNG is yet another factor to consider: improper use of a device may not be identified by the more well-known test batteries and incorrect configuration can be as damaging as any other form of non-randomness. The Comscire PQ32MU performs well on most tests but struggles with the Rabbit and Crush tests.

Table 10.7 shows the results of Ent for the QRNG. DESFire results are not shown to avoid repetition. A summary of the 100 samples tested shows that Post-processed Quantis data, and the PQ32MU, passes the χ^2 and serial correlation tests with no issues. All devices pass the other tests, hence their omission from this table. However, the raw Quantis data fails the χ^2 test dramatically. Furthermore, the 4M and its USB variant perform quite poorly on the serial correlation test at the bit level. This emphasizes the need to test sequences across multiple block sizes to identify issues that may occur at lower or higher orders of output. Unlike the EV1, raw Quantis data does not provide an easily identifiable or consistent bias across

Table 10.7 ENT results

Device	Samples #	Bytes		Bits	
		χ^2 passed	Serial corr. passed	χ^2 passed	Serial corr. passed
Quantis 16M	100	10	99	0	100
Post 16M	100	100	96	100	96
Quantis 4M	100	0	99	0	49
Post 4M	100	100	99	100	100
Quantis USB	100	0	92	0	81
Post USB	100	100	94	100	100
Comscire PQ32MU	100	100	99	100	100

samples. The bias appears to drift between samples, with the only constant being a tendency to express a 10^{-6} bias above the normal for byte values 0–5. Even this is not a representative trend, with only 38% of samples showing this particular trait.

Figure 10.3 shows the χ^2 statistics for raw Quantis samples from all the 16M and 4M devices. The results for the Quantis USB are omitted, as the USB is effectively a 4M in different packaging and provides similar results.

The 16M (a) fails the χ^2 test for 90 of its samples. The mean statistic for the 16M is approximately 350. This is above the acceptable maximum threshold for this test. The 4M is significantly worse, with a mean statistic of 506. Unlike the 16M, the 4M shows no passes at all (the USB reports similar results). In fact, the minimum statistic for the 4M was 407. This is significantly above the maximum threshold for the χ^2 test.

The experiments conducted over these QRNGs show that established tests do not always identify issues that more recent (or just less well-known) tests highlight. The TestU01 battery reinforces the results of the Ent test, by providing a wider variety of more sophisticated tests that prove that there are issues beyond simple deviation from the normal distribution of values at the byte and bit level. As TestU01 is designed to provide the tools to test TRNG, this battery would ideally be made a mandatory recommendation for TRNG and QRNG testing. Dieharder and NIST SP800-22 will remain in use, as they are effective at identifying egregious issues with RNG output, but the extension of the minimum recommended number of tests is very much needed at this time. Post-processed and raw data should be tested and the results clearly marked to show users how the improper configuration of software post-processing can be identified and resolved. One should also consider that if IoT QRNGs are sought-after, how does one implement a post-processing algorithm (which are known for their high memory requirements) in such a small package? Resource limitations may prevent effective post-processing of QRNG output, the consequences of which are made clear in the preceding work.

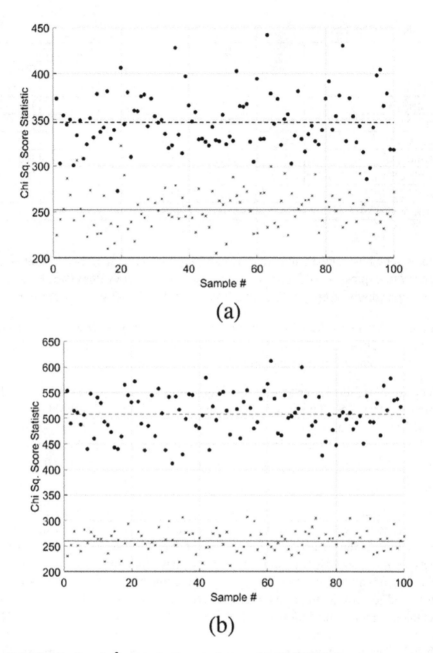

Fig. 10.3 Distribution of χ^2 scores for Quantis devices. (**a**) 16M. (**b**) 4M

10.5 Conclusion

There are many complex issues to consider when evaluating RNGs for use in security systems. Device specifications, the use of off-device entropy pools, post-processing, and output speed are all critical to the evaluation process. Each element should be tested in isolation, but only the whole device may be certified, leading to issues when considering black-box design philosophy and resource-constrained devices.

The DESFire EV1 has been found to output biased values from its TRNG, but this does not necessarily mean that the RNG itself is at fault. Subsequent work with the EV2 has found no issues with its RNG. Combined with conversations with NXP's engineers, this indicates that the issue may instead be in the whitening function employed to remove bias from the raw TRNG output. The EV1 results highlight two key issues; the role of black box design in complicating the evaluation process, and the quality control challenges facing small-scale robust TRNGs. Quantis QRNGs also require post-processing, as demonstrated by the exceptionally poor results shown by raw data over a variety of statistical tests. Rigorous testing of RNG with multiple input and processing dependencies should require results demonstrating the performance of both raw and processed output of such devices. This will aid in the identification of implementation errors.

Reliance on Dieharder and NIST SP800-22 cannot continue to the exclusion of new tests, such as those employed by TestU01. There is a wealth of academic literature on the subject of statistical tests of randomness and efforts must be made to identify which of these will provide the next wave of reliable tests of randomness. Finally, it is important to consider how tests may be evaded by manipulation of RNG output; future work will focus on how some simple manipulations result in predictable data that passes current statistical tests of randomness.

11

Embedded Systems and Bug Discovery

Aurélien Francillon, Sam L. Thomas, and Andrei Costin

Abstract The goal of this chapter is to introduce the reader to the domain of bug discovery in embedded systems which are at the core of the Internet of Things. Embedded software has a number of particularities which makes it slightly different to general purpose software. In particular, embedded devices are more exposed to software attacks but have lower defense levels and are often left unattended. At the same time, analyzing their security is more difficult because they are very "opaque", while the execution of custom and embedded software is often entangled with the hardware and peripherals. These differences have an impact on our ability to find software bugs in such systems. This chapter discusses how software vulnerabilities can be identified, at different stages of the software life-cycle, for example during development, during integration of the different components, during testing, during the deployment of the device, or in the field by third parties.

11.1 The Challenges of Embedded Devices and Software

We argue that the problem of embedded software security is due to multiple factors, including a systematic lack of transparency, control, and resistance to attacks. A particular way to improve this is to analyze the software of these devices, with the particular goal of identifying software vulnerabilities in order to correct them as early as possible.

A. Francillon (✉)
EURECOM, Sophia Antipolis, France
e-mail: aurelien.francillon@eurecom.fr

S. L. Thomas
University of Birmingham, Birmingham, United Kingdom

A. Costin
Faculty of Information Technology, University of Jyväskylä, Jyväskylä, Finland

11.1.1 Lack of Transparency

Today, many smart devices are compromised during massive attacks, and may be abused to form large *botnets* (networks of compromised devices). Record-high Distributed Denial of Service (DDoS) attacks (i.e., network flooding) reportedly generated between 620 Gbps and 1 Tbps of traffic [241, 344]. These DDoS attacks were reported to use several hundred thousand compromised embedded/smart devices, comprising dozens of different models of Commercial Off-The-Shelf (COTS) products like IP/CCTV cameras and home routers. Most of those devices were compromised using default or hard-coded credentials set by the manufacturer [345]. Malware running on such devices has complete control over the traffic that is generated, and most smart devices do not embed any infection detection or prevention mechanism. Worse yet, the users or owners of the device are often not aware of the problem, and unable to solve it. In fact, devices are not designed to be inspected and modified by end-users (e.g., to perform forensics as discussed in Chap. 13).

11.1.2 Lack of Control

Another important problem is that smart devices are generally provided as a fixed software (i.e., firmware) and hardware platform, often tied to a cloud service and bundled together as a closed system that the user has little control over. An example of the negative consequences of this customer lock-out is the *Revolv* smart thermostat. *Revolv*'s manufacturer was acquired by its competitor Nest, and after a year Nest stopped the cloud service, rendering the *Revolv* thermostats installed in homes impossible to use [271]. Users often have no choice regarding which software the device should run, or which cloud service to use, or what the device should do. Choosing, installing and using alternative software for such devices is difficult, if not impossible, often due to the single-purpose nature of the hardware and software design, the lack of public documentation, in addition to any anti-tampering measures imposed by the manufacturer.

11.1.3 Lack of Resistance to Attacks

In practice, Internet scanning botnets are active enough that some devices will be compromised within a few minutes after being connected to the Internet [344]. To be considered trustworthy, devices need to have a certain level of resistance to attacks. This is astonishing, because in essence many of the recurring security issues with smart devices have already been "solved" for many years. If vulnerabilities and corresponding attack situations could ultimately be avoided, it is important to ask who is responsible for the damage caused by compromised smart devices, beyond the malware author. The device owner may be legally responsible, but often the end-user does not have any means to detect or prevent such compromises, or to apply a secure configuration. On the other hand, the manufacturers currently often have no legal liability, and thus no incentive (e.g., economic, legal) to prevent a potential vulnerability and compromise.

11.1.4   Organization of This Chapter

Solving these problems requires analyzing the software and firmware for the embedded devices, and identifying and fixing their vulnerabilities. This chapter describes the possible steps to systematically and consistently achieve this goal. We first provide a classification of embedded systems that is well adapted to their analysis. We then describe the possible steps for their analysis. We start with ways to obtain the software to analyze, which is often a challenge in itself for embedded devices. We then describe how to perform static analysis on the firmware packages obtained, which has many advantages such as speed and scalability. We then describe techniques which can be used to dynamically analyze the firmware, which in contrast to static analysis has the advantage of larger code coverage and lower false positive rates.

11.1.5   Classification of Embedded Systems

A general definition of embedded systems is hard to establish [261]. However, two widely accepted differences separate embedded devices from modern general-purpose computers, such as ordinary desktop PCs or smartphones, namely: (a) they are designed to fulfill a *specific purpose*, and (b) they heavily interact with the physical world via *peripherals*. The aforementioned two criteria cover a wide variety of devices, ranging from hard-disk controllers to home routers, from digital cameras to Programmable Logic Controllers (PLCs). These families can be further classified according to several aspects, such as their actual computing power [171], the extent to which they interact with their computing and physical environment, their field of usage, or the timing constraints imposed on them.

Unfortunately, these classifications tell us very little about the type of security mechanisms that are available on a given device. Muench et al. [430] classifies embedded systems according to the type of operating system (OS) they use. While the operating system is certainly not the only source of security features, it provides several security primitives, handles recovery from faulty states, and often serves as a building block for additional and more complex security mechanisms. We therefore classify embedded devices using the following taxonomy:

Type-0:   Multipurpose / non-embedded systems.

We use Type-0 in order to reference traditional general-purpose systems.

Type-I: General purpose OS-based devices (e.g., Linux-based).

The Linux OS kernel is widely used in the embedded world. However, in comparison to the traditional GNU/Linux found on desktops and servers, embedded systems typically follow more minimalist approaches. For example, a very common configuration that can be found in consumer-oriented products as well as in Industrial Control Systems (ICS) is based on the Linux kernel coupled with `BusyBox` and `uClibc`.

Type-II: Embedded OS-based devices.

These dedicated operating systems targeted at embedded devices systems are particularly suitable for devices with low computation power, which is typically enforced on embedded systems for cost reasons. Operating systems such as `uClinux` or `FreeRTOS` are suitable for systems without a Memory Management Unit (MMU) and are usually adopted on single-purpose user electronics, such as IP cameras, DVD players and Set-Top Boxes (STB).

Type-III: Devices without OS-Abstraction.

These devices adopt a so called "monolithic firmware", whose operation is typically based on a single control loop and interrupts triggered by the peripherals in order to handle external events. Monolithic firmware can be found in a large variety of controllers of hardware components, such as CD-readers, WiFi-cards or GPS-dongles.

11.2 Obtaining Firmware and Its Components

Even though complete black box analysis of embedded devices is possible to some degree and in certain situations, obtaining the firmware significantly helps and makes more advanced analyses possible. There are two main ways to obtain the firmware for a given device—as a firmware package (e.g., online, support media) and through extraction from the device itself.

11.2.1 Collecting Firmware Packages

The environments in which embedded systems are deployed are heterogeneous, spanning a variety of devices, vendors, CPU/hardware architectures, instruction sets, operating systems, and custom components. This makes the task of compiling a *representative* and *balanced* dataset of firmware packages a difficult problem to solve. The lack of centralized points of collection, such as the ones provided by software/app marketplaces, antivirus vendors, or public sandboxes in the malware analysis field, makes it difficult for researchers to gather large and well triaged datasets. Firmware often needs to be downloaded from vendor Web pages and FTP sites, and it is not always simple, even for a human, to tell whether or not two firmware packages are for the same physical device.

One challenge often encountered in firmware analysis and reverse engineering processes is the difficulty of reliably extracting meta-data from a firmware package. This meta-data might include, the device's vendor, its product code and purpose, its firmware version, or its processor architecture, among countless other details.

11.2.2   *Extracting Firmware from Devices*

Obtaining the firmware from an online repository as a firmware package is convenient and thus preferred, however it is not always possible. First, the firmware may not be available, e.g., because there is no update yet, nor one planned. Sometimes the firmware is only distributed through authorized and qualified maintenance agents, e.g., in case of industrial or critical systems. It is also common that the firmware is not distributed at all in an attempt to prevent counterfeit products, reverse engineering of the software or protecting its security.

In such cases the best (and sometimes the only) solution is to extract the firmware from the device itself. There are multiple possible ways to approach this ([529] and [564] provide a detailed overview of the process), each approach having its own set of benefits and issues. In the simplest case, the firmware can be extracted by connecting to a debug interface (e.g., JTAG, and serial ports such as UART, SPI, I2C). It is important to note that JTAG is a low level protocol and many different mechanisms can be implemented on top of it. Debug mechanisms allow dumping some memories (e.g., ROM, RAM or Flash memories behind a Flash controller), but not necessarily others. When Flash memory is soldered onto a Printed Circuit Board (PCB) and is independent from the processor, it is possible to de-solder it and extract its contents using a Flash programmer/reader. Unfortunately, the variety of Flash memory standards, types and pinouts is huge. One can design their own Flash chip adapter for reading and dumping the memory contents (e.g., code, data) [75]. However, some cheap universal programmers may be sufficient for dumping sufficiently many models of Flash memories [38]. Finally, the advanced Flash programmers support even hundreds of thousands of different Flash memory models [198].

However, when the device is a Flash microcontroller, the Flash memory is integrated within the microcontroller and is typically not directly accessible. In such cases, the microcontrollers themselves provide mechanisms to access Flash memory areas, but often such mechanisms come with some Flash area protection mechanisms, which are often arbitrary and microcontroller specific. Such protection mechanisms can sometimes be bypassed due to vulnerabilities in the implementation of the protections themselves [447, 556]. However, such attacks may not always succeed, and one may be left with using more costly invasive hardware attacks such as Linear Code Extraction (LCE) [549] or direct memory readout using a microscope [158] as the only option available.

11.2.3 Unpacking Firmware

The next step towards the analysis of a firmware package is to unpack and extract the files or resources it contains. The output of this phase largely depends on the type of firmware, as well as the unpacking and extraction tools employed. In some examples, executable code and resources (such as graphics files or HTML code) might be embedded directly into a binary blob that is designed to be directly copied into memory by a bootloader and then executed. Some other firmware packages are distributed in a compressed and obfuscated package which contains a block-by-block image copy of the Flash memory. Such an image may consist of several partitions containing a bootloader, a kernel, a file system, or any combination of these.

11.2.4 Firmware Unpacking Frameworks

The main tools to unpack arbitrary firmware packages are: binwalk [263], FRAK [161], Binary Analysis Toolkit (BAT) [558] and Firmware.RE [155] (Table 11.1 compares the performance of each framework):

- Binwalk is perhaps the best known and most used firmware unpacking tool developed by Craig Heffner [263]. It uses pattern matching to locate and carve files from a binary blob. Additionally, it also extracts some meta-data such as license strings.
- FRAK is an unpacking toolkit first presented by Cui et al. [162]. It reportedly[1] supports a limited number of device vendors and models, such as HP printers and Multi-Function Peripherals (MFP).
- The Binary Analysis Toolkit (BAT), formerly known as GPLtool, was originally designed by Armijn Hemel and Tjaldur software in order to detect GPL license violations [269, 558]. To do so, it recursively extracts files from a binary blob and matches strings with a database of known strings from GPL projects and licenses. BAT also supports file carving similar to binwalk, as well as a very flexible plugin-oriented extension interface.

---

[1]Even though the authors mention that the tool would be made publicly available, it has yet to be released.

Table 11.1 Comparison of the unpacking performance of Binwalk, BAT, FRAK and Firmware.RE on a few example firmware packages (according to [155])

Device	Vendor	OS	Binwalk	BAT	FRAK	Firmware.RE
PC	Intel	BIOS	✗	✗	✗	✗
Camera	STL	Linux	✗	✓	✗	✓
Router	Bintec	–	✗	✗	✗	✗
ADSL gateway	Zyxel	ZynOS	✓	✓	✗	✓
PLC	Siemens	–	✓	✓	✗	✓
DSLAM	–	–	✓	✓	✗	✓
PC	Intel	BIOS	✓	✓	✗	✓
ISDN server	Planet	–	✓	✓	✗	✓
Voip	Asotel	Vxworks	✓	✓	✗	✓
Modem	–	–	✗	✗	✗	✓
Home automation	Belkin	Linux	✗	✗	✗	✓
			55%	64%	0%	82%

- Firmware.RE [155] extends BAT with additional unpacking methods and specific analyses to perform automated large-scale analyses. When released, it achieved a lower false positive rate when unpacking firmware compared to binwalk.

11.2.5 Modifying and Repacking Firmware

Modifying and repacking a firmware could be one optional step during the analysis of the firmware and device security. The modifications could be performed either at the level of the entire firmware package, or at the level of individually unpacked files (that are finally repacked back into a firmware package). Such a step could be useful in testing several things. First, it can check whether a particular firmware has error, modification and authenticity checks for new versions of firmware. If such checks are missing or improperly implemented, the firmware update mechanism can then be used as an attack vector, or as a way to perform further analysis of the system [57, 162]. Second, it can be used to augment the firmware with additional security-related functionality, such as exploits, benign malware and more advanced analysis tools. For example, this could be useful when there are no other ways to deliver an exploit (e.g., non-network local exploits such as kernel privilege escalation), or provide some (partial) form of introspection into the running device/firmware [163].

The firmware-mod-kit tool [262] is perhaps the most well-known (and possibly among the very few) firmware modification tools. Unfortunately, it supports a limited number of firmware formats, and while it can be extended to support more formats, to do so requires substantial manual effort. Further, for some formats it relies on external tools to perform some of the repacking. These tools are developed and maintained by different persons or entities in different shapes and forms, thus there is no uniform way to modify and repack firmware packages.

11.3   Static Firmware Analysis

Once the code is extracted further analysis can be performed. There are two main classes of analysis that can be preformed on a generic computing system—static analysis and dynamic analysis. In principle, the distinction between the two is easy: in static analysis the code is analyzed without executing it, but instead only reasoning about it, while in the dynamic setting the analysis is performed on the code while it is executed. With more advanced analysis techniques, however, this frontier is slightly blurred. For example, symbolic execution allows one to analyze software by considering some variables to have an unknown value (i.e., they are unconstrained). Symbolic execution is sometimes considered static analysis and at other times dynamic analysis. In this section, we will first describe simple static analysis which can be efficiently performed on firmware packages, then we will discuss more advanced static analysis approaches. Finally, we will cover the limitations of static analysis and in the next section focus on the dynamic analysis on firmware packages.

11.3.1   Simple Static Analysis on Firmware Packages

11.3.1.1   Configuration Analysis

For a large majority of complex embedded devices (i.e., those of Type-I as described in Sect. 11.1.5), while service configuration is stored within the file-system of the device, user-configurable information is often stored elsewhere—within a region of memory called Non-Volatile Random Access Memory (NVRAM) which retains its state between power cycles (similar to Flash memory in some ways). Many devices treat NVRAM as a key-value store and include utilities such as nvram-get and nvram-set, as well as dedicated libraries to get and set values stored there. On a router, for example, the current Wi-Fi passphrase and web-based configuration interface credentials, will often be stored within the NVRAM, which will be queried by software in order to facilitate the authentication of the device and its services.

All other device configuration, without performing a firmware upgrade, will be static. As a result of this, any, e.g., hard-coded passwords or certificates (as noted in [151]), can be leveraged by an adversary to compromise a device. To this end, Costin et al. [155] show many instances where devices are configured with user accounts and passwords that are weak, missing entirely, or stored in plain-text. Therefore, a first step in static analysis of firmware is to examine the configuration of its services: to check for improperly configured services, e.g., due to use of

```
mount -t proc proc /proc
mount -t ramfs ramfs /var
mkdir /var/tmp
mkdir /var/ppp/
mkdir /var/log
mkdir /var/run
mkdir /var/lock
mkdir /var/flash
#iwcontrol is required for RTL8185 Wireless driver
#iwcontrol auth &

#busybox insmod /lib/modules/2.4.26-uc0/kernel/drivers/usb/quickcam.o

/bin/webs -u root -d /www -i /var/run/thttpd.pid &
#ifconfig wlan0 up promisc
```

Fig. 11.1 Example of a boot script taken from an IP camera

unsafe defaults and hard-coded credentials. Configuration files are of further use in estimating the set of programs utilized and the initial global configuration of a device, in the absence of physical access to it. For example, by examination of its boot scripts, we are able to learn which services present in its firmware (among potentially hundreds) are actually utilized by the device, this can aid in reducing the amount of time taken by more complex analysis approaches described later.

Manual methods are often sufficient for analysis of a few firmware images and, with limited scope, analysis of things such as the device's configuration. For example, to estimate the set of processes started by a firmware one can inspect the contents of a boot script, e.g., /etc/rcS.

Figure 11.1 details such a boot script taken from the firmware of an IP camera. We are able to observe that the device's primary functionality is orchestrated by the /bin/webs binary, which we would then analyze further using the methods detailed in Sect. 11.3.2.

11.3.1.2 Software Version Analysis

Many devices are not designed to receive firmware updates. This prohibits patching against known security vulnerabilities and can often render a device useless to an end-user. This prevents abusing the firmware update as an attack vector. However, when a vulnerability is discovered, the only effective mitigation is to replace the device with a new one.

Many devices are designed to be updated and vendors provide firmware updates. However, the mechanisms for applying those updates are often not standardized and are largely ad-hoc. They also heavily rely on the end-user's diligence (to identify that an update is available) and action (to actually apply the updates). The end-result of this is that an overwhelming majority of devices are left unpatched against known vulnerabilities. Thus, a further step in the analysis of firmware is to identify the versions of software (both programs and libraries) it contains, and correlate those versions with known vulnerabilities (e.g., CVE database).

There are several possible approaches to perform this. For example, [155] use fuzzy hashing [340, 507] as a method to correlate files in firmware images. The effectiveness of the approach was demonstrated in several examples, in particular uncovering many IoT and embedded devices being so-called "white label" products.[2] Finally, machine learning can be used to identify firmware images [157] or to search for known vulnerabilities [585].

11.3.2   Static Code Analysis of Firmware Packages

Developing tools for performing automated static code analysis on embedded device firmware presents a number of complexities compared to performing analyses on software for commodity PC systems (i.e., Type-0 devices). The first challenge is the diversity of CPU architectures. This alone restricts the amount of existing tooling that can be used, and when attempting large scale analysis tools will inevitably have to deal with firmware from a number of distinct architectures. To facilitate the analysis in this case, the algorithms will either have to be reimplemented for each architecture being analyzed, or the architecture-specific disassembled firmware instructions will have to be lifted to a common, so-called Intermediate Language (IL) or Intermediate Representation (IR). A further difficulty for more simple devices (e.g., those of Type-III) is the often non-standard means by which different device firmware executes (e.g., it could be interrupt driven) and interacts with the memory and external peripherals. More complex firmware (e.g., that of Type-I devices) tends to more closely follow the execution behavior of more conventional devices (those of Type-0).

11.3.2.1   Code Analysis of Embedded Firmware

Despite the increased complexity of performing automated analysis of embedded device firmware, a number of techniques have been proposed for both targeted and large-scale static analysis. Eschweiler et al. [202] and Feng et al. [212] use numeric feature vectors to perform graph-based program comparisons [191] efficiently. They encode control-flow and instruction information in these feature vectors to identify known vulnerabilities in device firmware. Both methods provide a means of querying a data-set of binaries using a reference vulnerability as input and identifying the subset of binaries that contain constructs that are *similar* (but not necessarily the same) to those of the input vulnerability. The work in [585] improves the performance of these approaches by relying on Neural Networks.

---

[2]Generic products which are sold under a known brand.

11.3.2.2   Discovering Backdoors with Static Analysis

Aside from vulnerability discovery, a small body of work has attempted to automatically identify backdoor-like constructs in device firmware. Static analysis is most suited to detecting such constructs due to the fact it can achieve full program coverage. Dynamic analysis is less adequate in this case, as it relies solely on execution traces that can be captured and analyzed stemming from triggering standard program behaviors (which, by definition [551], a backdoor is not).

HumIDIFy[3] [552] uses a combination of Machine Learning (ML) and static analysis to identify anomalous and unexpected behavior in services commonly found in Linux-based firmware. ML is used first to identify the type of firmware binaries, e.g., a web-server, this then drives classification-specific static analysis on each binary. HumIDIFy attempts to validate that binaries do not perform any functionality outside of what is expected of the type of software they are identified as. For example, HumIDIFy is able to detect a backdoor within a web-server taken from Tenda router firmware[4] that contains an additional UDP listening thread which executes shell commands provided to it (without authentication) as the root user.

Stringer[5] [550] attempts to locate backdoor-like behavior in Linux-based firmware. It automatically discovers comparisons with static data that leads to execution of *unique* program functionality, which models the situation of a backdoor providing access to undocumented functionality via a hard-coded credential pair or undocumented command. Stringer provides an ordering of the functions within a binary based on how much their control-flow is influenced by static data comparisons that *guard* access to functionality not otherwise reachable. The authors demonstrate Stringer is able to detect both undocumented functionality and hard-coded credential backdoors in devices from a number of manufacturers.

Firmalice [528] is a tool for detecting authentication bypass vulnerabilities and backdoors within firmware by symbolic execution. It takes a so-called security policy as input, which specifies a condition a program (or firmware) will exhibit when it has reached an authenticated state. Using this security policy, it attempts to prove that it is possible to reach an authenticated state by discovering an input that when given to the program satisfies the conditions to reach that state. To discover such an input, Firmalice employs symbolic execution on a program slice taken from a program point acting as an input source to the point reached that signals the program is in an authenticated state. If it is able to satisfy all of the constraints such that a path exists between these two points, and an input variable can be concretised that satisfies those constraints, then it has discovered an authentication bypass backdoor (and a triggering input)—such an input will not be discoverable in a non-backdoored authentication routine. Unfortunately, Firmalice requires a degree of manual intervention to perform its analysis, such as identifying the security policy,

---

[3] Available as open-source: https://github.com/BaDSeED-SEC/HumIDIFy.

[4] http://www.devttys0.com/2013/10/from-china-with-love/.

[5] Available as open-source: https://github.com/BaDSeED-SEC/strngr.

input points and privileged program locations. It is therefore not easily adaptable for large-scale analysis.

11.3.2.3   Example Static Analysis to Discover Code Parsers

In order to interact with remote servers or connecting clients (e.g., for remote configuration), most firmware for networked embedded devices will contain client/server components, e.g., a web-server, or proprietary, domain-specific client/server software. In all cases, the firmware itself or software contained within it (for more complex devices) will implement parsers for handling the messages of the protocols required to communicate with corresponding client/server entities. Such parsers are a common source of bugs, whether their implementation incorrectly handles input in a way that causes a memory corruption, or permits an invalid state transition in a protocol's state machine logic. Thus, identifying these constructs in binary software is useful as a premise to performing targeted analyses. To this end, Cojocar et al. [150], propose PIE, a tool to automatically detect parsing routines in firmware binaries. PIE utilizes a supervised learning classifier trained on a number of simple features of the LLVM IL representation of firmware components known to contain parsing logic. Such features include: basic block count, number of incoming edges to blocks, and number of callers (for functions). PIE provides a means to identify specific functions responsible for performing parsing within an input firmware package, or software component. Stringer [550], described in Sect. 11.3.2.2, similarly provides a means of automatically identifying parser routines (for text-based input); in addition to identifying routines, it is also able to identify the individual (text-based) commands, processed by the parser.

11.4   Dynamic Firmware Analysis

Static analysis is indeed a robust technique that can help discover a wide range of vulnerability classes, such as misconfigurations or backdoors. However, it is not necessarily best suited for other types of vulnerabilities, especially when they depend on the complex runtime state of the program.

Similar to static analysis, powerful dynamic analysis techniques and tools have been developed for traditional systems and general purpose computers. However, the unique characteristics and challenges of the embedded systems make it difficult, if not impossible, to directly apply those proven methods. To this end, there are several distinct directions for dynamic analysis of embedded systems and we briefly discuss them below.

11.4.1 Device-Interactive Dynamic Analysis Without Emulation

When the device is present for analysis, the simplest form of device-interactive dynamic analysis is to test the devices in a "black-box" manner. The general idea of this approach is to setup and run the devices under analysis as in normal operation (e.g., connect to Ethernet LAN, WLAN, smartphone), and then test it with various tools and manual techniques (e.g., generic or specialized fuzzers, web penetration) and observe their behavior via externally observable side-effects such as device reboots, network daemon crashes, or XSS artifacts [439]. Similar approaches and results were reported by several independent and complementary works [259, 280, 292].

While being simple and easy to perform, this type of dynamic analysis has certain limitations, some of which are due to the "black-box" nature of the approach. For example, it is challenging to know what is happening with the entire system/device while the dynamic analysis is performed, i.e., the introspection of the system is missing or is hard to achieve. Also, in this approach it is not easy to control in detail what specifically is being executed and analyzed, the analysis being mostly driven by the data and actions fed to the device. In addition to this, some types of vulnerabilities might not have side-effects that are immediately [430] or externally visible (e.g., a crash of a daemon which does not necessarily expose a network port), therefore those bugs could be missed or misinterpreted during the analysis.

11.4.2 Device-Interactive Dynamic Analysis with Emulation

As an extension to the aforementioned approach, emulation can be coupled with device-interactive dynamic analysis to provide the required depth and breadth, therefore outperforming other static or dynamic analysis methods. The general idea of this approach is to split the execution of the embedded firmware between the analysis host and the actual running device. The analysis host is connected to the device via a debug (e.g., JTAG) or serial (e.g., UART) interface. Therefore one requirement is that the device under analysis must provide at least such an interface, whether documented or not. The analysis host then runs a dynamic analysis environment which is typically an emulator (e.g., QEMU-based) augmented or extended with additional layers and plugins such as symbolic execution and taint analysis. The analysis host has access to the execution and memory states both for the emulator and for the running device. The firmware is being analyzed first in the extended emulator environment. During the firmware emulation and analysis, certain parts of the analyzed firmware are transferred for execution by the analysis host from the emulator to the running device. This is sometimes required, for example, when the firmware needs to perform an I/O operation with a peripheral present on the devices but not in the emulator. The execution and state transfer to and from the device occur via the connected debug or serial interface. On the one hand, by using this approach it is possible to control exactly what is to be analyzed because the emulator is under the full supervision of the analysis host. On the other hand, this approach enables broader and deeper coverage of the execution because the device can complement the execution of firmware parts that are impossible to execute within the emulator.

This is the approach followed by Avatar [591] which aims at providing symbolic execution with S2E [140], while Avatar2 [429] focuses on better interoperability with more tools. Prospect [312] explores forwarding at the system calls level and Surrogates [341] provides a very fast debug interface. Inception [125] provides an analysis environment to use during testing when source code is available.

11.4.3 Device-Less Dynamic Analysis and Emulation

Performing dynamic analysis in a device-interactive manner certainly has its benefits, however such an approach has a number of limitations and is hard to fully automate. Firstly, it is not easy to scale the human operator's interventions and expertise required for many of the tasks related to the approach of device interaction with emulation. Secondly, it is challenging to automate and scale the logistics operations related to acquisition, tear-down, connection, configuration and reset of a large number of devices. Therefore, dynamic analysis techniques that are easier and more feasible to scale and automate are required. One such technique is the device-less analysis based on full or partial emulation.

Davidson et al. [175] presented the FIE tool that detects bugs in firmware of the MSP430 microcontroller family. FIE leverages KLEE [120] to perform symbolic execution of firmware in order to detect memory safety violations (e.g., buffer overflows and out-of-bounds memory accesses), and misuse of peripherals (e.g., attempted writes to read-only memory). FIE needs the availability of the source code, which is uncommon, and is able to handle a variety of the nuances and challenges faced during automated analysis of firmware, especially when dealing with firmware for Type-III devices. However, when reading I/O from a device, the values read are always assumed to return unconstrained (completely symbolic) values which leads to a state explosion problem. This limits the size of the programs which can be analyzed.

In [156], the authors perform device-less dynamic security analysis via automated and large-scale emulation of embedded firmware. Similarly, FIRMA-DYNE [137] presents an automated and scalable system for performing emulation and dynamic analysis of Linux-based embedded firmware.

The general idea of both works is to crawl and then unpack firmware packages into minimal root filesystems (i.e., `rootfs`) that can subsequently be virtualized and executed as a whole via "system emulation" (as opposed to "user emulation") using for example QEMU [69]. The emulator is first used to start an architecture-specific emulation host OS, such as Debian for ARM or MIPS depending on the architecture of the device whose firmware is being dynamically analyzed. Then the firmware root filesystem is uploaded to the emulation host OS, where its Linux boot sequence scripts are initiated, most likely in a `chroot` environment under the emulation host OS. Once the firmware's Linux boot sequence concludes, various services (e.g., a web server, SSH, telnet, and FTP) of the device/firmware under analysis should be running, and are ready for logging, tracing, instrumentation and debugging. The work in [137] extends this approach by running a custom operating system kernel which is able to emulate some of the missing drivers.

11.5   Conclusion

We have provided a short overview of the field: from our excursus, it is clear that analyzing the software of IoT/embedded devices and finding security vulnerabilities within them is still a challenging task. While multiple directions and techniques are being actively explored and developed within the field, more research, insights and tools are still required.

Unfortunately, the existing proven techniques (e.g., static, dynamic, hybrid analysis) cannot be applied in a straightforward manner to embedded devices and their software/firmware. One reason for this is the high heterogeneity and fragmentation of the technological space that supports embedded/IoT systems. Another reason is the "opaque" nature of embedded devices, which can be seen as akin to the "security by obscurity" principle. Such reasons make embedded systems harder to analyze compared to more traditional systems.

Indeed, the current embedded firmware "population" may still contain many latent backdoors and vulnerabilities, both known and unknown. However, as we detailed in this chapter, positive and promising avenues for the detection of embedded software bugs are becoming increasingly available. Such avenues include large-scale analysis and correlation techniques, hybrid/dynamic analysis of emulated firmware or running devices, and advanced techniques to specifically detect backdoors.

Part V
Privacy on IoT Systems and their Forensic Analysis

12

Ubiquitous Computing Systems: Privacy Risks

Agusti Solanas, Edgar Batista, Fran Casino, Achilleas Papageorgiou, and Constantinos Patsakis

Abstract Ubiquitous computing systems are commonplace. They have opened the door to great benefits for society as a whole. However, they have to be used with care, otherwise they can cause serious risks for their users. In this chapter, we analyze the privacy risks of ubiquitous computing systems from a new individual-centred perspective based on five privacy dimensions, namely identity, location, footprint, query and intelligence. We describe each dimension and provide an introductory view of the main privacy risks of these systems. Also, we discuss some of the challenges that derive from new trends in the field.

12.1 Introduction

The widespread deployment of ubiquitous computing systems (UCS) is a commonplace reality. Despite their youth, the adoption of ICT together with the generalization of the Internet [294] have enabled the early consolidation of UCS in our daily lives. Nowadays, it is not surprising to find people using multiple computing devices: from traditional computers or laptops, to smart phones or even trendy smart watches or fitness trackers equipped with plenty of built-in sensors and powerful computing capabilities. In addition, to make things even more complex, interactions do not take place between humans and machines only, but among machines too. Those machine-to-machine interactions are magnified with the adoption of the Internet of Things (IoT), which implies a strengthening of the overall sensing capabilities of the machines ecosystem which allows further

A. Solanas
Universitat Rovira i Virgili, Tarragona, Catalonia, Spain

E. Batista
SIMPPLE, Tarragona, Catalonia, Spain

F. Casino · A. Papageorgiou · C. Patsakis (✉)
University of Piraeus, Piraeus, Greece
e-mail: kpatsak@unipi.gr

processing [437]. In a nutshell, the consolidation of these technologies has paved the way for what has been called the third era of modern computing [424].

Following the increasing use of UCS, it was inevitable that they would become able to sense, collect and store huge amounts of information, which quite frequently refer to people. From a global perspective, this results in a tremendous increase in the data generated (and stored) in the digital world and, in fact, according to IBM, by 2017 90% of all data ever created had been created just in the previous 2 years [290]. It is worth noting that most of this data is sensor-based data gathered by UCS. In this situation of rapid growth of heterogeneous data, big data technologies has emerged as a solution for their management and processing [293].

People, consciously or not, provide vast amounts of personal information (e.g., locations, preferences) to digital services in exchange for an improved user experience and personalized results. In the UCS context, the storage and processing of large amounts of data could jeopardize privacy. Thus, it must be preserved by computer systems and technologies should be revisited as they evolve to guarantee individuals' privacy and to foster awareness. Interestingly enough, about two decades ago, in the late 1990s, initial studies evaluated people's awareness regarding privacy in the digital world due to the rise of the Internet and e-commerce. This was done by profiling individuals [351] and evaluating their *comfortability* in providing different types of information [8]. At that time, people could have hardly imagined the effects of the new digital era and its influence on today's lives. Thus, recent studies aim at evaluating the levels of concern of people regarding ubiquitous tracking and recording technologies [438], and their main concerns regarding their loss of control over their privacy [352]. Currently, the adoption of big data motivates the redefinition and analysis of privacy concerns on UCS [400].

Already identified as one of the most challenging issues, privacy is not a new addition to the ubiquitous computing field [578]. Unfortunately, determining whether a given UCS is privacy-friendly is not straightforward, since current techniques are based on individual analyses. In this context, understanding the purpose of UCS, how they work, and why they work that way, are key questions that emerge from the analysis of their privacy features [348, 513]. The increasing number and variety of UCS makes the assessment of the proper management of personal data in all UCS devices very difficult. Additionally, new advances in the privacy and security fields (e.g., recent attacks, vulnerable technologies and protocols) do not guarantee to an adequate level that a certain UCS will always remain safe, and this motivates the periodical review of UCS privacy-related analyses. It should also be highlighted that the recent implementation of the General Data Protection Regulation [547] requires the privacy impact assessment of all services that process sensitive user data, along with other requirements such as consent management, mechanisms to allow data portability, and erasure of user data [486]. All in all, interest in UCS privacy is justifiably growing.

12.1.1   Goal and Plan of the Chapter

In this chapter we analyze the current state of UCS from a privacy perspective. To do so, we identify, describe and explain the most relevant privacy risks that derive from the deployment and use of UCS. However, since privacy is a multifaceted topic, understanding it holistically might be difficult for non-expert readers. Hence, we propose the use of a 5-dimensional approach to analyze privacy and we classify the identified privacy risks into five privacy dimensions: *identity privacy*, *query privacy*, *location privacy*, *footprint privacy*, and *intelligence privacy*. This 5-D approach, which has been previously used in the context of smart cities, will help readers grasp the difficulties and nuances of privacy protection in a compartmental way, which will finally lead to a wider and more comprehensive understanding of the problem. Therefore, the ultimate goal of the chapter is to increase awareness on privacy risks related to UCS.

The rest of the chapter is organized as follows: Sect. 12.2 summarizes previous work related to the identification of threats in UCS and reports the most relevant classifications and analysis of privacy-related issues. Section 12.3 describes our 5-D classification of privacy risks in UCS. Moreover, possible countermeasures, some practical scenarios and privacy enhancing technologies will be discussed, to better illustrate each privacy threat. Next, Sect. 12.4 provides readers with a glimpse into the future of privacy protection in the context of UCS, by analyzing the impact of new technologies and services. Finally, the chapter ends in Sect. 12.5 with a summary of the main contributions and with some thoughts regarding the importance of increasing awareness on privacy-related issues in UCS.

12.2   Background and Previous Work on Privacy in UCS

Regardless of the context or application area of the UCS at hand, its design involves several challenging steps, from the proper selection of hardware and technology (e.g., microelectronics, power supplies, sensors, communications, localization technology, M2M interactions and human-machine interfaces [518]), to the implementation of a system that addresses security risks [119, 352] (e.g., large number of nodes, resource constraints, authentication-related challenges, unauthorized access to devices or networks) and privacy issues. Regarding the latter, some studies have analyzed the privacy issues of UCS. Kušen and Strembeck published, very recently (i.e., 2017), a systematic literature review on the security of UCS and they identified vulnerabilities, threats, attacks, and some defenses. Within the last category they consider several options (i.e., trust computation and management, cryptographic protocols, authentication and access control, and privacy protection mechanisms).

They identified the most common privacy protection mechanisms found in the literature [352] as follows:

- Masking mechanisms that preserve individuals' privacy by hiding their identities.
- Privacy protection layer for mobile apps, that imply security analyses, configuration and proper regulation of permissions. Especially when it has been repeatedly proven that leaks are common [459].
- Obfuscation, based on deliberately degrading the quality of the information.
- Proximity detection schemes, that are founded on trust computation based on *encounters*, which require a coincidence in space and time and a mutual interest between the components performing the computation.
- Game-based approaches, to find the optimal privacy protection mechanism depending on the requirements and needs of participants by following several rounds in a game between the attacker and the user.
- Consents and notifications.
- Negotiation approaches, in which privacy settings may be modified and configured to enable different services.
- RFID-based methods, that use RFID devices that simulate multiple RFID tags simultaneously.
- Other techniques such as tag identification schemes or recommendation systems for private location-sharing services.

In this study, the authors found that 29% of the privacy measures were related to masking mechanisms, these being the most frequently used. Although most research on privacy in UCS is focused on the aforementioned privacy protection mechanisms, it is worth noting that privacy may also be considered as a requirement by design. Along this line, Duan and Canny[190] advocate for the principle of *data discretion* in which, in their own words, *"users should have access and control of data about them, and should be able to determine how it is used."*.

Moreover, in [357] Langheinrich stresses the importance of including privacy considerations in the early stages of system design. He proposes six principles to guide the development of privacy-preserving ubiquitous systems as follows:

- Notice: Users should always be aware of what data is being collected.
- Choice and Consent: Users should be able to choose whether it is used.
- Anonymity, Pseudonymity: Should apply when identity is not needed.
- Meeting Expectations: Systems should mimic real-world norms.
- Security: Different amounts of protection depending on the situation.
- Access and Recourse: Users should have access to data about them.

Also, Langheinrich, in [358], proposed a privacy awareness system (PawS) to enforce users' participation and to give them the ability to respect other user's safety, property, or privacy, and to rely on social norms, legal deterrence, and law enforcement to create a reasonable expectation that people will follow such rules.

In addition, PawS elaborates on four principles that complement the previous and that are prevalent in a ubiquitous computing environment:

- Notice: The ability of the environment not only to set privacy policies but also to implement efficient ways to communicate these to the user.
- Choice and consent: The provision to the data subject of the choice and ability to agree or to oppose a policy in a functional way.
- Proximity and locality: Mechanisms to encode and use locality information for collected data in order to achieve access restrictions based on the location of the person.
- Access and recourse: The system must give access to the user's data and also provide him with all of the essential information regarding the activity history of the usage of his data.

For the above principles to be fulfilled Langheinrich suggests a series of mechanisms, namely machine-readable privacy policies, policy announcement mechanisms, privacy proxies, policy-based data access.

In UCS we want technologies to fade into the background and become invisible to the user, hence, the location of the user should not be an obstacle. In this sense, Location Based Services (LBS) [346] are one of the main enablers of UCS. The research on privacy protection in LBS is vast [29, 342, 460, 533, 573]. In this line, several dimensions of privacy could be identified [395, 461] but in most cases, research articles focus on only one at a time: identity [76, 85], data [454, 484, 571], location [30, 408, 506, 599] and footprint [7, 123].

12.3 5-D Classification and Analysis of Privacy Risks

From Sect. 12.2 it can be derived that most of the efforts have been oriented towards the suggestion of measures to protect privacy (fighting against specific privacy issues). Also, some efforts have been devoted to the analysis and proposal of privacy principles and properties to be fulfilled. However, there is a lack of conceptual models that allow researchers and practitioners to analyze UCS privacy holistically. With the aim to fill this gap we build upon the ideas of Martínez et al. in [395] to suggest a 5-dimensional privacy model for UCS.

The 5-dimensional privacy model results from the combination of two simpler privacy models (i.e., the 3-D Conceptual Framework for Database Privacy [187] and the W^3-privacy model for location-based services [461]), and it was already used within the context of smart cities [395]. However, in this chapter we revisit the model and adapt it to the nuances of UCS. Moreover, we provide more detailed insights regarding the scope of each dimension with regard to individuals' privacy, in opposition to corporations' privacy, which in the original model was called "owner privacy" and we have renamed it for the sake of clarity as "intelligence privacy". In our model, we identify five privacy dimensions: (1) *identity* privacy, (2) *query* privacy, (3) *location* privacy, (4) *footprint* privacy, and (5) *intelligence* privacy. Next, for each dimension, we detail the definition, risks, countermeasures and practical scenarios within the context of UCS.

12.3.1 Identity Privacy

In the context of UCS, service providers cover some needs of their clients through a variety of added-value services. In order to use such services, generally, providers require clients to identify themselves using different kinds of identification mechanism to control who is accessing the services. Although this requirement is reasonable in most cases from the providers' perspective, it might not be always convenient from the users' perspective, they might prefer to avoid the disclosure of their identities.

Identity privacy refers to the preservation and non-disclosure of the identities of individuals to service providers when using their UCS-based services. The identification of users (e.g., by using their full name, the SSN) commonly improves their experience since it enables the outcomes of the service to be personalized in accordance with users' preferences. However, identification procedures based on this kind of personal data allow providers to uniquely identify their clients and track their use of the provided service (or services). As a result, privacy advocates have raised concern about user profiling.

Disclosing real identities to service providers enables the possibility for those providers to create digital profiles with personal information and, as a result of combining information from multiple providers (or from multiple services offered by the same provider) they could infer personal information such as daily activities, habits and routines. The more information providers collect and the more UCS services deployed, the more accurate and realistic these digital profiles can become. With the creation of users' profiles, additional concerns such as the trustworthiness of the providers, the purposes of the gathered data, and the potential privacy impact in the case of misuse or theft arise.

Using pseudonyms might help to preserve identity privacy. However, this is a choice that is frequently not in the hands of users but providers, who decide which information they require for validation. The idea behind pseudonyms is simple and builds upon linking a certain pseudonym or pseudonyms to an individual's identity in a secret, unique and non-trivial way. Users might create and control their own pseudonyms, but this task might be difficult for most users and it is handed over to pseudonymisers (i.e., third parties that do the job). In this case, the trust is placed in those pseudonymisers. Hence, using a single pseudonymiser might not be enough for some users. With the aim to improve the privacy-resistance of a single-pseudonymiser approach, multiple and geographically distributed pseudonymisers can be used instead [462].

It is worth noting that often users are identified by means of the devices they use. We observe several risk levels depending on the nature of the UCS device in place. The riskier situation arises with UCS devices that normally belong to a unique individual (e.g., smart watches, smart glasses or fitness trackers). In this situation, to preserve the identity privacy of individuals, the relationship between each individual and his/her device must be unknown. Hence, pseudonyms could be helpful but clearly are not enough to prevent the disclosure of identities. A similar, though not so risky scenario is that where we have UCS devices providing services to a controlled group of people, such as the UCS devices in a smart home or in an autonomous vehicle. In this scenario, services are provided to their owners. As in the previous situation, the relationship between individuals and devices should be unknown. However, in this case, if the service identifies the device, it cannot identify a single individual, since he/she is somehow anonymized within the group. The more people using the same device, the more preserved their identities will be. This example could be extended to larger systems such as smart cities in which services are provide to the entire population in which case, the identity of the users is practically guaranteed. Despite the above, we suggest the use of attribute based credentials [84, 244] as the best option to protect identity privacy in the UCS context, especially when using a single device.

12.3.2   Query Privacy

Usually, UCS provide services on demand, i.e., upon the reception of requests from consumers. Normally, these requests can be understood as queries that users create to obtain a specific service. Although queries do not necessarily include personal identifiers, they have to be managed carefully since they could disclose much personal information. In this context, *query privacy* refers to the privacy preservation of the queries sent by users to UCS service providers.

By collecting queries from anonymous users, one could profile them and infer their habits and preferences. More importantly, some queries could enable the identification of such "anonymous" users [9]. In this situation, users tend to trust providers, however, this has proven to be a suboptimal solution. Thus, with the aim to avoid the need to trust providers, scenarios where services can be used by providing minimal query information would be suitable from the privacy perspective (i.e., putting in place the principle of data minimization). By doing so, users make more difficult for service providers to learn information.

Most users are not trained to tune their queries, hence, in general, *query privacy* concerns can be mitigated by using Private Information Retrieval (PIR) techniques. By definition, PIR-based schemes are cryptographic protocols that retrieve records from databases while masking the identity of the retrieved records from the database owners [589]. From the UCS-based services perspective, PIR tools could be used by consumers to query service providers. By doing so, the correlation between queries and individuals could be broken and profiling becomes much more difficult.

Queries and their results can be easily analyzed by UCS-based service providers unless the proper countermeasures are put in place. For example, providers of fitness services could infer habits and routines when interacting with the fitness trackers since they collect a variety of health-related data (e.g., physiologic, biometric, exercise, calorie intake). Furthermore, UCS-based services in smart homes and autonomous vehicles might also put in danger *query privacy* since the submitted queries could be used to extract information about daily habits, such as work schedules or sleep routines. Finally, one of the most challenging UCS services that could endanger *query privacy* are those related to voice recognition, since they listen to and record the exact query. For this kind of service, it would be necessary to guarantee that the signal processing is done on the device, which currently is not the case for most services.

12.3.3   Location Privacy

One of the most significant revolutions provided by UCS is their capability to bring computation anywhere. The deployment of UCS devices around the globe has indirectly led to the control and monitoring of their physical location.

This situation may raise some privacy concerns since location of users of such devices could be inferred. Location data needs to be carefully managed. It is worth noting that with location information, other sensitive data could be inferred, e.g., health-related data, religious or political beliefs, or even social relationships. The importance of preserving individuals' location privacy in the context of UCS-based services justifies its addition as an independent dimension to be analyzed. *Location privacy* concentrates on guaranteeing the preservation of the physical location of individuals when accessing UCS-based services.

Classical location-based services (LBS), which could be integrated into UCS devices, require location data to provide their services (e.g., roadside assistance, real-time traffic information or proximity-based marketing). Normally, UCS service providers receive location information directly from individuals that use their services. For instance, requiring the weather forecast information or the best route to go to a specific location according to the real-time state of the traffic are services where individuals disclose their location information explicitly. Besides, many UCS devices, such as smartphones, smart watches, fitness trackers or autonomous vehicles, already integrate built-in sensors with location capabilities, commonly GPS-based.

Moreover, there are situations in which UCS providers could infer the location of individuals by using proximity data. For instance, video surveillance systems could identify individuals (e.g., by using face recognition) and associate their location with that of the camera, without the intervention of the user. Also, in the case of autonomous cars and smart homes, the location of users is indirectly disclosed since it coincides with the location of the car and the home, respectively.

The sensitiveness of location data fosters the search for solutions that allow the hiding of location information while preserving functionality. For example, in scenarios where the location of the UCS changes over time, collaboration mechanisms between nearby UCS devices/users could mask exact locations, so that the location data sent to the providers would not directly disclose the real location. Similarly, if collaboration protocols are not suitable, real locations could be also protected by means of cloaking services [248] or by determining the proximity to entities without revealing their whereabouts [342, 460]. However, this could result in a degradation of the quality of the results obtained and users might look for the right balance between location details disclosure and the quality of the results.

12.3.4   Footprint Privacy

While providing clients with the requested services, service providers collect information about them. They store the activities that individuals perform, mainly for traceability and analytical purposes. As a result, large amounts of microdata (i.e., individual records containing information collected from individuals) are stored. Roughly speaking, UCS providers collect microdata sets with information detailing the use and traffic on their services, that is, the footprint left by the users on the services. Privacy concerns might emerge once these microdata sets are published or released to external third parties, since these parties could be able to retrieve meaningful information about individuals. In addition, if third parties obtain microdata sets from several service providers used by the same user, further knowledge could be inferred about the individuals' actions. To address these concerns, *footprint privacy*, considers the control of the information that can be retrieved or inferred from microdata sets.

Any UCS service provider collecting and storing information about the activities of their consumers might raise footprint privacy concerns. In previously discussed privacy dimensions, users played a key role in protecting their privacy by putting in place the right countermeasures. However, in the footprint privacy dimension, most of the effort to guarantee privacy is handed over to the provider, and hence it has to be enforced by law (as in fact it is). This privacy dimension will mainly be preserved when service providers apply the proper countermeasures before releasing microdata sets. Otherwise, the privacy of individuals whose data have been collected would be jeopardized.

Statistical disclosure control (SDC) techniques have been used to protect the privacy of users, whose data is stored in microdata sets. Footprint privacy is, hence, normally preserved by applying those techniques. Proposed SDC techniques (e.g., noise addition, rank swapping or micro-aggregation [534], to name a few) aim to prevent linkage between individuals' identities and some of their data (i.e., footprint data) by distorting it. It is worth noting that footprint data does not include identifiers. However, the combination of quasi-identifier attributes might lead to the reidentification of users. Yet, the distortion applied to the data to enhance privacy is not free, since the quality and the utility of the data decrease. So, when using SDC techniques a trade-off between privacy and data utility needs to be considered [287].

12.3.5   Intelligence Privacy

In the current globalization context, there are numerous service providers offering similar products and services, which results in an increase in the number of competitors. Data collected by each provider is, in many cases, very valuable, and it is used to extract knowledge and provide customer-oriented, personalized or added-value services. Hence, sharing and releasing this data is not a common practice, especially if competitors have a chance to take advantage from such data. However, in some cases, organizations (not necessarily competitors) could take mutual benefit by collaborating, but they do not want to share their data. This situation is covered by what we have called *intelligence privacy*. In this dimension, the goal is to allow the collaboration among several organizations so that all could make joint queries to databases to obtain joint information in such a way that only the results are revealed (i.e., the actual information in the databases of each company is not shared or revealed).

To clarify the concept of intelligence privacy let us have a look at the following example of manufacturers of autonomous and intelligent vehicles. Each vehicle manufacturer integrates many built-in sensors on vehicles to gather, store and analyze the status of the car, the nearby environment and further driving-related parameters. Since these data are highly sensitive, manufacturers might decide not to share them. However, collaboration among manufacturers by sharing data could be extremely useful to improve safety on roads and to avoid collisions. In this sense, each manufacturer (even if they compete) would benefit from the collaboration, that is, to obtain joint results, but they want to avoid sharing their intelligence data.

In this situation of mutual distrust, Privacy-Preserving Data Mining (PPDM) techniques emerge as the natural solution to protect *intelligence privacy* [12]. PPDM methods are applicable once independent entities want to collaborate to obtain common results that benefit both of them, but without sharing their data since they do not trust each other. In such scenario, by applying PPDM to the queries submitted across several organization databases, the amount of information transferred to every party is controlled, and this does not pose risks that original data will be revealed, only the results.

It is worth emphasizing that *Intelligence Privacy* considers data belonging to companies (e.g., the heat dissipated by the front-left wheel brake). Thus, data collected by companies but belonging to individuals should not be considered under this dimension because they belong to the users and not to the companies, and hence they should be managed as such.

12.4   Future Trends and Challenges

Privacy has often been considered from a data-oriented perspective. The goal was to protect the data regardless of their origin. Data, in this sense, were seen as something of value that belong to whoever has the ability to collect, store and exploit them and, following this line, privacy protection has been mixed with related problems such as access control, network and database security, and the like. However, to understand privacy we have to put the focus on people and, from there, we should rethink the whole architecture that aims at protecting it.

Although some people support the idea of companies' privacy (i.e., our concept of *intelligence privacy*), privacy issues mainly affect people. There is no doubt about the importance of protecting people's privacy and to do so we state that the focus should be put on people and become personalized. In the years to come, we will see many changes related to how privacy is understood, how the focus will shift from data privacy to people's privacy, and how the latter is protected in practice. We see some fundamental changes that are taking place already and are going to fully develop in the years to come.

12.4.1 Privacy by Design

The addition of privacy at the very beginning of the design process [357] is going to change many ideas and bad practices that are common nowadays. This principle is especially important when we consider the UCS that surround us all the time. Take as an example the face recognition technology that allows access to our mobile phones. In the early days of this technology (and similar ones), biometric information was sent to servers over the Internet, analyzed, and the authentication result was sent back to the edge device. Clearly, this procedure has many points of failure from a privacy perspective. Now most of these technologies are executed on the device, and as a result the data is privately stored by the user and privacy risks are lessened. Emerging technologies based on context-awareness (e.g., smart homes, smart cities, intelligent transportation systems, smart healthcare systems [535, 536]) must be designed with privacy at their core, otherwise we will make the same mistakes of the past and we will need to address privacy as an additional layer outside the system instead of an inner component.

12.4.2 Individual-Centred Privacy

We are shifting towards an individual-centred privacy in which the focus is on the user of the technology and privacy is going to be protected by understanding the personal dimensions of users. As we introduced in this chapter, those dimensions respond to questions such as Who am I? (Identity Privacy), Where am I? (Location Privacy), What do I need? (Query Privacy), What have I done? (Footprint Privacy). This paradigm shift is especially relevant when we consider the impact of wearable devices (e.g., smart phones, smart watches, smart glasses). Most of the data that they generate are sensitive, personal data about their users, hence the important thing here is not the data per se but its relationship to users and their privacy dimensions.

12.4.3 Growing Importance of Legislation

Since the beginning of the twenty-first century, researchers have proposed concepts such as data minimization to improve privacy protection. However, these ideas are taking shape along with others such as consent as a result of the enforcement of the Global Data Protection Regulation (GDPR) [547]. In this sense, it could be said that the ideas were there, but it took almost 20 years to provide them with the right embodiment to be enforced. Clearly, the role of legislation and law enforcers will be fundamental for the protection of privacy, since technology alone can hardly protect all privacy dimensions that affect people.

Lately, there has been a lot of controversy around the impact of the GDPR in the technological context, affecting trendy fields such as UCS, IoT and Big Data. With the aim to enhance individuals' privacy and strengthen the protection of personal data, GDPR unifies data protection laws across EU member states. Law experts agree that GDPR has caused a major overhaul of data protection laws across EU. Thus, to preserve individuals' privacy and guarantee their rights, UCS need to be designed to protect individuals data.

To prevent potential data misuse, GDPR limits the processing of personal data, places higher importance on individuals' consents, and strengthens the rights of individuals to control their data. Also, it introduces reinforcements on the conditions for processing personal data. Hence, processing is only allowed when individuals give explicit and informed consent for such processing according to some well-defined and unambiguous purposes and uses. These requirements pose many challenges for UCS (e.g., obtaining consent in public environments, clearly defining the purposes of processing). In addition, GDPR introduces the right to withdraw this consent (i.e., revocation of consent) easily and at any time, thus denying the future processing of these data if no legal basis justifies their storage.

Also, GDPR considers the right of individuals to obtain their data in a structured, commonly used, interoperable and machine-readable format. This is indeed very challenging, since the heterogeneity of UCS leads to a wide spectrum of information to be returned, ranging from health-related data, wearable trackers, and opinions to even biometric and financial data [562].

For the processing of personal data, UCS must put in place appropriate means to guarantee privacy. For instance, encryption and pseudonymisation could be used to ensure confidentiality. However, despite these techniques, UCS are not free of attacks that open the door to personal data breaches and scenarios where data is compromised. In this context, considering that GDPR establishes the obligation to communicate data breaches to supervisory authorities within 72 h, monitoring systems should permanently keep track of UCS activities and look for abnormal behavior that could compromise personal data [176].

The effect of GDPR on privacy protection will be varied, and the years to come will see a very interesting transformation of the field of privacy protection as a result of its deployment and enforcement.

12.5 Conclusions

Privacy is a fundamental right that has to be protected, and Ubiquitous Computing Systems (UCS) are so intricately fused with our daily lives that they must play a key role in this endeavor. In this chapter, we have provided an overview of the privacy issues that might arise as a result of the generalization of UCS.

We have briefly summarized the state of the art on the matter and we have proposed a 5-dimensional framework that allows the analysis of privacy protection from an individual perspective, in opposition to the older approach centred on data. In our model, we focused on individual dimensions (i.e., identity, location, query, and footprint). Also, for the sake of completeness we have considered a dimension for companies (i.e., intelligence privacy). We believe that this high-level model of privacy dimensions will help researchers and practitioners to approach the difficult problem of analyzing and guaranteeing individuals' privacy in a more comprehensive way.

Also, we have analyzed some of the main changes that we expect to affect privacy in UCS now and in the years to come. Along this line, we emphasized three fundamental trends, namely the consolidation of the privacy-by-design approach, the paradigm shift from data privacy to individuals' privacy, and the growing importance of legislation. Overall, this chapter had the goal of improving people's awareness on privacy issues that affect us all. We hope that these lines have helped readers realize the importance and fragility of their privacy in the technological world in which we live today.

13

Internet of Things Forensics: Research Opportunities and Issues

Sasa Mrdovic

Abstract This chapter provides an overview of research opportunities and issues in IoT forensics. It gives a quick introduction to forensics and digital forensics. Key specifics of IoT forensics are explained. Issues that arise from IoT related challenges in all phases of a forensic investigation are presented. Some opportunities that IoT brings to forensics are pointed out. An example of an IoT forensics case is provided. A detailed research overview is given, providing information on the main research directions with a brief overview of relevant papers. The chapter concludes with some ideas for future research.

13.1 Introduction

IoT, like any other system, needs a way to analyze things that happened within a system. When such analysis is performed for legal reasons it is called forensics. IoT brings many opportunities and issues in its forensics. Collection of forensic data from devices with very limited interfaces and capabilities for data storage and processing is challenging. On the other hand, aggregation of little data pieces from these devices can provide an unprecedented picture of events from various perspectives. That opens up a new chapter in digital forensics.

The future prevalence of connected things will provide an abundance of forensically relevant data. Our digitally connected lives leave traces that might lead to a golden age of forensics. Hard evidence will replace unreliable human recollection.

The opportunities of IoT forensics come with a price. The first issue that comes to mind is privacy. Fortunately, researchers are aware of this challenge and are working on addressing it, in general IoT and especially in IoT forensics. The focus of this chapter is mostly on the difficulties that a forensic investigator faces with IoT specific challenges.

S. Mrdovic (✉)
University of Sarajevo, Sarajevo, Bosnia and Herzegovina
e-mail: smrdovic@etf.unsa.ba

The chapter is organized in the following way. Section 13.2 provides a short introduction to general and then digital forensics, and ends with IoT forensics specifics. Open questions and hurdles that IoT forensics faces are presented in Sect. 13.3. Section 13.4 deals with opportunities that IoT forensics provide. An example of an IoT forensics case is presented in Sect. 13.5. An overview of IoT research with a focus on new approaches is the subject of Sect. 13.6. The last section presents conclusions and future research directions.

13.2 Forensics

Forensic science, usually called forensics, encompasses scientific methods used with the purpose of answering legal questions that generally arise in court cases and criminal investigations. One of the main activities in forensics is evidence collection and analysis. Evidence collection and handling has its procedures that should ensure that [286]:

- evidence is obtained legally, by court order or by order of an authorized institution or person;
- there is a chain of custody, which ensures that collected evidence is unaltered from the moment it was collected until the moment it is presented.

13.2.1 Digital Device Forensics

Digital forensics deals with evidence in a digital form. Digital, or sometimes called electronic, evidence is easy to change. Every access to a file on a digital device (PC, smart phone, IoT device) changes the file's last access time, and thus changes the file in a way that might constitute evidence. This is an example of a change that is neither malicious nor substantial but might be considered evidence tampering. An even bigger issue is the possibility of intentional malicious alterations. To ensure digital evidence integrity and its usability in court, procedures for electronic evidence and handling are in use [208].

The first step is the creation of a forensically correct evidence copy. The forensic copy is bit-by-bit identical to an original digital record. This must be done by tools developed for this purpose that are evaluated and tested to confirm their operation in accordance with a requirements specification [305]. Before and after copying bits, the tools create a cryptographic hash of the original and copied data to confirm data integrity during the copy making process. These tools also keep a log of all steps taken to ensure the existence of the mentioned chain of evidence. Further evidence analysis is performed on the copy, which ensures that the original evidence is unaltered and available in case it's needed for new analysis.

There is an ethical question of data privacy regarding digital evidence from any device that holds personal data. Digital devices are part of our everyday life. All of them, ranging from personal devices such as smart phones or personal computers to cloud and IoT devices, process and store huge amounts of data about personal users' private lives. Most of that data is not relevant in any particular case that triggered evidence collection from that digital device. Nevertheless, a forensic investigator frequently needs to examine a variety of files to be able to establish which ones are relevant to an investigation and which ones are not. Digital device examination is a significant invasion of privacy. For this reason, it is necessary to clearly define what kind of data and evidence an investigator should look for, to protect user privacy as much as possible. This issue in regard to IoT will be further addressed later.

The fact that digital evidence can be on a number of different devices in a variety of formats represents an additional challenge. These devices can be computers, smart phones, digital cameras, GPS devices, or any other device (thing) that stores data in a digital form (and it seems that it will eventually include everything). Each of these devices might store data on a different medium in a different way. Luckily there is some *de facto* standardization that usually makes it a little easier. Digital records on devices are created by different software that use different data formats. To read and understand a particular data format one needs specialized knowledge and tools. For this reason, evidence collection from special devices is often performed by a specialist in that area.

13.2.2   Other Digital Forensics

There are other sources of digital forensic data. Collecting data from those has some issues that are similar to IoT forensics. In reviewing them we can identify what differentiates IoT evidence collection.

All issues mentioned in the previous subsection relate to digital evidence that exist in the memory of a device. That memory is usually non-volatile. Volatile, working memory, like RAM, can contain forensically interesting data. The creation of an evidence copy of such memory must be done without powering down the device, this is known as live forensics. That procedure generally alters memory content and must be thoroughly documented.

Similar issues exist within network forensics. Some of the evidence can be collected from network devices, like routers, firewalls, etc., but most of it exists only in flight. That data can be captured only at the time it passes through a device processing it. There are devices and procedures for storing that network data. Nevertheless, it is impractical to capture and save all network data, due to its volume, however there are other issues such as the number and location of sniffing devices needed [174]. The question of privacy here is much larger as the network data might include a lot of information that is not related to the legal case in question [10]. Therefore, a narrow investigation focus is of utmost importance.

The more recent development in digital forensics is the need for cloud forensics. In its essence it should not differ much from device and network forensics, however it does. The cloud is built on a virtual infrastructure that is shared among many users of a particular cloud service provider. That presents a challenge for forensics because it is hard to locate, identify and separate data or virtual resources relevant for an investigation. In addition, there is no easy way to get access to the cloud infrastructure needed for creation of forensics copies. Data processing is decentralized and data cannot be collected without the cooperation of cloud service providers. Data decentralization might mean that parts of that data are stored in different jurisdictions where different authority can apply [483].

13.2.3   The Need for IoT Forensics

IoT forensics encompass these forensics: device, live, network and cloud. 'Things' might be devices with permanent storage with familiar file systems and file formats. Such 'things' can be treated as any other digital device. Unfortunately, 'things' might use proprietary file systems and formats. They might not even have permanent memory that holds user data and a limited power supply that severely limits duration or even prevents live forensics. 'Things' might have limited amount of RAM and transfer all their data immediately. That data can be transferred in an open standard or a proprietary closed format. Network data can be encrypted. IoT data is often processed in the cloud located in an unknown location that can be on the other side of the planet. All this makes IoT forensics different and more challenging than traditional digital forensics.

An IoT ecosystem, especially for forensic purposes, is divided into three areas: (IoT) device forensics, network forensics and cloud forensics [592]. Although all three of them are important, the focus of this chapter is on (IoT) device forensics. It is in line with the focus of this book on ubiquitous computing systems. The other two areas are more mature. Here they are briefly covered, to the extent required to understand IoT systems forensics.

One of the first papers on IoT forensics [455] created a list of differences to traditional digital forensics. A more recent paper [131], in an IEEE Security and Privacy issue devoted to digital forensics, extended that list. The differences found are the source of specific issues and opportunities in IoT forensics that are discussed in the next two sections.

13.3   Challenges in IoT Forensics

Issues specific to IoT forensics are systematized here based on the available literature. Initially, the general issues are presented followed by others as they occur in successive phases of a forensic investigation.

13.3.1 General Issues

There is a lack of a methodology and framework for IoT forensics. Even in digital forensics there is no single universally accepted methodology, but there are a few that are recognized and used by practitioners and researchers. IoT forensics is still in its infancy and relies on methodologies and frameworks from standard digital forensics that might not be fully adequate.

There is a lack of appropriate tools for IoT forensics. New software and hardware will be needed. A good overview of available forensics tools and their suitability for IoT is given in [559]. After a thorough analysis the authors concluded that existing traditional computer forensic tools are insufficient for cyber-crime investigations in IoT systems.

Since IoT is everywhere, it might be difficult to establish which jurisdiction a case might fall under as there will often be more than one involved. IoT systems can have devices in different jurisdictions as well as different cloud locations and providers. This is not too dissimilar to the Internet with its worldwide reach. IoT just expands the issue from the digital to the physical world.

13.3.2 Evidence Identification, Collection and Preservation

With IoT forensics the first thing to do is to identify the available sources of evidence. The investigator must establish which devices recorded relevant data. The question that needs to be answered is how IoT interacts with its surroundings. The investigator can then know which of the possible available sources to use. In addition, information on where and in which format data is saved must be obtained. Before collecting evidence, constraints to data collection (physical, proprietary standards, legal) should be checked.

Detecting the presence of IoT systems [258], and identification of IoT devices that can provide evidence in an investigation can also be challenging [264]. In addition, the device might contain data on different users not just the one(s) relevant to the investigation. Identification of data of a particular user is not an easy task.

A wide array of different devices makes it difficult to have a standardized approach to evidence collection. Data extraction is made difficult by the limited capabilities of devices, their various interfaces, and their storage formats. Data extraction without making changes to the device or data can potentially be difficult, which is an issue in forensics and can even be considered evidence tampering. On-board data storage is generally not accessible via traditional digital forensic methods [576]. There are limited methods to create forensic images of a given IoT device [152]. It can be difficult or even impossible to collect residual evidence from the device in a forensically sound manner [188, 405]. Encryption of data can make it difficult or impossible to collect evidence. Cumulative datasets may exist in multiple locations [576].

A crime scene in IoT involves physical things and the environment. It can be very difficult to preserve it in its entirety. IoT elements might be interacting autonomously. That can make it impossible to identify the boundaries of a crime scene and separate it from its surroundings [152].

There is a practical question if an IoT device needs to be kept as evidence or not. By its removal from the IoT environment there is an obvious loss of functionality.

13.3.3 *Evidence Analysis and Correlation*

The first issue for a digital forensics investigator when faced with an IoT system is how to analyze evidence from the physical world. IT knowledge might not be enough and expertise from related disciplines can be required [374].

The main issue at this stage of the investigation is the amount of data that an IoT system might produce. That amount can be overwhelming for an investigator [455] and the tools used [559]. The number of possible evidence sources in IoT is much higher than in standard digital forensics. Each source might produce a lot of data, for instance if it is a sensor that measures some physical property in small time intervals.

Since the evidence comes from a high number of heterogeneous sources it is more difficult to correlate. Creating a time-line is important in forensics. With a variety of devices with possibly unsynchronized clocks it can be very challenging to do [152]. All this is an issue in reconstructing events of interest. More evidence should mean better reconstruction but requires a lot of effort that might not be worth it [131].

The issue of privacy is most present in this phase. Aggregation and analysis enables pieces of evidence to be put together, and to establish someone's identity and actions. That is a good thing if the identity belongs to the person being investigated, however it is difficult to know in advance. Data collected from an IoT system might contain a lot of information on individuals not relevant to the investigation [440]. It is best to filter that data out at the time of collection but it is generally not possible due to time and resource limitations in that phase. Even the data on individuals relevant to the investigation might contain personal information that is not important. This issue also exists for standard digital forensics, however in IoT the data is collected continuously and indiscriminately from within the sensors' reach, and usually when individuals are involved this happens without their knowledge.

13.3.4 *Presentation*

Presenting forensic findings in a case involving IoT can be challenging. It is a new forensics and legal field. The courts are just learning to accept virtual evidence and this physical/virtual combination that IoT brings might be confusing.

There is also an additional question in this phase, as well as in the others, of whether a court will accept the methodology and tools used since they are not yet standardized.

There are several issues that are more relevant for forensic practitioners than researchers, but should be mentioned. How much court knowledge and understanding of IoT operations should be assumed? Should IoT devices be brought to court and an explanation provided on how they work before presenting evidence from them? Should an IT or an IoT expert present evidence? [374].

13.4   Opportunities of IoT Forensics

Fortunately, we do not only encounter challenges with IoT forensics. There are also opportunities. Some of them are presented in this section.

IoT brings new sources of evidence to general forensics. IoT records events from the physical environment, which were not recorded and stored before. They are now even stored as digital data. That enables much easier search, filtering, cross-relating, aggregation and other data operations that are helpful in turning data into evidence. IoT systems can contain contextual evidence collected without the individual who committed the crime being aware. This all happens automatically, without any user interaction as a side effect of the IoT operation [264].

IoT evidence, both for physical and digital forensics, is also harder to destroy [131]. It usually is not just one piece of evidence and it is generally stored in the cloud out of the reach of people who may want to delete it. As mentioned in the previous paragraph, usually suspects are not even aware of the evidence being collected. If that is the case they will not see the need and will not try to delete collected evidence.

IoT offers more evidence sources than standard digital forensics. Connected things provide an abundance of forensically relevant data. All devices that might collect, process, store or exchange data are interesting as possible sources of evidence. Even the smallest sensor that transmits a single value of measurement of a single physical quantity might be important. A composite picture of events can be constructed from all the data collected from the IoT systems. For example, the location of a suspect at a particular time can be established by correlating data from different IoT devices from various locations the suspect frequents. Wearable activity monitors can also help identify the approximate location of the suspect [592].

13.5   An Example of an IoT Forensics Case

To present how the above-mentioned IoT forensics challenges and opportunities can relate to a "real" case, a DFRWS IoT forensics Challenge will be used. The Digital Forensic Research Workshop (DFRWS) is a top forensics conference. It has a yearly forensics challenge, and in 2017 the focus was on IoT. The challenge is open to the public but it is particularly directed towards forensic researchers and practitioners. It is intended to motivate new approaches to IoT forensic analysis. The submitted solutions had to include source code openly available under a free software license with supporting documentation. Explanations of the procedure used to analyze the data needed for reaching conclusions were also required. There were four submissions. The winners were announced in May 2018. The challenge details and all submissions with explanations and tools used are available on a github repository for the challenge [302]. All people interested in practical aspects of IoT forensics are strongly advised to read the challenge and check out all proposed solutions. It is state of the art in this area at the time of writing. A lot can be learned from the solutions, explanations and tools.

The case scenario is simple. A woman has been murdered. Her husband has called an ambulance. The husband claims to have been at home at the time of the murder. Contestants had to analyze available artifacts for forensically interesting information and try to conclude who killed the woman.

An overview of general IoT forensics issues, analyzed in Sect. 13.3.1, as they relate to this case are given below.

- **Tools:** The fact that there is a challenge to develop new tools shows that existing tools, either free open source or proprietary commercial, are inadequate for IoT forensics. All submitted solutions used a combination of existing and tools specifically developed for this purpose.
- **Jurisdiction:** In this case there were no jurisdiction issues. Investigators had access to all data collected. In this case the husband provided credentials for cloud stored data. In reality, such credentials might be missing and a court warrant can be required to obtain cloud data that can potentially be in a different country.

Evidence identification, collection and preservation challenges, described in Sect. 13.3.2, which this case brings are presented next. In this particular case the investigators were provided with a list of digital devices found on the scene and the images or data from the devices including the cloud provider network traffic dump. A quick overview of issues police might have faced during relevant data collection is provided.

- **Identification of devices with relevant evidence:** There are some obvious devices that might contain relevant data such as the victim's mobile phone and the smart wristband she was wearing, as well as the husband's mobile phone. Since the husband claimed to have been watching TV using a Raspberry Pi as a smart device at the time of the murder, data from that Raspberry Pi is also of interest. There was a smart Amazon Echo speaker in the apartment that might have recorded something of interest for the investigation. Three sensors, a main sensor, a bedroom door sensor, and a motion sensor, connected to a Samsung SmartThings hub were found. A Google OnHub AP/Router provided Internet access and it had forensically interesting data. It was connected to the

Samsung SmartThings hub and an IPTime network switch. Finding all these devices required effort and knowledge given by the police officers who were on the scene. In this case they missed the smart power outlet.

- **Data extraction/image creation:** Getting relevant data from the devices in a forensically sound manner depends on the type of the device. Creating an image of a mobile phone can be challenging without credentials. Since a Raspberry Pi holds all its data on its SD memory card, imaging it is not difficult. IoT devices like the wristband and the sensors usually do not store any data. Data they generate can be found on the mobile phones used to control them, in the cloud of the smart service provider, or in a network traffic dump. Data collected from the Amazon Echo device can be obtained partly from the device and partly from the cloud. Access to the cloud data here was possible as the victim's husband provided the password. In some other cases, the password might not be available and cloud data would be more difficult to get. Network traffic is usually not logged on a permanent basis. In this case it was possible to obtain a diagnostic report from the OnHub AP/router in Google's protocol buffer specification format and a SmartHome network traffic dump for a period of one relevant hour.
- **Encryption:** It was not an issue in this case since the credentials for the devices and the accounts were available. In general, in the case of encrypted data on devices, or network dumps of encrypted traffic, collection of data in readable format might be impossible.
- **Multiple data locations:** Data was saved on multiple locations: devices and clouds.
- **Crime scene preservation:** Police arrived at the crime scene a short time after the relevant event. Data was collected in a timely manner and there was no need for additional crime scene preservation.

The practical issues of evidence analysis and correlation (Sect. 13.3.3) in this case are explained next.

- **Physical world data expertise:** There was no need for expertise on the data collected from the physical world. All events were simple (opening, closing, motion, steps) and were easy to interpret. That should be expected in current home automation, but in an industrial environment or a smart city this would have been different.
- **Amount of data:** The total amount of compressed data was over 6 GB. It was only a small household of two persons and a relatively short period of time. One can only imagine the data amount expected in a case involving an open space in a smart city.
- **Correlation/time-line:** The analyzed data was from six different devices and locations. For analysis, knowledge was required on how each of the devices and services, which were sources of data, worked and what the collected data meant. Significant effort was required to establish how the devices were connected and how all the data correlated. The time-line was a little easier to establish since all the devices had working and fairly synchronized clocks.

- **Privacy:** Analysis revealed a lot of personal data on the victim and her husband. The history of their phone usage, which included messages, application usage, locations visited, and health data collected from the health devices, among other information, was available to the investigators. Some of their physical conversations, the commands they gave to their smart devices, their movement through the home, and their TV viewing habits were also disclosed. Some data, such as the victim's phone messages and Echo-recorded conversations, were crucial for the investigation, but some, such as the husband's TV viewing habits, were not.

- **Effort needed:** The challenge was open for 3 months. Even after that period, none of the four teams that submitted solutions could be certain that their explanation of the events was completely correct. In total 18 highly skilled professionals worked for 3 months. It was a significant effort and as it was a murder case a human life was at stake. In real life, it is hard to imagine having so many experts available for an investigation. In the author's opinion, that fact might be the biggest practical problem of IoT forensics. Real forensic investigations are not like the CSI program we see on TV.

The challenges of how IoT forensics can present findings, as described in Sect. 13.3.4, are described below for this particular case. The details of the solutions that the competing teams provided were very technical. They were difficult to read and understand for non-experts. They were not written for the court, but for an expert panel. In reality, an additional effort would be needed to prepare the case presentation in front of a judge and jury. In this case it should have been possible to explain to the general public the sequence of events established after the forensic investigation. Technical details need to be kept to a minimum and should be presented as an appendix to the written report.

This case clearly shows the opportunities that IoT forensics can bring. Without IoT forensics the main, and probably only, evidence would have come from eyewitnesses. There might not have been any eyewitnesses, or they could have been hard to find. The case would have had to rely on memories that might have been incomplete, unreliable and subject to change.

IoT forensics enabled the collection of more reliable evidence. That evidence was used to reconstruct the sequence of events that led to the murder. The sensors provided data on door opening and movement. That data enabled investigators to establish the presence of a third person. The smart loudspeaker data contained parts of relevant conversation that confirmed the presence of a third person arguing with the victim. The victim's phone data showed unfriendly conversation between the victim and the coworker she seems to have been having an affair with. That enabled us to establish the identity of a suspect. Data from the smart TV confirmed that the husband was watching TV at the time of the attack on his wife.

13.6   Research Overview

Here we present and analyze the research directions in the literature that address the above-described issues and proposed solutions. IoT forensics research is in its early stages. It did not really start until 2013. It seems that researchers are just beginning to scratch the surface of this vast area. This opens up opportunities for young researchers to join in and offer fresh ideas. Most of the published papers expand on previous results in standard digital, network, cloud and mobile forensics. Several research directions can be identified. The following overview is organized into subsections, with papers that propose similar ideas grouped together and ordered by publication year. Some papers might belong to multiple subsections but are referred to in just the one that corresponds to its main contribution.

13.6.1   New Models and Frameworks

The biggest number of papers belongs to this group. It is understandable as models and frameworks need to define and provide some direction and standardization for researchers and professionals. Unfortunately, none of the proposed models and frameworks has been widely accepted and most of the proposals are still of theoretical nature. A brief overview of papers follows.

In addition to defining challenges and IoT differences, as mentioned in Sect. 13.2.3, [455] proposed some approaches to address challenges. Authors proposed a zone-based method for approaching IoT related investigations. They call them 1-2-3 zones. Zones loosely correspond to three areas of IoT forensics: device, network and cloud. Zone 1 is an internal network with all devices and software. Zone 2 covers hardware and software at the network border that provides communication services from outside networks. It can include a firewall and IDS. Zone 3 is everything outside of the network being investigated and includes cloud and ISP, among other things. Zones enable work in parallel or they focus on the one that is most urgent. Authors also propose a preparation phase for IoT forensics methodology. Future papers confirm the need for the phase where data collection devices are installed in advance. The paper proposes another important concept, Next Best Thing (NBT). It can be expected that in IoT some sources of evidence will not be available or reliable. The NBT model suggests that forensically interesting data can be acquired from devices that are either directly connected or somehow related to the object of forensic interest, as authors call it.

Another IoT digital forensic investigation model is presented in [470]. The model divides IoT into a number of zones, similar to [455]. It includes concepts for base device identification, a location finder represented by zones. The conceptual idea is on the right track, but the paper does not propose how the model could be implemented.

Yet another framework is proposed in [318]. That framework is created to comply with ISO/IEC 27043:2015, the international standard for incident investigation principles and processes. The authors hope that their approach to the standardization and creation of a framework will enable tool development. Their framework consists of distinct processes: proactive process, IoT forensics, and the reactive process. The proactive process is similar to the preparation phase in other models and frameworks. IoT forensics is the same as in [592]. The reactive process consists of initialization, acquisition and investigation which happens after an incident is identified in an IoT-based environment.

Harbawi and Varol [258] propose a theoretical framework that should improve the evidence acquisition model for IoT forensics. They address the problem of the identification of the main source of digital evidence in IoT. A Last-on-Scene (LoS) algorithm is proposed, consisting of seven steps for things-of-interest identification. It extends ideas from [455] and [470]. After things of interest are defined, a modified digital forensic procedure consisting of seven steps is proposed. The authors also propose an online management platform that manages and clusters IoT digital forensic cases, but the paper does not elaborate further than platform general specifications.

Zia et al. [602] propose adding application specific forensics to digital forensics model. They argue that to ensure the collection of evidence in the context of specific IoT applications it is important to have application-specific forensics in place. This application specific component feeds data into the digital forensics component of their model. It provides relevant data for the IoT application in question. That enables focused extraction of artifacts relevant to the investigation. The authors picked the top three most popular IoT applications at the time of writing: Smart Home, Wearables and Smart City. For each of these they defined items of forensic interest in a complete IoT system: device, network and cloud. With this approach the IoT forensic process should be focused on important data but is still holistic.

Privacy protection in IoT forensics is the focus of [440]. It proposes a Privacy-aware IoT forensics model (PRoFIT) that takes into consideration the privacy requirements established by the ISO/IEC 29100:2011 privacy framework. The model, similarly to others, relies on a preparatory phase. In this phase a piece of software may be installed to assist and advise the user about the information contained in the device according to privacy policies and forensic restrictions. Data collection is based on informed user consent. The logic is that enough IoT users will provide this consent and have the software installed. In that case at the time of the investigation a lot of data will be readily available. There might always be a need for court-ordered data collection but less than without the preparation step. The model presents privacy protection aspects through the rest of the investigation process. It includes asking the user's consent whenever there is a need in the investigation to share user data with someone who was not included in previous consents.

The same authors combined their work on PRoFIT [440] with Digital witness [442] to advance IoT forensics while providing user control of private data in [441]. Digital Witness is, exactly what its name suggests, a device which is able to collaborate in the management of electronic evidence. To stimulate a willingness among citizens to collaborate and allow their devices to be Digital Witnesses they need assurance about the protection of their personal information on such devices. The paper shows how it is possible and feasible to have a PRoFIT-compliant Digital Witness. The authors evaluate and confirm their approach in two cases: social malware and warehouse registration.

13.6.2   Preparation Step with Repository

Most of the proposed models and frameworks define the need for a preparation phase in IoT forensics. Such a phase has been suggested for other types of digital forensics. In IoT, due to the lack of logging and local data preservation, a type of pre-prepared local data repository of potential evidence seems to be the most warranted. The following papers offer some ideas on how this can be achieved.

The work in [456], from the same authors as [455], proposes a concept that introduces a device in between the local IoT network and the home firewall (Internet/Cloud) that provides security and forensic services. It is an end-user-managed solution which is unusual and has its pros and cons. The device provides standard security services like IDS/IPS, network monitoring, logging and threshold establishment. Once something happens that causes a crossing of a set threshold the forensic services are activated. They include data compression, parsing and differentiation, storage, time-line creation, alerting, preparation and presentation of results. It is an interesting idea but relies on the end user who might want to hide certain events. Authors also mentioned issues, common with all systems that monitor network traffic, when encryption, compression and steganography are used on the network data. In addition, a device that sits in the path of network traffic might become a bottleneck.

The FAIoT paper [592] formally defined IoT forensics and listed its challenges. It proposed a forensics-aware model for the IoT infrastructures (FAIoT). The model is supposed to help researchers focus on a specific research sub-problem of the IoT forensics problem domain. The FAIoT consists of three parts: a secure evidence preservation module, a secure provenance module, and access to evidence through an API. The authors propose a centralized trusted evidence repository as a new service available for all the IoT devices. Since the repository should handle very large datasets, the authors propose the use of the Hadoop Distributed File System (HDFS). To ensure a proper chain of custody by preserving the access history of that evidence, a provenance aware file system [433] for the repository is proposed. FAIoT could help with IoT forensics investigation but at this stage it is more a conceptual design than a practically usable system.

One more paper that proposes a preparatory phase in order to obtain evidence is [405]. It argues that collection of IoT devices states can enable an investigator to create a clear picture of the events that have occurred. The authors propose a centralized controller that can be connected to devices, controllers (hubs) and the cloud to acquire IoT states. This controller can only read the state and cannot change it. It logs states with time stamps in secure storage with hashes for integrity. The authors provide a proof of concept implementation of their controller using an open source IoT device controller, OpenHAB. It is connected to one device (IP camera), one controller (Insteon Hub) and a cloud account for a device (Nest thermostat). Analysis of the logged states enables reconstruction of scenarios of events in the physical world.

Wang et al. [572] propose a system that ensures data provenance. It ensures that it is possible to establish where a piece of data came from as well as the processes and methodology by which it was produced. It enables a holistic explanation of the system activities, including malicious behaviors. With data provenance, the sequences of activities in an IoT system can be connected with causal relationships. It replaces isolated logging and the analysis of individual devices. The authors implemented this idea with a centralized auditing system for a Samsung SmartThings platform called ProvThing. They showed that, through optimization, real-time system auditing is possible with minimal overhead.

13.6.3   Real-World Systems

The paper "Digital forensic approaches for Amazon Alexa ecosystem" [145] discusses practical issues when carrying out the forensic analysis of IoT systems present in many households. It proposes a combination of cloud-native forensics with forensics of companion devices, and this is called client-side forensics. Since Alexa is a cloud based assistant, most of its data is in the cloud. The authors used unofficial Alexa APIs to access its cloud data. Analysis of network traffic with the Alexa cloud-using proxy, enabled the authors to establish that the data are returned in the JSON format. This reveals issues with cloud forensics retrieving data that might not be available in its raw form but only through calls to predefined query functions, and these functions might not be documented. In this manner the authors were able to obtain some Alexa-native artifacts. Alexa is usually managed through a mobile application or the web. The authors apply forensics of mobile applications and web browsers to retrieve additional artifacts from the client. To automate this process of data collection, visualization and evaluation, the authors created CIFT (Cloud-based IoT Forensic Toolkit). The paper emphasizes the need for a holistic approach to data collection and analysis. The DFRWS Challenge, presented previously, had a practical scenario with more popular home IoT devices, including Alexa Echo, a smart speaker that is part of the Alexa Echo system.

In [494] the authors investigate what data can be collected in IoT attacks and what can be reconstructed from that data. They used a hub and sensors from "sen.se" as well as the Samsung hub, both for the home environment. After a 20-day period of operation, the collected data was analyzed. The authors explain the challenges they faced even with this small system. The paper shows how with a small number of simple sensors different attack scenarios can be identified, interpreted, data preserved and analyzed and presented in a way that is easy to understand. It clearly demonstrates the power and opportunities that come from IoT forensics.

13.7   Conclusion and Future Research Directions

IoT forensics is a new area open for research. There is already a need for practical solutions to questions that arise during investigations that include IoT. That need will help advance the research through practice.

The omnipresence of IoT makes it an ideal tool for evidence collection. As part of its normal operation IoT collects data from its surroundings. That data, from different IoT devices, can be correlated to create a very detailed reconstruction of events. Suspects can easily be unaware of recordings and usually cannot destroy the evidence.

Although this seems like a dream come true for surveillance agencies it can be perceived as "scary" for the common citizen. IoT forensics, with data correlation, can enable the emergence of personally identifiable information from, what seems like, irrelevant pieces of data. The issue of privacy in IoT is a very important one and needs to be adequately addressed.

With the opportunities it offers, IoT forensics has also some issues. New devices, new interfaces, new storage media, new file systems, new network protocols, dispersed cloud storage, unclear authority and jurisdiction are just some of those. The amount of data that needs to be preserved, stored and processed is huge. Even the presentation of the results can be challenging.

IoT forensics research so far has three main directions: the creation of new models and interfaces, the creation of systems with a pre-prepared repository for evidence, and forensics of real-world IoT systems. It seems to be at its beginning, so there are definitely many opportunities for further research.

From the author's point of view two new technologies, blockchain and SDN, can play an important role in that future research. IoT's distributed nature seems to be a good fit for blockchain which is built to, among other things, ensure integrity which is important for forensics. SDN can play a key role in relevant IoT traffic filtering which can be set up on an ad hoc basis.

References

1. 3GPP. ETSI (2014-10). Universal Mobile Telecommunications System (UMTS); LTE; 3G Security; Specification of the 3GPP confidentiality and integrity algorithms; Document 2: Kasumi specification (3GPP TS 35.202 version 12.0.0 Release 12), 2014.

2. Mohamed Ahmed Abdelraheem. Estimating the probabilities of low-weight differential and linear approximations on PRESENT-like ciphers. In Taekyoung Kwon, Mun-Kyu Lee, and Daesung Kwon, editors, *ICISC 12: 15th International Conference on Information Security and Cryptology*, volume 7839 of *Lecture Notes in Computer Science*, pages 368–382, Seoul, Korea, November 28–30, 2013. Springer.

3. Mohamed Ahmed Abdelraheem, Javad Alizadeh, Hoda A. Alkhzaimi, Mohammad Reza Aref, Nasour Bagheri, and Praveen Gauravaram. Improved linear cryptanalysis of reduced-round SIMON-32 and SIMON-48. Cryptology ePrint Archive, Report 2015/988, 2015. http://eprint.iacr.org/2015/988.

4. Mohamed Ahmed Abdelraheem, Javad Alizadeh, Hoda A. Alkhzaimi, Mohammad Reza Aref, Nasour Bagheri, Praveen Gauravaram, and Martin M. Lauridsen. Improved linear cryptanalysis of reduced-round SIMON. Cryptology ePrint Archive, Report 2014/681, 2014. http://eprint.iacr.org/2014/681.

5. Farzaneh Abed, Eik List, Stefan Lucks, and Jakob Wenzel. Cryptanalysis of the speck family of block ciphers. Cryptology ePrint Archive, Report 2013/568, 2013. http://eprint.iacr.org/2013/568.

6. Farzaneh Abed, Eik List, Stefan Lucks, and Jakob Wenzel. Differential and linear cryptanalysis of reduced-round simon. Cryptology ePrint Archive, Report 2013/526, 2013. http://eprint.iacr.org/2013/526.

7. Osman Abul and Cansın Bayrak. From location to location pattern privacy in location-based services. *Knowledge and Information Systems*, Jan 2018.

8. Mark S. Ackerman, Lorrie Faith Cranor, and Joseph Reagle. Privacy in e-commerce: examining user scenarios and privacy preferences. In *EC*, pages 1–8, 1999.

9. Eytan Adar. User 4xxxxx9: Anonymizing query logs. In *Proc of Query Log Analysis Workshop, International Conference on World Wide Web*, 2007.

10. Mikhail Afanasyev, Tadayoshi Kohno, Justin Ma, Nick Murphy, Stefan Savage, Alex C. Snoeren, and Geoffrey M. Voelker. Privacy-preserving network forensics. *Commun. ACM*, 54(5):78–87, May 2011.

11. Dakshi Agrawal, Josyula R. Rao, Pankaj Rohatgi, and Kai Schramm. Templates as Master Keys. In *CHES*, volume 3659, pages 15–29. Springer, August 29 – September 1 2005. Edinburgh, UK.

12. Rakesh Agrawal and Ramakrishnan Srikant. Privacy-Preserving Data Mining. *ACM Sigmod Record*, 29(2):439–450, 2000.

13. Martin Ågren and Martin Hell. Cryptanalysis of the stream cipher bean. In *Security of*

Information and Networks, SIN 2011, Sydney, Australia, November 14–19, 2011, pages 21–28, 2011.

14. Martin Ågren, Martin Hell, Thomas Johansson, and Willi Meier. Grain-128a: a new version of Grain-128 with optional authentication. *International Journal of Wireless and Mobile Computing*, 5(1):48–59, 2011.

15. Siavash Ahmadi, Zahra Ahmadian, Javad Mohajeri, and Mohammad Reza Aref. Low-data complexity biclique cryptanalysis of block ciphers with application to piccolo and HIGHT. *IEEE Trans. Information Forensics and Security*, 9(10):1641–1652, 2014.

16. Toru Akishita and Harunaga Hiwatari. Very compact hardware implementations of the blockcipher clefia. In *Selected Areas in Cryptography, SAC 2011, Ontario, Canada, August 11–12, 2011*, pages 278–292, 2011.

17. Martin R. Albrecht, Benedikt Driessen, Elif Bilge Kavun, Gregor Leander, Christof Paar, and Tolga Yalçin. Block ciphers - focus on the linear layer (feat. PRIDE). In Juan A. Garay and Rosario Gennaro, editors, *Advances in Cryptology – CRYPTO 2014, Part I*, volume 8616 of *Lecture Notes in Computer Science*, pages 57–76, Santa Barbara, CA, USA, August 17–21, 2014. Springer.

18. Javad Alizadeh, Nasour Bagheri, Praveen Gauravaram, Abhishek Kumar, and Somitra Kumar Sanadhya. Linear cryptanalysis of round reduced SIMON. Cryptology ePrint Archive, Report 2013/663, 2013. http://eprint.iacr.org/2013/663.

19. Hoda A. Alkhzaimi and Martin M. Lauridsen. Cryptanalysis of the SIMON family of block ciphers. Cryptology ePrint Archive, Report 2013/543, 2013. http://eprint.iacr.org/2013/543.

20. Riham AlTawy, Raghvendra Rohit, Morgan He, Kalikinkar Mandal, Gangqiang Yang, and Guang Gong. sliscp: Simeck-based permutations for lightweight sponge cryptographic primitives. In *Selected Areas in Cryptography, SAC 2017, Ottawa, Canada, August 16–18, 2017*, pages 129–150, 2018.

21. Frederic Amiel, Benoit Feix, and Karine Villegas. Power analysis for secret recovering and reverse engineering of public key algorithms. In Carlisle Adams, Ali Miri, and Michael Wiener, editors, *Selected Areas in Cryptography*, volume 4876 of *Lecture Notes in Computer Science*, pages 110–125. Springer, 2007.

22. Elena Andreeva, Begül Bilgin, Andrey Bogdanov, Atul Luykx, Bart Mennink, Nicky Mouha, and Kan Yasuda. Ape: Authenticated permutation-based encryption for lightweight cryptography. In *Fast Software Encryption, FSE 2014, London, UK, March 3–5, 2014*, pages 168–186, 2015.

23. Ralph Ankele, Subhadeep Banik, Avik Chakraborti, Eik List, Florian Mendel, Siang Meng Sim, and Gaoli Wang. Related-key impossible-differential attack on reduced-round skinny. In Dieter Gollmann, Atsuko Miyaji, and Hiroaki Kikuchi, editors, *ACNS 17: 15th International Conference on Applied Cryptography and Network Security*, volume 10355 of *Lecture Notes in Computer Science*, pages 208–228, Kanazawa, Japan, July 10–12, 2017. Springer.

24. Ralph Ankele and Eik List. Differential cryptanalysis of round-reduced sparx-64/128. Cryptology ePrint Archive, Report 2018/332, 2018. https://eprint.iacr.org/2018/332.

25. Cédric Archambeau, Éric Peeters, François-Xavier Standaert, and Jean-Jacques Quisquater. Template Attacks in Principal Subspaces. In *CHES*, volume 4249 of *LNCS*, pages 1–14. Springer, October 10–13 2006. Yokohama, Japan.

26. Frederik Armknecht, Matthias Hamann, and Vasily Mikhalev. Lightweight authentication protocols on ultra-lightweight RFIDs – myths and facts. In *Workshop on RFID Security – RFIDSec'14*, Oxford, UK, July 2014.

27. Frederik Armknecht and Vasily Mikhalev. On lightweight stream ciphers with shorter internal states. In Gregor Leander, editor, *Fast Software Encryption – FSE 2015*, volume 9054 of *Lecture Notes in Computer Science*, pages 451–470, Istanbul, Turkey, March 8–11, 2015. Springer.

28. Tomer Ashur and Yunwen Liu. Rotational cryptanalysis in the presence of constants. *IACR Transactions on Symmetric Cryptology*, 2016(1):57–70, 2016. http://tosc.iacr.org/index.php/ToSC/article/view/535.

29. Philip Asuquo, Haitham Cruickshank, Jeremy Morley, Chibueze P. Anyigor Ogah, Ao Lei, Waleed Hathal, Shihan Bao, and Zhili Sun. Security and privacy in location-based services for vehicular and mobile communications: An overview, challenges and countermeasures. *IEEE Internet of Things Journal*, pages 1–1, 2018.

30. Mehrnaz Ataei and Christian Kray. Ephemerality is the new black: A novel perspective on location data management and location privacy in lbs. In Georg Gartner and Haosheng Huang, editors, *Progress in Location-Based Services 2016*, pages 357–373, Cham, 2017. Springer International Publishing.

31. Giuseppe Ateniese, Bernardo Magri, and Daniele Venturi. Subversion-resilient signature schemes. In Indrajit Ray, Ninghui Li, and Christopher Kruegel, editors, *Proceedings of the 22nd ACM SIGSAC Conference on Computer and Communications Security, Denver, CO, USA, October 12–16, 2015*, pages 364–375. ACM, 2015.

32. Jean-Philippe Aumasson and Daniel J. Bernstein. SipHash: A fast short-input PRF. In Steven D. Galbraith and Mridul Nandi, editors, *Progress in Cryptology - INDOCRYPT 2012: 13th International Conference in Cryptology in India*, volume 7668 of *Lecture Notes in Computer Science*, pages 489–508, Kolkata, India, December 9–12, 2012. Springer.

33. Jean-Philippe Aumasson, Luca Henzen, Willi Meier, and María Naya-Plasencia. Quark: A lightweight hash. *Journal of Cryptology*, 26(2):313–339, April 2013.

34. Jean-Philippe Aumasson, Philipp Jovanovic, and Samuel Neves. Norx8 and norx16: Authenticated encryption for low-end systems. IACR Cryptology ePrint Archive 2015/1154, 2015.

35. Jean-Philippe Aumasson, Philipp Jovanovic, and Samuel Neves. NORX v3.0. candidate for the CAESAR competition. https://norx.io, 2016.

36. Jean-Philippe Aumasson, Simon Knellwolf, and Willi Meier. Heavy quark for secure aead. In *Directions in Authenticated Ciphers, DIAC 2012, Stockholm, Sweden, July 05–06, 2012*, 2012.

37. Jean-Philippe Aumasson, Samuel Neves, Zooko Wilcox-O'Hearn, and Christian Winnerlein. BLAKE2: Simpler, smaller, fast as MD5. In Michael J. Jacobson Jr., Michael E. Locasto, Payman Mohassel, and Reihaneh Safavi-Naini, editors, *ACNS 13: 11th International Conference on Applied Cryptography and Network Security*, volume 7954 of *Lecture Notes in Computer Science*, pages 119–135, Banff, AB, Canada, June 25–28, 2013. Springer.

38. Autoelectric. XGecu TL866II. http://autoelectric.cn/EN/TL866_main.html.

39. Roberto Avanzi. The QARMA block cipher family – almost MDS matrices over rings with zero divisors, nearly symmetric Even-Mansour constructions with non-involutory central rounds, and search heuristics for low-latency S-boxes. Cryptology ePrint Archive, Report 2016/444, 2016. http://eprint.iacr.org/2016/444.

40. Gildas Avoine, Muhammed Ali Bingöl, Ioana Boureanu, Srdjan Čapkun, Gerhard Hancke, Süleyman Kardaş, Chong Hee Kim, Cédric Lauradoux, Benjamin Martin, Jorge Munilla, Alberto Peinado, Kasper Bonne Rasmussen, Dave Singelée, Aslan Tchamkerten, Rolando Trujillo-Rasua, and Serge Vaudenay. Security of distance-bounding: A survey. *ACM Comput. Surv.*, 51(5):94:1–94:33, September 2018.

41. Gildas Avoine, Muhammed Ali Bingöl, Süleyman Kardaş, Cédric Lauradoux, and Benjamin Martin. A formal framework for analyzing RFID distance bounding protocols. In *Journal of Computer Security - Special Issue on RFID System Security, 2010*, volume 19, pages 289–317, 2011.

42. Gildas Avoine, Xavier Bultel, Sébastien Gambs, David Gérault, Pascal Lafourcade, Cristina Onete, and Jean-Marc Robert. A terrorist-fraud resistant and extractor-free anonymous distance-bounding protocol. In *ACM on Asia Conference on Computer and Communications Security*, ASIA CCS '17, pages 800–814, New York, NY, USA, 2017. ACM.

43. Gildas Avoine, Xavier Carpent, and Julio Hernandez-Castro. Pitfalls in ultralightweight authentication protocol designs. *IEEE Trans. Mob. Comput.*, 15(9):2317–2332, 2016.

44. Gildas Avoine, Xavier Carpent, and Benjamin Martin. Strong Authentication and Strong Integrity (SASI) is not that Strong. In S.B. Ors Yalcin, editor, *Workshop on RFID Security – RFIDSec'10*, volume 6370 of *Lecture Notes in Computer Science*, pages 50–64, Istanbul, Turkey, June 2010. Springer.

45. Gildas Avoine and Aslan Tchamkerten. An efficient distance bounding RFID authentication protocol: Balancing false-acceptance rate and memory requirement. In *International Conference on Information Security (ISC) 2009*, volume 5735 of *Lecture Notes in Computer Science*, pages 250–261. Springer, 2009.

46. Yossi Azar, Andrei Z. Broder, Anna R. Karlin, and Eli Upfal. Balanced allocations. *SIAM J. Comput.*, 29(1):180–200, 1999.

47. Steve Babbage. Improved "exhaustive search" attacks on stream ciphers. In *European Convention on Security and Detection*, pages 161–166. IET, May 1995.

48. Steve Babbage and Matthew Dodd. The MICKEY stream ciphers. In *New Stream Cipher Designs - The eSTREAM Finalists*, pages 191–209, 2008.

49. Stéphane Badel, Nilay Dagtekin, Jorge Nakahara, Khaled Ouafi, Nicolas Reffé, Pouyan Sepehrdad, Petr Susil, and Serge Vaudenay. ARMADILLO: A multi-purpose cryptographic primitive dedicated to hardware. In Stefan Mangard and François-Xavier Standaert, editors, *Cryptographic Hardware and Embedded Systems – CHES 2010*, volume 6225 of *Lecture Notes in Computer Science*, pages 398–412, Santa Barbara, CA, USA, August 17–20, 2010. Springer.

50. Subhadeep Banik. Some results on Sprout. In *INDOCRYPT 2015*, volume 9462 of *LNCS*, pages 124–139. Springer, 2015.

51. Subhadeep Banik, Andrey Bogdanov, Takanori Isobe, Kyoji Shibutani, Harunaga Hiwatari, Toru Akishita, and Francesco Regazzoni. Midori: A block cipher for low energy. In Tetsu Iwata and Jung Hee Cheon, editors, *Advances in Cryptology – ASIACRYPT 2015, Part II*, volume 9453 of *Lecture Notes in Computer Science*, pages 411–436, Auckland, New Zealand, November 30 – December 3, 2015. Springer.

52. Subhadeep Banik, Takanori Isobe, Tingting Cui, and Jian Guo. Some cryptanalytic results on Lizard. *IACR Transactions on Symmetric Cryptology*, 2017(4):82–98, 2017.

53. Subhadeep Banik, Takanori Isobe, and Masakatu Morii. On design of robust lightweight stream cipher with short internal state. *IEICE Transactions*, 101-A(1):99–109, 2018.

54. Gaurav Bansod, Abhijit Patil, and Narayan Pisharoty. Granule: An ultra lightweight cipher design for embedded security. IACR Cryptology ePrint Archive 2018/600, 2018.

55. Achiya Bar-On, Itai Dinur, Orr Dunkelman, Virginie Lallemand, Nathan Keller, and Boaz Tsaban. Cryptanalysis of SP networks with partial non-linear layers. In Elisabeth Oswald and Marc Fischlin, editors, *Advances in Cryptology – EUROCRYPT 2015, Part I*, volume 9056 of *Lecture Notes in Computer Science*, pages 315–342, Sofia, Bulgaria, April 26–30, 2015. Springer.

56. Achiya Bar-On and Nathan Keller. A 2^{70} attack on the full MISTY1. In Matthew Robshaw and Jonathan Katz, editors, *Advances in Cryptology – CRYPTO 2016, Part I*, volume 9814 of *Lecture Notes in Computer Science*, pages 435–456, Santa Barbara, CA, USA, August 14–18, 2016. Springer.

57. Zachry Basnight, Jonathan Butts, Juan Lopez Jr., and Thomas Dube. Firmware modification attacks on programmable logic controllers. *International Journal of Critical Infrastructure Protection*, 2013.

58. Lejla Batina, Łukasz Chmielewski, Louiza Papachristodoulou, Peter Schwabe, and Michael Tunstall. Online template attacks. In Willi Meier and Debdeep Mukhopadhyay, editors, *Progress in Cryptology – INDOCRYPT 2014*, pages 21–36, Cham, 2014. Springer International Publishing.

59. Aurélie Bauer and Éliane Jaulmes. Correlation analysis against protected sfm implementations of rsa. In Goutam Paul and Serge Vaudenay, editors, *Progress in Cryptology - INDOCRYPT 2013*, volume 8250 of *Lecture Notes in Computer Science*, pages 98–115. Springer International Publishing, 2013.

60. Aurélie Bauer, Éliane Jaulmes, Emmanuel Prouff, and Justine Wild. Horizontal and vertical side-channel attacks against secure RSA implementations. In Ed Dawson, editor, *Topics in Cryptology – CT-RSA 2013*, volume 7779 of *Lecture Notes in Computer Science*, pages 1–17, San Francisco, CA, USA, February 25 – March 1, 2013. Springer.

61. Aurélie Bauer, Éliane Jaulmes, Emmanuel Prouff, and Justine Wild. Horizontal collision correlation attack on elliptic curves. In Tanja Lange, Kristin Lauter, and Petr Lisonek, editors, *SAC 2013: 20th Annual International Workshop on Selected Areas in Cryptography*, volume 8282 of *Lecture Notes in Computer Science*, pages 553–570, Burnaby, BC, Canada, August 14–16, 2014. Springer.

62. Aslı Bay, Ioana Boureanu, Aikaterini Mitrokotsa, Iosif Spulber, and Serge Vaudenay. The bussard-bagga and other distance-bounding protocols under attacks. In Mirosław Kutyłowski and Moti Yung, editors, *Information Security and Cryptology*, pages 371–391. Springer, 2013.

63. Adnan Baysal and Sühap Sahin. Roadrunner: A small and fast bitslice block cipher for low cost 8-bit processors. In *Lightweight Cryptography for Security and Privacy - 4th International Workshop, LightSec 2015, Bochum, Germany, September 10–11, 2015, Revised Selected Papers*, pages 58–76, 2015.

64. Ray Beaulieu, Douglas Shors, Jason Smith, Stefan Treatman-Clark, Bryan Weeks, and Louis Wingers. The SIMON and SPECK families of lightweight block ciphers. Cryptology ePrint Archive, Report 2013/404, 2013. http://eprint.iacr.org/2013/404.

65. Ray Beaulieu, Douglas Shors, Jason Smith, Stefan Treatman-Clark, Bryan Weeks, and Louis Wingers. The simon and speck lightweight block ciphers. In *Proceedings of the 52Nd Annual Design Automation Conference*, DAC '15, pages 175:1–175:6, New York, NY, USA, 2015. ACM.

66. Ray Beaulieu, Douglas Shors, Jason Smith, Stefan Treatman-Clark, Bryan Weeks, and Louis Wingers. Notes on the design and analysis of SIMON and SPECK. Cryptology ePrint Archive, Report 2017/560, 2017. http://eprint.iacr.org/2017/560.

67. G C Becker, Jennifer Cooper, E. DeMulder, Gilbert Goodwill, Jules Jaffe, G. Kenworthy, T. Kouzminov, Andrew Leiserson, Mark E. Marson, Pankaj Rohatgi, and Sami Saab. Test vector leakage assessment (tvla) methodology in practice. In *International Cryptographic Module Conference*, volume 1001, page 13, 2013.

68. Christof Beierle, Jérémy Jean, Stefan Kölbl, Gregor Leander, Amir Moradi, Thomas Peyrin, Yu Sasaki, Pascal Sasdrich, and Siang Meng Sim. The SKINNY family of block ciphers and its low-latency variant MANTIS. In Matthew Robshaw and Jonathan Katz, editors, *Advances in Cryptology – CRYPTO 2016, Part II*, volume 9815 of *Lecture Notes in Computer Science*, pages 123–153, Santa Barbara, CA, USA, August 14–18, 2016. Springer.

69. Fabrice Bellard. Qemu, a fast and portable dynamic translator. In *USENIX Annual Technical Conference, FREENIX Track*, volume 41, page 46, 2005.

70. Davide Bellizia, Milena Djukanovic, Giuseppe Scotti, and Alessandro Trifiletti. Template attacks exploiting static power and application to CMOS lightweight crypto-hardware. *I. J. Circuit Theory and Applications*, 45(2):229–241, 2017.

71. Richard Ernest Bellman. *Dynamic Programming*. Dover Publications, Incorporated, 2003.

72. Jens Bender, Marc Fischlin, and Dennis Kügler. Security analysis of the PACE key-agreement protocol. In Pierangela Samarati, Moti Yung, Fabio Martinelli, and Claudio Agostino Ardagna, editors, *Information Security, 12th International Conference, ISC 2009, Pisa, Italy, September 7–9, 2009. Proceedings*, volume 5735 of *Lecture Notes in Computer Science*, pages 33–48. Springer, 2009.

73. Jens Bender, Marc Fischlin, and Dennis Kügler. The PACE|CA Protocol for Machine Readable Travel Documents. In Roderick Bloem and Peter Lipp, editors, *Trusted Systems*, volume 8292 of *Lecture Notes in Computer Science*, pages 17–35. Springer International Publishing, 2013.

74. Samy Bengio, Gilles Brassard, Yvo G. Desmedt, Claude Goutier, and Jean-Jacques Quisquater. Secure implementation of identification systems. *Journal of Cryptology*, 4(3):175–183, January 1991.

75. Emma Benoit, Guillaume Heilles, and Philippe Teuwen. Quarkslab blog post: Flash dumping, September 2017. https://blog.quarkslab.com/flash-dumping-part-i.html.

76. Alastair R. Beresford and Frank Stajano. Mix zones: User privacy in location-aware services. In *2nd IEEE Conference on Pervasive Computing and Communications Workshops (PerCom 2004 Workshops), 14–17 March 2004, Orlando, FL, USA*, pages 127–131, 2004.

77. Thierry P. Berger, Joffrey D'Hayer, Kevin Marquet, Marine Minier, and Gaël Thomas. The GLUON family: A lightweight hash function family based on FCSRs. In Aikaterini Mitrokotsa and Serge Vaudenay, editors, *AFRICACRYPT 12: 5th International Conference on Cryptology in Africa*, volume 7374 of *Lecture Notes in Computer Science*, pages 306–323, Ifrance, Morocco, July 10–12, 2012. Springer.

78. Thierry P. Berger, Julien Francq, Marine Minier, and Gaël Thomas. Extended generalized feistel networks using matrix representation to propose a new lightweight block cipher: Lilliput. *IEEE Trans. Computers*, 65(7):2074–2089, 2016.

79. Daniel J. Bernstein. Chacha, a variant of salsa20. In Workshop Record of SASC, volume 8, 2008.

80. Daniel J. Bernstein. The Salsa20 family of stream ciphers. In *New Stream Cipher Designs - The eSTREAM Finalists*, pages 84–97, 2008.

81. G. Bertoni, J. Daemen, M. Peeters, and G. Van Assche. Keccak sponge function family main document. Submission to NIST (Round 2), 2009.

82. Guido Bertoni, Joan Daemen, Michaël Peeters, Gilles Van Assche, and Ronny Van Keer. Caesar submission: Ketje v2. candidate for the caesar competition. http://ketje.noekeon.org/, 2016.

83. Thomas Beth and Yvo Desmedt. Identification tokens – or: Solving the chess grandmaster problem. In Alfred J. Menezes and Scott A. Vanstone, editors, *Advances in Cryptology-CRYPTO' 90*, pages 169–176. Springer, 1991.

84. John Bethencourt, Amit Sahai, and Brent Waters. Ciphertext-policy attribute-based encryption. In *Security and Privacy, 2007. SP'07. IEEE Symposium on*, pages 321–334. IEEE, 2007.

85. Claudio Bettini, X. Sean Wang, and Sushil Jajodia. Protecting privacy against location-based personal identification. In Willem Jonker and Milan Petković, editors, *Secure Data Management*, pages 185–199. Springer, 2005.

86. Karthikeyan Bhargavan and Gaëtan Leurent. On the practical (in-)security of 64-bit block ciphers: Collision attacks on HTTP over TLS and OpenVPN. In Edgar R. Weippl, Stefan Katzenbeisser, Christopher Kruegel, Andrew C. Myers, and Shai Halevi, editors, *ACM CCS 16: 23rd Conference on Computer and Communications Security*, pages 456–467, Vienna, Austria, October 24–28, 2016. ACM Press.

87. Begül Bilgin, Andrey Bogdanov, Miroslav Knežević, Florian Mendel, and Qingju Wang. Fides: Lightweight authenticated cipher with side-channel resistance for constrained hardware. In Guido Bertoni and Jean-Sébastien Coron, editors, *Cryptographic Hardware and Embedded Systems – CHES 2013*, volume 8086 of *Lecture Notes in Computer Science*, pages 142–158, Santa Barbara, CA, USA, August 20–23, 2013. Springer.

88. Alex Biryukov and Eyal Kushilevitz. Improved cryptanalysis of RC5. In Kaisa Nyberg, editor, *Advances in Cryptology – EUROCRYPT'98*, volume 1403 of *Lecture Notes in Computer Science*, pages 85–99, Espoo, Finland, May 31 – June 4, 1998. Springer.

89. Alex Biryukov and Leo Perrin. State of the art in lightweight symmetric cryptography. Cryptology ePrint Archive, Report 2017/511, 2017. http://eprint.iacr.org/2017/511.

90. Alex Biryukov, Deike Priemuth-Schmid, and Bin Zhang. Multiset collision attacks on reduced-round SNOW 3G and SNOW 3G (+). In Jianying Zhou and Moti Yung, editors, *ACNS 10: 8th International Conference on Applied Cryptography and Network Security*, volume 6123 of *Lecture Notes in Computer Science*, pages 139–153, Beijing, China, June 22–25, 2010. Springer.

91. Alex Biryukov and Adi Shamir. Cryptanalytic time/memory/data tradeoffs for stream ciphers. In Tatsuaki Okamoto, editor, *Advances in Cryptology – ASIACRYPT 2000*, volume 1976 of *Lecture Notes in Computer Science*, pages 1–13, Kyoto, Japan, December 3–7, 2000. Springer.

92. Alex Biryukov, Adi Shamir, and David A. Wagner. Real time cryptanalysis of a5/1 on a pc. In *Fast Software Encryption, FSE 2000, New York, NY, USA, April 10–12, 2000*, pages 1–18, 2001.

93. Bruno Blanchet. An Efficient Cryptographic Protocol Verifier Based on Prolog Rules. In *IEEE Computer Security Foundations Workshop*, pages 82–96, Novia Scotia, Canada, 2001. IEEE.

94. Matt Blaze. Looking on the bright side of black-box cryptography (transcript of discussion). In *Security Protocols, 8th International Workshop, Cambridge, UK, April 3–5, 2000, Revised Papers*, pages 54–61, 2000.

95. Céline Blondeau and Benoît Gérard. Differential Cryptanalysis of PUFFIN and PUFFIN2, 11 2011.

96. Bluetooth^{TM}. Bluetooth specification, version 5.0, 2016.

97. Manuel Blum and Sampath Kannan. Designing programs that check their work. *J. ACM*, 42(1):269–291, 1995.

98. Martin Boesgaard, Mette Vesterager, Thomas Pedersen, Jesper Christiansen, and Ove Scavenius. Rabbit: A new high-performance stream cipher. In Thomas Johansson, editor, *Fast Software Encryption – FSE 2003*, volume 2887 of *Lecture Notes in Computer Science*, pages 307–329, Lund, Sweden, February 24–26, 2003. Springer.

99. Andrey Bogdanov, Ilya Kizhvatov, and Andrey Pyshkin. Algebraic methods in side-channel collision attacks and practical collision detection. In DipanwitaRoy Chowdhury, Vincent Rijmen, and Abhijit Das, editors, *Progress in Cryptology - INDOCRYPT 2008*, volume 5365 of *Lecture Notes in Computer Science*, pages 251–265. Springer, 2008.

100. Andrey Bogdanov, Miroslav Knežević, Gregor Leander, Deniz Toz, Kerem Varici, and Ingrid Verbauwhede. Spongent: A lightweight hash function. In Bart Preneel and Tsuyoshi Takagi, editors, *Cryptographic Hardware and Embedded Systems – CHES 2011*, volume 6917 of *Lecture Notes in Computer Science*, pages 312–325, Nara, Japan, September 28 – October 1, 2011. Springer.

101. Andrey Bogdanov, Lars R. Knudsen, Gregor Leander, Christof Paar, Axel Poschmann, Matthew J. B. Robshaw, Yannick Seurin, and C. Vikkelsoe. PRESENT: An ultra-lightweight block cipher. In Pascal Paillier and Ingrid Verbauwhede, editors, *Cryptographic Hardware and Embedded Systems – CHES 2007*, volume 4727 of *Lecture Notes in Computer Science*, pages 450–466, Vienna, Austria, September 10–13, 2007. Springer.

102. Andrey Bogdanov, Gregor Leander, Christof Paar, Axel Poschmann, Matthew J. B. Robshaw, and Yannick Seurin. Hash functions and RFID tags: Mind the gap. In Elisabeth Oswald and Pankaj Rohatgi, editors, *Cryptographic Hardware and Embedded Systems – CHES 2008*, volume 5154 of *Lecture Notes in Computer Science*, pages 283–299, Washington, D.C., USA, August 10–13, 2008. Springer.

103. Andrey Bogdanov, Florian Mendel, Francesco Regazzoni, Vincent Rijmen, and Elmar Tischhauser. ALE: AES-based lightweight authenticated encryption. In Shiho Moriai, editor, *Fast Software Encryption – FSE 2013*, volume 8424 of *Lecture Notes in Computer Science*, pages 447–466, Singapore, March 11–13, 2014. Springer.

104. Andrey Bogdanov and Christian Rechberger. A 3-subset meet-in-the-middle attack: Cryptanalysis of the lightweight block cipher KTANTAN. In Alex Biryukov, Guang Gong, and Douglas R. Stinson, editors, *SAC 2010: 17th Annual International Workshop on Selected Areas in Cryptography*, volume 6544 of *Lecture Notes in Computer Science*, pages 229–240, Waterloo, Ontario, Canada, August 12–13, 2011. Springer.

105. Julia Borghoff, Anne Canteaut, Tim Güneysu, Elif Bilge Kavun, Miroslav Knežević, Lars R. Knudsen, Gregor Leander, Ventzislav Nikov, Christof Paar, Christian Rechberger, Peter Rombouts, Søren S. Thomsen, and Tolga Yalçin. PRINCE - A low-latency block cipher for pervasive computing applications - extended abstract. In Xiaoyun Wang and Kazue Sako, editors, *Advances in Cryptology – ASIACRYPT 2012*, volume 7658 of *Lecture Notes in Computer Science*, pages 208–225, Beijing, China, December 2–6, 2012. Springer.

106. Christina Boura, María Naya-Plasencia, and Valentin Suder. Scrutinizing and improving impossible differential attacks: Applications to CLEFIA, Camellia, LBlock and Simon. In

Palash Sarkar and Tetsu Iwata, editors, *Advances in Cryptology – ASIACRYPT 2014, Part I*, volume 8873 of *Lecture Notes in Computer Science*, pages 179–199, Kaoshiung, Taiwan, R.O.C., December 7–11, 2014. Springer.

107. Ioana Boureanu, David Gerault, and Pascal Lafourcade. Fine-grained and application-ready distance-bounding security. Cryptology ePrint Archive, Report 2018/384, 2018.

108. Ioana Boureanu, Aikaterini Mitrokotsa, and Serge Vaudenay. On the pseudorandom function assumption in (secure) distance-bounding protocols. In Alejandro Hevia and Gregory Neven, editors, *Progress in Cryptology – LATINCRYPT 2012*, pages 100–120. Springer, 2012.

109. Ioana Boureanu, Aikaterini Mitrokotsa, and Serge Vaudenay. Towards secure distance bounding. In *Fast Software Encryption - 20th International Workshop, FSE 2013*, pages 55–67, Singapore, March 2013.

110. Ioana Boureanu, Aikaterini Mitrokotsa, and Serge Vaudenay. Practical and provably secure distance-bounding. In Yvo Desmedt, editor, *Information Security*, pages 248–258, Cham, 2015. Springer.

111. Ioana Boureanu and Serge Vaudenay. Optimal proximity proofs. In *Information Security and Cryptology - 10th International Conference, Inscrypt 2014, Beijing, China, December 13–15, 2014, Revised Selected Papers*, pages 170–190, 2014.

112. Stefan Brands and David Chaum. Distance-bounding protocols. In Tor Helleseth, editor, *Advances in Cryptology — EUROCRYPT '93*, pages 344–359. Springer, 1994.

113. Stefan Brands and David Chaum. Distance-bounding protocols. In Tor Helleseth, editor, *Advances in Cryptology – EUROCRYPT '93*, volume 765 of *Lecture Notes in Computer Science*, pages 344–359. Springer, 1994.

114. Agnès Brelurut, David Gerault, and Pascal Lafourcade. Survey of distance bounding protocols and threats. In Joaquin Garcia-Alfaro, Evangelos Kranakis, and Guillaume Bonfante, editors, *Foundations and Practice of Security*, pages 29–49, Cham, 2016. Springer.

115. Éric Brier, Christophe Clavier, and Francis Olivier. Correlation Power Analysis with a Leakage Model. In *CHES*, volume 3156 of *LNCS*, pages 16–29. Springer, August 11–13 2004. Cambridge, MA, USA.

116. Robert G Brown, Dirk Eddelbuettel, and David Bauer. Dieharder: A random number test suite. *Open Source software library, under development*, 2013.

117. Marco Bucci, Luca Giancane, Raimondo Luzzi, M. Marino, Giuseppe Scotti, and Alessandro Trifiletti. Enhancing power analysis attacks against cryptographic devices. *IET Circuits, Devices & Systems*, 2(3):298–305, 2008.

118. Xavier Bultel, Sébastien Gambs, David Gérault, Pascal Lafourcade, Cristina Onete, and Jean-Marc Robert. A prover-anonymous and terrorist-fraud resistant distance-bounding protocol. In *ACM Conference on Security & Privacy in Wireless and Mobile Networks*, WiSec '16, pages 121–133, New York, NY, USA, 2016. ACM.

119. Kang Byeong-Ho. Ubiquitous computing environment threats and defensive measures. *Int. J. Multimedia Ubiquit. Eng*, 2(1):47–60, 2007.

120. Cristian Cadar, Daniel Dunbar, and Dawson Engler. KLEE: Unassisted and Automatic Generation of High-coverage Tests for Complex Systems Programs. In *Proceedings of the 8th USENIX Conference on Operating Systems Design and Implementation*, OSDI '08, 2008.

121. Tom Caddy. Fips 140–2. In *Encyclopedia of Cryptography and Security*, pages 468–471. Springer, 2011.

122. Eleonora Cagli, Cécile Dumas, and Emmanuel Prouff. Convolutional neural networks with data augmentation against jitter-based countermeasures - profiling attacks without pre-processing. In *Cryptographic Hardware and Embedded Systems - CHES 2017 - 19th International Conference, Taipei, Taiwan, September 25–28, 2017, Proceedings*, pages 45–68, 2017.

123. Ying Cai and Ge Xu. Cloaking with footprints to provide location privacy protection in location-based services, August 15 2017. US Patent 9,736,685.

124. Seyit Ahmet Çamtepe and Bülent Yener. Combinatorial design of key distribution mechanisms for wireless sensor networks. *IEEE/ACM Trans. Netw.*, 15(2):346–358, 2007.

125. Giovanni Camurati and Aurélien Francillon. Inception: system-wide security testing of real-world embedded systems software. In *USENIX Security Symposium*, 2018.
126. Christophe De Cannière, Orr Dunkelman, and Miroslav Knežević. KATAN and KTANTAN - a family of small and efficient hardware-oriented block ciphers. In Christophe Clavier and Kris Gaj, editors, *Cryptographic Hardware and Embedded Systems – CHES 2009*, volume 5747 of *Lecture Notes in Computer Science*, pages 272–288, Lausanne, Switzerland, September 6–9, 2009. Springer.
127. Christophe De Cannière and Bart Preneel. Trivium. In *New Stream Cipher Designs - The eSTREAM Finalists*, pages 244–266, 2008.
128. Anne Canteaut, Thomas Fuhr, Henri Gilbert, María Naya-Plasencia, and Jean-René Reinhard. Multiple differential cryptanalysis of round-reduced PRINCE. In Carlos Cid and Christian Rechberger, editors, *Fast Software Encryption – FSE 2014*, volume 8540 of *Lecture Notes in Computer Science*, pages 591–610, London, UK, March 3–5, 2015. Springer.
129. Anne Canteaut, Virginie Lallemand, and María Naya-Plasencia. Related-key attack on full-round PICARO. In Orr Dunkelman and Liam Keliher, editors, *SAC 2015: 22nd Annual International Workshop on Selected Areas in Cryptography*, volume 9566 of *Lecture Notes in Computer Science*, pages 86–101, Sackville, NB, Canada, August 12–14, 2016. Springer.
130. Xavier Carpent. *RFID authentication and time-memory trade-offs*. PhD thesis, Catholic University of Louvain, Louvain-la-Neuve, Belgium, 2015.
131. Luca Caviglione, Steffen Wendzel, and Wojciech Mazurczyk. The future of digital forensics: Challenges and the road ahead. *IEEE Security & Privacy*, 15(6):12–17, 2017.
132. Avik Chakraborti, Anupam Chattopadhyay, Muhammad Hassan, and Mridul Nandi. TriviA: A fast and secure authenticated encryption scheme. In Tim Güneysu and Helena Handschuh, editors, *Cryptographic Hardware and Embedded Systems – CHES 2015*, volume 9293 of *Lecture Notes in Computer Science*, pages 330–353, Saint-Malo, France, September 13–16, 2015. Springer.
133. Nishanth Chandran, Vipul Goyal, Ryan Moriarty, and Rafail Ostrovsky. Position based cryptography. In *International Cryptology Conference on Advances in Cryptology – CRYPTO'09*, Lecture Notes in Computer Science, pages 391–407. Springer, 2009.
134. Suresh Chari, Charanjit Jutla, Josyula Rao, and Pankaj Rohatgi. Towards sound approaches to counteract power-analysis attacks. In *Advances in Cryptology - CRYPTO'99*, pages 791–791. Springer, 1999.
135. Suresh Chari, Josyula R. Rao, and Pankaj Rohatgi. Template Attacks. In *CHES*, volume 2523 of *LNCS*, pages 13–28. Springer, August 2002. San Francisco Bay (Redwood City), USA.
136. David Chaum and Torben P. Pedersen. Wallet databases with observers. In Ernest F. Brickell, editor, *Advances in Cryptology - CRYPTO '92, 12th Annual International Cryptology Conference, Santa Barbara, California, USA, August 16–20, 1992, Proceedings*, volume 740 of *Lecture Notes in Computer Science*, pages 89–105. Springer, 1992.
137. Daming D Chen, Manuel Egele, Maverick Woo, and David Brumley. Towards automated dynamic analysis for linux-based embedded firmware. In *ISOC NDSS 2016*, 2016.
138. Huaifeng Chen and Xiaoyun Wang. Improved linear hull attack on round-reduced Simon with dynamic key-guessing techniques. Cryptology ePrint Archive, Report 2015/666, 2015. http://eprint.iacr.org/2015/666.
139. Hung-Yu Chien. SASI: A new ultralightweight RFID authentication protocol providing strong authentication and strong integrity. *IEEE Transactions on Dependable and Secure Computing*, 4(4):337–340, December 2007.
140. Vitaly Chipounov, Volodymyr Kuznetsov, and George Candea. S2e: A platform for in-vivo multi-path analysis of software systems. *Acm Sigplan Notices*, 46(3):265–278, 2011.
141. Tom Chothia, Flavio D. Garcia, Joeri de Ruiter, Jordi van den Breekel, and Matthew Thompson. Relay cost bounding for contactless EMV payments. In Rainer Böhme and Tatsuaki Okamoto, editors, *Financial Cryptography and Data Security - 19th International Conference, FC 2015, San Juan, Puerto Rico, January 26–30, 2015, Revised Selected Papers*, volume 8975 of *Lecture Notes in Computer Science*, pages 189–206, Puerto Rico, January 2015. Springer.

142. Omar Choudary and Markus G. Kuhn. Efficient template attacks. In Aurélien Francillon and Pankaj Rohatgi, editors, *Smart Card Research and Advanced Applications - 12th International Conference, CARDIS 2013, Berlin, Germany, November 27–29, 2013. Revised Selected Papers*, volume 8419 of *LNCS*, pages 253–270. Springer, 2013.

143. Arka Rai Choudhuri and Subhamoy Maitra. Significantly improved multi-bit differentials for reduced round Salsa and ChaCha. *IACR Transactions on Symmetric Cryptology*, 2016(2):261–287, 2016. http://tosc.iacr.org/index.php/ToSC/article/view/574.

144. Jiali Choy, Huihui Yap, Khoongming Khoo, Jian Guo, Thomas Peyrin, Axel Poschmann, and Chik How Tan. SPN-hash: Improving the provable resistance against differential collision attacks. In Aikaterini Mitrokotsa and Serge Vaudenay, editors, *AFRICACRYPT 12: 5th International Conference on Cryptology in Africa*, volume 7374 of *Lecture Notes in Computer Science*, pages 270–286, Ifrance, Morocco, July 10–12, 2012. Springer.

145. Hyunji Chung, Jungheum Park, and Sangjin Lee. Digital forensic approaches for amazon alexa ecosystem. *Digital Investigation*, 22:S15–S25, 2017.

146. Jacek Cichoń, Zbigniew Golebiewski, and Mirosław Kutyłowski. From key predistribution to key redistribution. *Theor. Comput. Sci.*, 453:75–87, 2012.

147. Jacek Cichoń and Mirosław Kutyłowski. Anonymity and k-choice identities. In Dingyi Pei, Moti Yung, Dongdai Lin, and Chuankun Wu, editors, *Information Security and Cryptology, Third SKLOIS Conference, Inscrypt 2007, Xining, China, August 31 - September 5, 2007, Revised Selected Papers*, volume 4990 of *Lecture Notes in Computer Science*, pages 283–297. Springer, 2007.

148. Carlos Cid, Shinsaku Kiyomoto, and Jun Kurihara. The rakaposhi stream cipher. In *Information and Communications Security, ICICS 2009, Beijing, China, December 14–17, 2009*, pages 32–46, 2009.

149. Jolyon Clulow, Gerhard P Hancke, Markus G Kuhn, and Tyler Moore. So near and yet so far: Distance-bounding attacks in wireless networks. In *European Workshop on Security in Ad-hoc and Sensor Networks*, volume 4357 of *Lecture Notes in Computer Science*, pages 83–97. Springer, 2006.

150. Lucian Cojocar, Jonas Zaddach, Roel Verdult, Herbert Bos, Aurélien Francillon, and Davide Balzarotti. PIE: Parser Identification in Embedded Systems. *Annual Computer Security Applications Conference (ACSAC)*, December 2015.

151. SEC Consult. House of Keys: Industry-Wide HTTPS Certificate and SSH Key Reuse Endangers Millions of Devices Worldwide. *Blog, Nov, 25, 2015.*

152. Mauro Conti, Ali Dehghantanha, Katrin Franke, and Steve Watson. Internet of things security and forensics: Challenges and opportunities. *Future Generation Computer Systems*, 78:544–546, 2018.

153. Jean-Sbastien Coron, Aline Gouget, Thomas Icart, and Pascal Paillier. Supplemental access control (pace v2): Security analysis of pace integrated mapping. *IACR Cryptology ePrint Archive*, 2011:58, 2011.

154. Jean-Sébastien Coron. Resistance against differential power analysis for elliptic curve cryptosystems. In *Proceedings of the First International Workshop on Cryptographic Hardware and Embedded Systems*, CHES '99, pages 292–302, London, UK, UK, 1999. Springer-Verlag.

155. Andrei Costin, Jonas Zaddach, Aurélien Francillon, and Davide Balzarotti. A Large Scale Analysis of the Security of Embedded Firmwares. In *Proceedings of the 23rd USENIX Security Symposium (USENIX Security)*, August 2014.

156. Andrei Costin, Apostolis Zarras, and Aurélien Francillon. Automated Dynamic Firmware Analysis at Scale: A Case Study on Embedded Web Interfaces. In *11th ACM Asia Conference on Computer and Communications Security (ASIACCS, ASIACCS 16*, May 2016.

157. Andrei Costin, Apostolis Zarras, and Aurélien Francillon. Towards automated classification of firmware images and identification of embedded devices. In *IFIP International Conference on ICT Systems Security and Privacy Protection*, pages 233–247. Springer, 2017.

158. Franck Courbon, Sergei Skorobogatov, and Christopher Woods. Reverse engineering flash EEPROM memories using scanning electron microscopy. In *Smart Card Research and Advanced Applications - 15th International Conference, CARDIS 2016*, pages 57–72, 2016.

159. Nicolas T. Courtois. An improved differential attack on full GOST. In *The New Codebreakers - Essays Dedicated to David Kahn on the Occasion of His 85th Birthday*, pages 282–303, 2016.

160. Cas Cremers, Kasper B. Rasmussen, Benedikt Schmidt, and Srdjan Capkun. Distance hijacking attacks on distance bounding protocols. In *IEEE Symposium on Security and Privacy*, SP '12, pages 113–127, Washington, DC, USA, 2012. IEEE.

161. Ang Cui. Embedded Device Firmware Vulnerability Hunting with FRAK. *DefCon 20*, 2012.

162. Ang Cui, Michael Costello, and Salvatore J Stolfo. When Firmware Modifications Attack: A Case Study of Embedded Exploitation. In *Proceedings of the 20th Symposium on Network and Distributed System Security*, NDSS '13. The Internet Society, 2013.

163. Ang Cui and Salvatore J. Stolfo. Defending Embedded Systems with Software Symbiotes. In Robin Sommer, Davide Balzarotti, and Gregor Maier, editors, *Recent Advances in Intrusion Detection*, volume 6961 of *Lecture Notes in Computer Science*, pages 358–377. Springer, 2011.

164. Joan Daemen, René Govaerts, and Joos Vandewalle. A new approach to block cipher design. In Ross J. Anderson, editor, *Fast Software Encryption – FSE'93*, volume 809 of *Lecture Notes in Computer Science*, pages 18–32, Cambridge, UK, December 9–11, 1994. Springer.

165. Joan Daemen, Michaël Peeters, Gilles Van Assche, and Vincent Rijmen. Nessie proposal: NOEKEON, 2000. http://gro.noekeon.org/.

166. Joan Daemen and Vincent Rijmen. *The Design of Rijndael: AES - The Advanced Encryption Standard*. Springer-Verlag, 2002.

167. Yibin Dai and Shaozhen Chen. Cryptanalysis of full PRIDE block cipher. *Science China Information Sciences*, 60(5):052108, Sep 2016.

168. Boris Danev, Heinrich Luecken, Srdjan Capkun, and Karim El Defrawy. Attacks on physical-layer identification. In *ACM Conference on Wireless Network Security*, WiSec '10, pages 89–98, New York, NY, USA, 2010. ACM.

169. Paolo D'Arco and Alfredo De Santis. On Ultra-Lightweight RFID Authentication Protocols. *IEEE Transactions on Dependable and Secure Computing*, 99(PrePrints), 2010.

170. Paolo D'Arco and Roberto De Prisco. Design weaknesses in recent ultralightweight RFID authentication protocols. In *ICT Systems Security and Privacy Protection - 33rd IFIP TC 11 International Conference, SEC 2018, Held at the 24th IFIP World Computer Congress, WCC 2018, Poznan, Poland, September 18–20, 2018, Proceedings*, pages 3–17, 2018.

171. Lyla B Das. *Embedded Systems: An Integrated Approach*. Pearson Education India, 2012.

172. Sourav Das and Dipanwita Roy Chowdhury. Car30: a new scalable stream cipher with rule 30. *Cryptography and Communications*, 5(2):137–162, 2013.

173. Mathieu David, Damith Chinthana Ranasinghe, and Torben Bjerregaard Larsen. A2U2: A stream cipher for printed electronics RFID tags. *2011 IEEE International Conference on RFID*, pages 176–183, 2011.

174. Sherri Davidoff and Jonathan Ham. *Network forensics: tracking hackers through cyberspace*, volume 2014. Prentice hall Upper Saddle River, 2012.

175. Drew Davidson, Benjamin Moench, Thomas Ristenpart, and Somesh Jha. FIE on Firmware: Finding Vulnerabilities in Embedded Systems Using Symbolic Execution. In *Proceedings of the 22nd USENIX Security Symposium*, SEC '13, 2013.

176. Simon Davies. The Data Protection Regulation: A Triumph of Pragmatism over Principle? *European Data Protection Law Review*, 2:290, 2016.

177. Alexandre Debant, Stéphanie Delaune, and Cyrille Wiedling. Proving physical proximity using symbolic models. Technical report, Univ Rennes, CNRS, IRISA, France, February 2018.

178. Yvo Desmedt. Major security problems with the "unforgeable" (feige-)fiat-shamir proof of identity and how to overcome them. In *Securicom 88, 6th worldwide congress on computer and communications security and protection*, pages 147–159. SEDEP Paris France, 1988.

179. Lin Ding and Jie Guan. Cryptanalysis of mickey family of stream ciphers. *Security and Communication Networks*, 6(8):936–941, 2013.

180. Lin Ding, Chenhui Jin, Jie Guan, and Qiuyan Wang. Cryptanalysis of lightweight wg-8 stream cipher. *IEEE Transactions on Information Forensics and Security*, 9(4):645–652, 2014.

181. Daniel Dinu, Léo Perrin, Aleksei Udovenko, Vesselin Velichkov, Johann Großschädl, and Alex Biryukov. Design strategies for ARX with provable bounds: Sparx and LAX. In Jung Hee Cheon and Tsuyoshi Takagi, editors, *Advances in Cryptology – ASIACRYPT 2016, Part I*, volume 10031 of *Lecture Notes in Computer Science*, pages 484–513, Hanoi, Vietnam, December 4–8, 2016. Springer.

182. Dumitru-Daniel Dinu, Alex Biryukov, Johann Großschädl, Dmitry Khovra-Tovich, Yann Le Corre, and Léo Perrin. FELICS – fair evaluation of lightweight cryptographic systems. In NIST Workshop on Lightweight Cryptography 2015. National Institute of Standards and Technology (NIST), 2015.

183. Itai Dinur. Improved differential cryptanalysis of round-reduced Speck. Cryptology ePrint Archive, Report 2014/320, 2014. http://eprint.iacr.org/2014/320.

184. Itai Dinur and Jérémy Jean. Cryptanalysis of fides. In *Fast Software Encryption, FSE 2014, London, UK, March 3–5, 2014*, pages 224–240, 2015.

185. Christoph Dobraunig, Maria Eichlseder, Daniel Kales, and Florian Mendel. Practical key-recovery attack on mantis5. *IACR Trans. Symmetric Cryptol.*, 2016(2):248–260, 2017.

186. Christoph Dobraunig, Maria Eichlseder, Florian Mendel, and Martin Schläffer. Ascon v1.2. candidate for the CAESAR competition. http://ascon.iaik.tugraz.at/, 2016.

187. Josep Domingo-Ferrer. A three-dimensional conceptual framework for database privacy. In *Workshop on Secure Data Management*, pages 193–202. Springer, 2007.

188. Christian D'Orazio, Kim-Kwang Raymond Choo, and Laurence T. Yang. Data exfiltration from internet of things devices: ios devices as case studies. *IEEE Internet of Things Journal*, 4(2):524–535, 2017.

189. Saar Drimer and Steven J. Murdoch. Keep your enemies close: Distance bounding against smartcard relay attacks. In *USENIX security symposium*, volume 312, 2007.

190. Yitao Duan and John Canny. Protecting user data in ubiquitous computing: Towards trustworthy environments. In *International Workshop on Privacy Enhancing Technologies*, pages 167–185. Springer, 2004.

191. Thomas Dullien and Rolf Rolles. Graph-based comparison of executable objects. In *Symposium sur la Securite des Technologies de lInformation et des Communications*, SSTIC '05, 2005.

192. Orr Dunkelman, Nathan Keller, and Adi Shamir. A practical-time related-key attack on the kasumi cryptosystem used in gsm and 3g telephony. In *Advances in Cryptology CRYPTO 2010, Santa Barbara, California, USA, August 15–19, 2010*, pages 393–410, 2010.

193. Ulrich Dürholz, Marc Fischlin, Michael Kasper, and Cristina Onete. A formal approach to distance bounding RFID protocols. In *Information Security Conference ISC 2011*, volume 7001 of *Lecture Notes in Computer Science*, pages 47–62. Springer, 2011.

194. François Durvaux, Mathieu Renauld, François-Xavier Standaert, Loic van Oldeneel tot Oldenzeel, and Nicolas Veyrat-Charvillon. Cryptanalysis of the ches 2009/2010 random delay countermeasure. *IACR Cryptology ePrint Archive*, 2012:38, 2012.

195. Stefan Dziembowski and Krzysztof Pietrzak. Leakage-resilient cryptography. In *Foundations of Computer Science, 2008. FOCS'08. IEEE 49th Annual IEEE Symposium on*, pages 293–302. IEEE, 2008.

196. Thomas Eisenbarth, Timo Kasper, Amir Moradi, Christof Paar, Mahmoud Salmasizadeh, and Mohammad T. Manzuri Shalmani. On the Power of Power Analysis in the Real World: A Complete Break of the KeeLoq Code Hopping Scheme. In *CRYPTO*, volume 5157 of *Lecture Notes in Computer Science*, pages 203–220. Springer, August 17–21 2008. Santa Barbara, CA, USA.

197. Thomas Eisenbarth, Sandeep S. Kumar, Christof Paar, Axel Poschmann, and Leif Uhsadel. A survey of lightweight-cryptography implementations. *IEEE Design & Test of Computers*, 24(6):522–533, 2007.

198. Elnec.   Elnec beeprog2.   https://www.elnec.com/en/products/universal-programmers/
     beeprog2/.
199. EMVCo. Book C-2 kernel 2 specification v2.5. EMV contactless specifications for payment
     system, March 2015.
200. Daniel W. Engels, Markku-Juhani O. Saarinen, Peter Schweitzer, and Eric M. Smith. The
     hummingbird-2 lightweight authenticated encryption algorithm. In *RFID. Security and
     Privacy - 7th International Workshop, RFIDSec 2011, Amherst, USA, June 26–28, 2011,
     Revised Selected Papers*, pages 19–31, 2011.
201. İmran Ergüler and Orhun Kara. A new approach to keystream based cryptosystems. In *SASC
     2008, Workshop Record,*, pages 205–221. SASC, 2008.
202. Sebastian Eschweiler, Khaled Yakdan, and Elmar Gerhards-Padilla. discovRE: Efficient
     Cross-Architecture Identification of Bugs in Binary Code. In *ISOC NDSS 2016*, 2016.
203. Muhammed F. Esgin and Orhun Kara. Practical cryptanalysis of full Sprout with TMD
     tradeoff attacks. In *Selected Areas in Cryptography - SAC 2015*, pages 67–85, 2015.
204. ETSI/SAGE. Specification of the 3gpp confidentiality and integrity algorithms uea2 & uia2.
     document 2: Snow 3g specification. technical report, etsi/sage, 2006.
205. ETSI/SAGE. Specification of the 3gpp confidentiality and integrity algorithms 128-eea3 &
     128-eia3. document 2: Zuc specification, version 1.6, 2011.
206. Limin Fan, Hua Chen, and Si Gao.   A general method to evaluate the correlation of
     randomness tests. In *International Workshop on Information Security Applications*, pages
     52–62. Springer, 2013.
207. Xinxin Fan, Kalikinkar Mandal, and Guang Gong. Wg-8: A lightweight stream cipher
     for resource-constrained smart devices. In *Quality, Reliability, Security and Robustness in
     Heterogeneous Networks, Qshine 2013, Greader Noida, India, January 11–12, 2013, Revised
     Selected Papers*, pages 617–632, 2013.
208. Dan Farmer and Wietse Venema. *Forensic Discovery*. Addison-Wesley Professional, 2005.
209. Horst Feistel. Cryptography and computer privacy. *Scientific American*, 228(5):15–23, 1973.
210. Benoit Feix, Mylène Roussellet, and Alexandre Venelli. Side-channel analysis on blinded
     regular scalar multiplications. In Willi Meier and Debdeep Mukhopadhyay, editors, *Progress
     in Cryptology - INDOCRYPT 2014: 15th International Conference in Cryptology in India*,
     volume 8885 of *Lecture Notes in Computer Science*, pages 3–20, New Delhi, India,
     December 14–17, 2014. Springer.
211. Martin Feldhofer and Christian Rechberger. A case against currently used hash functions
     in rfid protocols. In *On the Move to Meaningful Internet Systems, OTM 2006, Montpellier,
     France, October 29 - November 3, 2006*, pages 372–381, 2006.
212. Qian Feng, Rundong Zhou, Chengcheng Xu, Yao Cheng, Brian Testa, and Heng Yin. Scalable
     Graph-based Bug Search for Firmware Images. In *ACM CCS 2016*, 2016.
213. Xiutao Feng and Fan Zhang. A practical state recovery attack on the stream cipher sablier v1.
     IACR Cryptology ePrint Archive 2014/245, 2014.
214. Niels Ferguson, Stefan Lucks, Bruce Schneier, Doug Whiting, Mihir Bellare, Tadayoshi
     Kohno, Jon Callas, and Jesse Walker. The skein hash function family (version 1.3). www.
     skein-hash.info/sites/default/files/skein1.3.pdf, 2010.
215. Niels Ferguson, Doug Whiting, Bruce Schneier, John Kelsey, Stefan Lucks, and Tadayoshi
     Kohno. Helix: Fast encryption and authentication in a single cryptographic primitive. In
     Thomas Johansson, editor, *Fast Software Encryption – FSE 2003*, volume 2887 of *Lecture
     Notes in Computer Science*, pages 330–346, Lund, Sweden, February 24–26, 2003. Springer.
216. Marc Fischlin and Cristina Onete. Terrorism in distance bounding: Modeling terrorist-
     fraud resistance. In *Applied Cryptography and Network Security*, ACNS'13, pages 414–431.
     Springer, 2013.
217. International Organization for Standardization.   Standardization and related activities –
     general vocabulary (iso/iec guide no. 2), 2004.
218. International Organization for Standardization. Information technology – security techniques
     – lightweight cryptography – part 2: Block ciphers (iso/iec standard no. 29192–2), 2012.

219. A. P. Fournaris, L. Papachristodoulou, and N. Sklavos. Secure and efficient rns software implementation for elliptic curve cryptography. In *2017 IEEE European Symposium on Security and Privacy Workshops (EuroS PW)*, pages 86–93, April 2017.

220. Apostolos P. Fournaris. *Fault and Power Analysis Attack Protection Techniques for Standardized Public Key Cryptosystems*, pages 93–105. Springer International Publishing, Cham, 2017.

221. Aurélien Francillon, Boris Danev, and Srdjan Capkun. Relay attacks on passive keyless entry and start systems in modern cars. In *Network and Distributed System Security Symposium (NDSS)*. Eidgenössische Technische Hochschule Zürich, Department of Computer Science, 2011.

222. Lishoy Francis, Gerhard Hancke, Keith Mayes, and Konstantinos Markantonakis. Practical NFC peer-to-peer relay attack using mobile phones. In *International Workshop on Radio Frequency Identification: Security and Privacy Issues*, pages 35–49. Springer, 2010.

223. Kai Fu, Meiqin Wang, Yinghua Guo, Siwei Sun, and Lei Hu. MILP-based automatic search algorithms for differential and linear trails for speck. In Thomas Peyrin, editor, *Fast Software Encryption – FSE 2016*, volume 9783 of *Lecture Notes in Computer Science*, pages 268–288, Bochum, Germany, March 20–23, 2016. Springer.

224. Ximing Fu, Xiaoyun Wang, Xiaoyang Dong, and Willi Meier. A key-recovery attack on 855-round trivium. Cryptology ePrint Archive, Report 2018/198, 2018. https://eprint.iacr.org/2018/198.

225. Daniel Genkin, Adi Shamir, and Eran Tromer. Acoustic cryptanalysis. *Journal of Cryptology*, 30(2):392–443, Apr 2017.

226. Carmina Georgescu, Emil Simion, Alina-Petrescu Nita, and Antonela Toma. A view on nist randomness tests (in) dependence. In *Electronics, Computers and Artificial Intelligence (ECAI), 2017 9th International Conference on*, pages 1–4. IEEE, 2017.

227. Benoît Gérard, Vincent Grosso, María Naya-Plasencia, and François-Xavier Standaert. Block ciphers that are easier to mask: How far can we go? In Guido Bertoni and Jean-Sébastien Coron, editors, *Cryptographic Hardware and Embedded Systems – CHES 2013*, volume 8086 of *Lecture Notes in Computer Science*, pages 383–399, Santa Barbara, CA, USA, August 20–23, 2013. Springer.

228. Vahid Amin Ghafari and Honggang Hu. Fruit-80: A secure ultra-lightweight stream cipher for constrained environments. *Entropy*, 20(3):180, 2018.

229. Benedikt Gierlichs, Lejla Batina, Pim Tuyls, and Bart Preneel. Mutual information analysis. In Elisabeth Oswald and Pankaj Rohatgi, editors, *Cryptographic Hardware and Embedded Systems – CHES 2008*, pages 426–442. Springer, 2008.

230. Benedikt Gierlichs, Kerstin Lemke-Rust, and Christof Paar. Templates vs. Stochastic Methods. In *CHES*, volume 4249 of *LNCS*, pages 15–29. Springer, October 10–13 2006. Yokohama, Japan.

231. Henri Gilbert, Matthew Robshaw, and Hervé Sibert. An active attack against HB^+ – a provably secure lightweight authentication protocol. *IET Electronics Letters*, 41(21):1169–1170, October 2005.

232. Henri Gilbert, Matthew J. B. Robshaw, and Yannick Seurin. Good variants of HB+ are hard to find. In Gene Tsudik, editor, *FC 2008: 12th International Conference on Financial Cryptography and Data Security*, volume 5143 of *Lecture Notes in Computer Science*, pages 156–170, Cozumel, Mexico, January 28–31, 2008. Springer.

233. Henri Gilbert, Matthew J. B. Robshaw, and Yannick Seurin. $HB^\sharp$: Increasing the security and efficiency of HB^+. In Nigel P. Smart, editor, *Advances in Cryptology – EUROCRYPT 2008*, volume 4965 of *Lecture Notes in Computer Science*, pages 361–378, Istanbul, Turkey, April 13–17, 2008. Springer.

234. Henri Gilbert, Matthew JB Robshaw, and Yannick Seurin. How to encrypt with the LPN problem. In *International Colloquium on Automata, Languages, and Programming*, pages 679–690. Springer, 2008.

235. R. Gilmore, N. Hanley, and M. O'Neill. Neural network based attack on a masked implementation of aes. In *2015 IEEE International Symposium on Hardware Oriented Security and Trust (HOST)*, pages 106–111, May 2015.

236. Jovan Dj. Golic. Cryptanalysis of alleged A5 stream cipher. In Walter Fumy, editor, *Advances in Cryptology – EUROCRYPT'97*, volume 1233 of *Lecture Notes in Computer Science*, pages 239–255, Konstanz, Germany, May 11–15, 1997. Springer.

237. Jovan Dj. Golíc. Cryptanalysis of alleged A5 stream cipher. In Walter Fumy, editor, *Advances in Cryptology – EUROCRYPT 97*, volume 1233 of *Lecture Notes in Computer Science*, pages 239–255. Springer, 1997.

238. Zheng Gong, Pieter H. Hartel, Svetla Nikova, Shaohua Tang, and Bo Zhu. Tulp: A family of lightweight message authentication codes for body sensor networks. *J. Comput. Sci. Technol.*, 29(1):53–68, 2014.

239. Zheng Gong, Svetla Nikova, and Yee Wei Law. KLEIN: A new family of lightweight block ciphers. In *RFID. Security and Privacy - 7th International Workshop, RFIDSec 2011, Amherst, USA, June 26–28, 2011, Revised Selected Papers*, pages 1–18, 2011.

240. T. Good and M. Benaissa. Hardware performance of estream phase-iii stream cipher candidates. In *In SASC 2008*, pages 163–174, 2008.

241. Dan Goodin. Record-breaking ddos reportedly delivered by >145k hacked cameras. Ars Technica, 09 2016.

242. Xavier Torrent Gorjón. Protecting against relay attacks forging increased distance reports. Research Project, Universiteit van Amsterdam, 2015.

243. Louis Goubin and Jacques Patarin. Des and differential power analysis the "duplication" method. In *Cryptographic Hardware and Embedded Systems*, pages 728–728. Springer, 1999.

244. Vipul Goyal, Omkant Pandey, Amit Sahai, and Brent Waters. Attribute-based encryption for fine-grained access control of encrypted data. In *Proceedings of the 13th ACM conference on Computer and communications security*, pages 89–98. Acm, 2006.

245. Hannes Gross, Erich Wenger, Christoph Dobraunig, and Christoph Ehrenhfer. Ascon hardware implementations and side-channel evaluation. *Microprocessors and Microsystems*, 22(1):1–10, 2016.

246. Vincent Grosso, Gaëtan Leurent, François-Xavier Standaert, Kerem Varici, Françcois Durvaux, Lubos Gaspar, and Stéphanie Kerckhof. SCREAM & iSCREAM, side-channel resistant authenticated encryption with masking. submission to the caesar competition, 2014.

247. Vincent Grosso, Gaëtan Leurent, François-Xavier Standaert, and Kerem Varici. LS-designs: Bitslice encryption for efficient masked software implementations. In Carlos Cid and Christian Rechberger, editors, *Fast Software Encryption – FSE 2014*, volume 8540 of *Lecture Notes in Computer Science*, pages 18–37, London, UK, March 3–5, 2015. Springer.

248. Marco Gruteser and Dirk Grunwald. Anonymous usage of location-based services through spatial and temporal cloaking. In *Proceedings of the 1st International Conference on Mobile Systems, Applications and Services*, pages 31–42, 2003.

249. Christoph G Günther. A universal algorithm for homophonic coding. In *Workshop on the Theory and Application of of Cryptographic Techniques*, pages 405–414. Springer, 1988.

250. Jian Guo, Jérémy Jean, Ivica Nikolic, Kexin Qiao, Yu Sasaki, and Siang Meng Sim. Invariant subspace attack against Midori64 and the resistance criteria for S-box designs. *IACR Transactions on Symmetric Cryptology*, 2016(1):33–56, 2016. http://tosc.iacr.org/index.php/ToSC/article/view/534.

251. Jian Guo, Thomas Peyrin, and Axel Poschmann. The PHOTON family of lightweight hash functions. In Phillip Rogaway, editor, *Advances in Cryptology – CRYPTO 2011*, volume 6841 of *Lecture Notes in Computer Science*, pages 222–239, Santa Barbara, CA, USA, August 14–18, 2011. Springer.

252. Jian Guo, Thomas Peyrin, Axel Poschmann, and Matthew J. B. Robshaw. The LED block cipher. In Bart Preneel and Tsuyoshi Takagi, editors, *Cryptographic Hardware and Embedded Systems – CHES 2011*, volume 6917 of *Lecture Notes in Computer Science*, pages 326–341, Nara, Japan, September 28 – October 1, 2011. Springer.

253. Matthias Hamann, Matthias Krause, and Willi Meier. LIZARD – A lightweight stream cipher for power-constrained devices. *IACR Transactions on Symmetric Cryptology*, 2017(1):45–79, 2017.

254. Gerhard P. Hancke and Markus G. Kuhn. An RFID distance bounding protocol. In *Conference on Security and Privacy for Emergency Areas in Communication Networks (SecureComm) 2005*, pages 67–73. IEEE, 2005.

255. Gerhard P Hancke and Markus G Kuhn. Attacks on time-of-flight distance bounding channels. In *ACM conference on Wireless network security*, pages 194–202. ACM, 2008.

256. Gerhard P Hancke, KE Mayes, and Konstantinos Markantonakis. Confidence in smart token proximity: Relay attacks revisited. *Computers & Security*, 28(7):615–627, 2009.

257. Lucjan Hanzlik, Łukasz Krzywiecki, and Mirosław Kutyłowski. Simplified PACE|AA protocol. In Robert H. Deng and Tao Feng, editors, *Information Security Practice and Experience - 9th International Conference, ISPEC 2013, Lanzhou, China, May 12–14, 2013. Proceedings*, volume 7863 of *Lecture Notes in Computer Science*, pages 218–232. Springer, 2013.

258. Malek Harbawi and Asaf Varol. An improved digital evidence acquisition model for the internet of things forensic i: A theoretical framework. In *2017 5th International Symposium on Digital Forensic and Security (ISDFS)*, pages 1–6, April 2017.

259. Mária Hatalová. *Security of small office home routers*. PhD thesis, Masarykova univerzita, Fakulta informatiky, 2015.

260. George Hatzivasilis, Konstantinos Fysarakis, Ioannis Papaefstathiou, and Charalampos Manifavas. A review of lightweight block ciphers. *J. Cryptographic Engineering*, 8(2):141–184, 2018.

261. Steve Heath. *Embedded systems design*. Newnes, 2002.

262. C Heffner and J Collake. Firmware mod kit-modify firmware images without recompiling, 2015.

263. Craig Heffner. binwalk – firmware analysis tool designed to assist in the analysis, extraction, and reverse engineering of firmware images. https://github.com/ReFirmLabs/binwalk.

264. Robert Hegarty, David J Lamb, and Andrew Attwood. Digital evidence challenges in the internet of things. In *Tenth International Network Conference (INC 2014)*, 2014.

265. Martin Hell, Thomas Johansson, Alexander Maximov, and Willi Meier. The grain family of stream ciphers. In *New Stream Cipher Designs*, pages 179–190. Springer, 2008.

266. Martin Hell, Thomas Johansson, Er Maximov, and Willi Meier. A stream cipher proposal: Grain-128. In *2006 IEEE International Symposium on Information Theory*, pages 1614–1618, July 2006.

267. Martin Hell, Thomas Johansson, and Willi Meier. Grain: a stream cipher for constrained environments. *IJWMC*, 2(1):86–93, 2007.

268. Martin E. Hellman. A cryptanalytic time-memory trade-off. *IEEE Trans. Information Theory*, 26(4):401–406, 1980.

269. Armijn Hemel, Karl Trygve Kalleberg, Rob Vermaas, and Eelco Dolstra. Finding Software License Violations Through Binary Code Clone Detection. In *Proceedings of the 8th Working Conference on Mining Software Repositories*, MSR '11. ACM, 2011.

270. Luca Henzen, Flavio Carbognani, Norbert Felber, and Wolfgang Fichtner. Vlsi hardware evaluation of the stream ciphers salsa20 and chacha, and the compression function rumba. In *2nd International Conference on Signals, Circuits and Systems, SCS 2008, Monastir, Tunisia, November 7–9, 2008*, pages 1–5, 2008.

271. Alex Hern. Revolv devices bricked as Google's Nest shuts down smart home company. The Guardian, April 2016. https://www.theguardian.com/technology/2016/apr/05/revolv-devices-bricked-google-nest-smart-home.

272. Julio Hernandez-Castro and David F Barrero. Evolutionary generation and degeneration of randomness to assess the indepedence of the ent test battery. In *Evolutionary Computation (CEC), 2017 IEEE Congress on*, pages 1420–1427. IEEE, 2017.

273. Julio C. Hernandez-Castro, Pedro Peris-Lopez, Raphael C.W. Phan, and Juan M. Estevez-Tapiador. Cryptanalysis of the David-Prasad RFID Ultralightweight Authentication Protocol.

In S.B. Ors Yalcin, editor, *Workshop on RFID Security – RFIDSec'10*, volume 6370 of *Lecture Notes in Computer Science*, pages 22–34, Istanbul, Turkey, June 2010. Springer.

274. A. Heuser, S. Picek, S. Guilley, and N. Mentens. Lightweight ciphers and their side-channel resilience. *IEEE Transactions on Computers*, PP(99):1–1, 2017.

275. Annelie Heuser, Michael Kasper, Werner Schindler, and Marc Stöttinger. A New Difference Method for Side-Channel Analysis with High-Dimensional Leakage Models. In Orr Dunkelman, editor, *CT-RSA*, volume 7178 of *Lecture Notes in Computer Science*, pages 365–382. Springer, 2012.

276. Annelie Heuser, Stjepan Picek, Sylvain Guilley, and Nele Mentens. Side-channel analysis of lightweight ciphers: Does lightweight equal easy? In *Radio Frequency Identification and IoT Security - 12th International Workshop, RFIDSec 2016, Hong Kong, China, November 30 - December 2, 2016, Revised Selected Papers*, pages 91–104, 2016.

277. Annelie Heuser, Olivier Rioul, and Sylvain Guilley. Good is Not Good Enough — Deriving Optimal Distinguishers from Communication Theory. In Lejla Batina and Matthew Robshaw, editors, *CHES*, volume 8731 of *Lecture Notes in Computer Science*. Springer, 2014.

278. Annelie Heuser, Werner Schindler, and Marc Stöttinger. Revealing side-channel issues of complex circuits by enhanced leakage models. In Wolfgang Rosenstiel and Lothar Thiele, editors, *DATE*, pages 1179–1184. IEEE, 2012.

279. Annelie Heuser and Michael Zohner. Intelligent Machine Homicide - Breaking Cryptographic Devices Using Support Vector Machines. In Werner Schindler and Sorin A. Huss, editors, *COSADE*, volume 7275 of *LNCS*, pages 249–264. Springer, 2012.

280. Hewlett Packard Enterprise (HPE). Internet of things research study – 2015 report, 2015.

281. Shoichi Hirose, Kota Ideguchi, Hidenori Kuwakado, Toru Owada, Bart Preneel, and Hirotaka Yoshida. A lightweight 256-bit hash function for hardware and low-end devices: Lesamnta-LW. In Kyung Hyune Rhee and DaeHun Nyang, editors, *ICISC 10: 13th International Conference on Information Security and Cryptology*, volume 6829 of *Lecture Notes in Computer Science*, pages 151–168, Seoul, Korea, December 1–3, 2011. Springer.

282. Deukjo Hong, Jung-Keun Lee, Dong-Chan Kim, Daesung Kwon, Kwon Ho Ryu, and Dong-Geon Lee. LEA: A 128-bit block cipher for fast encryption on common processors. In Yongdae Kim, Heejo Lee, and Adrian Perrig, editors, *WISA 13: 14th International Workshop on Information Security Applications*, volume 8267 of *Lecture Notes in Computer Science*, pages 3–27, Jeju Island, Korea, August 19–21, 2014. Springer.

283. Deukjo Hong, Jaechul Sung, Seokhie Hong, Jongin Lim, Sangjin Lee, Bon-Seok Koo, Changhoon Lee, Donghoon Chang, Jesang Lee, Kitae Jeong, Hyun Kim, Jongsung Kim, and Seongtaek Chee. HIGHT: A new block cipher suitable for low-resource device. In Louis Goubin and Mitsuru Matsui, editors, *Cryptographic Hardware and Embedded Systems – CHES 2006*, volume 4249 of *Lecture Notes in Computer Science*, pages 46–59, Yokohama, Japan, October 10–13, 2006. Springer.

284. Nicholas J. Hopper and Manuel Blum. Secure human identification protocols. In Colin Boyd, editor, *Advances in Cryptology – ASIACRYPT 2001*, volume 2248 of *Lecture Notes in Computer Science*, pages 52–66, Gold Coast, Australia, December 9–13, 2001. Springer.

285. Gabriel Hospodar, Benedikt Gierlichs, Elke De Mulder, Ingrid Verbauwhede, and Joos Vandewalle. Machine learning in side-channel analysis: a first study. *Journal of Cryptographic Engineering*, 1:293–302, 2011. 10.1007/s13389-011-0023-x.

286. Max Houck and Jay Siegel. *Fundamentals of Forensic Science*. Academic Press. Elsevier Science & Technology Books, 2015.

287. Anco Hundepool, Josep Domingo-Ferrer, Luisa Franconi, Sarah Giessing, Eric Schulte Nordholt, Keith Spicer, and Peter-Paul De Wolf. *Statistical disclosure control*. John Wiley & Sons, 2012.

288. Darren Hurley-Smith and Julio Hernandez-Castro. Bias in the mifare desfire ev1 trng. In *Radio Frequency Identification: 12th International Workshop, RFIDsec 2016, Hong Kong, China, November 30-December 2, 2016*. Springer International Publishing, 2016.

289. Darren Hurley-Smith and Julio Hernandez-Castro. Certifiably biased: An in-depth analysis of a common criteria eal4+ certified trng. *IEEE Transactions on Information Forensics and Security*, 13(4):1031–1041, 2018.

290. IBM Marketing Cloud. 10 Key Marketing Trends for 2017 and Ideas for Exceeding Customer Expectations, 2017.

291. ICAO. Machine Readable Travel Documents - Part 11: Security Mechanism for MRTDs. Doc 9303, 2015.

292. Independen Security Evaluators. Exploiting SOHO Routers, April 2013.

293. insideBIGDATA. Guide to the Intelligent Use of Big Data on an Industrial Scale, 2017. Special Research Report.

294. Internet World Stats. Internet usage statistics, the internet big picture, 2017.

295. ISO. Iso/iec directives, part 1 – consolidated jtc 1 supplement 2017 – procedures specific to jtc 1.

296. ISO. Iso/iec directives, part 2 – principles and rules for the structure and drafting of iso and iec documents (2018).

297. Takanori Isobe, Toshihiro Ohigashi, and Masakatu Morii. Slide cryptanalysis of lightweight stream cipher rakaposhi. In *Advances in Information and Computer Security, IWSEC 2012, Fukuoka, Japan, November 7–9, 2012*, pages 138–155, 2012.

298. ISO/IEC. ISO/IEC JTC1 SC17 WG3/TF5 for ICAO: Supplemental Access Control for Machine Readable Travel Documents v1.1. Technical Report, April 15 2014.

299. Maryam Izadi, Babak Sadeghiyan, Seyed Saeed Sadeghian, and Hossein Arabnezhad Khanooki. MIBS: A new lightweight block cipher. In Juan A. Garay, Atsuko Miyaji, and Akira Otsuka, editors, *CANS 09: 8th International Conference on Cryptology and Network Security*, volume 5888 of *Lecture Notes in Computer Science*, pages 334–348, Kanazawa, Japan, December 12–14, 2009. Springer.

300. Goce Jakimoski and Samant Khajuria. ASC-1: An authenticated encryption stream cipher. In Ali Miri and Serge Vaudenay, editors, *SAC 2011: 18th Annual International Workshop on Selected Areas in Cryptography*, volume 7118 of *Lecture Notes in Computer Science*, pages 356–372, Toronto, Ontario, Canada, August 11–12, 2012. Springer.

301. Gareth James, Daniela Witten, Trevor Hastie, and Robert Tibsihrani. *An Introduction to Statistical Learning*. Springer Texts in Statistics. Springer, 2001.

302. Joshua James and Eoghan Casey. dfrws2017-challenge. https://github.com/dfrws/dfrws2017-challenge, 2018.

303. Pieter Janssens. Proximity check for communication devices, April 2015.

304. Jérémy Jean, Ivica Nikolić, and Thomas Peyrin. Joltik v1. submission to the caesar competition, 2014.

305. Keith J. Jones, Richard Bejtlich, and Curtis W. Rose. *Real Digital Forensics: Computer Security and Incident Response*. Addison-Wesley Professional, 2005.

306. Anthony Journault, François-Xavier Standaert, and Kerem Varici. Improving the security and efficiency of block ciphers based on ls-designs. *Des. Codes Cryptography*, 82(1–2):495–509, 2017.

307. Lyndon Judge, Michael Cantrell, Cagil Kendir, and Patrick Schaumont. A modular testing environment for implementation attacks. In *2012 ASE/IEEE International Conference on BioMedical Computing (BioMedCom)*, pages 86–95, Dec 2012.

308. Ari Juels. RFID Security and Privacy: A Research Survey. *IEEE Journal on Selected Areas in Communications*, 24(2):381–394, February 2006.

309. Ari Juels and Stephen A Weis. Authenticating pervasive devices with human protocols. In *Advances in Cryptology–CRYPTO 2005*, pages 293–308. Springer, 2005.

310. Ari Juels and Stephen A. Weis. Authenticating pervasive devices with human protocols. In Victor Shoup, editor, *Advances in Cryptology – CRYPTO 2005*, volume 3621 of *Lecture Notes in Computer Science*, pages 293–308, Santa Barbara, CA, USA, August 14–18, 2005. Springer.

311. Pascal Junod. On the complexity of matsuis attack. In *Selected Areas in Cryptography, SAC 2001 Toronto, Ontario, Canada, August 1617, 2001*, pages 199–211, 2001.

312. Markus Kammerstetter, Christian Platzer, and Wolfgang Kastner. Prospect: peripheral proxying supported embedded code testing. In *Proceedings of the 9th ACM symposium on Information, computer and communications security*, pages 329–340. ACM, 2014.

313. Orhun Kara, İmran Ergüler, and Emin Anarim. A new security relation between information rate and state size of a keystream generator. *Turkish Journal of Electrical Engineering & Computer Sciences*, 24(3):1916–1929, 2016.

314. Orhun Kara and Muhammed F. Esgin. On analysis of lightweight stream ciphers with keyed update. *IEEE Trans. Computers*, 68(1):99–110, 2019.

315. Ferhat Karakoç, Hüseyin Demirci, and A. Emre Harmanci. Itubee: A software oriented lightweight block cipher. In *Lightweight Cryptography for Security and Privacy - Second International Workshop, LightSec 2013, Gebze, Turkey, May 6–7, 2013, Revised Selected Papers*, pages 16–27, 2013.

316. Chris Karlof, Naveen Sastry, and David Wagner. Tinysec: A link layer security architecture for wireless sensor networks. In *Embedded networked sensor systems, SenSys04, Baltimore, USA, November 03–05, 2004*, pages 162–175, 2004.

317. Pierre Karpman and Benjamin Grégoire. The Littlun S-box and the fly block cipher. Lightweight Cryptography Workshop, October 17–18 2016, NIST, 2016.

318. Victor R. Kebande and Indrakshi Ray. A generic digital forensic investigation framework for internet of things (IoT). In *4th IEEE International Conference on Future Internet of Things and Cloud, FiCloud 2016, Vienna, Austria, August 22–24, 2016*, pages 356–362, 2016.

319. John Kelsey, Bruce Schneier, and David Wagner. Mod n cryptanalysis, with applications against RC5P and M6. In Lars R. Knudsen, editor, *Fast Software Encryption – FSE'99*, volume 1636 of *Lecture Notes in Computer Science*, pages 139–155, Rome, Italy, March 24–26, 1999. Springer.

320. John Kelsey, Bruce Schneier, and David A. Wagner. Related-key cryptanalysis of 3-way, biham-des, cast, des-x, newdes, rc2, and tea. In *Information and Communication Security, First International Conference, ICICS'97, Beijing, China, November 11–14, 1997*, pages 233–246, 1997.

321. Yahya S Khiabani and Shuangqing Wei. A joint shannon cipher and privacy amplification approach to attaining exponentially decaying information leakage. *Information Sciences*, 357:6–22, 2016.

322. Yahya S Khiabani, Shuangqing Wei, Jian Yuan, and Jian Wang. Enhancement of secrecy of block ciphered systems by deliberate noise. *IEEE Transactions on Information Forensics and Security*, 7(5):1604–1613, 2012.

323. Umar Mujahid Khokhar, Muhammad Najam-ul-Islam, and Shahzad Sarwar. A new ultra-lightweight RFID authentication protocol for passive low cost tags: KMAP. *Wireless Personal Communications*, 94(3):725–744, 2017.

324. Dmitry Khovratovich and Christian Rechberger. The local attack: Cryptanalysis of the authenticated encryption scheme ale. In *Selected Areas in Cryptography, SAC 2013, Burnaby, Canada, August 14–16, 2013*, pages 174–184, 2013.

325. Handan Kılınç and Serge Vaudenay. Optimal proximity proofs revisited. In Tal Malkin, Vladimir Kolesnikov, Allison Bishop Lewko, and Michalis Polychronakis, editors, *ACNS 15: 13th International Conference on Applied Cryptography and Network Security*, volume 9092 of *Lecture Notes in Computer Science*, pages 478–494, New York, NY, USA, June 2–5, 2015. Springer.

326. Handan Kılınç and Serge Vaudenay. Formal analysis of distance bounding with secure hardware. Cryptology ePrint Archive, Report 2018/440, 2018.

327. Wolfgang Killmann and Werner Schindler. Ais 31: Functionality classes and evaluation methodology for true (physical) random number generators, version 3.1. *Bundesamt fur Sicherheit in der Informationstechnik (BSI), Bonn*, 2001.

328. Chong Hee Kim, Gildas Avoine, François Koeune, François-Xavier Standaert, and Olivier Pereira. The Swiss-Knife RFID distance bounding protocol. In *Information Security and Cryptology (ICISC) 2008*, volume 5461 of *Lecture Notes in Computer Science*, pages 98–115. Springer, 2008.

329. Jaehun Kim, Stjepan Picek, Annelie Heuser, Shivam Bhasin, and Alan Hanjalic. Make some noise: Unleashing the power of convolutional neural networks for profiled side-channel analysis. Cryptology ePrint Archive, Report 2018/1023, 2018. https://eprint.iacr.org/2018/1023.

330. Aleksandar Kircanski and Amr M. Youssef. Differential fault analysis of rabbit. In *Selected Areas in Cryptography, SAC 2009, Calgary, Alberta, Canada, August 13–14, 2009*, pages 197–214, 2009.

331. Marek Klonowski, Mirosław Kutyłowski, Michał Ren, and Katarzyna Rybarczyk. Mixing in random digraphs with application to the forward-secure key evolution in wireless sensor networks. *TOSN*, 11(2):29:1–29:27, 2015.

332. Marek Klonowski and Piotr Syga. Enhancing privacy for ad hoc systems with predeployment key distribution. *Ad Hoc Networks*, 59:35–47, 2017.

333. Lars R. Knudsen, Gregor Leander, Axel Poschmann, and Matthew J. B. Robshaw. PRINT-cipher: A block cipher for IC-printing. In Stefan Mangard and François-Xavier Standaert, editors, *Cryptographic Hardware and Embedded Systems – CHES 2010*, volume 6225 of *Lecture Notes in Computer Science*, pages 16–32, Santa Barbara, CA, USA, August 17–20, 2010. Springer.

334. Lars R. Knudsen and Havard Raddum. On Noekeon, 2001.

335. Çetin Kaya Koç. *Cryptographic Engineering*. Springer Publishing Company, Incorporated, 1st edition, 2008.

336. Paul Kocher, Joshua Jaffe, and Benjamin Jun. Differential power analysis. In *Advances in Cryptology Proceedings of Crypto 99*, pages 388–397. Springer-Verlag, 1999.

337. Paul Kocher, Ruby Lee, Gary McGraw, and Anand Raghunathan. Security as a new dimension in embedded system design. In *Proceedings of the 41st Annual Design Automation Conference*, DAC '04, pages 753–760, New York, NY, USA, 2004. ACM. Moderator-Ravi, Srivaths.

338. Paul C. Kocher. Timing Attacks on Implementations of Diffie-Hellman, RSA, DSS, and Other Systems. In *Proceedings of CRYPTO'96*, volume 1109 of *LNCS*, pages 104–113. Springer-Verlag, 1996.

339. Paul C. Kocher, Joshua Jaffe, and Benjamin Jun. Differential power analysis. In *Proceedings of the 19th Annual International Cryptology Conference on Advances in Cryptology*, CRYPTO '99, pages 388–397, London, UK, UK, 1999. Springer-Verlag.

340. Jesse D. Kornblum. Identifying Almost Identical Files Using Context Triggered Piecewise Hashing. In *Proceedings of the Digital Forensic Workshop*, 2006.

341. Karl Koscher, Tadayoshi Kohno, and David Molnar. Surrogates: enabling near-real-time dynamic analyses of embedded systems. In *Proceedings of the 9th USENIX Conference on Offensive Technologies*. USENIX Association, 2015.

342. Panayiotis Kotzanikolaou, Constantinos Patsakis, Emmanouil Magkos, and Michalis Korakakis. Lightweight private proximity testing for geospatial social networks. *Computer Communications*, 73:263–270, 2016.

343. Takuma Koyama, Yu Sasaki, and Noboru Kunihiro. Multi-differential cryptanalysis on reduced DM-PRESENT-80: Collisions and other differential properties. In Taekyoung Kwon, Mun-Kyu Lee, and Daesung Kwon, editors, *ICISC 12: 15th International Conference on Information Security and Cryptology*, volume 7839 of *Lecture Notes in Computer Science*, pages 352–367, Seoul, Korea, November 28–30, 2013. Springer.

344. Brian Krebs. KrebsOnSecurity Hit With Record DDoS. Krebs On Security, September 2016.

345. Brian Krebs. Who Makes the IoT Things Under Attack? Krebs On Security, October 2016.

346. Jukka M Krisp. *Progress in location-based services*. Springer, 2013.

347. J. Krumm and E. Horvitz. Locadio: inferring motion and location from wi-fi signal strengths. In *The First Annual International Conference on Mobile and Ubiquitous Systems: Networking and Services, 2004. MOBIQUITOUS 2004.*, pages 4–13, August 2004.

348. John Krumm. *Ubiquitous Computing Fundamentals*. CRC Press, 2016.

349. Przemysław Kubiak and Mirosław Kutyłowski. Supervised usage of signature creation devices. In Dongdai Lin, Shouhuai Xu, and Moti Yung, editors, *Information Security and*

Cryptology - 9th International Conference, Inscrypt 2013, Guangzhou, China, November 27–30, 2013, Revised Selected Papers, volume 8567 of *Lecture Notes in Computer Science*, pages 132–149. Springer, 2013.

350. Naveen Kumar, Shrikant Ojha, Kritika Jain, and Sangeeta Lal. Bean: a lightweight stream cipher. In *Security of Information and Networks, SIN 09, Famagusta, North Cyprus, October 06–10, 2009*, pages 168–171, 2009.

351. Ponnurangam Kumaraguru and Lorrie Faith Cranor. Privacy indexes: A survey of Westin's studies. Technical Report CMU-ISRI-5-138, Carnegei Mellon University, 2005.

352. Ema Kušen and Mark Strembeck. Security-related Research in Ubiquitous Computing–Results of a Systematic Literature Review. *arXiv preprint arXiv:1701.00773*, 2017.

353. Satoh Labs and Morita Tech. Sasebo/sakura project. http://satoh.cs.uec.ac.jp/SAKURA/index.html.

354. Satoh Labs and Morita Tech. Sasebo/sakura quick start source codes. http://satoh.cs.uec.ac.jp/SAKURA/hardware.html.

355. Virginie Lallemand and María Naya-Plasencia. Cryptanalysis of full Sprout. In *Advances in Cryptology – CRYPTO 2015*, volume 9215 of *LNCS*, pages 663–682. Springer, 2015.

356. Jingjing Lan, Jun Zhou, and Xin Liu. An area-efficient implementation of a message authentication code (mac) algorithm for cryptographic systems. In *TENCON 1016, Singapore, Singapore, November 22–25, 2016*, pages 601–617, 2016.

357. Marc Langheinrich. Privacy by design – principles of privacy-aware ubiquitous systems. In Gregory D. Abowd, Barry Brumitt, and Steven Shafer, editors, *Ubicomp 2001: Ubiquitous Computing*, pages 273–291. Springer, 2001.

358. Marc Langheinrich. A privacy awareness system for ubiquitous computing environments. In *international conference on Ubiquitous Computing*, pages 237–245. Springer, 2002.

359. Gregor Leander, Mohamed Ahmed Abdelraheem, Hoda AlKhzaimi, and Erik Zenner. A cryptanalysis of PRINTcipher: The invariant subspace attack. In Phillip Rogaway, editor, *Advances in Cryptology – CRYPTO 2011*, volume 6841 of *Lecture Notes in Computer Science*, pages 206–221, Santa Barbara, CA, USA, August 14–18, 2011. Springer.

360. Gregor Leander, Brice Minaud, and Sondre Rønjom. A generic approach to invariant subspace attacks: Cryptanalysis of robin, iSCREAM and Zorro. In Elisabeth Oswald and Marc Fischlin, editors, *Advances in Cryptology – EUROCRYPT 2015, Part I*, volume 9056 of *Lecture Notes in Computer Science*, pages 254–283, Sofia, Bulgaria, April 26–30, 2015. Springer.

361. Gregor Leander, Christof Paar, Axel Poschmann, and Kai Schramm. New lightweight DES variants. In Alex Biryukov, editor, *Fast Software Encryption – FSE 2007*, volume 4593 of *Lecture Notes in Computer Science*, pages 196–210, Luxembourg, Luxembourg, March 26–28, 2007. Springer.

362. Pierre L'Ecuyer and Richard Simard. Testu01: Ac library for empirical testing of random number generators. *ACM Transactions on Mathematical Software (TOMS)*, 33(4):22, 2007.

363. Liran Lerman, Gianluca Bontempi, and Olivier Markowitch. Power analysis attack: An approach based on machine learning. *Int. J. Appl. Cryptol.*, 3(2):97–115, June 2014.

364. Liran Lerman, Gianluca Bontempi, and Olivier Markowitch. A machine learning approach against a masked AES - Reaching the limit of side-channel attacks with a learning model. *J. Cryptographic Engineering*, 5(2):123–139, 2015.

365. Liran Lerman, Stephane Fernandes Medeiros, Gianluca Bontempi, and Olivier Markowitch. A Machine Learning Approach Against a Masked AES. In *CARDIS*, Lecture Notes in Computer Science. Springer, November 2013. Berlin, Germany.

366. Liran Lerman, Stephane Fernandes Medeiros, Nikita Veshchikov, Cédric Meuter, Gianluca Bontempi, and Olivier Markowitch. Semi-supervised template attack. In Emmanuel Prouff, editor, *COSADE 2013, Paris, France, 2013, Revised Selected Papers*, pages 184–199. Springer, 2013.

367. Liran Lerman, Romain Poussier, Gianluca Bontempi, Olivier Markowitch, and François-Xavier Standaert. Template attacks vs. machine learning revisited (and the curse of dimensionality in side-channel analysis). In Stefan Mangard and Axel Y. Poschmann, editors, *Constructive Side-Channel Analysis and Secure Design - 6th International Workshop,*

COSADE 2015, Berlin, Germany, April 13–14, 2015. Revised Selected Papers, volume 9064 of *Lecture Notes in Computer Science*, pages 20–33. Springer, 2015.

368. Gaëtan Leurent. Differential forgery attack against lac. In *Selected Areas in Cryptography, SAC 2015, Sackville, Canada, August 12–14, 2015*, pages 217–224, 2016.

369. Gaëtan Leurent. Improved differential-linear cryptanalysis of 7-round chaskey with partitioning. In Marc Fischlin and Jean-Sébastien Coron, editors, *Advances in Cryptology – EUROCRYPT 2016, Part I*, volume 9665 of *Lecture Notes in Computer Science*, pages 344–371, Vienna, Austria, May 8–12, 2016. Springer.

370. T. Li, H. Wu, X. Wang, and F. Bao. Sensec design. i^2r sensor network flagship project (snfp: security part): Technical report-tr v1.0, 2005.

371. Zheng Li, Xiaoyang Dong, and Xiaoyun Wang. Conditional cube attack on round-reduced ascon. *IACR Trans. Symmetric Cryptol.*, 2017(1):175–202, 2017.

372. Chae Hoon Lim and Tymur Korkishko. mCrypton - a lightweight block cipher for security of low-cost RFID tags and sensors. In Jooseok Song, Taekyoung Kwon, and Moti Yung, editors, *WISA 05: 6th International Workshop on Information Security Applications*, volume 3786 of *Lecture Notes in Computer Science*, pages 243–258, Jeju Island, Korea, August 22–24, 2006. Springer.

373. Li Lin, Wenling Wu, and Yafei Zheng. Automatic search for key-bridging technique: Applications to LBlock and TWINE. In Thomas Peyrin, editor, *Fast Software Encryption – FSE 2016*, volume 9783 of *Lecture Notes in Computer Science*, pages 247–267, Bochum, Germany, March 20–23, 2016. Springer.

374. Jigang Liu. Iot forensics issues, strategies, and challenges. In *A presentation at 12th IDF Annual Conference*, 2015.

375. Yifei Liu, Timo Kasper, Kerstin Lemke-Rust, and Christof Paar. E-passport: Cracking basic access control keys. In Robert Meersman and Zahir Tari, editors, *On the Move to Meaningful Internet Systems 2007: CoopIS, DOA, ODBASE, GADA, and IS, OTM Confederated International Conferences CoopIS, DOA, ODBASE, GADA, and IS 2007, Vilamoura, Portugal, November 25–30, 2007, Proceedings, Part II*, volume 4804 of *Lecture Notes in Computer Science*, pages 1531–1547. Springer, 2007.

376. Yunwen Liu, Glenn De Witte, Adrin Ranea, and Tomer Ashur. Rotational-xor cryptanalysis of reduced-round speck. *IACR Transactions on Symmetric Cryptology*, 2017(3):24–36, Sep. 2017.

377. Yunwen Liu, Qingju Wang, and Vincent Rijmen. Automatic search of linear trails in ARX with applications to SPECK and chaskey. In Mark Manulis, Ahmad-Reza Sadeghi, and Steve Schneider, editors, *ACNS 16: 14th International Conference on Applied Cryptography and Network Security*, volume 9696 of *Lecture Notes in Computer Science*, pages 485–499, Guildford, UK, June 19–22, 2016. Springer.

378. Zongbin Liu, Qinglong Zhang, Cunqing Ma, Changting Li, and Jiwu Jing. Hpaz: a high-throughput pipeline architecture of zuc in hardware. In *Design, Automation & Test in Europe, DATE 2016, Dresden, Germany, March 14–18, 2016*, pages 269–272, 2016.

379. NXP Semiconductors Ltd. *MF1PLUSx0y1 Public Datasheet*. NXP Semiconductors.

380. Jiqiang Lu. Related-key rectangle attack on 36 rounds of the XTEA block cipher. *Int. J. Inf. Sec.*, 8(1):1–11, 2009.

381. Yi Lu, Willi Meier, and Serge Vaudenay. The conditional correlation attack: a practical attack on bluetooth encryption. In *Advances in Cryptology CRYPTO 2005, Santa Barbara, California, USA, August 14–18, 2005*, pages 97–117, 2005.

382. Mark Luk, Ghita Mezzour, Adrian Perrig, and Virgil Gligor. Minisec: A secure sensor network communication architecture. In *6th International Symposium on Information Processing in Sensor Networks, IPSN 2007, Cambridge, MA, USA, April 25–27, 2007*, pages 479–488, 2007.

383. Hanguang Luo, Guangjun Wen, Jian Su, and Zhong Huang. SLAP: succinct and lightweight authentication protocol for low-cost RFID system. *Wireless Networks*, 24(1):69–78, 2018.

384. Atul Luykx, Bart Preneel, Elmar Tischhauser, and Kan Yasuda. A MAC mode for lightweight block ciphers. In Thomas Peyrin, editor, *Fast Software Encryption – FSE 2016*, volume 9783 of *Lecture Notes in Computer Science*, pages 43–59, Bochum, Germany, March 20–23, 2016. Springer.

385. Zhen Ma, Tian Tian, and Wen-Feng Qi. Internal state recovery of Grain v1 employing guess-and-determine attack. *IET Information Security*, 11(6):363–368, 2017.

386. Houssem Maghrebi, Thibault Portigliatti, and Emmanuel Prouff. Breaking cryptographic implementations using deep learning techniques. In *Security, Privacy, and Applied Cryptography Engineering - 6th International Conference, SPACE 2016, Hyderabad, India, December 14–18, 2016, Proceedings*, pages 3–26, 2016.

387. Subhamoy Maitra, Santanu Sarkar, Anubhab Baksi, and Pramit Dey. Key recovery from state information of Sprout: Application to cryptanalysis and fault attack. Cryptology ePrint Archive, Report 2015/236.

388. Hamid Mala, Mohammad Dakhilalian, and Mohsen Shakiba. Cryptanalysis of mcrypton - A lightweight block cipher for security of RFID tags and sensors. *Int. J. Communication Systems*, 25(4):415–426, 2012.

389. Stefan Mangard, Elisabeth Oswald, and Thomas Popp. *Power Analysis Attacks: Revealing the Secrets of Smart Cards*. Springer, December 2006. ISBN 0-387-30857-1, http://www.dpabook.org/.

390. Stefan Mangard, Elisabeth Oswald, and Thomas Popp. *Power Analysis Attacks: Revealing the Secrets of Smart Cards (Advances in Information Security)*. Springer, feb 2007.

391. Charalampos Manifavas, George Hatzivasilis, Konstantinos Fysarakis, and Yannis Papaefstathiou. A survey of lightweight stream ciphers for embedded systems. *Security and Communication Networks*, 9(10):1226–1246, 2016.

392. Konstantinos Markantonakis, Lishoy Francis, Gerhard Hancke, and Keith Mayes. Practical relay attack on contactless transactions by using nfc mobile phones. *Radio Frequency Identification System Security: RFIDsec*, 12:21, 2012.

393. George Marsaglia. Diehard, a battery of tests for random number generators. *CD-ROM, Department of Statistics and Supercomputer Computations Research Institute, Florida State University, USA*, 1995.

394. George Marsaglia. The marsaglia random number cdrom including the diehard battery of tests of randomness, 1995.

395. Antoni Martínez-Ballesté, Pablo A. Pérez-Martínez, and Agusti Solanas. The pursuit of citizens' privacy: A privacy-aware smart city is possible. *IEEE Communications Magazine*, 51(6):136–141, 2013.

396. Kinga Marton and Alin Suciu. On the interpretation of results from the nist statistical test suite. *Science and Technology*, 18(1):18–32, 2015.

397. James L Massey. Some applications of source coding in cryptography. *Transactions on Emerging Telecommunications Technologies*, 5(4):421–430, 1994.

398. Mitsuru Matsui. New block encryption algorithm MISTY. In Eli Biham, editor, *Fast Software Encryption – FSE'97*, volume 1267 of *Lecture Notes in Computer Science*, pages 54–68, Haifa, Israel, January 20–22, 1997. Springer.

399. Tsutomu Matsumoto, Shinichi Kawamura, Kouichi Fujisaki, Naoya Torii, Shuichi Ishida, Yukiyasu Tsunoo, Minoru Saeki, and Atsuhiro Yamagishi. Tamper-resistance standarization research committee report. The 2006 Symposium on Cryptography and Information Security, 2006.

400. Tobias Matzner. Why privacy is not enough privacy in the context of "ubiquitous computing" and "big data". *Journal of Information, Communication and Ethics in Society*, 12(2):93–106, 2014.

401. S. Mauw, Z. Smith, J. Toro-Pozo, and R. Trujillo-Rasua. Distance-bounding protocols: Verification without time and location. In *IEEE Symposium on Security and Privacy*, volume 00, pages 152–169, 2018.

402. Rita Mayer-Sommer. Smartly Analyzing the Simplicity and the Power of Simple Power Analysis on Smartcards. In *CHES*, volume 1965 of *LNCS*, pages 78–92. Springer, May 14–16 2001. http://citeseer.nj.nec.com/mayer-sommer01smartly.html.

403. BD McCullough. A review of testu01. *Journal of Applied Econometrics*, 21(5):677–682, 2006.

404. Kerry A. McKay, Larry Bassham, Meltem Sönmez Turan, and Nicky Mouha. Nistir 8114 - report on lightweight cryptography, 2016.

405. Christopher Meffert, Devon Clark, Ibrahim Baggili, and Frank Breitinger. Forensic state acquisition from internet of things (fsaiot): A general framework and practical approach for iot forensics through iot device state acquisition. In *Proceedings of the 12th International Conference on Availability, Reliability and Security*, ARES '17, pages 56:1–56:11, New York, NY, USA, 2017. ACM.

406. Simon Meier, Benedikt Schmidt, Cas Cremers, and David Basin. The tamarin prover for the symbolic analysis of security protocols. In *International Conference on Computer Aided Verification*, CAV'13, pages 696–701. Springer, 2013.

407. Daniel Mellado, Eduardo Fernández-Medina, and Mario Piattini. A common criteria based security requirements engineering process for the development of secure information systems. *Computer standards & interfaces*, 29(2):244–253, 2007.

408. Imran Memon, Qasim Ali Arain, Muhammad Hammad Memon, Farman Ali Mangi, and Rizwan Akhtar. Search me if you can: Multiple mix zones with location privacy protection for mapping services. *International Journal of Communication Systems*, 30(16), 2017.

409. Nele Mentens, Jan Genoe, Bart Preneel, and Ingrid Verbauwhede. A low-cost implementation of Trivium. In *SASC 2008*, pages 197–204, 2008.

410. Thomas S. Messerges. Using Second-Order Power Analysis to Attack DPA Resistant Software. In *CHES*, volume 1965 of *LNCS*, pages 238–251. Springer-Verlag, August 17–18 2000. Worcester, MA, USA.

411. Thomas S. Messerges, Ezzy A. Dabbish, and Robert H. Sloan. Investigations of power analysis attacks on smartcards. In *Proceedings of the USENIX Workshop on Smartcard Technology on USENIX Workshop on Smartcard Technology*, WOST'99, pages 17–17, Berkeley, CA, USA, 1999. USENIX Association.

412. Thomas S. Messerges, Ezzy A. Dabbish, and Robert H. Sloan. Power Analysis Attacks of Modular Exponentiation in Smartcards. In Çetin Kaya Koç and Christof Paar, editors, *CHES*, volume 1717 of *LNCS*, pages 144–157. Springer, 1999.

413. Miodrag J Mihaljevic. A framework for stream ciphers based on pseudorandomness, randomness and coding. In *Enhancing Cryptographic Primitives with Techniques from Error Correcting Codes*, pages 117–139. IOS Press, Amsterdam, The Netherlands, 2009.

414. Miodrag J Mihaljević. An approach for light-weight encryption employing dedicated coding. In *Global Communications Conference, 2012 IEEE*, pages 874–880. IEEE, 2012.

415. Miodrag J. Mihaljevic, Sugata Gangopadhyay, Goutam Paul, and Hideki Imai. Generic cryptographic weakness of k-normal boolean functions in certain stream ciphers and cryptanalysis of grain-128. *Periodica Mathematica Hungarica*, 65(2):205–227, 2012.

416. Miodrag J. Mihaljevic, Sugata Gangopadhyay, Goutam Paul, and Hideki Imai. Internal state recovery of grain-v1 employing normality order of the filter function. *IET Information Security*, 6(2):55–64, 2012.

417. Miodrag J. Mihaljevic, Sugata Gangopadhyay, Goutam Paul, and Hideki Imai. Internal state recovery of keystream generator LILI-128 based on a novel weakness of the employed boolean function. *Inf. Process. Lett.*, 112(21):805–810, 2012.

418. Miodrag J Mihaljević and Hideki Imai. An approach for stream ciphers design based on joint computing over random and secret data. *Computing*, 85(1–2):153–168, 2009.

419. Miodrag J Mihaljević and Hideki Imai. Employment of homophonic coding for improvement of certain encryption approaches based on the lpn problem. In *Symmetric Key Encryption Workshop, SKEW*, pages 16–17, 2011.

420. Miodrag J Mihaljević and Frédérique Oggier. Security evaluation and design elements for a class of randomised encryptions. *IET Information Security*, 13(1):36–47, 2019.

421. Vasily Mikhalev, Frederik Armknecht, and Christian Müller. On ciphers that continuously access the non-volatile key. *IACR Transactions on Symmetric Cryptology*, 2016(2):52–79, 2016. http://tosc.iacr.org/index.php/ToSC/article/view/565.

422. Vasily Mikhalev, Frederik Armknecht, and Christian Müller. On ciphers that continuously access the non-volatile key. *IACR Transactions on Symmetric Cryptology*, 2016(2):52–79, 2017.

423. Thomas M. Mitchell. *Machine Learning*. McGraw-Hill, Inc., New York, NY, USA, 1 edition, 1997.

424. Seyyed Mohamamd Reza Moosavi and Abolghasem Sadeghi-Niaraki. A survey of smart electrical boards in ubiquitous sensor networks for geomatics applications. *The International Archives of Photogrammetry, Remote Sensing and Spatial Information Sciences*, 40(1):503, 2015.

425. Amir Moradi. Statistical tools flavor side-channel collision attacks. In David Pointcheval and Thomas Johansson, editors, *Advances in Cryptology - EUROCRYPT 2012*, volume 7237 of *Lecture Notes in Computer Science*, pages 428–445. Springer, 2012.

426. Amir Moradi, Axel Poschmann, San Ling, Christof Paar, and Huaxiong Wang. Pushing the limits: A very compact and a threshold implementation of AES. In Kenneth G. Paterson, editor, *Advances in Cryptology – EUROCRYPT 2011*, volume 6632 of *Lecture Notes in Computer Science*, pages 69–88, Tallinn, Estonia, May 15–19, 2011. Springer.

427. Athanassios Moschos, Apostolos P. Fournaris, and Odysseas Koufopavlou. A flexible leakage trace collection setup for arbitrary cryptographic ip cores. In *2018 IEEE International Symposium on Hardware Oriented Security and Trust (HOST)*, pages 138–142, April 2018.

428. Nicky Mouha, Bart Mennink, Anthony Van Herrewege, Dai Watanabe, Bart Preneel, and Ingrid Verbauwhede. Chaskey: An efficient MAC algorithm for 32-bit microcontrollers. In Antoine Joux and Amr M. Youssef, editors, *SAC 2014: 21st Annual International Workshop on Selected Areas in Cryptography*, volume 8781 of *Lecture Notes in Computer Science*, pages 306–323, Montreal, QC, Canada, August 14–15, 2014. Springer.

429. Marius Muench, Dario Nisi, Aurélien Francillon, and Davide Balzarotti. Avatar2: A Multi-target Orchestration Platform. In *Workshop on Binary Analysis Research (colocated with NDSS Symposium)*, BAR 18, February 2018.

430. Marius Muench, Jan Stijohann, Frank Kargl, Aurélien Francillon, and Davide Balzarotti. What you corrupt is not what you crash: Challenges in fuzzing embedded devices. In *ISOC NDSS 2018*, 2018.

431. Umar Mujahid, Muhammad Najam-ul Islam, and Ali Shami. RCIA: A new ultralightweight RFID authentication protocol using recursive hashing. *International Journal of Distributed Sensor Networks*, December 2014.

432. Frédéric Muller. Differential attacks against the helix stream cipher. In *Fast Software Encryption, FSE 2004, Delhi, India, February 5–7 , 2004*, pages 94–108, 2004.

433. Kiran-Kumar Muniswamy-Reddy, David A. Holland, Uri Braun, and Margo Seltzer. Provenance-aware storage systems. In *Proceedings of the Annual Conference on USENIX '06 Annual Technical Conference*, ATEC '06, pages 4–4, Berkeley, CA, USA, 2006. USENIX Association.

434. Radu Muresan and Stefano Gregori. Protection Circuit against Differential Power Analysis Attacks for Smart Cards. *IEEE Trans. Computers*, 57(11):1540–1549, 2008.

435. Mara Naya-Plasencia and Thomas Peyrin. Practical cryptanalysis of armadillo2. In *Fast Software Encryption, FSE 2012, Washington, DC, USA, March 19–21, 2012*, pages 146–162, 2012.

436. Roger M. Needham and David J. Wheeler. Tea extensions. Technical report, Computer Laboratory, University of Cambridge, 1997.

437. Irene C. L. Ng and Susan Y. L. Wakenshaw. The internet-of-things: Review and research directions. *International Journal of Research in Marketing*, 34(1):3–21, 2017.

438. David H. Nguyen and Gillian R. Hayes. Information privacy in institutional and end-user tracking and recording technologies. *Personal and Ubiquitous Computing*, 14(1):53–72, 2010.

439. Marcus Niemietz and Jörg Schwenk. Owning your home network: Router security revisited. In *9th Workshop on Web 2.0 Security and Privacy (W2SP) 2015*, 2015.

440. Ana Nieto, Ruben Rios, and Javier Lopez. A methodology for privacy-aware iot-forensics. In *2017 IEEE Trustcom/BigDataSE/ICESS*, pages 626–633, Aug 2017.

441. Ana Nieto, Ruben Rios, and Javier Lopez. Iot-forensics meets privacy: Towards cooperative digital investigations. *Sensors*, 18(2), 2018.

442. Ana Nieto, Rodrigo Roman, and Javier López. Digital witness: Safeguarding digital evidence by using secure architectures in personal devices. *IEEE Network*, 30(6):34–41, 2016.

443. Ivica Nikolic, Lei Wang, and Shuang Wu. Cryptanalysis of round-reduced \mathttled. In *Fast Software Encryption - 20th International Workshop, FSE 2013, Singapore, March 11–13, 2013. Revised Selected Papers*, pages 112–129, 2013.

444. NIST. Cryptographic standards and guidelines: Aes development. https://csrc.nist. gov/Projects/Cryptographic-Standards-and-Guidelines/Archived-Crypto-Projects/AES-Development.

445. NXP. Nxp mifare plus ev1 – latest features on highest security level scalable – flexible – future proof, April 2016.

446. NXP. Nxp mifare desfire ev2 – contactless IC for next-generation, multi-application solutions in smart cities, May 2018.

447. Johannes Obermaier and Stefan Tatschner. Shedding too much light on a microcontroller's firmware protection. In *11th USENIX Workshop on Offensive Technologies (WOOT 17)*, Vancouver, BC, 2017. USENIX Association.

448. National Institute of Standards and Technology. *NIST SP800-22 Revision 1a – A Statistical Test Suite for Random And Pseudorandom Number Generators for Cryptographic Applications*. Retrieved from: https://nvlpubs.nist.gov/nistpubs/Legacy/SP/nistspecialpublication800-22r1a.pdf 16:53 21/05/2018.

449. National Institute of Standards and Technology. *NIST SP800-90 B – Reccommendation for the Entropy Sources used for Random Bit Generation*. Retrieved from: https://nvlpubs.nist. gov/nistpubs/SpecialPublications/NIST.SP.800-90B.pdf 17:33 21/05/2018.

450. Colin O'Flynn. Chipwhisperer. https://wiki.newae.com/Main_Page.

451. Colin O'Flynn and Zhizhang (David) Chen. *ChipWhisperer: An Open-Source Platform for Hardware Embedded Security Research*, pages 243–260. Springer International Publishing, Cham, 2014.

452. Frédérique Oggier and Miodrag J Mihaljević. An information-theoretic security evaluation of a class of randomized encryption schemes. *IEEE Transactions on Information Forensics and Security*, 9(2):158–168, 2014.

453. Miyako Ohkubo, Koutarou Suzuki, and Shingo Kinoshita. Cryptographic Approach to "Privacy-Friendly" Tags. In *RFID Privacy Workshop*, MIT, Massachusetts, USA, November 2003.

454. Femi Olumofin, Piotr K. Tysowski, Ian Goldberg, and Urs Hengartner. Achieving efficient query privacy for location based services. In Mikhail J. Atallah and Nicholas J. Hopper, editors, *Privacy Enhancing Technologies*, pages 93–110. Springer, 2010.

455. Edewede Oriwoh, David Jazani, Gregory Epiphaniou, and Paul Sant. Internet of things forensics: Challenges and approaches. In *9th IEEE International Conference on Collaborative Computing: Networking, Applications and Worksharing, Austin, TX, USA, October 20–23, 2013*, pages 608–615, 2013.

456. Edewede Oriwoh and Paul Sant. The forensics edge management system: A concept and design. In *2013 IEEE 10th International Conference on Ubiquitous Intelligence and Computing and 2013 IEEE 10th International Conference on Autonomic and Trusted Computing, UIC/ATC 2013, Vietri sul Mare, Sorrento Peninsula, Italy, December 18–21, 2013*, pages 544–550, 2013.

457. Khaled Ouafi, Raphael Overbeck, and Serge Vaudenay. On the security of HB# against a man-in-the-middle attack. In Josef Pieprzyk, editor, *Advances in Cryptology – ASIACRYPT 2008*, volume 5350 of *Lecture Notes in Computer Science*, pages 108–124, Melbourne, Australia, December 7–11, 2008. Springer.

458. Khaled Ouafi and Serge Vaudenay. Smashing SQUASH-0. In Antoine Joux, editor, *Advances in Cryptology – EUROCRYPT 2009*, volume 5479 of *Lecture Notes in Computer Science*, pages 300–312, Cologne, Germany, April 26–30, 2009. Springer.

459. Achilleas Papageorgiou, Michael Strigkos, Eugenia A. Politou, Efthimios Alepis, Agusti Solanas, and Constantinos Patsakis. Security and privacy analysis of mobile health applications: The alarming state of practice. *IEEE Access*, 6:9390–9403, 2018.

460. Constantinos Patsakis, Panayiotis Kotzanikolaou, and Mélanie Bouroche. Private proximity testing on steroids: An ntru-based protocol. In *Security and Trust Management - 11th International Workshop, STM 2015, Vienna, Austria, September 21–22, 2015, Proceedings*, pages 172–184, 2015.

461. Pablo A. Pérez-Martínez and Agusti Solanas. W3-privacy: the three dimensions of user privacy in lbs. In *12th ACM Intl. Symp. Mobile Ad Hoc Networking and Computing*, 2011.

462. Pablo A. Pérez-Martínez, Agusti Solanas, and Antoni Martínez-Ballesté. Location Privacy Through Users' Collaboration: A Distributed Pseudonymizer. In *Proceedings of the 3rd International Conference on Mobile Ubiquitous Computing, Systems, Services and Technologies (UBICOMM)*, pages 338–341, 2009.

463. Pedro Peris-Lopez, Julio Hernandez-Castro, Juan M. Estévez-Tapiador, and Arturo Ribagorda. Advances in ultralightweight cryptography for low-cost RFID tags: Gossamer protocol. In Kyo-Il Chung, Kiwook Sohn, and Moti Yung, editors, *WISA 08: 9th International Workshop on Information Security Applications*, volume 5379 of *Lecture Notes in Computer Science*, pages 56–68, Jeju Island, Korea, September 23–25, 2009. Springer.

464. Pedro Peris-Lopez, Julio C. Hernandez-Castro, Juan M. Estevez-Tapiador, Tieyan Li, and Jan C.A. van der Lubbe. Weaknesses in Two Recent Lightweight RFID Authentication Protocols. In *Workshop on RFID Security – RFIDSec'09*, Leuven, Belgium, July 2009.

465. Pedro Peris-Lopez, Julio C. Hernandez-Castro, Juan M. Estevez-Tapiador, and Arturo Ribagorda. EMAP: An Efficient Mutual Authentication Protocol for Low-Cost RFID Tags. In *OTM Federated Conferences and Workshop: IS Workshop – IS'06*, volume 4277 of *Lecture Notes in Computer Science*, pages 352–361, Montpellier, France, November 2006. Springer.

466. Pedro Peris-Lopez, Julio C. Hernandez-Castro, Juan M. Estevez-Tapiador, and Arturo Ribagorda. LMAP: A Real Lightweight Mutual Authentication Protocol for Low-cost RFID tags. In *Workshop on RFID Security – RFIDSec'06*, Graz, Austria, July 2006. Ecrypt.

467. Pedro Peris-Lopez, Julio C. Hernandez-Castro, Juan M. Estevez-Tapiador, and Arturo Ribagorda. M2AP: A Minimalist Mutual-Authentication Protocol for Low-cost RFID Tags. In Jianhua Ma, Hai Jin, Laurence Tianruo Yang, and Jeffrey J. P. Tsai, editors, *International Conference on Ubiquitous Intelligence and Computing – UIC'06*, volume 4159 of *Lecture Notes in Computer Science*, pages 912–923, Wuhan and Three Gorges, China, September 2006. Springer.

468. Pedro Peris-Lopez, Julio C. Hernandez-Castro, Raphael C.-W. Phan, Juan M. E. Tapiador, and Tieyan Li. Quasi-Linear Cryptanalysis of a Secure RFID Ultralightweight Authentication Protocol. In *6th China International Conference on Information Security and Cryptology – Inscrypt'10*, Shanghai, China, October 2010. Springer.

469. Léo Perrin and Dmitry Khovratovich. Collision spectrum, entropy loss, T-sponges, and cryptanalysis of GLUON-64. In Carlos Cid and Christian Rechberger, editors, *Fast Software Encryption – FSE 2014*, volume 8540 of *Lecture Notes in Computer Science*, pages 82–103, London, UK, March 3–5, 2015. Springer.

470. Sundresan Perumal, Norita M. Norwawi, and Valliappan Raman. Internet of things (IoT) digital forensic investigation model: Top-down forensic approach methodology. In *2015 Fifth International Conference on Digital Information Processing and Communications (ICDIPC)*, pages 19–23, Oct 2015.

471. Petter Pessl and Michael Hutter. Pushing the limits of sha-3 hardware implementations to fit on rfid. In *Cryptographic Hardware and Embedded Systems, CHES 2013, Santa Barbara, CA, USA, August 20–23, 2013*, pages 126–141, 2013.

472. Christophe Petit and Jean-Jacques Quisquater. Cryptographic hash functions and expander graphs: The end of the story? In *The New Codebreakers - Essays Dedicated to David Kahn on the Occasion of His 85th Birthday*, pages 304–311, 2016.

473. Raphael C.-W. Phan. Cryptanalysis of a New Ultralightweight RFID Authentication Protocol - SASI. *IEEE Transactions on Dependable and Secure Computing*, 99(1), 2008.

474. Raphael C.-W. Phan and Adi Shamir. Improved related-key attacks on desx and desx+. *Cryptologia*, 32(1):13–22, 2008.

475. Stjepan Picek, Annelie Heuser, Cesare Alippi, and Francesco Regazzoni. When theory meets practice: A framework for robust profiled side-channel analysis. Cryptology ePrint Archive, Report 2018/1123, 2018. https://eprint.iacr.org/2018/1123.

476. Stjepan Picek, Annelie Heuser, and Sylvain Guilley. Template attack versus bayes classifier. *Journal of Cryptographic Engineering*, 7(4):343–351, Nov 2017.

477. Stjepan Picek, Annelie Heuser, Alan Jovic, Lejla Batina, and Axel Legay. The secrets of profiling for side-channel analysis: feature selection matters. *IACR Cryptology ePrint Archive*, 2017:1110, 2017.

478. Stjepan Picek, Annelie Heuser, Alan Jovic, Shivam Bhasin, and Francesco Regazzoni. The curse of class imbalance and conflicting metrics with machine learning for side-channel evaluations. *IACR Transactions on Cryptographic Hardware and Embedded Systems*, 2019(1):209–237, Nov. 2018.

479. Stjepan Picek, Annelie Heuser, Alan Jovic, and Axel Legay. Climbing down the hierarchy: Hierarchical classification for machine learning side-channel attacks. In Marc Joye and Abderrahmane Nitaj, editors, *Progress in Cryptology - AFRICACRYPT 2017: 9th International Conference on Cryptology in Africa, Dakar, Senegal, May 24–26, 2017, Proceedings*, pages 61–78, Cham, 2017. Springer International Publishing.

480. Stjepan Picek, Annelie Heuser, Alan Jovic, Axel Legay, and Karlo Knezevic. Profiled sca with a new twist: Semi-supervised learning. Cryptology ePrint Archive, Report 2017/1085, 2017. https://eprint.iacr.org/2017/1085.

481. Stjepan Picek, Annelie Heuser, Alan Jovic, Simone A. Ludwig, Sylvain Guilley, Domagoj Jakobovic, and Nele Mentens. Side-channel analysis and machine learning: A practical perspective. In *2017 International Joint Conference on Neural Networks, IJCNN 2017, Anchorage, AK, USA, May 14–19, 2017*, pages 4095–4102, 2017.

482. Stjepan Picek, Ioannis Petros Samiotis, Jaehun Kim, Annelie Heuser, Shivam Bhasin, and Axel Legay. On the performance of convolutional neural networks for side-channel analysis. In Anupam Chattopadhyay, Chester Rebeiro, and Yuval Yarom, editors, *Security, Privacy, and Applied Cryptography Engineering*, pages 157–176, Cham, 2018. Springer International Publishing.

483. Ameer Pichan, Mihai Lazarescu, and Sie Teng Soh. Cloud forensics: Technical challenges, solutions and comparative analysis. *Digital Investigation*, 13:38–57, 2015.

484. Aniket Pingley, Nan Zhang, Xinwen Fu, Hyeong-Ah Choi, Suresh Subramaniam, and Wei Zhao. Protection of query privacy for continuous location based services. In *INFOCOM 2011. 30th IEEE International Conference on Computer Communications, Joint Conference of the IEEE Computer and Communications Societies, 10–15 April 2011, Shanghai, China*, pages 1710–1718, 2011.

485. Gilles Piret, Thomas Roche, and Claude Carlet. PICARO - a block cipher allowing efficient higher-order side-channel resistance. In Feng Bao, Pierangela Samarati, and Jianying Zhou, editors, *ACNS 12: 10th International Conference on Applied Cryptography and Network Security*, volume 7341 of *Lecture Notes in Computer Science*, pages 311–328, Singapore, June 26–29, 2012. Springer.

486. Eugenia Politou, Efthimios Alepis, and Constantinos Patsakis. Forgetting personal data and revoking consent under the gdpr: Challenges and proposed solutions. *Journal of Cybersecurity*, page tyy001, 2018.

487. Axel Poschmann, San Ling, and Huaxiong Wang. 256 bit standardized crypto for 650 GE - GOST revisited. In Stefan Mangard and François-Xavier Standaert, editors, *Cryptographic Hardware and Embedded Systems – CHES 2010*, volume 6225 of *Lecture Notes in Computer Science*, pages 219–233, Santa Barbara, CA, USA, August 17–20, 2010. Springer.

488. David Martin Ward Powers. Evaluation: from precision, recall and f-factor to roc, informedness, markedness and correlation, 2007.

489. Sihang Pu, Yu Yu, Weijia Wang, Zheng Guo, Junrong Liu, Dawu Gu, Lingyun Wang, and Jie Gan. Trace augmentation: What can be done even before preprocessing in a profiled sca? In Thomas Eisenbarth and Yannick Teglia, editors, *Smart Card Research and Advanced Applications*, pages 232–247, Cham, 2018. Springer International Publishing.

490. Kexin Qiao, Lei Hu, and Siwei Sun. Differential security evaluation of simeck with dynamic key-guessing techniques. Cryptology ePrint Archive, Report 2015/902, 2015. http://eprint.iacr.org/2015/902.

491. Lingyue Qin, Huaifeng Chen, and Xiaoyun Wang. Linear hull attack on round-reduced simeck with dynamic key-guessing techniques. In Joseph K. Liu and Ron Steinfeld, editors, *ACISP 16: 21st Australasian Conference on Information Security and Privacy, Part II*, volume 9723 of *Lecture Notes in Computer Science*, pages 409–424, Melbourne, VIC, Australia, July 4–6, 2016. Springer.

492. Cai Qingling, Zhan Yiju, and Wang Yonghua. A Minimalist Mutual Authentication Protocol for RFID System & BAN Logic Analysis. In *ISECS International Colloquium on Computing, Communication, Control, and Management – CCCM'08.*, volume 2, pages 449–453, August 2008.

493. Jean-Jacques Quisquater and David Samyde. Electromagnetic analysis (ema): Measures and counter-measures for smart cards. In Isabelle Attali and Thomas Jensen, editors, *Smart Card Programming and Security*, pages 200–210. Springer, 2001.

494. KM Sabidur Rahman, Matt Bishop, and Albert Holt. Internet of things mobility forensics. *Researchgate. net*, 2017.

495. Rambus. Dpa workstation testing platform. http://info.rambus.com/hubfs/rambus.com/Gated-Content/Cryptography/DPA-Workstation-Product-Brief.pdf.

496. Kasper Bonne Rasmussen and Srdjan Čapkun. Location privacy of distance bounding protocols. In *Conference on Computer and Communications Security (CCS)*, pages 149–160. ACM, 2008.

497. Shahram Rasoolzadeh, Zahra Ahmadian, Mahmoud Salmasizadeh, and Mohammad Reza Aref. An improved truncated differential cryptanalysis of KLEIN. *Tatra Mountains Mathematical Publications*, 67:135–147, 2017.

498. Christian Rechberger and Elisabeth Oswald. Practical Template Attacks. In *WISA*, volume 3325 of *LNCS*, pages 443–457. Springer, August 23-25 2004. Jeju Island, Korea.

499. Michał Ren, Tanmoy Kanti Das, and Jianying Zhou. Diverging keys in wireless sensor networks. In Sokratis K. Katsikas, Javier López, Michael Backes, Stefanos Gritzalis, and Bart Preneel, editors, *Information Security, 9th International Conference, ISC 2006, Samos Island, Greece, August 30 - September 2, 2006, Proceedings*, volume 4176 of *Lecture Notes in Computer Science*, pages 257–269. Springer, 2006.

500. Mathieu Renauld, François-Xavier Standaert, Nicolas Veyrat-Charvillon, Dina Kamel, and Denis Flandre. A formal study of power variability issues and side-channel attacks for nanoscale devices. In Kenneth G. Paterson, editor, *Advances in Cryptology - EUROCRYPT 2011 - 30th Annual International Conference on the Theory and Applications of Cryptographic Techniques, Tallinn, Estonia, May 15-19, 2011. Proceedings*, volume 6632 of *Lecture Notes in Computer Science*, pages 109–128. Springer, 2011.

501. Riscure. Inspector: The side channel test tool. https://www.riscure.com/security-tools/inspector-sca/.

502. Ronald L. Rivest. The RC5 encryption algorithm. In Bart Preneel, editor, *Fast Software Encryption – FSE'94*, volume 1008 of *Lecture Notes in Computer Science*, pages 86–96, Leuven, Belgium, December 14–16, 1995. Springer.

503. Ronald L Rivest and Alan T Sherman. Randomized encryption techniques. In *Advances in Cryptology*, pages 145–163. Springer, 1983.

504. Phillip Rogaway, Mihir Bellare, and John Black. Ocb: A block-cipher mode of operation for efficient authenticated encryption. *ACM Transactions on Information and System Security*, 6(3):365–403, 2003.

505. Michael Roland, Josef Langer, and Josef Scharinger. Applying relay attacks to google wallet. In *Near Field Communication (NFC), 2013 5th International Workshop on*, pages 1–6. IEEE, 2013.

506. John D. Roth, Murali Tummala, John C. McEachen, and James W. Scrofani. On location privacy in LTE networks. *IEEE Trans. Information Forensics and Security*, 12(6):1358–1368, 2017.

507. Vassil Roussev. Data Fingerprinting with Similarity Digests. In *IFIP International Conference on Digital Forensics*, pages 207–226, 2010.

508. Andrew Rukhin, Juan Soto, and James Nechvatal. A statistical test suite for random and pseudorandom number generators for cryptographic applications. nist dtic document. *NIST SP800-22*, 2010.

509. Andrew Rukhin, Juan Soto, James Nechvatal, Miles Smid, and Elaine Barker. A statistical test suite for random and pseudorandom number generators for cryptographic applications. Technical report, DTIC Document, 2001.

510. Alexander Russell, Qiang Tang, Moti Yung, and Hong-Sheng Zhou. Cliptography: Clipping the power of kleptographic attacks. In Jung Hee Cheon and Tsuyoshi Takagi, editors, *Advances in Cryptology - ASIACRYPT 2016 - 22nd International Conference on the Theory and Application of Cryptology and Information Security, Hanoi, Vietnam, December 4-8, 2016, Proceedings, Part II*, volume 10032 of *Lecture Notes in Computer Science*, pages 34–64, 2016.

511. Karmakar Sandip, Mukhopadhyay Debdeep, and Roy Chowdhury Dipanwita. Cavium strengthening trivium stream cipher using cellular automata. *Journal of Cellular Automata*, 7(2):179–197, 2012.

512. Yu Sasaki and Yosuke Todo. New differential bounds and division property of Lilliput: Block cipher with extended generalized Feistel network. In Roberto Avanzi and Howard M. Heys, editors, *SAC 2016: 23rd Annual International Workshop on Selected Areas in Cryptography*, volume 10532 of *Lecture Notes in Computer Science*, pages 264–283, St. John's, NL, Canada, August 10–12, 2016. Springer.

513. Florian Schaub, Bastian Könings, and Michael Weber. Context-adaptive privacy: Leveraging context awareness to support privacy decision making. *IEEE Pervasive Computing*, 14(1):34–43, 2015.

514. Werner Schindler and Wolfgang Killmann. Evaluation criteria for true (physical) random number generators used in cryptographic applications. In *International Workshop on Cryptographic Hardware and Embedded Systems*, pages 431–449. Springer, 2002.

515. Werner Schindler, Kerstin Lemke, and Christof Paar. A Stochastic Model for Differential Side Channel Cryptanalysis. In LNCS, editor, *CHES*, volume 3659 of *LNCS*, pages 30–46. Springer, Sept 2005. Edinburgh, Scotland, UK.

516. Tobias Schneider and Amir Moradi. Leakage assessment methodology. In *International Workshop on Cryptographic Hardware and Embedded Systems*, pages 495–513. Springer, 2015.

517. Friedhelm Schwenker and Edmondo Trentin. Pattern classification and clustering: A review of partially supervised learning approaches. *Pattern Recognition Letters*, 37:4–14, 2014.

518. Jaydip Sen. Ubiquitous computing: Potentials and challenges. *arXiv preprint arXiv:1011.1960*, 2010.

519. Mohammad Hossein Faghihi Sereshgi, Mohammad Dakhilalian, and Mohsen Shakiba. Biclique cryptanalysis of MIBS-80 and PRESENT-80 block ciphers. *Security and Communication Networks*, 9(1):27–33, 2016.

520. Adi Shamir. SQUASH - a new MAC with provable security properties for highly constrained devices such as RFID tags. In Kaisa Nyberg, editor, *Fast Software Encryption – FSE 2008*, volume 5086 of *Lecture Notes in Computer Science*, pages 144–157, Lausanne, Switzerland, February 10–13, 2008. Springer.

521. Jinyong Shan, Lei Hu, Ling Song, Siwei Sun, and Xiaoshuang Ma. Related-key differential attack on round reduced RECTANGLE-80. Cryptology ePrint Archive, Report 2014/986, 2014. http://eprint.iacr.org/2014/986.

522. Claude Shannon. Communication theory of secrecy systems. *Bell System Technical Journal*, 28(4):656–715, 1949.

523. Danping Shi, Lei Hu, Siwei Sun, Ling Song, Kexin Qiao, and Xiaoshuang Ma. Improved linear (hull) cryptanalysis of round-reduced versions of SIMON. Cryptology ePrint Archive, Report 2014/973, 2014. http://eprint.iacr.org/2014/973.

524. Zhenqing Shi, Xiutao Feng, Dengguo Feng, and Chuankun Wu. A real-time key recovery attack on the lightweight stream cipher a2u2. In *Cryptology and Network Security, CANS 2012, Darmstadt, Germany, December 12-14, 2012*, pages 12–22, 2012.

525. Zhenqing Shi, Bin Zhang, and Dengguo Feng. Practical-time related-key attack on hummingbird-2. *IET Information Security*, 9(6):321–327, 2015.

526. Kyoji Shibutani, Takanori Isobe, Harunaga Hiwatari, Atsushi Mitsuda, Toru Akishita, and Taizo Shirai. Piccolo: An ultra-lightweight blockcipher. In Bart Preneel and Tsuyoshi Takagi, editors, *Cryptographic Hardware and Embedded Systems – CHES 2011*, volume 6917 of *Lecture Notes in Computer Science*, pages 342–357, Nara, Japan, September 28 – October 1, 2011. Springer.

527. Taizo Shirai, Kyoji Shibutani, Toru Akishita, Shiho Moriai, and Tetsu Iwata. The 128-bit blockcipher CLEFIA (extended abstract). In Alex Biryukov, editor, *Fast Software Encryption – FSE 2007*, volume 4593 of *Lecture Notes in Computer Science*, pages 181–195, Luxembourg, Luxembourg, March 26–28, 2007. Springer.

528. Yan Shoshitaishvili, Ruoyu Wang, Christophe Hauser, Christopher Kruegel, and Giovanni Vigna. Firmalice-automatic detection of authentication bypass vulnerabilities in binary firmware. In *NDSS*, 2015.

529. O. Shwartz, Y. Mathov, M. Bohadana, Y. Oren, and Y. Elovici. Reverse engineering iot devices: Effective techniques and methods. *IEEE Internet of Things Journal*, pages 1–1, 2018.

530. Siang Meng Sim and Lei Wang. Practical forgery attacks on scream and iscream. http://www1.spms.ntu.edu.sg/~syllab/m/images/b/b3/ForgeryAttackonSCREAM.pdf.

531. Mridula Singh, Patrick Leu, and Srdjan Capkun. UWB with pulse reordering: Securing ranging against relay and physical layer attacks. IACR ePrint Report 2017/1240, December 2017.

532. Sergei Skorobogatov and Christopher Woods. In the blink of an eye: There goes your AES key, 2012.

533. Agusti Solanas and Josep Domingo-Ferrer. Location privacy in location-based services: Beyond ttp-based schemes. In *In Proceedings of the 1st international workshop on privacy in location-based applications (PILBA)*, pages 12–23, 2008.

534. Agusti Solanas and Antoni Martínez-Ballesté. V-MDAV: a multivariate microaggregation with variable group size. In *17th COMPSTAT Symposium of the IASC*, pages 917–925, 2006.

535. Agusti Solanas, Constantinos Patsakis, Mauro Conti, Ioannis S. Vlachos, Victoria Ramos, Francisco Falcone, Octavian Postolache, Pablo A. Pérez-Martínez, Roberto Di Pietro, Despina N. Perrea, and Antoni Martínez-Ballesté. Smart health: A context-aware health paradigm within smart cities. *IEEE Communications Magazine*, 52(8):74–81, 2014.

536. Agusti Solanas, Jens H. Weber, Ayse Basar Bener, Frank van der Linden, and Rafael Capilla. Recent advances in healthcare software: Toward context-aware and smart solutions. *IEEE Software*, 34(6):36–40, 2017.

537. Ling Song, Zhangjie Huang, and Qianqian Yang. Automatic differential analysis of ARX block ciphers with application to SPECK and LEA. In Joseph K. Liu and Ron Steinfeld, editors, *ACISP 16: 21st Australasian Conference on Information Security and Privacy, Part II*, volume 9723 of *Lecture Notes in Computer Science*, pages 379–394, Melbourne, VIC, Australia, July 4–6, 2016. Springer.

538. Juan Soto. Statistical testing of random number generators. In *Proceedings of the 22nd National Information Systems Security Conference*, volume 10, page 12. NIST, 1999.

539. Luigi Sportiello and Andrea Ciardulli. Long distance relay attack. In *International Workshop on Radio Frequency Identification: Security and Privacy Issues*, pages 69–85. Springer, 2013.

540. Frank Stajano. *Security for Ubiquitous Computing*. John Wiley and Sons, February 2002.

541. François-Xavier Standaert, Gilles Piret, Gaël Rouvroy, Jean-Jacques Quisquater, and Jean-Didier Legat. ICEBERG: An involutional cipher efficient for block encryption in reconfigurable hardware. In Bimal K. Roy and Willi Meier, editors, *Fast Software Encryption – FSE 2004*, volume 3017 of *Lecture Notes in Computer Science*, pages 279–299, New Delhi, India, February 5–7, 2004. Springer.

542. François-Xavier Standaert, Gilles Piret, Neil Gershenfeld, and Jean-Jacques Quisquater. SEA: A scalable encryption algorithm for small embedded applications. In *Smart Card Research and Advanced Applications, 7th IFIP WG 8.8/11.2 International Conference, CARDIS 2006, Tarragona, Spain, April 19-21, 2006, Proceedings*, pages 222–236, 2006.

543. Yue Sun, Meiqin Wang, Shujia Jiang, and Qiumei Sun. Differential cryptanalysis of reduced-round ICEBERG. In Aikaterini Mitrokotsa and Serge Vaudenay, editors, *AFRICACRYPT 12: 5th International Conference on Cryptology in Africa*, volume 7374 of *Lecture Notes in Computer Science*, pages 155–171, Ifrance, Morocco, July 10–12, 2012. Springer.

544. Tomoyasu Suzaki, Kazuhiko Minematsu, Sumio Morioka, and Eita Kobayashi. TWINE: A lightweight, versatile block cipher. In *ECRYPT Workshop on Lightweight Cryptography*, pages 146–169, 2011.

545. Biaoshuai Tao and Hongjun Wu. Improving the biclique cryptanalysis of aes. In *Information Security and Privacy, ACISP 2015, Brisbane, Australia, June 29 - July 1, 2015*, pages 39–56, 2015.

546. The European Parliament and the Council of the European Union. Regulation (EU) No 910/2014 of the European Parliament and of the Council of 23 July 2014 on electronic identification and trust services for electronic transactions in the internal market and repealing Directive 1999/93/ec. Available at: http://eur-lex.europa.eu/legal-content/EN/TXT/?uri= uriserv:OJ.L_.2014.257.01.0073.01.ENG, 2014.

547. The European Parliament and the Council of the European Union. Regulation (EU) 2016/679 of the European Parliament and of the Council of 27 April 2016 on the protection of natural persons with regard to the processing of personal data and on the free movement of such data, and repealing Directive 95/46/ec (General Data Protection Regulation). *Official Journal of the European Union*, 119(1), 2016.

548. Pierre-Henri Thevenon and Olivier Savry. Implementation of a countermeasure to relay attacks for contactless hf systems. In *Radio Frequency Identification from System to Applications*. InTech, 2013.

549. Olivier Thomas and Dmitry Nedospasov. On the impact of automating the ic analysis process. BlackHat 2015, August 2015.

550. Sam L. Thomas, Tom Chothia, and Flavio D. Garcia. Stringer: Measuring the Importance of Static Data Comparisons to Detect Backdoors and Undocumented Functionality. In *Proceedings of the 22nd European Symposium on Research in Computer Security*, ESORICS '17, 2017.

551. Sam L. Thomas and Aurélien Francillon. Backdoors: Definition, Deniability and Detection. In *Symposium on Research in Attacks, Intrusion, and Defenses (RAID)*. Springer, September 2018.

552. Sam L. Thomas, Flavio D. Garcia, and Tom Chothia. HumIDIFy: A Tool for Hidden Functionality Detection in Firmware. In *Proceedings of the 14th International Conference on Detection of Intrusions and Malware, and Vulnerability Assessment*, DIMVA '17, 2017.

553. Peter Thueringer, Hans De Jong, Bruce Murray, Heike Neumann, Paul Hubmer, and Susanne Stern. Decoupling of measuring the response time of a transponder and its authentication, November 2008.

554. Yun Tian, Gongliang Chen, and Jianhua Li. A new ultralightweight RFID authentication protocol with permutation. *IEEE Communications Letters*, 16(5):702–705, May 2012.

555. Yun Tian, Gongliang Chen, and Jianhua Li. Quavium - a new stream cipher inspired by trivium. *Journal of Computers*, 7(5):1278–1283, 2012.

556. Andrew Tierney (@cybergibbons). Bypassing code readout protections on microcontrollers, January 2018.

557. K. Tiri and I. Verbauwhede. A logic level design methodology for a secure dpa resistant asic or fpga implementation. In *Proceedings Design, Automation and Test in Europe Conference and Exhibition*, volume 1, pages 246–251 Vol.1, Feb 2004.

558. Tjaldur Software Governance Solutions. Binary Analysis Tool (BAT).

559. Jevgenijus Toldinas, Algimantas Venčkauskas, Šarūnas Grigaliūnas, Robertas Damaševičius, and Vacius Jusas. Suitability of the digital forensic tools for investigation of cyber crime in the internet of things and services. In *The 3rd International Virtual Research Conference In Technical Disciplines*, pages 86–97, October 2015.

560. Meltem Sönmez Turan, Ali DoĞanaksoy, and Serdar Boztaş. On independence and sensitivity of statistical randomness tests. In *International Conference on Sequences and Their Applications*, pages 18–29. Springer, 2008.

561. Pascal Urien and Selwyn Piramuthu. Elliptic curve-based rfid/nfc authentication with temperature sensor input for relay attacks. *Decis. Support Syst.*, 59:28–36, March 2014.

562. Lachlan Urquhart, Neelima Sailaja, and Derek McAuley. Realising the right to data portability for the domestic internet of things. *Personal and Ubiquitous Computing*, pages 1–16, 2017.

563. Jordi van den Breekel, Diego A. Ortiz-Yepes, Erik Poll, and Joeri de Ruiter. EMV in a nutshell. June, KPMG, IBM Research Zurich, Radboud University Nijmegen, 2016.

564. S. Vasile, D. Oswald, and T. Chothia. Breaking all the things - a systematic survey of firmware extraction techniques for iot devices. In *CARDIS*, 2018.

565. Rajesh Velegalati and Jens-Peter Kaps. Introducing FOBOS: Flexible Open-source BOard for Side-channel analysis. Work in Progress (WiP), Third International Workshop on Constructive Side-Channel Analysis and Secure Design, COSADE 2012, May 2012.

566. Rajesh Velegalati and Jens-Peter Kaps. Towards a Flexible, Opensource BOard for Side-channel analysis (FOBOS). Cryptographic architectures embedded in reconfigurable devices, CRYPTARCHI 2013, June 2013.

567. José Vila and Ricardo J. Rodríguez. Practical experiences on NFC relay attacks with android: Virtual pickpocketing revisited. In Stefan Mangard and Patrick Schaumont, editors, *Radio Frequency Identification. Security and Privacy Issues - 11th International Workshop, RFIDsec 2015, New York, NY, USA, June 23-24, 2015, Revised Selected Papers*, volume 9440 of *Lecture Notes in Computer Science*, pages 87–103, New York City, USA, June 2015. Springer.

568. John Walker. Ent, a pseudorandom number sequence test program. Fourmilab, 2008.

569. Cheng Wang and Howard M. Heys. An ultra compact block cipher for serialized architecture implementations. In *Proceedings of the 22nd Canadian Conference on Electrical and Computer Engineering, CCECE 2009, 3-6 May 2009, Delta St. John's Hotel and Conference Centre, St. John's, Newfoundland, Canada*, pages 1085–1090, 2009.

570. Jian Wang, Jiaqi Mu, Shuangqing Wei, Chunxiao Jiang, and Norman C Beaulieu. Statistical characterization of decryption errors in block-ciphered systems. *IEEE Transactions on Communications*, 63(11):4363–4376, 2015.

571. Jinbao Wang, Zhipeng Cai, Yingshu Li, Donghua Yang, Ji Li, and Hong Gao. Protecting query privacy with differentially private k-anonymity in location-based services. *Personal and Ubiquitous Computing*, Mar 2018.

572. Qi Wang, Wajih Ul Hassan, Adam Bates, and Carl Gunter. Fear and logging in the internet of things. *Network and Distributed Systems Symposium*, Feb 2018.

573. Shengling Wang, Qin Hu, Yunchuan Sun, and Jianhui Huang. Privacy preservation in location-based services. *IEEE Communications Magazine*, 56(3):134–140, MARCH 2018.

574. Dai Watanabe, Kota Ideguchi, Jun Kitahara, Kenichiro Muto, Hiroki Furuichi, and Toshinobu Kaneko. Enocoro-80: A hardware oriented stream cipher. In *Proceedings of the The Third International Conference on Availability, Reliability and Security, ARES 2008, March 4-7, 2008, Technical University of Catalonia, Barcelona , Spain*, pages 1294–1300, 2008.

575. Dai Watanabe, Kazuto Okamoto, and Toshinobu Kaneko. A hardware-oriented light weight pseudo-random number generator enocoro-128v2. In *SCIS 2010, 3D1-3, (2010). In Japanese*, 2010.

576. Steve Watson and Ali Dehghantanha. Digital forensics: the missing piece of the internet of things promise. *Computer Fraud & Security*, 2016(6):5–8, 2016.

577. Shuangqing Wei, Jian Wang, Ruming Yin, and Jian Yuan. Trade-off between security and performance in block ciphered systems with erroneous ciphertexts. *IEEE Transactions on Information Forensics and Security*, 8(4):636–645, 2013.

578. Mark Weiser. The computer for the 21st century. *Mobile Computing and Communications Review*, 3(3):3–11, 1999.

579. Oscar Williams-Grut. Hackers once stole a casino's high-roller database through a thermometer in the lobby fish tank. Business Insider, 2018.

580. Ian H. Witten and Eibe Frank. *Data Mining: Practical Machine Learning Tools and Techniques, Second Edition (Morgan Kaufmann Series in Data Management Systems)*. Morgan Kaufmann Publishers Inc., San Francisco, CA, USA, 2005.

581. Hongjun Wu. Acorn: A lighweight authenticated cipher (v3). Candidate for the CAESAR Competition, 2016.

582. Wenling Wu, Shuang Wu, Lei Zhang, Jian Zou, and Le Dong. Lhash: A lightweight hash function. In *Information Security and Cryptology - 9th International Conference, Inscrypt 2013, Guangzhou, China, November 27-30, 2013, Revised Selected Papers*, pages 291–308, 2013.

583. Wenling Wu and Lei Zhang. LBlock: A lightweight block cipher. In Javier Lopez and Gene Tsudik, editors, *ACNS 11: 9th International Conference on Applied Cryptography and Network Security*, volume 6715 of *Lecture Notes in Computer Science*, pages 327–344, Nerja, Spain, June 7–10, 2011. Springer.

584. Minm Xie, Jingjing Li, and Yuechuan Zang. Related-key impossible differential cryptanalysis of lblock. *Chinese Journal of Electronics*, 26(1):35–41, 2017.

585. Xiaojun Xu, Chang Liu, Qian Feng, Heng Yin, Le Song, and Dawn Song. Neural network-based graph embedding for cross-platform binary code similarity detection. In *ACM SIGSAC Conference on Computer and Communications Security*, CCS '17, 2017.

586. Dai Yamamoto, Kouichi Itoh, and Jun Yajima. A very compact hardware implementation of the kasumi block cipher. In *4th IFIP WG 11.2 International Workshop WISTP 2010, Passau, Germany, April 12-14, 2010*, pages 293–307, 2010.

587. Gangqiang Yang, Xinxin Fan, Mark Aagaard, and Guang Gong. Design space exploration of the lightweight stream cipher wg-8 for fpgas and asics. In *Workshop on Embedded Systems Security, WESS'13, Article No. 8, Montreal, Quebec, Canada, September 29 - October 04, 2013*, 2013.

588. Gangqiang Yang, Bo Zhu, Valentin Suder, Mark D. Aagaard, and Guang Gong. The simeck family of lightweight block ciphers. In Tim Güneysu and Helena Handschuh, editors, *Cryptographic Hardware and Embedded Systems – CHES 2015*, volume 9293 of *Lecture Notes in Computer Science*, pages 307–329, Saint-Malo, France, September 13–16, 2015. Springer.

589. Sergey Yekhanin. Private Information Retrieval. *Communications of the ACM*, 53(4):68–73, 2010.

590. Adam L. Young and Moti Yung. *Malicious cryptography - exposing cryptovirology*. Wiley, 2004.

591. Jonas Zaddach, Luca Bruno, Aurélien Francillon, and Davide Balzarotti. Avatar: A Framework to Support Dynamic Security Analysis of Embedded Systems' Firmwares. In *NDSS 2014*, February 2014.

592. Shams Zawoad and Ragib Hasan. FAIoT: Towards building a forensics aware eco system for the internet of things. In *2015 IEEE International Conference on Services Computing, SCC 2015, New York City, NY, USA, June 27 - July 2, 2015*, pages 279–284, 2015.

593. Bin Zhang and Xinxin Gong. Another tradeoff attack on Sprout-like stream ciphers. In *ASIACRYPT 2015*, volume 9453 of *LNCS*, pages 561–585. Springer, 2015.

594. Bin Zhang, Zhenqing Shi, Chao Xu, Yuan Yao, and Zhenqi Li. Sablier v1. Candidate for the CAESAR Competition, 2014.
595. Bin Zhang, Chao Xu, and Willi Meier. Fast near collision attack on the Grain v1 stream cipher. In Jesper Buus Nielsen and Vincent Rijmen, editors, *Advances in Cryptology – EUROCRYPT 2018, Part II*, volume 10821 of *Lecture Notes in Computer Science*, pages 771–802, Tel Aviv, Israel, April 29 – May 3, 2018. Springer.
596. Lei Zhang, Wenling Wu, Yanfeng Wang, Shengbao Wu, and Jian Zhang. LAC: A lightweight authenticated encryption cipher. Candidate for the CAESAR Competition, 2014.
597. Liwei Zhang, A. Adam Ding, Francois Durvaux, Francois-Xavier Standaert, and Yunsi Fei. Towards sound and optimal leakage detection procedure. Cryptology ePrint Archive, Report 2017/287, 2017. http://eprint.iacr.org/2017/287.
598. WenTao Zhang, ZhenZhen Bao, DongDai Lin, Vincent Rijmen, BoHan Yang, and Ingrid Verbauwhede. Rectangle: a bit-slice lightweight block cipher suitable for multiple platforms. *Science China Information Sciences*, 58(12):1–15, 2015.
599. Huang Zhangwei and Xin Mingjun. A distributed spatial cloaking protocol for location privacy. In *2010 Second International Conference on Networks Security, Wireless Communications and Trusted Computing*, volume 2, pages 468–471, April 2010.
600. Yingxian Zheng, Yongbin Zhou, Zhenmei Yu, Chengyu Hu, and Hailong Zhang. How to Compare Selections of Points of Interest for Side-Channel Distinguishers in Practice? In Lucas C. K. Hui, S. H. Qing, Elaine Shi, and S. M. Yiu, editors, *ICICS 2014, Revised Selected Papers*, pages 200–214, Cham, 2015. Springer International Publishing.
601. Shuangyi Zhu, Yuan Ma, Jingqiang Lin, Jia Zhuang, and Jiwu Jing. More powerful and reliable second-level statistical randomness tests for nist sp 800-22. In *International Conference on the Theory and Application of Cryptology and Information Security*, pages 307–329. Springer, 2016.
602. Tanveer Zia, Peng Liu, and Weili Han. Application-specific digital forensics investigative model in internet of things (iot). In *Proceedings of the 12th International Conference on Availability, Reliability and Security*, ARES '17, pages 55:1–55:7, New York, NY, USA, 2017. ACM.

Permissions

All chapters in this book were first published in SUCSST, by Springer; hereby published with permission under the Creative Commons Attribution License or equivalent. Every chapter published in this book has been scrutinized by our experts. Their significance has been extensively debated. The topics covered herein carry significant information for a comprehensive understanding. They may even be implemented as practical applications or may be referred to as a beginning point for further studies.

The contributors of this book come from diverse backgrounds, making this book a truly international effort. We would like to thank all the contributing authors for lending their expertise to make the book truly unique. They have played a crucial role in the development of this book. Without their invaluable contributions this book wouldn't have been possible. They have made vital efforts to compile up to date information on the varied aspects of this subject to make this book a valuable addition to the collection of many professionals and students.

This book was conceptualized with the vision of imparting up-to-date and integrated information in this field. To ensure the same, a matchless editorial board was set up. Every individual on the board went through rigorous rounds of assessment to prove their worth. After which they invested a large part of their time researching and compiling the most relevant data for our readers.

The editorial board has been involved in producing this book since its inception. They have spent rigorous hours researching and exploring the diverse topics which have resulted in the successful publishing of this book. They have passed on their knowledge of decades through this book. To expedite this challenging task, the publisher supported the team at every step. A small team of assistant editors was also appointed to further simplify the editing procedure and attain best results for the readers.

Apart from the editorial board, the designing team has also invested a significant amount of their time in understanding the subject and creating the most relevant covers. They scrutinized every image to scout for the most suitable representation of the subject and create an appropriate cover for the book.

The publishing team has been an ardent support to the editorial, designing and production team. Their endless efforts to recruit the best for this project, has resulted in the accomplishment of this book. They are a veteran in the field of academics and their pool of knowledge is as vast as their experience in printing. Their expertise and guidance has proved useful at every step. Their uncompromising quality standards have made this book an exceptional effort. Their encouragement from time to time has been an inspiration for everyone.

The publisher and the editorial board hope that this book will prove to be a valuable piece of knowledge for students, practitioners and scholars across the globe.

Index